GOLD
WAS THE
MORTAR

GOLD WAS THE MORTAR

THE ECONOMICS OF CATHEDRAL BUILDING

HENRY KRAUS

BARNES & NOBLE

NEW YORK

This 2009 edition published by Barnes & Noble, Inc.,
by arrangement with Lillian Hamerslough.

Barnes & Noble, Inc.
122 Fifth Avenue
New York, NY 10011

ISBN: 978-1-4351-0512-6

Printed and bound in the United States of America

10 9 8 7 6 5 4 3 2 1

Contents

Illustrations

Acknowledgments

THE RESEARCH THAT WAS REQUIRED FOR THIS BOOK WAS FACILITATED BY GRANTS from the Bollingen, Chapelbrook and Samuel H. Kress Foundations. Obtaining this aid was made possible by the generous endorsements of Professors Harry Bober of New York University, Albert Elsen of Stanford University and Meyer Schapiro of Columbia University, all of whom expressed a continuing, warm interest in the work, especially as it appeared in parallel writings published by the *Gazette des Beaux-Arts*. Professor Schapiro also read the typed manuscript of the book and his suggestions were extremely helpful.

The author and publishers are grateful to the following for permission to reproduce the figures listed: Roger-Viollet, Paris, Fig. 2; Dépt des Estampes, Bibliothèque Nationale, Paris, Figs 3, 5, 7, 10, 18; Martin Frishman, London, Fig. 4; Réunion des Musées Nationaux, Paris, Fig. 6; Archives Photographiques, Paris, Figs 8, 12, 13, 14, 15, 16, 17, 20, 23, 24, 25, 31, 32, 33, 34, 35, 36, 38; Pascal Corbierre, Paris, Figs 9, 37, 40; Bibliothèque d'Amiens (drawing by Charles Pinsard, nineteenth century), Fig. 11; Lilliane Marroig, Lyon, Fig. 19; Collections des Archives Nationales, Paris, Fig. 21; National Monuments Record, London, Figs 26, 27, 28, 29, 30. Fig. 1 is an engraving from A. Seyboth, *Das alte Strassburg*, 1890; Fig. 22 is a sixteenth-century engraving from J. Schilter, *Chronike von Königshoven*, 1698; Fig. 39 is an engraving from P. Langlois, *Histoire du prieuré du Mont-aux-Malades-lès-Rouen*, 1851.

1. Medieval Strasbourg

The Cathedral and the People

THE CATHEDRAL TOWERED OVER THE MEDIEVAL CITY, BUT THE PEOPLE were not cowed. It was their church, they had helped erect it, with their sinew, with their wit, with their farthings and their pounds.

They were one, too, with its spiritual message, its offer of salvation, its promise of eternal bliss.

That, though, was not the whole content of their thought or striving. The engraving reflects the wider boundaries of their interest: their city hall, their treasury, their hospital.

And still the medieval church reached man in every phase of his experience. The contact may have been benign, it may have been bitter. The cathedral's varying splendour would mirror the conditions of this relationship.

Introduction

⌒

THIS IS A BOOK ABOUT THE CREATION OF EIGHT CATHEDRALS, BUT IT IS NOT their detailed building history. Excellent monographs are available for most of them as well as specialized technical, stylistic or iconographic studies. The book does not attempt to assemble or update these data either, though it makes frequent use of their information.

To say that the book is about the financing of the eight cathedrals would risk giving a very limited notion of its scope or interest. And yet there have been exciting books written in modern times about the creation of a personal fortune. A medieval cathedral's monetary adventures are often far from dull.

The noblest monuments repeatedly got entangled in problems about money. A cathedral was terribly costly, a truly stupendous financial undertaking for its time.[1] Lack of funds could lengthen the building period inordinately, stretches of three hundred years or more being on the record. Steady availability of finance might, in contrast, reduce the construction time to as little as seventy-five. Chartres, a prodigious exception, was done in thirty-five.

Many things could affect the readiness of money, and it is with the examination of this subject that the book essentially deals. Anything that advanced or hindered a cathedral's progress was of interest to it. It will probably surprise the reader to discover the wide range of factors that was involved, which reflects the vast importance of the church and its cathedral in medieval life.

This book is by no means unique in concerning itself with the financing of great churches. Every serious monograph of a cathedral makes some attempt to dig out the more substantial sources of its building funds.[2] But it is not enough to put the questions: What? Who? When? For all the important answers will not then be forthcoming. We must also ask: Why? Without a doubt, it is this book's leading interrogation. Works that pose it consistently, it must be said, are rare.

By focusing this work on French monuments, it has been possible to study their building records against France's broad historic backdrop. The creation of the cathedrals coincided with that country's greatest national surge and was inevitably favoured by it. Churches in the territories conquered by the French often experienced the opposite fate. Thus, the building of the cathedrals of Poitiers and Toulouse was impeded by the subjugation of their domains.

Conversely, the swift evolution of the Gothic style in France was largely helped by the treasure that came from these and other conquests. Notre-Dame de Paris was a documented beneficiary. The expansionist French drive began in the twelfth century, and the great building impulse that coincided with it expressed itself preponderantly in the new architectural mode, which thereafter was associated with French church-building.

The Gothic style, an historically evolved form that was influenced by many currents, is as difficult to describe as it is to account for. Technical elements that are intimately related to it, such as the cross-ribbed vault, the pointed arch or the flying buttress are all found in other styles. Nor is height its exclusive feature. What probably can be said to be the predominant aim of Gothic builders was to bring light and air into the great church vessel through the elimination of the cumbersome masses of earlier structures and by the wide opening out of the window spaces.

All of this entailed a more complex and finer fabric than was customary in previous construction, which, together with the richer decorative sparkle that generally characterized the new churches, added greatly to their cost. Such a development would have been impossible without the tremendous growth of wealth that took place in the thirteenth century. Since the bourgeoisie was both an important vehicle for and recipient of this enrichment, it is not surprising that the active participation of this class in a cathedral-building programme could add significantly to its speed and lustre.

Yet this collaboration was not certain nor even indispensable. In fact, it was at times virtually refused by churchmen who for prestige or other reasons wished to keep commoners aloof from their cathedral even at the risk of losing their patronage. But medieval man was deeply devout. Turned away from the bishop's church, he found other pious attachments, which became the primary outlets of his benevolence, a development that this book broadly documents. The great variation in burgher donorship to cathedral-building projects seemed puzzling at first sight. Could it have been due to the church's known antagonism to the bourgeois commune? This would have resulted in bitter conflict in any city where the bishop was the sovereign, and thus reduced the flow of the citizens' benefactions.

The postulate was verified at Lyon, among other places, where the archbishop's blazing opposition to the burghers' political and social aspirations not only made an active ally of the latter to the French in their conquest of that great province but also froze the commoners' aid to the metropolitan church. Yet the same did not occur at Strasbourg, though its prelate was likewise the segnior of that city. Unforeseen circumstances at the Rhine metropolis brought about a close political and even military collaboration between bishop and burghers, who often became sophisticated warriors in the feudal epoch, either under the banner of their segnior or in the city militia. In the long run, the city–church co-operation at Strasbourg resulted in far-going benefit to the Münster. In fact, the municipality took over full control of the cathedral's construction at the midpoint and never surrendered it thereafter.

Such a role for the citizens was highly exceptional, however. The church was far better equipped financially for this task and normally made the major contribution to it. And yet it is surprising how often an outstanding episcopacy would fail to conduct an adequate cathedral-building enterprise. The possession of great wealth by prelates and dignitaries did not always benefit their church. Like any laymen, they would often be preoccupied with purely mundane goals. Impassioned builders among the ecclesiastics, contrary to all romantic notions, were relatively rare, and the prescribed assignment of one-fourth of church income for building purposes was frequently disregarded.

The outlay of treasure for church-building in the Middle Ages was none the less enormous,[3] but planning was not always judicious and the competitive quest of funds from the faithful often taxed a city's possibilities. The financial needs of a cathedral under construction were so great that coercive methods had repeatedly to be used to keep the flow of contributions focused on this goal. Parish churches, in particular, were frequently called on to make great sacrifices over lengthy periods. For these reasons, too, the patronage of citizens to the secondary churches has had to be closely investigated.

Functional elements required for a city's commercial life, particularly in an advanced communal town, likewise often cut deeply into the funds that would nominally be available for patronage. On the other hand, civic expenditure was in itself a sign of economic vitality, hence a potential supplementary source of benevolence. It is not surprising that Amiens, where communal power was mated with the most cordial churchburgher relations, should have achieved one of the most resplendent of French cathedrals.

The eight cathedrals in this book were not chosen for their style, dimension or luxuriance but rather for the variety of their problems and building experience. The exclusion of this or that church need not surprise the reader, since there could have been a number of equally interesting selections which were limited only by time and space. Strasbourg, which was German in the medieval period, was an early choice whose historic panorama, so different from that of French towns, promised to be particularly instructive. The verification of this prospect prompted the addition of an English cathedral to our list,[4] York being eventually chosen, though it was by no means meant to be regarded as a model of building experience in that country.

The great amount of research called for by this work was only partly lightened by the virtual elimination from its scope of stylistic or technical aspects. But the broad orbit of the book still made widespread claims, in addition to the general historical background, regarding the knowledge of each city's commercial life, its political establishment, the citizens' organizations, church structure and economy, financial systems and various other subjects. Above all, the sources of donorship had to be scanned in early cartularies and obituaries or in inventories prepared by later archivists of now-vanished documents and most particularly in the burghers' wills, when available.

Let the reader not be dismayed by the prospect of a dense thicket of documents in this book. The body of the text has been kept in a cursive style, while the considerable corroborative material in the Notes can be consulted as the reader's time, interest or enjoyment dictates, or can even remain virtually disregarded without danger of marring his overall appreciation of the work. Somehow it gives me much pleasure to think that notes occupying several pages can be compressed into a sentence or two of text. This seems to vouch for the continued wide accessibility of information that is becoming more and more difficult to assimilate in an ever more specialized world.

1

PARIS

*The
Golden Legend*

Paris Cathedral Chronology

1163/64	New building begun at choir, replacing much smaller church of seventh century. But work on part of the façade sculpture (south portal) was done somewhat earlier (c.1150–60). This consisted of the tympanum lintel and archivolt sculpture, carved in Romanesque style and later re-employed in the Gothic portal of Ste-Anne.
1177	Choir, including double aisles of ambulatory, completed though not yet vaulted. Choir consecrated 1182.
1180–96	Transept and nave built except for final western bay; completed shortly after Maurice de Sully's death, around 1200.
1200–20	Façade portals and Gallery of Kings of Judah above them completed; earlier Ste-Anne sculpture re-employed; Judgment Day and other sculpture of central portal carved.
1220–30	Major changes launched, including choir and nave vaulting, enlargement of windows, nave flying-buttresses doubled, etc. Earlier stained-glass windows reglazed.
1220–5	Façade level of rose window completed.
1225–50	Remainder of façade is built, including high gallery and towers.
1235	Chantry chapels of nave begun, built between vertical buttresses, starting at the west and south (Ste-Anne Chapel). Dating is incomplete, but chapels adjoining transept were probably done in late 1250s.
1250; 1258	Elongation of transept begun, on north by Pierre de Montreuil, on south by Jean de Chelles, as recorded in carved Gothic inscription at bottom of piers on both sides of south portal.
1254–c.1320	Chapels of apse done. Paid for by various donors, including burghers, bishops and kings, and separately built; last one completed c.1320.
c.1300–50	Creation of the choir enclosure (partly missing) and roodscreen (entirely vanished) by Pierre de Chelles, Jean Ravy and Jean le Bouteiller, each working at a separate period.

2. Notre-Dame de Paris, the golden legend

NOTRE-DAME DE PARIS'S STORY IS A GOLDEN LEGEND. COULD LESS BE EXPECTED
of the capital city of France, which in the thirteenth century enjoyed the most
spectacular growth in all its long and brilliant history?[1] Begun in 1163, virtually
completed by 1235, soon after undergoing a basic reconstruction,[2] the cathedral had
few of the financial trials that were the lot of the churches of Lyon, Toulouse, Poitiers
and other cities outside the royal domain. What wars there were were wars of conquest, for others to suffer, and by the time of the Hundred Years catastrophe, Paris's
cathedral was already fully built.

Paris, too, was singularly free of civil strife during the building period. The royal
presence was so overpowering as to discourage any thrust of popular insurgency.
What dozens of French towns could attain—the commune—the Paris municipality
never won, its powers remaining forever fragmentary.[3] Throughout the twelfth
century and well into the thirteenth the great city's political structure was centred

on a small band of merchants who monopolized commerce on the Seine.[4] When the municipality later took control of a few secondary responsibilities, it was through this already organized Hanse, somewhat transformed but still activated by a small group of wealthy burghers. The great mass of the population remained outside the political pale.[5]

The famous revolt led by Etienne Marcel in 1358 was an historical maverick, erupting from the crushing defeat of French arms at Poitiers by the English, their capture of King Jean II and his long imprisonment in London. After Etienne Marcel's exemplary punishment, some of his most intimate associates were promptly taken back to the royal bosom and Paris's top bourgeoisie resumed their traditional role of court favourites, their fortunes waxing in service of the king.[6]

This posture of Paris's affluent burghers was already well established by the end of the twelfth century. A famous act is on record, undertaken by King Philippe-Auguste on his departure for the Crusade of 1190, in which he is shown assigning seven commoners the important task of supervising the banking of royal revenues during his absence.[7] Little more than a decade later, when Philippe made his first great conquests in the north-west and west, a number of Parisian burghers were among those called on to help organize the absorption of these new domains and to guide the flood of gold from them into the royal coffers.

These newly accrued riches made France the wealthiest kingdom of Europe. The addition of Normandy and Languedoc alone, both in the first half of the thirteenth century, is estimated to have doubled the royal revenues.[8] In later chapters we shall see how the draining off of treasure from conquered provinces slowed or even permanently attenuated their cathedrals. The reverse was true for Paris and the Île de France, where a great 'mantle' of Gothic masterpieces was fostered by their extraordinary enrichment. What has often been dubbed the royal French style was as much the result of these favouring circumstances as of aesthetic creativity.

The extent to which Notre-Dame itself benefited from expropriated wealth is obscured by the almost total lack of building fabric records. But signs of the swelling gains of other Paris churches are eloquent. St Louis (1226–70) alone was to endow at least a dozen religious units in the capital.[9] While his predilection for praying communities won him the caustic observation of A.-L. Millin, the famous registrar of monuments in the revolutionary period, that he 'spent more on the monks than Louis XIV and Louis XV did on their mistresses,'[10] the haloed monarch's benefactions did include one of Paris's brightest gems, the Sainte-Chapelle, as well as the great Abbey of Royaumont, situated about twenty miles to the north of the capital.

A direct line on revenues drawn from the subjected lands to a religious monument has been established by us for the latter unit, perhaps St Louis's most splendid foundation in the greater Paris region. This monastery was endowed with a great permanent yearly revenue of 500 livres (about $400,000 or £220,000 in contemporary terms; for explanation see Glossary, under 'Money'), extracted from peasants in the king's newly acquired Norman domains (see Chapter 8). A similar origin was that of the important Priory of St-Bernard at Paris, which was founded by St Louis's brother, Alphonse de Poitiers, who based its yearly *rente* of 140 livres on the royal earnings at La Rochelle, capital of the conquered coastal province of Aunis.[11]

These outstanding foundations were matched, often on hardly a more modest scale, by a number of the crown's officers who served in the occupied lands. One of the most magnificent of these was founded by a minor rural lordling of the Île de France. Such were Pierre de Thillay's beginnings, in any case, until he built up his years of dedicated service to Philippe-Auguste (1180–1223) into an important family seigniory—in Normandy. The soaring change in Pierre's fortune was the result of great and repeated gratuities by the king to his first bailiff of that conquered province, compounded by supposedly voluntary gifts by local nobles to the powerful royal official.[12]

Whatever the source, this carpetbagger of old France used his great gains in a most exemplary manner, whether viewed from the expectation of a patriot or a good Christian. (The use of the term carpetbagger is a bit irregular since the American carpetbagger from the North who operated in the South after the Civil War was a private adventurer, whereas Pierre de Thillay and others like him were hired officials.) A large part of these riches he allowed to remain in their original form of landed property in the heart of Normandy, onto which he grafted a good loyal French family, a permanent settler in the conquered land. Pierre must have been too old to pull up stakes himself and he had no son who could establish the family name in the important seigniory of Mesnil-Mauger. But he did have a daughter, Héloise, whom he married off to another small seignior from his region. Accordingly, it was Eudes de Tremblay who had the distinction of making this brilliant implantation.[13]

For his offering to God, Pierre de Thillay chose to build what has been called 'the finest rural hospital in the diocese of Paris', the Hôtel-Dieu of Gonesse. One wonders that he did not establish it too in Normandy, as Guillaume Acarin, a cleric who was his close associate throughout his royal service, had done, founding a collegiate church at Caen and becoming its first dean.[14] Perhaps Pierre's choice was dictated by sentimental attachment to his old king. Was it not at Gonesse that Philippe-Auguste was born, in 1160, a son at last—as his father Louis VII had exultantly proclaimed: 'A child of the better sex!' The monarch described himself as thrilled to the marrow by this event, after long decades of being 'horrified . . . by the succession of my daughters', and handsomely rewarded the guard who announced the great news to him that early morning.[15]

Pierre de Thillay's hospital and chapel were worthy of a king's consecration. They were endowed so solidly, with lands, vineyards, houses at Paris, a rich tithe, that the foundation has come down into modern times.[16] Here Pierre and his wife Aveline were buried, and, while their monument has disappeared, the historian Jean Lebeuf described it as he saw it early in the eighteenth century, the effigied founders 'with an arc over their heads on which were written Latin verses very difficult to read'.[17]

The commemorative plaque, which can be seen today at the reconstructed Hôtel-Dieu de Gonesse, attaches his endless string of Norman seigniories to Pierre de Thillay's name: Mesnil-Mauger, Friebois, Barneville, Amundeville, Quisberville, etc. From these the uninitiated visitor might be inclined to identify a high noble of ancient strain, whose baronial domains were presumably an accumulation of feudal conquests or of generations of inter-family alliances rather than the acquisitions of an honest functionary prodigally rewarded for his loyal services to his king.

Among the many other itinerant royal agents who returned to the Paris area to invest part of their booty in spiritual goods were a number of burghers. One of the best known, Jean Sarrazin, served both St Louis and Alphonse, the former as chamberlain, for many years. Jean was an open-handed donor to several Parisian churches, being responsible for the foundation of a number of chaplaincies, one of them at Notre-Dame.[18] Another member of Alphonse's 'family', Pierre Apothicaire, was equally lavish in pious gifts, having donated 700 livres ($560,000 or £308,000) 'and more' to the Paris Abbey of St-Victor. More important, he apparently paid for the erection of one of Notre-Dame's chantry chapels and established a private chaplain in it.[19]

Still another chaplaincy founder at the cathedral was Aléaume Hécelin, a recipient of great royal favours, one of which brought him the remunerative sinecure of surveyor of Paris's streets.[20] Aléaume's father had served Philippe-Auguste as bailiff of Gisors, one of the districts of Normandy, for a number of years, and put part of his accumulated gains into a Paris hospice and chapel.[21] Two half-brothers, Guillaume Escuacol and Jean Palée, likewise operators in Normandy, built two chapels, one at Paris, the other at their native village of Rennemoulin, which they endowed with vines, quitrents and other revenues to support the priest who daily praised their names.[22]

One of Guillaume Escuacol's assignments while royal bailiff of Rouen was confiscation of the wealth of the Jews. This consisted mainly of taking over their debtors' lists and collecting the principal for the king, for which Guillaume was credited with the important sum of 12,340 livres, in itself worthy of a princely reward.[23] Twenty years later, in 1230, the Jews of Normandy had evidently recouped their fortunes sufficiently to justify another confiscatory effort. This one was ordered by the young St Louis and turned over for accomplishment to still another Paris agent, Nicolas Arrode,[24] part of whose spoils went to the foundation of a chapel, built in the cemetery of the famous Paris priory, St-Martin-des-Champs.[25]

Aside from the frankly extortionate role of the French army of occupation and its civilian adherents, the spiritual side of absorption was not neglected. The regional hierarchy was conciliated and those won to the crown rapidly advanced. Gillebert de Saane, a modest Norman cleric, made a spectacular rise in this way by the grace of royal favours, finally serving as high-treasurer of the Rouen church under Archbishop Eudes Rigaud. The latter was the intimate friend of St Louis, and held the top ecclesiastic post of the conquered province for several decades.

Evidence of Gillebert de Saane's attachment to the French crown appears in the list of his known benefactions, the most important of which were established at Paris rather than in his native Normandy. These included the foundation of a chapel at Notre-Dame together with a chaplaincy. For the financing of the chaplaincy we have a rare document showing the direct transfer of a gift from the king to Gillebert, 'my beloved clerk'.[26] Previously another important plum had fallen into the Norman's lap: the post of canon at the cathedral.

Gillebert de Saane's major endowment was a college at Paris University, which he founded and completely financed, reserving its benefits to students from Normandy. It was one of a number of similar foundations that were limited to scholars from a newly acquired region. While no doubt dictated by an esteem for learning, these establishments consciously or unconsciously served the purpose of building ties between the conquered provinces and France. This conclusion seems particularly warranted in the case of two other Paris colleges that were established by three brothers of a remarkable Norman family, the Harcourts, whose fidelity to France won two bishoprics, canonries at Notre-Dame and many other honours.[27]

Although Notre-Dame's cartulary is very deficient in naming donors to its building fund, it is surprising that the two lone gifts by royalty to the cathedral fabric that are to be found in its cartulary are not supplemented by grants listed in other sources. We have collated a number of royal foundations at the cathedral but they are almost all for prayers and masses for their founders' personal salvation.[28] Even so, added together they would not have paid for the construction of a single bay of the fifteen that proceeded in steady majestic sequence down Notre-Dame's choir and nave. The densely carved façade was undertaken without pause less than four decades after the foundation stone was laid 130 metres to the east. Money never seemed to be lacking for this stupendous accomplishment.

It strikes one as particularly strange that St Louis's name does not appear in a single act of patronage toward Notre-Dame. The enormous cost of his two Crusades— well over a million livres for his first,[29] enough to build the cathedral several times over—could hardly have been the explanation, considering the king's many other charities and the fabulous revenues that he drew from all the conquered territories. A more reasonable explanation is that Notre-Dame's primary structure was almost completed when the boy-king took the crown, while its partial reconstruction was only getting under way at the end of his reign, when his mind was totally taken with preparations, especially financial, for his second Crusade.

The bourgeoisie's patronage role during the cathedral's first building is shrouded by the lack of fabric records or other pertinent documents. However, we can be sure that their potential aid was not neglected by the church authorities. There is a sermon, for example, by Notre-Dame's founding bishop, Maurice de Sully, in which he appeals to the merchants to place their hopes for felicity in fostering monuments to the Virgin rather than in material wealth.[30] My own list of important burgher foundations at Notre-Dame includes two chaplaincies (provisions for a personal priest in perpetuity) that were established during the earlier construction period. Later, this type of bourgeois benefaction was multiplied enormously (see Note 48).

An unfortunate circumstance that clouds the extent of the burghers' assistance to Notre-Dame is the almost total destruction of its old stained glass (largely by order of the cathedral canons long before the Revolution), which in Chartres, Bourges,

3. Notre-Dame's sole guild-given lancet: showing the central roundel at the apex of the now vanished stained-glass window that represented Crispin and Crispinian, the patron saints of the shoe-makers' guild, whose confraternity was once active in this chapel

Le Mans, Rouen and other cathedrals was a notable medium of middle-class donorship. This tragic loss prompted me to search old graphics and other sources for possible references to the vanished glass, from which I collated a certain number of attributions but only a single one which related to the burghers. It was a small roundel showing St Crispin and his brother at their shoe-making trade, an obvious reference to the guild that had once been active in this chapel.[31]

Can we assume that there were other examples of guild-donated lancets that have disappeared without leaving a trace? There is little likelihood of this, for the evidence is quite strong that while allowing the wealthiest of burghers to establish remunerative chaplaincies whose daily masses would be discreetly attended by a few members of the family, Notre-Dame's canons were not willing to extend the same hospitality to groups of artisans and tradesmen. Already by the end of the twelfth century, all ordinary sacerdotal activity had been shifted to neighbouring parish churches.[32] The cathedral of France's royal city was reserved for a more exalted existence, the shoemakers' chapel remaining an unexplained exception.

Everything indicates that the remarkable feat of building Notre-Dame in less than seventy-five years was the financial accomplishment basically of its ecclesiastic family. Because of the absence of a fabric register, this conclusion must remain largely inferential.[33] Nevertheless, the cathedral's obituaries testify eloquently to the loyalty of its great clerical family to their church. Many of their bequests were modest enough, providing for a good meal for their fellow clerics, for example, or even only an extra plate, on some holiday. But an astonishing number of the testators made the church community their sole heir, their benefactions often running to hundreds and in several cases thousands of livres.

Some of these gifts that are cited in the churchmen's obituaries[34] were specifically marked for building operations, thus giving us by inadvertence a few dated guidelines that are verified by documentation. It is interesting that among the most munificent donors were the two bishops whose careers bracketed Notre-Dame's construction. Maurice de Sully (d.1196) not only launched the new building in 1163/64 but fervently pursued it throughout his life both as fund-raiser and donor. His bequest of 100 livres to buy lead for the nave roof indicates the almost incredible speed of construction during his episcopacy. A significant interim donor was Canon Jean de Paris, who left money around 1270 'for work on the transepts recently begun'. But the most generous donor of all was certainly Bishop Simon Matiffas de Buci (d.1304), whose benefactions exceeding 5,000 livres included a great allowance for the creation of the three axis chapels, which were to round off the cathedral's far-ranging reconstruction in the early years of the fourteenth century.

Paris's church was a very wealthy one, its great revenues deriving as much from propertied holdings (both in the city and throughout the diocese) and seigniorial taxes as from strictly church sources. These revenues could be augmented by the sale of part of the church's temporality during a building campaign, as seems to have happened at Notre-Dame.[35] Animated appeals for donations and other special measures were not lacking either, and in the end resources for the great project were clearly adequate. An indirect proof of this appears from the great amount of supplementary construction that was undertaken simultaneously. Most important was the vast new episcopal palace that Maurice de Sully initiated just a few years after he began building Notre-Dame. Aside from residential quarters, assembly halls and business offices, this imposing structure (which was destroyed in the Revolution of 1830) also enclosed a double chapel, a treasury and a donjon for the prelate's clerical prisoners. The chapter likewise had a number of construction projects under way.[36]

So often do we find ecclesiastics who were without interest in their own cathedral that we tend to forget that this was one of their major responsibilities and are inclined to attribute exceptional merit to those who did make a decent contribution. It is a sobering fact that even Notre-Dame's canons were eager to shift this burden to any other shoulders that would bear it and that the cathedral's remarkable building record was to a significant extent due to heavy sacrifices of the chapter's 2,000 serfs.

It was hardly voluntary! In fact, the money in question, which stemmed from a head-tax (*taille*) that the chapter repeatedly imposed on its subjects during the first construction period, became the object of a prolonged and bitter conflict, whose true meaning long remained obscure. The reason for this was that the queen-dowager, Blanche of Castille, got involved in the contestation at its high point and thereafter was credited with having emancipated the chapter's serfs. This she had neither the intention nor the right to do, as the French scholar, Marc Bloch, has pointed out in a brilliant essay. In fact, the serfs' liberation did not take place until eleven years after the queen's death.[37]

No one would want to detract from Blanche's chivalric impulse on that occasion, however. When a new *taille* was announced by the chapter in 1250, the serfs refused to pay it on the grounds that they owed this tax only to the king, and sent a delegation to Paris to back up their claim. They were promptly imprisoned by the chapter in its hot and filthy jail. After a number of them died, the survivors managed to get a plea out to the queen mother, St Louis being away at the time on his first Crusade. On the strength of royal jurisdiction over appellate cases, the doughty Blanche led a troop of horses to the cathedral cloister, only to find the entire clerical family mysteriously absent. Since feudal rules forbade the queen's liberation of the prisoners, even if it were to save their lives, Blanche stepped into Notre-Dame to seek divine guidance. But while she was praying, one of her soldiers sprang the prison doors and released the unhappy men.[38]

The case went into arbitration soon afterwards, the commission consisting of three prelates, including the Bishop of Paris! The decision was foregone, in any case, since the issue was based on traditional feudal practice which an ecclesiastic board would certainly not upset. The major evidence came from Notre-Dame's canons themselves, who could point to incontrovertible proof that their serfs had paid a head-tax to them again and again, quoted instances going back as far as 1179. One canon asserted that it was hard to recall all the times it had been collected. Besides the cases enumerated, there were 'many others', he declared.[39]

Among the dates that were 'remembered', there were five that fell within the brief period of 1210 and 1232. Was it accidental that this covered a high point of work on the cathedral, when its stupendous façade was being created? Significantly, the reasons for the individual *tailles* listed by the canons usually referred to building projects: 'the chapterhouse'—'this chapter's cloister'—or 'St-Denis-du-Pas', a small church in the cathedral compound that had to be demolished and rebuilt to make space for the new edifice. Once, the tax was exacted 'to cover debts of the chapter', a catchall which could have included expenditures of the building fabric.

One *taille* imposed in 1219, to help pay for the erection of some capitular mansions, was actually opposed by a few of the canons, who argued that sufficient funds were available to cover these expenses. The majority group retorted that the chapter had an unlimited right to impose the tax 'at will' and as often as it wished.[40] But the debate implies that the cathedral building fund was amply supplied. In fact, no further tax was set between 1235 and 1250, which Marc Bloch attributes to the moral pressure of the dissenting canons. It is just as possible that the reason was the decrease in building expenditures since Notre-Dame's basic structure was completed around 1235 and work on the new transepts did not get into swing until the mid-century.

At that point, moreover, the serfs again supplied a substantial portion of the funds through payment of their manumission.[41] Since charges per head ran between 15 and 90 livres, Notre-Dame's receipts from this source mounted into the tens of thousands of livres. Where would the serfs have found such enormous sums? Marc Bloch suggests that the rich Paris burghers, whom we find hovering at all times about these incidents, were the financiers, loaning the money as a *surcens*, an increase in the feudal quitrent, which was in effect a kind of mortgage that was forever unredeemable.[42]

France's great successes in arms starting around 1200 not only brought huge stores of booty into the country but expanded immensely its economic potential, benefiting particularly the prosperity of its capital. This is nowhere better illustrated than in the advantage Paris merchants gained over their Rouen rivals following the French conquest of Normandy (see Chapter 8 for full details). The final outcome of this competition could never be in doubt. Paris eventually won free passage to and from the sea and Rouen's control even over its own port was seriously curtailed.

These advantages resulted in the enrichment of many individual Parisians. A pertinent example was that of Raoul de Pacy, whose boat loaded with wine was seized at Rouen for failure to pay the port tax. The dispute eventually came before the parlement, the crown's appellate court at Paris, which ruled that Rouen had no jurisdiction over wine from the Parisian merchant's vineyards, even though they were located in Normandy.[43] The decision itself is not so surprising but the inevitable question that rises from it is how this Paris burgher had acquired these distant vineyards in the conquered province. By royal gift? By purchase of a confiscated property?

There is an abundance of signs that the wealth of Paris's citizens increased enormously in the thirteenth century: through acquisition of important real-estate holdings both inside and outside the city; by purchase of noble fiefs; by the building of fine town houses and summer homes, the latter especially on the Seine's still sparsely settled Left Bank; by big loans to the king and other princes.[44] It would be impossible to sift out the part that was due to conquest and that which resulted from normal economic accumulation. But the data that are available leave no doubt about the great benefits accruing to Paris's burghers from the political successes of the crown.

It was this wealth of course that made possible their extraordinary patronage to the cathedral and to the numerous other churches of the capital. What was unique about this double munificence was the fact that its two elements could take place simultaneously. In other episcopal cities, even the most prosperous, as we shall see, secondary church-building usually had to cede to the needs of the cathedral. The enormous riches brought into the capital by the French conquests obviated such a compromise, so that a great multitude of parishes, convents and abbeys could rise in unison with the bishop's church at Paris.

4. Notre-Dame chantry chapels: built, from 1235 on, between the vertical buttresses, which can be seen rising above the chapel windows

Like a latterday homily is the story of Guillaume Poins-l'Asne, who started his career selling baked tidbits at Les Halles, Paris's great market, which was founded in 1137. When Guillaume had amassed his fortune, he had his old purveyor's platter encased in gold and silver, which he proudly displayed when giving testimonials in the parish churches about the goodness of the Lord and the rewards of bourgeois virtue. This humility did not bar the social ascension of Guillaume's family, however, his son becoming one of Paris's most esteemed doctors of theology.[45]

An important part of Guillaume Poins-l'Asne's fortune went toward founding a chapel and two private chaplaincies at his parish, the still-standing market church of St-Eustache, in 1224.[46] Numbers of other rich burghers did as much or more, the cathedral itself often being their beneficiary. While almost totally lacking in the first building period, evidence of bourgeois patronage at Notre-Dame during its major reconstruction beginning shortly before the middle of the century is extensive. However, this help did not stem from guilds or confraternities, for whose foundations I had at first searched in vain, but rather from affluent individuals to whom subsequently the investigation was extended.[47] For while the cathedral authorities were adamant in banning the mass guild rituals, they welcomed burgher foundations that operated more quietly.

The major portion of this patronage was found to have taken place around the creation of Notre-Dame's great belt of chantry chapels, which were built on the outside between the vertical buttresses, after which the aisle walls were broken through. Not only were there thirty-six chaplaincies established by the burghers in these units, or almost an average of one per chapel, but in a number of cases the funds for building the chapels themselves were likewise supplied by middle-class men and women. In fact, for this important sector of the cathedral's structure, Paris's bourgeoisie shared with the ecclesiastics the almost exclusive patronage role.[48]

Nevertheless, the cathedral's basic policy of class exclusion remained unchanged and the presence of even the wealthiest of burghers continued to be strictly limited. They were not, for example, accepted for burial at Notre-Dame, not even in the chapels for whose erection they paid. This ban extended even to so important a personage as Jean Sarrazin, St Louis's chamberlain and the treasurer of his household, who died around 1275. Though he did get a daily mass at the cathedral, founded for him by his wife Agnès, daughter of another important patrician family, the Barbettes, both had to go to the more hospitable Abbey of St-Victor to find their eternal repose.[49]

As a result of the rigid segregation practised by the cathedral canons, the overwhelming concentration of burgher benevolence in Paris went to the parish churches, convents and social welfare institutions. My hardly exhaustive survey of chaplaincies established by the middle class at churches other than Notre-Dame yielded close to three hundred such foundations.[50] Even more impressive are the innumerable proofs of bourgeois participation in the building and decoration of neighbourhood churches. Burghers were always active in this regard, as other studies will demonstrate. But the extent of their contribution at Paris was of an incomparable magnitude.[51]

Often the initial impulse for what eventually became a great church was a simple chapel fostered by a group of artisans or tradesmen or even by a single wealthy individual. This was the case with the church of St-Paul, which was to become one of Paris's most fashionable institutions. It was founded as a humble little oratory in the twelfth century by the city's cloth-fullers and shearers, who can be seen eventually in token of social ascension limiting membership in their confraternity to those 'sufficiently well-dressed'.[52] Around the same time, a man and his wife and another commoner were associated in establishing one of Paris's earliest university colleges, St-Honoré. The chapel that went with it was soon servicing the neighbourhood. It had a spectacular growth, being raised by the mid-century to the status of a collegiate church.[53]

The great market church of St-Eustache itself started as a chapel, founded by a burgher, Jean Allais, a performer of mystery plays. For unknown reasons, possibly as payment of a loan, Philippe-Auguste had granted Jean a penny tax on all fish sold at Les Halles. The mummer decided around 1200 to put up a chapel on the very spot where he had collected his mound of deniers. Was it from pride or the bite of conscience? In any case the chapel's success was so phenomenal that by 1223 it had to be rebuilt into a regular church (the first of several expansions), this time with the aid of all the parishioners.[54]

Proximity to the butchers' market was what gave St-Jacques-de-la-Boucherie its celebrated name. Often rebuilt, it was as early as 1217 that the parishioners are seen to be in charge of operations when their small twelfth-century edifice had to be expanded because of the rapidly increasing population of the quarter.[55] This was the pattern of all future rebuildings. For its final reconstruction, starting late in the fourteenth century, the wealthiest parishioners divided the financial responsibility, segment by assigned segment. No doubt there was a powerful appeal to the devout soul to pay for some important element of God's house, particularly if there was a crediting plaque put on each donated unit.

Thus, Jacqueline-the-Dyer paid for a pillar in the choir; Jean of Amiens and his wife for the aisle vaulting; Nicolas Boulard for another vault; the scribe Nicolas Flamel, a famed burgher art-patron, for a portal; and a number of others each financed a chapel.[56] Most unusual gift of all was that of Gilles Alain, against the wall of whose house the enlarged church would have to butt, requiring the sealing off of its windows. Gilles was willing to accept the inconvenience in return for a slight favour, that an opening the size of 'two fingers' be left in the church wall through which he could peek into the choir. In this manner Gilles's house became a sort of private chapel from which, like a lord, he could assist at mass without having to displace himself.[57]

A success story more in the medieval mode was that of St-Jean-en-Grève's transformation from an insignificant baptismal chapel of the merchants' church of St-Gervais into one of Paris's most magnificent structures.[58] An inspiration of medieval obscurantism, it was widely imitated for many centuries, finding expression particularly in art works, some of which can still be seen in Parisian churches, their time-obscured message occasionally explicated by propagandistic blurbs.[59]

It was the tale of the Jewish moneylender who obtained a communion wafer from a Christian woman as payment of the pledge on her Easter robe. The Jew then set out to destroy the mystic biscuit but it resisted every assault until the crime was discovered by an alert parishioner of St-Jean, who reported it to her priest. The Jew was duly burnt, his Talmud attached to his body by order of the king's provost: 'See if it will protect you from the flames!'[60] The donations of the vast crowds that were drawn to St-Jean thereafter allowed its being rebuilt in splendour, the miraculous wafer enshrined at the high altar in form of a vermilion sun beneath a cupola mounted on eight delicate marble columns. On the site of the Jew's house ('where the Lord was boiled'), a chapel was built at the cost of a devout burgher.[61]

Yet the ambivalent Middle Ages can show a fine humanitarian impulse to match every barbarity. At Paris, as at all other cities we shall study, burghers played the outstanding part in the establishment of social welfare institutions. This was true of the Hôtel-Dieu, the city's major hospital, whose cartulary records countless gifts by the people, including direct participation in the building and adornment of its two chapels, one of which, offered by Oudart de Mocreux, called for 'fine stained-glass windows'.[62] St-Lazare, the city's great leper-colony, was run by the bourgeoisie and mainly supported by it.[63] Even the Quinze-Vingts, the famous hospice for the blind to which St Louis's name is attached as founder, was almost from the start run by bourgeois 'masters', its solid revenues of 1,000 livres a year coming largely from middle-class donations, while at least two of its chapels were donated by them.[64]

Other charities established by the bourgeoisie often occasion surprise by their modern arrangements. Like low-cost housing for the poor, for example, to which the Flamels's name is attached.[65] One hospice, founded during the Hundred Years War to harbour orphans and homeless women, provided for wetnurses for sucklings. Other children, besides being fed, clothed and sheltered, were given elementary instruction and at a proper age were apprenticed to an artisan.[66] Various other places of refuge were endowed, for orphans whose mothers died giving birth, for widows past fifty, for destitute artisans, each operated by their own trade.[67] The curriers even installed a pioneering sick-benefit fund, which the guild statutes explain as being required by the 'grave and prolonged illnesses during which they cannot work and have to beg for their bread . . .'.[68]

France's great prosperity that marked most of the thirteenth and the first third of the fourteenth century was cut short by the outbreak of the cataclysmic Hundred Years War. This unexampled disaster wiped out most of the country's earlier conquests, while laying waste to large stretches of its territory and destroying vast resources and wealth. The losses in church architecture and art, by obliteration and arrested pro-duction, were certainly enormous. The decline in new work is particularly striking when contrasted with the accomplishment just prior to the great war, when many parts of France, and Paris especially, were enjoying one of the most creative periods in history.

In the capital, it was largely nourished by bourgeois gifts.[69] Great, indeed, was the affluence of the Parisian oligarchy. Jean Bouillart could buy for spot cash 970 livres worth (about $776,000 or £427,000) of woods from the king, who immediately accepted his homage on a noble fief,[70] which was tantamount to Jean's being ennobled. The Count of Savoy was mortgaged to the extent of 10,000 livres to a Paris master furrier, Gilbert Lescot, and had to surrender to him the Vicomté of Maulevrier in pay-ment of his debt.[71] Gandoufle d'Arcelles, an Italian banker turned Parisian, paid a *taille* on yearly earnings that would approximate to $3,150,000 (£1,730,000) today.[72]

Etienne Barbette had his own valet, falconer and chambermaid,[73] 'signs of riches' cited in the tax lists, each of which speaks volumes about the social climbing of the burghers, whose sons conducted mounted jousts that were attended by royalty.[74]

Paris's apical period of burgher art patronage in the first decades of the fourteenth century was the more remarkable in that these years were marked by a very serious political disturbance. The outburst occurred in 1306, brought on by King Philippe-le-Bel's imposition of a new currency (after repeated debasements of the old), which automatically trebled rents. The ruler's monetary manoeuvres were dictated by his protracted military campaigns in Flanders, for which the tax-raising methods of the day were wholly inadequate.[75] The revolt brought on the suppression of all burgher confraternities, which in the fourteenth century had come to play a leading role as the medium of their patronage.

It was not until 1320, several years after Philippe-le-Bel's death, that the fraternal groups were allowed to reassemble, under strict royal supervision, the re-establishing decree frankly stating that the close check was meant to prevent 'conspiracies'.[76] But this did not discourage the confraternities' massive reorganization, which resulted in the succeeding period in a dazzling agglomeration of church monuments and of decorative stone, glass and wood, the whole of it almost totally obliterated today.

Among the documentary or literary sources that tell about this vanished world of art, none is more touching than the story of the two musician-friends who were suddenly moved to pity by the sight of a poor paralysed woman who lay in her cart the whole year round near the home of one of them. The names of Jacques Grares and Huet le Guette appear on the roster of the thirty-seven 'minstrels' who founded the enabling confraternity in 1321, which built a hospice on this very spot, the crippled woman being given the first sleeping bench in it, where she lay until her death.[77]

Raising the money for the indispensable chapel, the famed St-Julien-des-Ménétriers, was tackled doggedly, the musicians taking up offerings at weddings or wherever else they played. In its foundation charter, they pledged for its continued sustenance not only all their personal belongings, 'present and future', and those of their wives, but their very lives.[78] On St-Julien's façade, which we know only from old engravings, a frieze of angels playing every type of instrument hinted at the minstrels' claim to a heavenly abode. The church was still erect in 1719, when a quadricentennial plaque was posted on it which superbly announced their role 'from time immemorial [as] founders, lay patrons, sole possessors, endowers, governors and administrators'.[79]

5. St-Julien-des-Ménétriers: the minstrels' chapel, built with their collections taken at weddings and other performances

Much higher on the bourgeois scale, no doubt, was the group responsible for the erection of Notre-Dame-de-Boulogne, near Paris, a replica of the shrine on the English Channel which housed the famous statue of the Virgin that had arrived mysteriously one day in a phantom boat and promptly began accomplishing its miracles. The pilgrimage to this holy place became for a time obligatory for stylish Parisians,[80] until merchants began to complain that it kept them too long away from their affairs. Why not build their own shrine-on-the-water nearer home? The idea caught fire. Two brothers who owned 7½ acres on the Seine a few miles downstream from Paris offered it as a site and the foundation was under way.

Despite its closeness to the capital, the trip to the new Boulogne, done on foot, to be sure, could simulate some of the hazardous conditions of an actual pilgrimage. There was a dense trackless wood to be traversed (the present Bois de Boulogne), where even an occasional boar or fox might be glimpsed. Consent of the king, the bishop, of the pope himself was obtained for their foundation by the spangled patrons, who lavished their donations on it. The church went up swiftly, radiant with a rich complement of stained-glass windows, frescoes and statuary.[81] And soon, too, this pious but splendid fraud was consecrated by its own set of miracles, to which the bishop obligingly attested.

The study of cathedrals is facilitated by their perennity. More than any other type of medieval monument they have survived, though they may have had to submit to many alterations in the process. Notre-Dame de Paris did not escape that kind of defacement: the destruction of virtually all of its old glass, of a considerable part of its sculpture, its roodscreen, much of its choir enclosure and its fourteenth-century stalls, to say nothing of the disfigurement due to the roughshod restorative methods of Viollet-le-Duc and his associates. Nevertheless, the cathedral looks essentially today as it did in the thirteenth century. And, above all, it is there.

The same cannot be said about the great body of Paris's medieval architectural patrimony, which counted two hundred religious structures as late as 1700 and of which hardly twenty now survive. The mortality of bourgeois-sponsored projects has been particularly high, leaving nothing but an engraving for St-Julien, a tower for St-Jacques-de-la-Boucherie, a bowdlerized version of Notre-Dame-de-Boulogne and for what was probably Paris's most splendid middle-class monument—St-Jacques-aux-Pèlerins—only five worn statues. But the pilgrim church did bequeath a surrogate in the form of its incomparable fabric records, which detail by detail preserve for our imagination its marvellous material substance.

It is difficult to describe the wonder of those confraternity rolls which have come down to us almost intact for the vital period of the pilgrim church's creation. Not only do they reveal every slightest gesture in its building story, the source of every denier received, the outlet of every livre spent. As precious as these factual data is the spiritual essence of the time itself which is released as one unwinds the lengthy scrolls at Paris's Public Welfare Archival Library, written in charming Old-French script.

While the participation of the burghers throughout its career gave St-Jacques its unique imprint, the founders were happy to share those honours with royalty, reflecting a common trend through much of the feudal period, when the bourgeoisie often found the king a vital champion of its soaring needs. Do we not find the king himself listed among the initial donors in the first great roll of 1319–24: 'Philip-the-Tall, whom may God absolve [for he was dead by then], by the hand of Croissant de Corbeil, Jew, 500 livres'?[82] (He was the king's banker.) This important donation was only the first of a continuing flow of gifts from members of the royal family, which, none the less, added up to only a fraction of the total amount contributed.

For St-Jacques-aux-Pèlerins was from the beginning and remained pre-eminently a bourgeois effort. In the first five years alone they paid out in building costs 5,772 livres,[83] enough to finance a cathedral. In addition, an annuity of 162 livres and 13 sous to cover the priests' salaries—four being planned at first, quickly raised to eight—was collected in 1323, indicating, besides, that the church must have already been racing vertiginously to its completion.[84]

But a much larger clerical family was even then foreseen, as can be glossed from one item in the 1319–24 roll, which calls for the making of twenty-eight stalls decorated with 'little animals', which may have been a reference to underseat carvings, or misericords.[85] These stalls could have been intended for the large number of individually endowed chaplaincies that were already anticipated and which would total close to fifty by the century's end.[86]

How that many daily masses could be fitted into the moderately sized church without utter chaos is hard to imagine. By 1343, with the edifice only recently terminated, the confraternity's governors can be seen assembling to discuss with the master-mason (architect) and master-carpenter this question of the lack of space and

6. A co-operative foundation of burghers and royalty, St-James-of-the-Pilgrims, once a splendid church and hospice, has left only five statues that are now at Cluny Museum: an Apostle. The sculptor could well have been Robert de Launay, who is documented as having done 'ten of the twelve' Apostles

the ways and means of overcoming it: 'To see and examine how and by how much the chapel would be expanded.'[87]

Nothing seemed too extravagant for the administrators of the pilgrim church to undertake, a confidence that was fully justified by the continuing stream of gifts. Four people in the early years bequeathed all or a major part of their worldly goods to it, one of them while on pilgrimage to Compostela, the great shrine of St-Jacques's patron. Ten donors gave a house or other important property and sixteen more gave either goodly sums of cash or yearly *rentes* worth 75 to 200 livres.[88]

In the case of William-with-the-Long-Nose, Englishman and beer-brewer, the 26 livres he donated in his will had to be dug out of his bin-hopper where he had hidden them.[89] It was only part of William's legacy since he had designated St-Jacques as sole heir to all his wealth, 'fixed or movable', the whole lot specifically assigned to the building fund. The same goal was undoubtedly intended by Philip-the-Mustardmaker, an inventory of whose worldly goods produced the not unimportant sum of 134 livres.[90]

One donor, Guillaume de Vertu, gave enough to cover the wages of a mason and his helper for forty days.[91] Others were privileged to know the very object that their gift would pay for, as was the case with Pierre de Clermont, butcher, whose 100 sous (5 livres) sufficed for the carving of the Gabriel of the great portal's Annunciation.[92] Others supplied six livres each for the making of the twelve Apostles who lined the nave on both sides in a stately procession that advanced solemnly toward the altar, where 'Our Lord'—costing seven livres—was waiting to receive them.[93] And in the end all the major elements of the church's embellishment are accounted for in this marvellous record: sculpture and stained-glass, small-art objects and goldsmith's work.

Almost it seems at one point that even medieval teratology had not been forgotten until one realizes that the 'ogre' referred to several times in the rolls is meant to designate the church organ,[94] for music must not be forgotten at St-Jacques, either. It is amazing, too, how much of the work is attributable to the responsible artists. We learn, for example, that there was once a series of murals devoted to the 'legend monsieur saint Jaques' done by Pierre de Broisselles (Brussels), who received 24 livres for the job.[95] Raoul de Heudicourt and his assistants did the important portal statues of the kneeling queen, her mother and four daughters, all encompassed by adoring angels, as well as a mammoth topical representation of the dedication ceremony, containing portraits of all the great ones present.[96]

We can no longer tell anything about the capacity for true portraiture possessed by St-Jacques's artists, since none of their work done 'from life' remains. But the confraternity rolls reveal that the patrons of this sculpture were preoccupied with the question of individuation from another order given by them for 'a bishop [to be done] in the semblance of mons. de Biauvais', the head of the Beauvais church, who was a kind of patron of the confraternity and sang the consecration mass at St-Jacques.[97] This personage is again named in a task assigned to sculptor and painter Robert de Launay: 'For a sketch of Monseigneur de Valois [the prince] and Monseigneur de Biauvais and to paint them, 40 sous'.[98]

Those four kneeling daughters at the side of Queen Jeanne, previously cited at the portal of the pilgrim church, could almost be considered a symbol of the exhaustion, after an astonishing three-hundred-and-fifty-years, of the 'direct' Capetian line. Philippe-le-Bel's three sons all died young, all had short reigns, all failed to leave viable offspring of the 'better sex'.[99] This resulted in the accession to the throne of a new lineage, that of the Valois, which was the precipitating cause of the Hundred Years War. This momentous tragedy could not yet be darkening people's minds when the sonless queen came to pray at St-Jacques. Her statue may even have been done before her husband's death, in 1322, when she certainly would have been asking divine intercession in the critical dynastic matter of her failure to produce a male heir for the king.

In addition to the listings of their donations, the confraternity rolls are rich in references to these rather pathetic royal figures. Queen Jeanne laid the foundation stone, which was specially cut for her, a hint that her delicate hands actually hefted it. It was no doubt smaller than the others which leading confrères, in a prudent reminder of their proprietorship, are described as having put down beside it.[100] It was a different Queen Jeanne, the wife of Philip-the-Tall's successor, his brother Charles, who in a gracious gesture donated a jewelled reliquary along with some gilt cloth to be sold for the benefit of the church.[101] Is it because jewels are commonly considered so inherent a part of a queen's personal array that this gift seems to transcend all other royal benefactions?

It needs no gift of divination to read into the queen's heart as to what she hoped to win by her alms and prayers. The latter reached the stage of paroxysm when this Jeanne's husband also died, in February 1328, not two months before their last child was born.[102] That it might be a son and hence take over the succession in his cradle, the queen planned the most persuasive gesture she could think of: the delivery would take place at St-Jacques's Hospital! The bourgeois administrators rose dutifully to their historic task: arranging to install the queen's lying-in bed in the hospice's 'new chambers', properly decorating them, constructing a new entrance, softening her arrival by covering the path with straw and hiring a 'tumbrel to remove the mud when the queen was carried back to Paris'.[103] Bearing a little girl, the confraternity rolls delicately neglected to add, whose illustrious name of 'Blanche' could only disguise the profound dismay that must have been felt by all.[104]

Thus, even in tragedy, was the most thoroughly bourgeois of Paris's churches identified with royalty. This relationship was all the more meaningful historically because of the broad spread of St-Jacques's membership, much different in this respect from that most exclusive of Paris confraternities, the Grande Confrérie Notre-Dame, to which a tight little group of high churchmen, nobility and even royalty belonged, and only burgher patricians who were 'well-revenued'.[105] It must be said, however, that the Grande Confrérie left no monument comparable to this one founded by the Confraternity of St-Jacques, whose popular character is illustrated by the attendance at its annual banquets, fully 1,536 participants being listed as early as 1327.[106]

No other loss among the endless desolation of Paris's medieval churches[107] is as acutely felt both in the aesthetic and social sense as is this one of St-James-of-the-Pilgrims. How sad that it should have weathered the War of Religions, as the French call the hostilities surrounding the Reformation, the Revolution of 1789, and other great upheavals, only to surrender at last to the reckless claims of nineteenth-century urban expansion.

When St-Jacques was destroyed, in 1808, the demolition squad did not even bother to smash the statuary, merely burying it helter-skelter in a great amorphous mound. By 1840, when a new building was planned on the site, the discovery of fourteen large statues by the excavators caused great surprise, as though they had been buried for centuries. A commission of the Société des Antiquaires (specialists in old art, not antique-dealers), sent out to study them, delivered their formal judgment that they had belonged to St-Jacques-aux-Pèlerins and represented Christ and the twelve Apostles.[108] One smaller figure, dressed as a pilgrim, must have been the modest donor, the commissioners conjectured, who wound up their report by suggesting that the government negotiate the purchase of the statues.

This was not done. Five of the great statues went to an appreciative sculptor as pay for his work on the department store of 'novelties' that was built on the

St-Jacques tumulus. Fortunately, the Cluny Museum was able to acquire these pieces in 1852 from the sculptor's widow, and they are there today. As for the nine remaining carvings, they were reinterred on the spot, except for three that got a reprieve: a beautiful seated St Jacques and two standing Apostles. These were implanted on the new store's façade, to justify the splendiferous name that its proprietors had thought up for their business:

AT THE SIGN OF THE STATUES OF ST-JACQUES

Soon, however, bits of the old carvings began to peel off and fall, and one day it was a big chunk that hurtled to the ground. The aroused authorities, in the name of public safety, ordered the entire group dislodged. But it was found that to do this in a way that could save the statues would be rather costly, so it was decided to destroy them as they were, *in situ*. Accordingly, with pickaxe and hammer they were pulverized to dust.[109]

Whatever we have been able to discover in the way of bourgeois church patronage, it can only be a fraction of what was originally bestowed, the flower of voluntary benevolence, wholeheartedly and devoutly given. This munificence will be seen to have been common to all the cities that we have studied, though it is especially striking in the case of Paris. Capital of a great conquering power, a goodly portion of its overwhelming spoils was lavished on aesthetic monuments, which were among the most refulgent that the Middle Ages created. The bourgeoisie shared importantly in both aspects of this historic phenomenon: in pocketing the expropriated wealth of the assimilated lands and in transmuting a part of it into splendid works of architecture and art.

They were by no means the only donors, for the patronage of pious aesthetic works was a universal feature of the Middle Ages. This was nowhere more glowingly illustrated than in Paris, one of the most affluent of all medieval cities. The wealth that poured into it from a dozen sources will probably never be fully evaluated and a huge amount of it was wasted on two ill-considered and extravagant Crusades. But its quantity was so great that what was spared could still endow this brilliant capital with unsurpassed economic and artistic riches. The latter, with which we are particularly concerned, found a double outlet of memorable scope at Paris: its marvellous, virtually twice-built cathedral and an almost endless number of important, simultaneously-created other monuments.

2

AMIENS

Cathedral and Commune

AMIENS CATHEDRAL CHRONOLOGY

1220   Destruction of Romanesque cathedral by fire in 1218 requires total recon-
        struction. Greatly enlarged, it is begun at the west while other buildings are
        temporarily maintained, St-Firmin-le-Confesseur serving as substitute cathedral.

1236   Nave is completed; also the lower west façade including the dense, magnificent
        sculpture of its portals.

1243   One of the façade towers had advanced sufficiently so that church-bells are cited
        in it by this date.

1247   Begun soon after 1236, when St-Firmin has been demolished, the apse ambula-
        tory and the radiating chapels are almost terminated by this date. The chapel
        lancets, mainly paid for by burghers or their organizations, are simultaneously
        glazed.

1258   Fire in the outer roofing of the choir halts construction, requiring some
        rebuilding.

1269   Choir is completed. Entire church's upper windows are glazed in following two
        decades.

Pre-1292 Chantry chapels along nave-aisles are added, following the Paris model of build-
        ing them between the vertical buttresses. The last two chapels are not done until
        1373–5, however.

1366   Work to complete the north tower is begun.

c.1401 South tower is terminated.

1508–19 The choir's 120 wooden stalls are carved. Probably France's finest set, they are
        still almost perfectly preserved.

Establishment of the Amiens commune,[1] in 1117, is often referred to as a revolution. Strange revolution in which the bourgeoisie had both the king and bishop as allies! The king's motive was control over the barons of the region and extension of the royal domain toward Flanders.[2] Louis VI was at the head of his troops when they and the armed burghers, including eighty women, stormed the citadel in the heart of the 'cité'.

But the entrenched count could not be dislodged. The king himself was gravely wounded and the attack was converted into a siege. It lasted two whole years, during which death poured down intermittently from the castle's parapets. When the stronghold fell at last, the king had only the burghers to depend on to hold the city for him. It was not until 1185 that the grandson of Louis VI, Philippe-Auguste, was able to conquer and definitively annex the county to the crown.[3] But by then the commune had firmly entrenched itself.

After the count's expulsion, the two other lay co-seigniors at Amiens—the *vidame* and the *châtelain*—stepped aside with more or less grace, donating their holdings in the city to religious groups or selling them to the commune.[4] Neither of the two remaining powers that thereafter faced the burghers—king or church—opposed their rise. Quite the contrary. The occasional inevitable differences that rose between the city and the bishop, which elsewhere might have provoked violent strife, were settled by periodic *concordiae* that stud the archives of this fortunate medieval community.[5] To all effects, the Amiens commune became the crown's principal ally in the region, a prodigal supplier of finances, the mainstay of the royal bastion.

The long span of peace that resulted from these accommodations greatly advantaged Amiens's economy. The latter was based on two major elements of trade, the one regional, wine, the other international, a blue dye.[6] Consumed chiefly by the drapery industries of Flanders, England and France, Picardy's woad was grown, processed and packed all within a radius of twenty kilometres of Amiens, along the valleys of the Somme, the Avre and the Encre. Preparation of the dye required much crushing and refining, with power derived from water or wind mills. All the country roundabout reverberated with the sound of turning wheels.[7] Many a proprietor owned one or more mills and often they figured in pious benefactions.[8] There was even one listed as the *moulin à waide* (woad) *de la ville*, for which the city's accounts for 1392 register the purchase of 'one bolt and one ring'.[9]

7. Seal of the commune of Amiens: the symbols illustrate how the burghers associated themselves with the fleur-de-lys of the French crown

Amiens's prelate, who sided with the burghers in 1117, was very much a maverick. Devout, peace-loving, ultimately canonized, Bishop St Geoffroy was a reluctant appointee, having to be virtually dragged out of retreat at the Abbey of Nogent when he assumed his post. Repeatedly thereafter we find him running back into the cloisters, from which he was always again summoned to his worldly assignment by his archbishop or some church council.[10] Whatever else might be conjectured about such a man, it is understandable that he should be sensitive to the yearnings of his flock, even if expressed as that shibboleth repulsive to most churchmen of his time—the commune.

Church and burghers at Amiens had various mutual grounds for their attachment, in addition. The prelate had often received the aid of the citizens during the repeated challenges of his more powerful and bellicose co-seigniors. Equally important were the economic advantages he obtained from them. There was no single phase of the city's commercial and industrial life in which the church was not involved, often co-operatively. Thus was consolidated an extraordinary friendship, which twice in less than a century produced a remarkable collaboration in cathedral-building campaigns.

Each time it was following a ravaging conflagration. After the first disaster, which occurred in 1137, the citizens and clergy met to determine how the reconstruction could be expedited. According to a hallowed legend drawn from a thirteenth-century breviary, the conferees reluctantly decided to parade the venerated bones of their first bishop, St Firmin, around the diocese in quest of funds. But the revered relic refused to move beyond a great stone at one of the city's gates. Whereupon the populace joyously returned the reliquary to the church, then vied with each other in offering gifts of 'gold necklaces, silver plate, precious stones, a great quantity of coins and rings and the elegant robes that they wore on holidays . . .'.[11]

This happy outcome of the fund drive may have been authentic enough. But we also possess more substantive proof of aid by commoners, in the form of two documents, dated 1145 and 1151. These two gifts, beyond their immediate purpose, helped establish the cathedral chapter as co-owner with the commune of the new Great Quay, the city's major river port. It was to this early commercial association between church and burghers that has been attributed the 'lasting peace' which blessed their relations for centuries.[12] The earlier and more important of the two gifts—made by 'burgher Nicolas son of burgher Mainier', who is qualified as 'illustrious' and 'dynamic' in that early episcopal text—embraced his house and lands and twelve serfs, in addition to the wharves.[13]

The great ceremonial that was arranged to envelop Nicolas's gift not only confirmed its importance but also reflected the stellar posture that a burgher could attain at that early date in the eyes of Amiens's hierarchy. By request of the donor and his wife, the presentation took place on Christmas Day and the proprietary charts were deposited on the Virgin's altar in the presence of numbers of witnesses, both lay and clerical. After the ceremony a great banquet was offered by the benefactors to the entire church family.[14]

One can imagine the bishop's gratitude for the splendid gift, which must have proved a genuine resource for the restitution of his damaged church. The extent of the ruin is not known. The cathedral could, at any event, be reconsecrated in fifteen years, which seems to delimit the destruction. The rebuilding could hardly have included any sweeping changes in the then modest structure. The church's financial needs were acute, as we learn from a pathetic letter that Amiens's Bishop Thierry wrote during this interval to Abbot Suger of St-Denis, who was king's regent while Louis VII was absent on the Second Crusade. In it the prelate pleaded his dire poverty for being unable to contribute a single penny to the ongoing campaign in the Holy Land.[15]

After the great fire of 1218, when the church of Amiens had to be totally rebuilt (starting in 1220), the burghers were again called on to assume a fundamental role. For the extent of their contribution, there is no masterbook of accounts or catalogue of gifts to enlighten us. Such records are rarely supplied by early church cartularies.[16] None the less, there is a considerable amount of indirect evidence of burgher patronage at Amiens, derived most notably from the inscriptions and heraldic symbols on the church's upper stained-glass windows, which the famous classicist, Charles Du Cange, transcribed in 1667.[17] The lancets themselves were destroyed during or shortly after the Revolution and no one had bothered to sketch them, though they must have been magnificent judging from the single window that survived the vandalism. Many other churches lost their glass in the pre-revolutionary period. The purpose was ostensibly to 'bring light' into the old edifices. Actually, abhorrence of 'gothic' art by the church canons was the hardly hidden motive of the vandalism.[18]

Du Cange recorded donor inscriptions for twenty-five of the cathedral's upper windows. Twelve of them identified burghers. Moreover, all but one of these was in

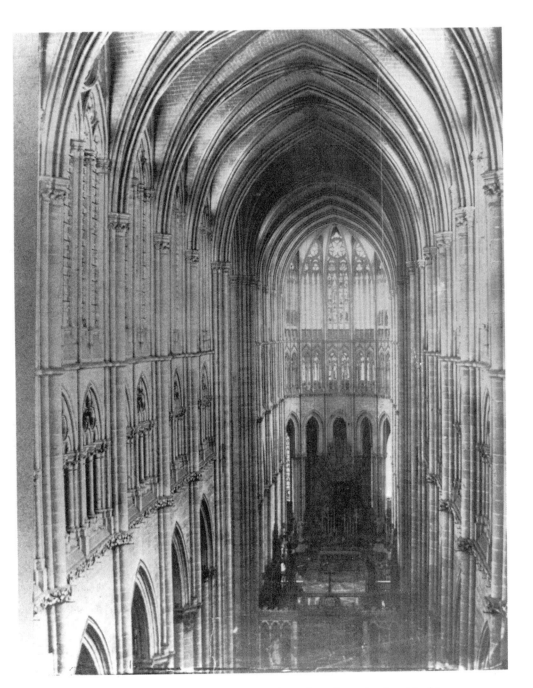

8. Amiens Cathedral: the great nave seen from the tribune level and looking east

some manner associated with woad, the great source of Amiens's wealth. A number of the city's leading bourgeois families—in whose coats-of-arms, significantly, the colour blue predominated—figured among these benefactors. Du Cange actually described one scene in the vanished donor panels representing a transaction between merchants who offered for sale sacks of the brightly tinctured dye to purchasers with glinting coins in their hands. The communal arms were also present among the donor panels, at times linked with those of André Malherbe, Amiens's greatest woad magnate, who participated in the payment of no fewer than six of the cathedral's great windows. One of the cathedral's three rose-windows also had a burgher donor.[19]

Notre-Dame's lower lancets were similarly adorned with painted glass. We are well informed about these windows also since a number of them survived into the present century, only to be destroyed by a lamentable accident.[20] Burgher purses played a large enabling role in their production too, though it was mainly confined to the seven chapels of the apse, built around the mid-century. In two of them all three lancets were paid for by individuals of the middle class or their guilds.[21] In the others, burgher aid can be conjectured from their foundations of chaplaincies and other indications.[22]

Such massive assistance by the bourgeoisie has by no means been an unfailing characteristic of cathedral building. As often as not, we shall see, they played but a minor role. Burgher patronage depended mainly on two factors: their economic situation and the state of their relations with the church. At Amiens, both of these elements were, for most of the critical construction period, at an optimum. While substantial burgher help was not indispensable for building a cathedral, the expeditiousness of construction and splendour of the edifice usually suffered from its absence. At Amiens the work progressed so fast that the basic vessel was completed in the quarter-century after 1220. This was all the more remarkable in that the funds came chiefly from local sources. Amiens was not a great pilgrimage centre.[23] Nor does it seem to have benefited from important gifts by royalty or the regional nobility or even by its affluent abbeys.[24]

However important the role of Amiens's burghers in the cathedral-building programme, it was almost certainly inferior to that of the clerical family, who, to all appearances, accepted their responsibility punctiliously. This, too, is more than can be said for various other churches. We have no precise information on how much money it took to keep up the phenomenal speed that was maintained over several decades at Amiens. From partial statistics gathered at several cathedrals, we can assume that as much as 1,500–2,500 livres a year were needed there. In addition, the Amiens fabric had some extraordinary expenses that concerned the cathedral construction only indirectly. These stemmed from the very limited space in the cathedral compound which required the demolition and re-erection elsewhere of several other units that stood on the assigned land, all of which was making itself felt before 1250, when the apse was fully built.[25]

But the bishop and his chapter (the latter being nominally in charge of the building fabric) did not seem to boggle at any outlay. Geoffroy d'Eu, who headed the church during this early construction period (1222–36), was one of those intoxicated builders of the age, whom we shall see now and again giving energetic impulsion to their cathedrals. In his quest for funds, we find this prelate even selling two of his most important revenue-earning properties, both to the commune, as it happened.[26]

Soon enough, however, such expedients would no longer be required as the gifts began streaming in. Within a few years there was even money left over for the chapter to make important property investments.[27] By 1234, in fact, the canons must have considered the financial situation so good and the building campaign so far advanced that they increased their own daily 'distributions'.[28] Would they have done so if the building programme lacked funds? Unfortunately, we shall find the canons in other cities doing exactly that. But not these at Amiens.

Nevertheless, the enormous outlay that was required exacted its price, which fell most heavily on the city's parish churches. Unlike Paris, where both the cathedral and subsidiary churches could be built simultaneously, the secondary units at Amiens were simply not allowed to allocate important funds for their own building needs during the cathedral's construction. One feels that Amiens's entire clergy, together with the bourgeoisie and the nobility, came to this joint decision. This was to be the period pre-eminently for concentration on the great cathedral, they agreed. Evidence of such an understanding is very persuasive.

Thus, of the eight parish churches within the walls, three were burnt down at the time of the 1218 fire, but remained unrebuilt throughout the rest of the thirteenth century and well on into the next.[29] Three others, which were built in the twelfth century or even earlier, were certainly in need of basic repair and enlargement to take care of the population growth, but received neither until the fifteenth or sixteenth century.[30] The last two—St-Firmin-le-Confesseur and St-Michel—were, it is true, rebuilt in the thirteenth century. But it is doubtful if this would have occurred if the cathedral's reconstruction had not required their being moved! Even so, work on the new St-Firmin went on for hardly more than ten years, when, once the choir was completed and partitioned off, operations on the rest of the church were abandoned for the better part of a century.[31]

There are, indeed, various signs that even the cathedral fabric suffered an eclipse of funds eventually. Aside from the inferential evidence that the chapter's investments in property virtually disappeared in the 1240s, there is the documented fact of an urgent meeting being called by the bishop, in 1236, at which all elements of the city's population were represented and where problems of the cathedral campaign, including money, were discussed.[32] Also, it is clear that work on the transept and apse, started around 1238, proceeded at a more leisurely pace than had been the case with the church's nave, where building operations had begun.[33]

The chevet's stone vaulting, it seems certain, could not have been initiated until after 1258, when the timber roofing was burnt out by a documented fire, traces of which Viollet-le-Duc, the well-known nineteenth-century architect and restorer, discovered on the upper chapel walls when he was repairing the cathedral. Building detail in the new section was also much less elegant, he found, than in the earlier-built areas, which he interpreted as indicating that even after the resumption of full-scale construction funds were less plentiful than before.[34]

By the mid-1240s the fabric fund was at such a low ebb that the bishop was prompted to a retaliatory act that could have endangered the commune's traditional amicable relationship with the church. Seventeen young clerics or students had been arrested by the king's bailiff and provost for having purportedly 'dishonoured' the former's daughter.[35] One of them was beaten to death when seized and five others were summarily executed. The bishop, gravely affronted in his judicial authority over the clergy (which included students), imposed a sharp judgment against the crown officials but also charged that the commune shared their guilt for allowing its prison in the *beffroi* (watchtower) to be used to lock up the young clerics. The case had to go before an arbitration board, which, dominated by churchmen, imposed a heavy fine on the city. It was ordered to found six chaplaincies, one for each of the deceased clerics. The cost was set at the monumental sum of 2,000 livres, about $1,600,000 (£880,000).[36]

9. Sellers of woad, donors of St-Nicolas Chapel; the inscription telling of this gift can be
seen above and at the left of the kneeling men

The 'award' was a windfall for the church exchequer, but the wisdom of imposing so drastic a fine on the commune strikes one as highly questionable. It seems to reveal a reckless eagerness to refill the fabric's coffers by any available means. But the fine could not have helped to speed up the lagging construction since it was not paid for almost twenty years—in 1262.[37] What appears to have been a particularly low period in fabric funds followed and with it a cooling off of the burghers' patronage.[38] How long this may have lasted is obscured by the fire of 1258 in the apse roofing which evidently required extensive repairs. These must have been completed by 1269, however, since upper choir windows were already being installed by that date, according to one of Du Cange's inscriptions. It belonged to a bishop. Indeed, not a single one of the eleven donors specified by the archivist in the upper choir was a burgher!

Had the 2,000 livres fine paid in 1262 left them short of funds, or in a bad humour toward the hierarchy? Both would have been ended by 1280 in any case when leaders (*maieurs*) of the guild of woad-merchants paid for a window in the transept. And in the following decade, during which the entire upper nave got its glass, all but one of its patrons were either the commune itself or wealthy woad-men, the richest of them all, André Malherbe, paying for half of the lancets.[39]

Clearly, then, the burghers' benevolence toward their cathedral had been restored by the 1280s. How strange, accordingly, that when the nave-aisle chantry chapels, a favourite zone of bourgeois patronage, were created, starting around 1290, only one of them was with some probability due to bourgeois largess.[40] A second chantry of the twelve has, in addition, generally been attributed to local woad-men. This is the famous St-Nicolas chapel, on whose outer wall has been superposed the well-known carving of two men standing before a sack of woad. The assignment of the chapel to these 'Amiens' merchants or their guild has seemed automatic. But it is palpably erroneous, if we but refer to the inscription on the stone, which identifies the donors as the two kneeling figures at the bottom of the relief, who are not Amiens men at all but people from the outlying region:

> THE GOOD PEOPLE FROM THE TOWNS ABOUT AMIENS WHO
> SELL WOAD HAVE BUILT THIS CHAPEL WITH THEIR ALMS.[41]

That there should have been a second decline so soon after the first in middle-class patronage during the creation of Amiens's chantries is a sobering element of our story. Over and over we shall be reminded by similar occurrences that even in the extraordinarily art-conscious Middle Ages, other considerations might take precedence over aesthetic ones, however important they might have seemed. In this particular case, as it happened, the cathedral's construction was the victim of a shattering calamity suffered by the Amiens woad-merchants. In fact, it is no exaggeration to say that this commercial disaster set the city on an economic decline from which it never completely recovered.

The first rude blow occurred in 1295, when the woad-men's goods warehoused in English ports were confiscated by King Edward I. It was an early act in the drapery war that was to rage between the two countries until the end of the century. Together with unpaid accounts, Amiens's total loss was 4,000 livres[42] (modern equivalent, $3,200,000 or £1,760,000), enough to build and furbish the entire series of lateral nave chantries at the cathedral. One of the big losers among the fifty-five Amiens woad-merchants expropriated by Edward was none other than André Malherbe, who had a warehouse at Lynn and whose agents sold his dyes throughout the English Midlands. Fortunately, by 1295, André's great church endowments had already been solidly financed.[43] He died soon after.

Even more grave than this stunning financial loss, moreover, was the virtual obliteration of the woad-producers' outlets, not only in England but also in the much more important drapery centres of Flanders, for which the Picard dye had been a major supplier. Here King Philippe-le-Bel's long-lasting war shut off the lucrative market for many more years with but intermittent periods of relief until competition from other sources broke Amiens's monopoly, reducing its prosperity accordingly. Added to these grim realities was the fact that the commune had, in 1292, just before the crisis onset, purchased the king's provostship (*prévôté*) in the city. For this ensemble of the crown's tax rights in trade and commerce, Amiens engaged itself to pay the huge yearly fee of 690 livres, which eventually proved to be an oppressive burden.[44]

It is a lucky circumstance that before this chain of calamities assailed it, Amiens's great cathedral was well along the way to completion. We shall not always find so happy a conjuncture. At Amiens itself, the competition between basic material needs and pious donorship must have been felt during the twelfth century already, when various urgent tasks had devolved on the young commune. These included the strengthening and expansion of the city walls, the building of roads and bridges, the dredging of its numerous canals, and most important of all the stupendous engineer-

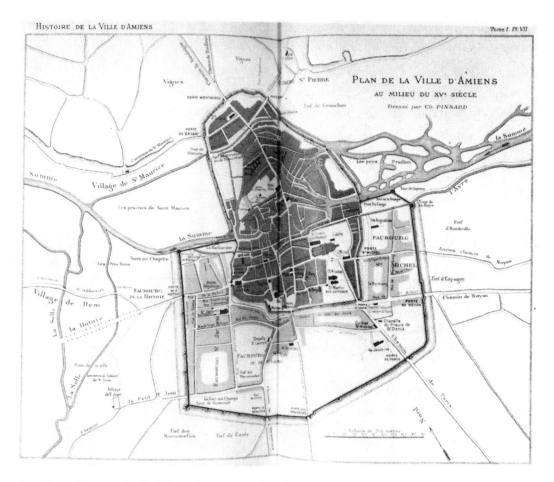

PLAN DE LA VILLE D'AMIENS
AU MILIEU DU XVᵉ SIÈCLE
Dressé par Ch. PINSARD

10. Map of Amiens in the fifteenth century. The Chemin de l'Eau, the artificial channel cut out by the commune in the twelfth century, forms a half-ellipse in the upper part of the photo. The Somme enters the city at the right and passes through it by way of ten or more branches, including the Chemin de l'Eau, all rejoining the stream's main body at the Port d'Amiens (at left), likewise built in the twelfth century. The great wall in the lower part of the map did not exist in the period that we are studying, when the entire city was enclosed in the map's dark section

ing exploit of cutting out a great new bed for the Somme. Called the Chemin de l'Eau, this artificial waterway traced a sweeping semi-ellipse around the town's lower quarters, enabling moderate-sized boats and barges loaded with precious woad to move unhampered past the city and out toward the English Channel.[45]

Of hardly less importance than all of this to its economic expansion was the process of building up the city's seigniory, without which its political power within the feudal system would have been most fragile.[46] The commune pursued this task relentlessly by the purchase of urban properties and feudal quitrents, including a number that had been taken over by the king from the count of Amiens. The city started this task early, and though it had to pay dearly for its acquisitions,[47] it pressed them so persistently that by 1228, according to a perceptive local historian, it had become 'the uncontested possessor of justice and landed seigniory' within the walls. This, he underscored, was the 'basis of its independence'.[48]

The advanced position of the commune of Amiens was consolidated, in 1292, by the outright purchase of the king's share of taxes on urban trade, to which we have already alluded. Though the commune paid 690 livres a year for these 'rights', only 400 livres actually came back to it in collections. The difference was no doubt compensated to some extent by what a leading authority, Augustin Thierry, has termed 'the increase of its jurisdiction [rights of justice] and political prerogatives'.[49] Other important acquisitions of a similar nature were the tax right on woollens and furs,[50] and that on woad, for which the city paid 1,000 livres in 1291.[51] And similar purchases continued on into the fourteenth century.[52] Even the strongest of medieval communes had to buy its 'liberties' in this manner and often enough it had to do so with its blood.

One wonders where all the money came from for these acquisitions. The answer is—from borrowing. The city had several ways of obtaining finance, at non-usurious rates of interest, that were widely current among medieval communities. The most common method used at Amiens was the *rente-à-vie*, a life annuity for which burghers invested a lump sum in cash. Also, the city took up orphans' inheritances and paid yearly stipends to their wards until their maturity. And it accepted the principal on pious bequests to churches from burghers' wills for anniversaries and chaplaincies, whose annuities it continued to dole out conscientiously for centuries.[53] All this borrowing added steadily to the city's debt, about which it seemed quite *insouciant* but which in the end became a source of economic distress.[54] The fact is that even the most liberated of medieval cities had insufficient tax rights to fund its manifold activities.

Amiens's extensive proprietary involvement eventually affected adversely its relations with church groups. A radical change in this respect was suddenly revealed, in 1264, in a dramatic outburst. The butt was only by accident the Dominican Order: it might have been any one of several other groups.[55] The friars, only recently established at Amiens—outside the walls, it should be clearly noted—managed to acquire two houses *inside* the city. Swiftly, even brutally, the authorities reacted, literally driving the monks from their property and forcing them to sell it to the municipality itself.[56] Significantly, a goods market was soon after erected on the land.[57]

One could almost be tempted to assume an anti-monastic or in any case an anti-Dominican prejudice on the part of Amiens's burghers. Neither would be true. None the less, it does seem amazing to find the Jacobins, who enjoyed an extraordinary prestige at the time, at least in the North, as the church's great lance against heresy, being treated so cavalierly by the Amiens commune. Moreover, the burghers knew only too well in what close affection the reigning king held the friars. In fact, in 1260, when these monks had acquired a first house inside the city, St Louis (Louis IX) had exerted all his influence to get the bishop's consent to their moving into it. The prelate, conscious of the city's opposition, delayed year after year before giving his approval.[58] Soon after it was obtained, the Dominicans got possession of the other two houses and their secret intention of moving their establishment within the walls became transparent. Then the city acted.

Other monastic orders met with the same savage opposition whenever they were considered to be endangering the commune's primary seigniory. This was true particularly of the Augustins, with whom, despite the royal sponsorship that they too enjoyed, the city conducted an endless vendetta. On one occasion, indeed, the city forced these monks to destroy various conventual buildings they had put up within the walls, including their very church and altar.[59] Other orders, like the Franciscans, who proved more accommodating[60]—that is, agreed to stay outside the walls—were managed with greater consideration. The most shining case of this kind was undoubtedly the Celestines, who got handsome grants from the commune, all in the suburbs, to be sure! Even former protagonists were eventually treated amicably, once the commune's seigniorial rights were beyond challenge.[61]

The danger to these rights that the monastic groups represented is revealed by a tell-tale little phrase that the city fathers often used in characterizing them. They were *gens de mainmorte*.[62] This meant that property falling into their 'dead hand' would be permanently withdrawn from communal control. How this could hurt the city is illustrated by the bicentenary struggle it had to pursue to force the church groups to pay their share of defence costs, for example.[63] Furthermore, churches always expected and often received extraordinary allowances in royal taxes on commodities put up for sale, including woad and wine, even though they were competitive with burghers' goods. Clerics even conducted public taverns to further these ends, despite repeated prohibition by prelates and popes.[64]

Nevertheless, it was not always possible to keep inner-city property from being assigned to church ownership. What if a burgher wanted to establish a chaplaincy (daily mass) and could only bequeath his house in its support? The city used a shrewd protective clause for such cases, which the recipient, church or chaplain, would have to sign, pledging that the property would remain 'taxable and justiciable' by the commune. The city's archives still contain dozens of these papers, dated from before the middle of the thirteenth century and going on into the fourteenth and beyond.[65]

While commerce was the goad of the burghers' unrelenting drive to secure their seigniory, at Amiens it was compounded by an almost fetishistic pursuit of space. This was a controlling element of many of the city's acts. Certainly it was a central factor in its antagonism to monastic groups. The root reason for this concern was the peculiarity of Amiens's topographic situation, its numerous river branches and tributaries slicing the city into a dozen segments, frequently overrunning their banks and sharply restricting the habitable and commercial areas.[66] This condition was further aggravated by the large number of mills used in woad-production, which dammed up the waterflow, established permanent swamps in numerous areas and intermittently seriously limited the city's water supply.[67]

Already in the high Middle Ages the walled *cité* of Amiens was one of the most exiguous known.[68] Its great economic development beginning in the late eleventh century multiplied its space needs, which could not be fully satisfied. Adding to this problem was the character of the city's commercial role chiefly as a distributing centre for woad and wine. This made the possession of a vast storage area indispensable. By ingenuity and at great expenditure in money and effort a solution was eventually found. But it remained partial and did not permanently relieve the city's spatial paranoia.

Amiens's vast system of medieval cellars was all but forgotten by the nineteenth century, when a series of accidents reminded inhabitants of their existence, dangerously honeycombing the entire subsoil of the city's centre. They were promptly filled in and covered over. But, as it happened by good fortune, the man who was assigned this job, Charles Pinsard, had the archaeological enterprise to take extensive measurements and even drawings of a number of these vaults, which now enrich the city's archives. They give us an impressive idea of the titanic effort that went into the making of the cellars. Pinsard counted several hundred of the subterranean chambers, which often underlay entire lengths of streets.[69]

Double- and even triple-storeyed, the storage areas transcended what we moderns would consider functional sufficiency in their fabrication. Entirely laid out in cut stone, the chambers were at times beautifully vaulted and embellished with carved capitals and friezes.[70] In fact, some resembled Gothic chapels or seemed to have served some other more refined purpose than the stowing of wine-casks and woad-sacks.[71] In their ensemble these great underground caves of Amiens today constitute a kind of buried medieval city, waiting for future generations of excavators to rediscover![72]

The imperious element of space could hardly have failed to affect the life and even structure of Amiens's churches. The cathedral's expansiveness—by far the most vast

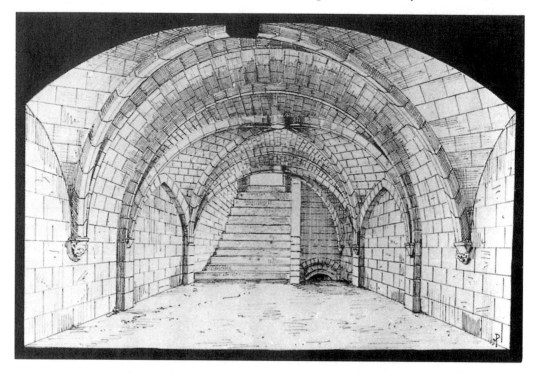

11. A medieval cellar of Amiens: one of the four hundred cellars filled in during the nineteenth century by city engineer, Charles Pinsard, who made sketches of a number of them before doing so. Note the elegant vaulting and the sculptured terminals

in all of France—was a reverse adaptation, its planners no doubt seeking to make up for deficiencies elsewhere.[73] Besides, as we have seen, several other units had to be sacrificed to it. Even so, the struggle for space inside the episcopal compound remained acute, one conflict between bishop and chapter over the size of the cloisters going on for decades.[74] The space allowances of the parishes were even more constricted. Their small number within the walls, eight, servicing a population of 15,000, was one result. And the churches themselves were undersized, barred from the most necessary growth for centuries, until the city walls were greatly expanded.

Thus, St-Firmin-à-la-Porte consisted of only a choir until 1490.[75] St-Firmin-en-Castillon had four bays in all and its chapels were not added until 1477.[76] St-Leu, the only parish built amid the rushing waters of the lower city, was never a big church and did not have its original fabric lengthened until 1481.[77] St-Michel remained forever narrow and deformed, crushed into the uneven space allotted it.[78] Even St-Martin-aux-Waides, the city's most active church, never possessed more than six bays. It must have been bursting at the seams when, in 1477, after repeated pleas, the commune granted its churchwardens all of two feet 'to enlarge their church and make it more beautiful, solemn and devout'.[79]

Another favourite of the burghers, St-Rémy, could not obtain a bit of additional building space from the commune until 1503, after its wardens had long complained that many of the parishioners attending mass had to stand outside 'in the cold, wind and rain'.[80] Not even was there room enough in the parishes to bury their dead, normally a considerable source of income. Interments, if they took place at all in the minuscule plots available, were eventually confined to children. Burials inside churches were also rigorously limited, mostly to the clergy. The *Epitaphier de Picardie* lists only one such burial of a burgher at Amiens in the pre-fifteenth-century period: but it was only his heart.[81]

But what Amiens's parish churches had to sacrifice in the way of structural splendour they often made up for by wealth of décor and the animation of their sacerdotal life. There is no doubt about the burghers' paramount role as patrons of the parishes, which developed notably once the cathedral's exigent financial priorities were disposed of. Unfortunately, because of the almost total devastation of the city's churches in modern times,[82] this contribution is known to us almost exclusively from early descriptions or by a few rare bits of art memorials. Nevertheless, these hints and remnants are of extraordinary interest historically since they are revealing about early 'bourgeois' art, which it would be far less likely to find at a cathedral.

A precious example of this kind is the thirteenth-century graved tombal portrait of Jehan Le Monnier, the son of a mayor of Amiens and head of the city mint, who died in his teens and whom we can still see at the Musée de Picardie, reclining on his eternal bed of roses.

We no longer have the effigy of Pierre Clabaut, another burgher patrician, on the other hand, but only the meticulous instructions he left in his will of 6 March, 1442, about the way he wanted his tomb fashioned:

> . . . handsome and noteworthy, cut from marble and richly worked in brass, like my father's . . . and I want my portrait to be etched on the brass and also that of my wife Isabel if she decides to be buried there, as well as those of my children. . . .[83]

And we have records of a few more such burial arrangements at important parishes like St-Martin-aux-Waides and St-Rémy.[84] Burghers also left provisions for prayers to be said on their behalf or even a daily mass (chaplaincy).[85] Jacques de Bonneville made a touching addition to the mass his brother Simon had established for himself at St-Rémy, paying for the founding of a bell which was to be tolled three times daily during its celebration.[86] Jacques must have been a music-loving man since he is also documented as having paid for the organ at St-Martin-aux-Jumeaux.[87]

The various signs of the burgher presence at St-Rémy are no more than might be expected of a church located in one of Amiens's busiest commercial quarters. Its original foundation, in 1107, significantly, was due to the city itself, which established it as an oratory, endowing it with a modest revenue of 8 livres a year.[88] Several times enlarged and rebuilt after that, it lasted until the Revolution, when it was withdrawn from the cult and sold on the auction block. What could be more appropriate than that a rich merchant should acquire it? Pulling down its sanctuary as though to divest it of its incantatory power, he had the rest of the old church transformed into a splendid town house.[89]

Even more circumstantial than our information about St-Rémy is what we know of St-Martin-aux-Waides, Amiens's pre-eminent bourgeois church, seat of its affluent and politically potent woad-men. The exterior of the church was, to judge from old engravings, nothing much to look at: small, almost shrunken, crushed by a dense surrounding mass of commercial structures. But the interior was, by all accounts, splendid, its decorative profusion manifesting itself particularly in the chapels that wealthy merchants built to house the daily masses that their 'perpetual' chaplains chanted for their everlasting repose.

We are largely beholden for this knowledge to the eighteenth-century chronicle of Jean Pagès, which describes in particular the stained glass in the church's chapels (now vanished with the edifice itself), rating it among the finest in the city. Pagès's account, unhappily, is quite fragmentary, conveying little idea of the glass's style or content. It does give a fillip to the imagination, nevertheless, when he pictures the donor of a John-the-Baptist lancet—Jean de St-Fuscien—'in a long magistrate's robe, with folded hands and kneeling on a prayer stool'.[90] Other window donors included some of Amiens's leading citizens, among them a member of the prominent Cocquerel family as well as that ubiquitous donor, André Malherbe, who paid for as many as three windows here.[91]

This art of St-Martin was a glowing background to what must have been a fervidly active church ritual. The 'merchants' mass' that started their busy day for the woad-men at 4 a.m. (5 a.m. in the winter) was only the first of a lengthy series.[92] Endowed with a number of burgher chaplaincies,[93] the church's offices must have been going on throughout the entire day, so that the merchant who had missed early mass could have left his stall or warehouse at almost any hour to make up for it. Here, too, would come the many woad-producers from the villages roundabout after they had deposited their sacks of dye.

Right next door to the church was the romantically named Hôtel du Noir Chevalier, the woad-men's mercantile seat. Here the dye was assayed and weighed and packed into barrels ready for shipment. Here, too, the tax on sales was collected, one of the city's two principal revenues, from which a deduction went to the woad-men's confraternity. This organization was almost indistinguishable from their business association. So also were the funds of the two groups. The confraternity paid for the 'merchants' mass' and a gamut of other pious and fraternal activities, most of which took place at St-Martin-aux-Waides.[94] And all was intermeshed for the woad-men, religion and professional and social life, joined in characteristic medieval unity.

Equally typical was the spontaneity with which the vibrant Amiens commune assumed civic responsibilities. The true make-up of the medieval citizen who helped build the great cathedrals cannot be fully grasped apart from this facet of his activities. Amiens's city archives, starting early in the twelfth century, reveal an ever-broadening list of accepted duties until their range takes on the aspect of a modern municipality. Besides the building and maintenance of walls, roads, waterways, bridges, quays, other functions included were the minting of money, training of a militia, supervision of trade and commerce, control of markets and the slaughter-house, regulation of quality in consumers' goods and of weights and measures, taxation, justice including capital cases, and many more.[95] Among the French cities that we shall study, Amiens takes the first rank in the breadth of its power and responsibilities.

Medieval man's fun-loving nature was also reflected in the many references to recreation in the aldermen's minutes. Great playing fields were set aside in the western marshes outside the walls where the city fathers themselves might participate zestfully in the Sunday sport.[96] A more patrician activity was the one their sons engaged in, around 1330, competing in tourneys of mounted chivalry against young burghers of Paris, Reims and Bruges.[97] Music, too, was encouraged and minstrels were never absent from an important city function.[98] Even the night guard at the city's watchtower was expected to jig and play the pipes on the upper platform for evening promenaders and it was considered a scandal when one tired old fellow refused to furnish this kind of recreation. He was summarily replaced.[99]

A watchtower, with its great bell for assembly and warning, had a very particular, a very sensitive meaning for the medieval burgher. It was no accident that the one at Amiens was the fruit of the city's first building act. After their victory of 1117, the people tore down the count's execrated *castillon* and with the same stones and on the same spot erected their *beffroi*. The archives show them lavishing treasure to decorate the watchtower with art.[100] It was no exception, moreover, for to medieval man sculpture and painting were an indispensable element of the uses of life. We find such expenditures also described at the *malemaison*, the old city hall,[101] and at the Hôtel des Cloquiers (*clochers* = belltowers), the hall of justice,[102] in both of which many stained-glass windows, often with the linked coats-of-arms of king and city, were installed, paid for out of the communal treasury.

But it was the splendour of the great gates, first seen by visiting notables, that was the most particular pride of the commune. All the gates were richly decorated, but none as grandly as the *Montrécu*,[103] for whose reconstruction, in 1390, we are favoured with a full report. The outlay was so great that the city, heavily indebted by the Hundred Years War, had to ask for a non-interest-bearing loan from the people. The response was breathtaking, with no fewer than 420 citizens from all the parishes subscribing 1,050 livres for this aesthetic purpose.[104]

It is revealing, also, how urgently the burghers undertook tasks concerned with disease and death. Burial was in most places during the medieval period the responsibility of the parish, which would have its plot near the church. Not so at space-restricted Amiens, where the great Cemetery of St-Denis located outside the walls accommodated most of the city's dead and where the authorities can be seen repeatedly expanding its terrain with purchases of fields and gardens.[105] By the fifteenth century, St-Denis had become a veritable *Campo Santo*, with cloisters and arcades and a chapel, all decorated with every type of art, most of it paid for by the burghers.[106]

Hôtel-Dieu, the city's leading hospital, though formally under the church's jurisdiction, was largely administered by the commune. It throve from innumerable burgher gifts, great and small.[107] One of the most important was that of its pioneer benefactor, Jean de Croy, who supplied the building site in the *basse-ville*, to which the hospital was shifted, in 1236, when it was necessary to clear its original site for the cathedral's mammoth construction programme.[108] Even more prodigal, perhaps, was the gift of Marie de Bethisy and her sister Isabelle, which consisted of a great batch of priceless quitrents on urban properties that were so important in the city's constant quest to expand its primary feudal seigniory.[109]

Names of all the city's leading families (and far more 'unknowns') can be found in Hôtel-Dieu's archives, some establishing daily masses at its chapel, others endowing some specific building element in the hospital's never-ceasing evolution, among the things listed being 'the cloisters', 'our oratory', 'to repair the walls', 'to build a house', etc.[110] Thus was social welfare happily joined to piety and to the extraordinary penchant of Amiens's bourgeoisie for architectural enterprise, which so much favoured the cathedral and many of its other churches.

That Amiens's citizens should have undertaken the full responsibility for its leper-colony as early as the twelfth century likewise reflects their alertness to the city's health problems.[111] Fortunately, the statutes of St-Lazare (or St-Ladre, as it was popularly called) have come down to us. They have been widely praised by modern specialists for their hygienic sagacity. An example was the rigid provisions for isolation of the stricken from critical areas like the cellar, the kitchen, the bakehouse, the well, and 'the barn where wheat and oats are threshed'. The sick must even stay away from the vineyard. Yet their care was amply provided for.[112] In the Middle Ages we often find frightful measures visited on lepers, as though their disease were proof of moral turpitude. The Amiens statutes contrast refreshingly by their humanity.

Amiens's burghers were also founders of a large number of smaller hospitals, or more properly hospices, homes for the aged, stopping-off places for poor travellers or pilgrims. One of the most important of these was attached to the Chapel of St-Quentin (both hospice and chapel were actually built by the commune), designed to service sick pilgrims who came to take the waters at the saint's miraculous fountain.[113] Most others were founded by individuals, by mayors or other leading citizens.[114] One of them was a charity of its most aristocratic family, the Cocquerels, who were fated to rise to eminence, one member, Firmin de Cocquerel, becoming dean of Paris cathedral, bishop of Noyon and king's chancellor under Philippe de Valois (1328–50).

Social advancement was by no means exceptional among Amiens's burghers, whose rise was often favoured by the church, another token of its cordial attitude. As early as the twelfth century, members of the rich middle class were allowed to join the cathedral chapter as canons, a practice that was frowned on by other hierarchies that we shall study.[115] The ultimate in social uplift was of course nobility, which could be attained by the king's accolade,[116] by marriage[117] or—and especially—by the purchase of noble fiefs.[118] Such an acquisition, with a particularly opulent buyer, might take in an entire domanial property, including justice and other feudal 'rights'. Thus, by one magic stroke—subject only to the king's ratification—a burgher could be endowed with the full dignity of the seigniorial estate.[119]

Amiens's bishop, who was the possessor of many such fiefs, did not hesitate to sell them to the bourgeoisie. This was far from being the universal practice of ecclesiastic seigniors. When Pierre Waignet bought several of these fiefs from the prelate, he made it clear that he was thus freeing himself of all charges that still marked the burgher's estate. The only duties that he now owed the prelate, he insisted, were those proper to a knight, such as attending his temporal court as his 'liege man'.[120] Another bourgeois of Amiens, 'Sire' Guillaume de Conti, held a fief of the bishop which was picturesquely described as being 'in full homage of mouth and hands'.[121] Even a 'demiselle', Jehanne du Cange, 'bourgeoise d'Amiens', was accepted as the bishop's liegewoman, performing several required acts of feudal homage toward him, such as serving him at the banquet of consecration.[122]

The inevitable result of this trend was to consolidate a cleavage among groups of the middle class, which had been a long time in the making. Amiens's commune itself was never truly democratic. From the beginning it had been run by a tight coterie of the wealthiest burghers to the exclusion of smaller tradesmen and artisans. There seems to have been no serious challenge to this situation throughout the twelfth and most of the thirteenth century. But that changed when economic conditions took a sharp decline late in the latter century.[123]

When dissatisfaction began to sputter among the city's underprivileged in the fourteenth century, it turned chiefly on the unfair tax system. In the case of wine, for instance, a major source of tax revenue, 85 per cent of the exactions were placed on the retail consumer, that is, on those in modest circumstances.[124] Moreover, many of the wealthiest citizens had found a tax-exempt loophole by turning their great storage cellars into taverns![125] An example was Jean de la Marche, head of the city mint, who, a document informs us, paid no tax 'for the wine he sold in his town house'.[126]

Chief complaint of the commoners was the mode of distributing the king's special tax (*aide*), which was levied more and more frequently under Philippe-le-Bel (1285–1314) in support of his war in Flanders. The patricians had control of collecting the tax and naturally favoured the method of imposing it on consumers' goods, whereas the commoners demanded a straight levy on wealth. All groups suffered, on the other hand, from the king's coin-debasing measures and from his trumped-up suppressions of longheld city privileges, only to sell them back at ruinous prices.[127]

The catastrophic early defeats of the Hundred Years War and the capture and long imprisonment of King Jean by the English set off a widespread disenchantment with the crown. At Amiens, this was especially marked among the upper bourgeoisie, who tried to lead the city, in 1358, into the movement initiated by Paris's famous provost of merchants, Etienne Marcel. The northern city suffered disastrously from the putting-down of this revolt, the entire suburban area being devastated, hundreds of houses and most of the outside churches being burnt to the ground. Seventeen of Amiens's top burghers, including the mayor and more than half the aldermen, were executed following the rout of the opposition forces.

This was the moment that the city's commoners chose to avenge themselves on the oligarchy, for they had remained in their great majority loyal to the king. The monarch showed his gratitude by ennobling one of them, Jean Boyleaue (literally, 'Waterdrinker'), a brewer who had fought sturdily against the patrician rebels.[128] And the lower orders rose in the succeeding period to the highest position they were ever to attain in the communal apparatus.[129] The most enterprising among them seized the opportunity to break into the patricians' monopoly in the all-important woad-trade, going into the country roundabout and buying up quantities of the dye directly from the producers.[130]

This aggressive pattern was crowned by a kind of revolution, in 1382, which was reflected most notably in the communal elections of that year, when an illiterate dyer, Henri de Roye, became the city's chief tax officer. But the king and the patricians had by this time patched up their differences and together suppressed the democratic revolt with harsh severity. The oligarchy was re-established at Amiens. But its instrument, the commune, never regained the broad power that had marked it in its most brilliant period, which we have been studying.[131]

As far as the construction of Amiens's majestic cathedral is concerned, these turbulent events were fortunately of no influence, since it was almost completely built when they occurred. In fact, the most striking aspect of the church's building history was its placidity, far different from the experience of other cities, as we shall learn. One important result of the favourable circumstances enjoyed by Amiens cathedral was the speed of its construction, in itself a partial shield to damaging historical or natural accidents.

But conflict was not totally absent from Amiens either, and even had some effect on the cathedral's construction, however serene it may have been as a whole. The commune itself had its part in these counter-currents. But what emerges with force is the positive overall role it played in the cathedral's story. Indeed, so many threads from the bourgeois loom have been woven into the church's fabric, one is almost inclined to conclude that it could not have been built without this collaboration.

That assumption would be misleading, for we shall see other cathedrals erected with far less participation of this kind. Their tasks were demonstrably the more burdensome because of it, to be sure. At Amiens, in contrast, the wealth of burgher patronage made it possible to fashion the grandiose church of Notre-Dame in a swift and continuous effort, thus contributing to its magnificent unity of structure and design.

What is all but lacking in this picture is the influence of the bourgeoisie on the content of the art. Almost total destruction of contemporary works at the burgher parishes, besides, has rendered the problem quite insoluble.[132] We can only assume that the middle-class impact must have been consequential, since so large a part of the city's art was paid for by it. But what is even more important, perhaps, is that the creation of this art was often a communal enterprise for which the combined bourgeoisie played the role of patron. This was a factor of historic moment, constituting a radical departure, a long step on the path to the secularization of art.

3

TOULOUSE

Orphan Cathedral

Toulouse Cathedral Chronology

*c.*1200	So-called 'Nave of Raymond VI' is begun in Gothic style. Decorative sculpture of the supplanted Romanesque church is re-employed in the new structure.
1213	Vaults of the nave's three bays are completed, after which work is halted following the defeat of the Toulousan forces at the Battle of Muret.
Post-1229	Façade is resumed after the Peace of Paris, including the rose-window, a diminished copy of the great rose of Notre-Dame de Paris.
1272	After a building pause of almost forty years, work resumes on a new choir under the inspiration of the extraordinary building bishop, Bertrand de l'Isle-Jourdain.
1286	Work ceases at the triforium level of the choir after Bishop Bertrand's death.
1305–1401	Virtually the only work done in the fourteenth century is the completion of four choir chapels of the seventeen projected and begun by Bertrand, each by a different bishop.
1439–51	The single portal of the façade is built with some carving that was destroyed in the Revolution; the tympanum, however, had no sculpture.
Early 1500s	Construction of the vault of the choir is projected but work does not get beyond the erection of a great pillar meant to support it.
1531	A single belltower, resembling a high donjon, is erected.
1609–11	Completion of the choir finally occurs in the seventeenth century following a fire that destroys its vault, which had remained all this time in timber. Reconstruction of the nave in the new style is planned, but is finally abandoned.

TOULOUSE IS THE CITY WHERE THE CATHEDRAL NEVER GOT PROPERLY BUILT. The anomaly was that two of its other churches were as splendid as any cathedral. All three—St-Etienne, St-Sernin and the Jacobins—have survived and are a source of confusion to the observant visitor who wonders about the inferiority of the bishop's church. The circumstances that brought on this incongruity are well worth studying. They are meshed with the entire tumultuous contemporary history of the great province.

The city's bourgeoisie, though it attained great power over a certain period, never played the kind of patronage role at the cathedral that we have seen in Amiens. Also, the Toulousan diocese was poor in temporal endowment. This should not have been an irremediable reason for the failure to construct a fine cathedral, since other resources might have been found, as occurred at Amiens. What was necessary, primarily, was a series of building-conscious and aggressive prelates. Toulouse had one such bishop at the end of the eleventh century, Izarn de Lavaur (1071–1105), and he almost pulled it off. In the end, however, his efforts resulted in hastening the construction of St-Sernin, his most formidable rival, instead. It was what we might call the first cathedral surrogate.

Bishop Izarn's design seemed at first to be headed for success. It was favoured by the circumstance that when he came to office the entire Catholic church was going through the regenerative process known as the 'Gregorian Reform'. This was characterized by a dual effort to repair its abject moral condition and to recapture church wealth, privileges and dignities that had fallen into lay hands during the high Middle Ages. Bishop Izarn wisely began by making an example of his own cathedral chapter, for whom he instituted communal living and other wholesome changes. To build up the fortunes of the diocese, one of the poorest in the southwest,[1] he used less commendable methods.

The prelate's impatient eye was inevitably drawn to St-Sernin. As it happened, this enormously affluent Benedictine abbey furnished him with ample excuse for intervening, since its adherents had abandoned the monastic life and had been selling or assigning away in fief many of its great properties. His corrective action took the form of putting the abbey under control of the powerful Cluny Order. But the move proved little more than a cover-up for Izarn's seizure of large portions of its revenues, which included, among other earnings, rights to the rich oblations and fees for burial. The latter especially were highly remunerative since great seigniors and even ecclesiastics preferred to be interred in St-Sernin's soil, virtue-drenched by the remains of many saints and martyrs.[2]

Its collection boxes were also eminently attractive, due to the church's drawing power as one of the main stopover points on the Compostela pilgrimage road, where St James's remains were considered to have been buried. Bishop Izarn claimed a major portion of the offerings, and to assure delivery confiscated the keys to the tomb of St Saturnin (Sernin), Toulouse's first bishop. This seizure was resisted by the combative abbey canons, many of whom were military men and sons of wealthy seigniors. But their revolt was put down with the help of Count Guillaume IV of Toulouse, who seems to have been a sincere dupe of Izarn's 'reform'. The insurgent canons were forcibly removed and a new set of submissive Cluniac monks from Moissac put in their places.

Bishop Izarn's bold exploit seemed at first fated for success. If consummated, it would have changed the destiny of the Toulouse see and more especially of its cathedral's building history. But Pope Gregory VII himself, for clouded reasons, possibly having to do with fear of the swelling power of Cluny, ordered a reversal of Izarn's actions.[3] Count Guillaume was promptly contrite, and proved it with important gifts to St-Sernin.[4] But the aggrieved bishop took many years to recover from his dashed hopes. Almost fifteen years later, before the church council at Nîmes (1095), he was still pleading for his right to a fourth of St-Sernin's oblations, declaring that without it he 'would not have enough to live on'.[5] Pope Urban II assured him that he would not let him starve. He seems to have meant hardly more than that.

St-Sernin was able to make its triumph stick by undertaking its own reform. It re-established the community of canons and began to buy or cajole back lost temporal riches as well as tithes and dependent churches that had fallen into lay hands.[6] These accomplishments reached their climax in a campaign to reconstruct its basilica,[7] for which task it was fortunate in winning the services of a great builder, Raymond Gayrard, a rich layman, probably even a burgher, who at the death of his wife took an oath of chastity and entered the community. Until his own death in 1118 he pursued this task singlemindedly, completing the church's beautiful chevet, its choir and transept as well as a considerable portion of the nave. He may have also built the cloister, which was destroyed in the nineteenth century, though some of its wondrous carved capitals were spared.[8]

Simultaneously with his attack on St-Sernin, Bishop Izarn made a reach for the fabulously wealthy local monastery, La Daurade, with hardly more success. Because it was equally in crying need of reform, the bishop succeeded in making a Cluniac priory of it. But it remained so for only a few decades, before reverting to the Benedictines. The bishopric seems to have benefited little here, in the temporal sense, either. Daurade's riches were made up chiefly of vast urban holdings, concentrated especially in long stretches on both sides of the Garonne, together with all milling and fishing rights, and in the great suburb of St-Cyprien across the river.[9]

One of the chief objectives of Bishop Izarn's seizure of St-Sernin had been its building fund. It is very likely that, had it succeeded, a new cathedral edifice would have been the beneficiary and St-Sernin's majesty would have been St-Etienne's. Even so the proud and ambitious prelate could hardly allow his rival to soar to new splendour while his own church bordered on dilapidation. Matching the basilica in industry if not in grandeur, Izarn succeeded in rebuilding St-Etienne. He even added a chapel nearby, pointedly naming it St-Jacques (St James) in the obvious hope that it would draw away from St-Sernin some of the pilgrim swarm bound for Compostela. A skull was obtained for display in the chapel sanctuary and word passed around that it was the head of the illustrious apostle. There is evidence of a certain success of these tactics.[10]

Overall, however, Izarn's cathedral did not benefit spectacularly. Its small stature (50 by 20 metres) and spare form (it had neither transept nor ambulatory)[11] contrasted mortifyingly with the magnificence of St-Sernin, which was surpassed only by Cluny among the great Romanesque basilicas. When, moreover, at the end of the twelfth century, it became a great challenge for cathedrals to rebuild in the lofty new Gothic style, such an ambition was far beyond the capacity of Toulouse's bishops. With no new Izarn appearing endowed with his exceptional drive, revenues declined almost to the vanishing point and donations were rare.[12] Nor did the citizens of Toulouse play the donorship role that we saw so brilliantly illustrated at Amiens. We need not go far in search of reasons. One of the things we shall witness over and over about cathedral-building is that popular support on its behalf depended very much on the church's own diligence. Where this was lacking, it would be highly improbable to find the parishioners stepping into the breach. The cathedral was the bishop-and-chapter's 'thing'. A parish church could, on the other hand, become the object of popular enterprise.

At Toulouse, an interesting early example of parishioner initiative was at the Dalbade ('white') church, which was located in one of the active commercial quar-

12. St-Sernin's majestic nave: looking toward the apse, beyond the choir

ters. Here, early in the twelfth century, the artisans and tradesmen are credited with having erected its first structure, which could hardly have been more than a chapel, and then rebuilt it at the end of the century. At that time, the contribution of the cutlers' guild or confraternity, for example, was so important as to merit it a private chantry, dedicated to its patron, St Eloi.[13]

The river fishermen also had an early chapel of their own. It was probably located across the Garonne, in the faubourg of St-Cyprien. The church was actually a converted house, and was called the Capelle Redonde because of its cylindrical form.[14] And the dyers, who together with the mill-operators made up Toulouse's two most important industrial groups, were early entrenched at St-Pierre-des-Cuisines, to which their boiling vats installed near the river evidently gave its unusual name ('of-the-kitchens'). The extent of parish influence here, which probably dated far back, was almost total by the fourteenth century, when the curé is seen, in an amazing document, pledging to give an accounting for the church's possessions 'at any moment at their pleasure' to the wardens, who included a parchment-maker, a jurist, a decorator and a currier.[15]

But, in the twelfth century, the bourgeoisie of Toulouse, as at Amiens, had other, more basic, preoccupations than church-building, whether it was parishes or the cathedral itself. The southern city never had a commune in the formal sense of the word, acknowledged by a charter with its more-or-less careful elaboration of structure and jurisdiction.[16] Nevertheless, by the end of the twelfth century and the early years of the thirteenth, the burghers' powers had evolved to such a degree as to dispense with such formalities.

Acquisition of this self-rule began in the usual fashion, with the purchase of rights and immunities from the counts, who had an insatiable need for money. One great drain was their extremely active role in the first Crusades. Even more exhausting were their constant wars with other powerful feudals of the region. The counts' territorial claims, which stretched all the way out to the Rhône, down to the Mediterranean and over to the Pyrenees, made them the greatest of French princes— on the map. But this vast paper empire was never firmly held. Even in Languedoc their great vassals were independent, and often belligerent, sovereigns. Through much of the twelfth century, the counts were forced to be absent from Toulouse, maintaining their capital at St-Gilles 150 miles away, while attempting to establish their claims to Provence and the east.

It was a time of golden opportunity for the Toulousan burghers. Left to defend themselves,[17] they organized their own militia, which, according to tradition, on one occasion trooped all the way to Orange beyond the Rhône to help their sovereign lift a siege.[18] They are supposed to have won some important grants as a reward. But it was the counts' bottomless financial needs that were the chief source of burgher privileges. Other rights they simply usurped during their rulers' prolonged absences, legitimizing them by use.[19] In the end, they enjoyed rights of administering justice, legislation, taxation, regulation of commerce and many others. Their trained militia was strong enough to undertake missions of economic conquest within a radius of fifty miles, capped by signed treaties with twenty-three towns and seigniors.[20]

Toulouse began to take on the aspect of an Italian city-state when in 1181 Count Raymond V, for reasons of feudal pride or greed, probably both, decided to put an end to its rise. He made a violent re-entry into his capital city, and there followed several years of strife, which mercifully for the burghers was broken at times by the prince's preoccupations with his powerful external enemies. His combats with the Anglo-Aquitainian forces led by Richard the Lion Heart, in 1188, appear to have so weakened him that the Toulousan consuls could face him with a kind of ultimatum. Raymond was forced to sign what was in effect a treaty with them, in 1189, by which fundamental power passed over to the city.[21]

This victory inaugurated what historians have called Toulouse's 'age of liberty'. It lasted about forty years, reaching its apogee during the Albigensian crusade. The latter is known as the church's desperate combat against the Catharist heresy, the most perilous threat it was to face prior to the Reformation. But it was as much a war of conquest which French royalty and its northern baronial allies waged against the disintegrating Languedocian dynasty. For the south, this struggle took on the aspect of a national resistance, in which Toulouse's 'people in arms' fought with extraordinary valour.[22] Indeed, it was outside its walls that the northern commander-in-chief, Simon de Montfort, was killed in 1218, by a rock hurled from a projectile-thrower operated 'by young girls and married women', according to a famed troubadour's account.[23]

But the ultimate defeat of the south, which occurred in 1229, led soon after to the absorption of Languedoc by France. It also resulted in a progressive loss of Toulouse's civil liberties. In truth, the process had begun even before the crown took over the great province in 1249. This occurred in the person of Alphonse de Poitiers, St Louis's brother, who married the daughter of Toulouse's last native count, Raymond VII, as was arranged by the 1229 peace treaty. Raymond, too enfeebled to undertake ambitious forays, turned his bent lance against the city consulate.[24] The latter's decline, despite spurts of resistance, was in any case inevitable, after the assumption of power by the Capetians. By the time of Alphonse's death in 1271, Toulouse was a town 'decorated by privileges' but no longer free.[25]

That the curve of the Toulousan church's fortunes should have been almost exactly the reverse of the consulate's is hardly coincidental. The bishops from the beginning fervidly embraced the fight against the heresy (in which many prominent burghers were involved), sharing responsibility for some of the worst atrocities of this oft-told horror story. They opened their own city by deception to the northern invaders, calling on them repeatedly to destroy it, which almost happened once when Simon de Montfort succeeded in setting fire to several quarters. Another time, the bishop cast some of the leading citizens held as hostages into his dungeons, and only the payment of a huge ransom saved their lives.[26] Most fateful of all, the Toulouse church opened its arms to the Inquisition.

The rewards of this policy completely reversed the bishopric's feeble political position and unfolded almost unlimited resources for its enrichment. By the end of Bishop Fulcrand's term (1179–1200) the episcopacy had reached so low a state that the prelate had to beg his chapter for a canon's 'portion', the daily distribution of one pint of wine and a pound of bread. A thirteenth-century chonicler tells us that Fulcrand's total income came from a feudal oven (where people were required to bake their bread) and a few farms. His successor, Raymond de Rabastens (1202–5), mortgaged off even this pittance to pay for suits he conducted for the restoration of lost episcopal revenues.[27]

When Bishop Foulques (1206–30), one of Toulouse's more notable prelates, took the mitre, his entire income was said to be 'one hundred less four sous' (less than five livres) and he did not dare to send his mules down to the river to water out of fear of seizure by his creditors, burghers who had cited him before the consular court.[28] Once a troubadour, Foulques was the son of a rich Marseille merchant. But it was not with the paternal wealth that he built up his bishopric. Coming to office as the church's attack on the Albigensian heterodoxy reached its crisis, Foulques benefited enormously from his impassioned advocacy. Historically, his greatest fame stems from his espousal of Dominick of Guzman's mission. Out of his great poverty he endowed the founder of the Dominican Order, turning over to him a small church, a hospital and a cut of the diocesan tithes, the last being the portion that the episcopacy was required to use for church construction.[29]

Bread-on-the-water alms were never better rewarded. Foulques's gains began to be gathered up a bit earlier, in fact, when Simon de Montfort's victories resulted in massive expropriations of the crusade's opponents. The nucleus of the northern general's grants to the Toulousan see was the Château of Verfeil, an opulent seigniory that encompassed twenty villages, together with abundant appurtenances of every kind, including many serfs.[30]

Verfeil's punishment in being bound over to the church was for the latter a bit of precious revenge going back to St Bernard's time. Then, too, the people of this town had been charged with heresy, symbolized by the breaking of crosses, against which the great monk-diplomat was sent to sermonize. But his audience drowned out his voice and finally walked out on him. As he withdrew, Bernard called down an anathema on the city: 'Green-Leaf, may God wither you!' he cried out in a blood-curdling pun.[31]

This gift of Verfeil to the Toulousan church was but one of a long series whose itemized documentation is now lost. Half a century later, in 1289, a document which constituted an agreement over seigniorial boundaries between king and bishop credited the prelate with an endless list of possessions. Some, it must be said, could have come by purchase. But this in itself would have been proof of a phenomenal upturn in the bishop's fortunes. Their probable source is revealed by the inadvertent reference in the document to former owners of the properties listed. One, part of the château and domain of Castelmauroi, had come from Raymond Unaud, *condemned for heresy*. Another, the fief of Castelviel and land of Pressac, had belonged to Bernard Signier, citizen of Toulouse, likewise *condemned for heresy*.[32]

Whatever the sources of its newfound fortunes, the Toulousan church, starting with Bishop Foulques, became immensely wealthy. Now at last it could put an end to the disgrace of its puny cathedral, whose proportions hardly exceeded those of a moderate-sized parish church.[33] Episcopal dignity required a more stately edifice. Indeed, a partial reconstruction of St-Etienne had been launched in the late twelfth or early thirteenth century. But, strange as it may seem, this was not undertaken at the initiative of the bishops.[34]

There is a strong tradition attributing the effort to the Count of Toulouse, who was allegedly eager to prove his piety and thus deprive his enemies of their claim that

13. 'Raymond VI's Nave': view of the western part of the Cathedral of St-Etienne, built in the early thirteenth century. Note its simplicity of style and its extremely modest proportions

he was 'soft' on the heresy. The three bays that were built, still standing, have long borne the name of 'Raymond VI's Nave'. The count's coat-of-arms was prominently displayed at several places (though these could have been put in later) and he is said to have refused to abandon construction work on it during the turmoil of Simon de Montfort's first siege of Toulouse in 1211.[35]

Raymond VI's fragment has been extravagantly praised. This is hard to understand in the light of all the Gothic marvels that already existed early in the thirteenth century.[36] Frugality ruled in the entire effort. The only stone sculptures are a few bits that were saved from the part of Izarn's church that was pulled down to make way for the new nave. Brick was used exclusively for the walls (see note 93 for lack of stone in Toulouse region, hence its costliness), which were kept very thin, and there were no aisles, arcades or other costly features. Raymond had to run off in 1213 after the disastrous defeat of the southern forces at Muret, and work evidently halted until after the Paris treaty of 1229, when the façade, unadorned but for its rose-window copied in shrunken form from Notre-Dame de Paris, was completed. And nothing more was added to St-Etienne for forty years.

In view of the extraordinary growth in the church's wealth, such a failure seems contradictory. Could it have been that the fight against the heresy was so costly that funds for church-building were simply unavailable? As a matter of fact, the military expenditures were enormous. But this aspect of the struggle was soon ended and, besides, expropriations of the victims proved in the long run far greater than the costs of the conquest.[37] The Toulousan church, as we have seen, was a prime beneficiary in this positive balance.

But there is better proof, substantive proof, that lack of money was not the reason for the continued neglect of Toulouse's cathedral. For the cathedral *was* built. However, this was not the official edifice. It was once again a cathedral surrogate, the second of its kind erected in as many centuries, each of which left St-Etienne an orphan. It was on this substitute cathedral, the Dominicans' monumental Jacobins church, as it was to be called, that the thoughts of Toulouse's bishops, first Foulques, then Raymond de Falgar (1230–70), were focused.

On this second great rival of St-Etienne were showered all the graces of the Toulousan see. It may seem strange that two successive bishops should have made such a choice to the detriment of their own cathedral. Yet they could hardly have seen the Jacobins as a substitute. To these embattled men it must have symbolized something far more vital: the defensive arm of the church in its life-and-death grapple with its greatest peril. Though the church they built was heightened and refurbished in the following century, its early proportions already far exceeded those of 'Raymond VI's Nave'.

Even today, when still only partially restored, and despite the loss of its splendid decoration (including nineteen great stained-glass lancets) during the nineteenth century, when it served as an army stable, the Jacobins is extraordinarily impressive. Its

14. Les Jacobins, the interior: showing the great capacity of the 'Preachers'' church, opened wide by its central pillars to the large audiences for which it was intended by these battlers against the Albigensian heresy

central pillars, resembling graceful, towering palms whose spreading fronds mate the vaulting, opened the church of the Preachers to the great audiences for which it was designed. Even in its own time the Jacobins must have possessed the aura of a cathedral and it was for a considerable period the administrative and political heart of the Toulousan diocese.

It must have been Foulques himself, who, in 1229, got the fabulously wealthy capitalist, Pons de Capdenier, to donate the extensive site on which the new church was initiated. This greatest of all Toulouse's bourgeois benefactors had no reason to defend his orthodoxy. But the times, which held 'big business' as hardly better than usury and usury akin to heresy, were uncertain. Had not that other great merchant and church patron, Pons David, been dug up from his grave in 1215 and flung out of consecrated ground by this same irate bishop?[38] Old age may have mellowed Foulques's truculent spirit. He could look back with satisfaction on the brilliant successes of his episcopacy and of orthodoxy as a whole. He must have regarded the Jacobins project as capping his career. He laid down its foundation stone—and died the very next day.

However, by designating the Dominican Provincial, Raymond de Falgar, as his successor, Foulques had made certain that the needed funds and energies would be centred on this task. The new bishop himself made over important recorded sums to its fabric.[39] But there could hardly have been any monetary problem for the first church and convent of the Dominican Order, which already by 1230 was manifestly intended for a refulgent destiny. In 1233, it was given charge of the Inquisition in the entire south and though it had no formal claim to the enormous fortune that was expropriated through this agency, it is more than mere conjecture that the Dominicans in general and the Jacobins church in particular received ample appreciative rewards from it.

It is certain, on the other hand, that if the friars had had to depend on burgher donations for their great building programme (aside from the church, a number of conventual and accessory structures had to be erected), it hardly would have got off the ground. For, up to the end of the century, they got gifts of some importance from only five members of the bourgeoisie.[40] And the record is as complete as anything that has come down for that period, since it was compiled by the excellent scribes and chroniclers that the literate, efficient Dominicans chose from their own ranks.

The most famous among them, Bernard Gui, when transcribing the history of the building of the Jacobins, lists few gifts altogether from whatever source for this great enterprise. And yet money came from somewhere for the many purchases (of land and houses) which he records as being made in the van of the advancing church.[41] The strong presumption is that a major source was funds deflected from confiscations. It is even likely that the exorbitant living expenses filed by the Dominican Inquisitors, about which the pope himself complained, may have concealed sizeable appropriations to this building fund.[42]

Ten times as many paid acquisitions (approximately sixty of them) as donations are listed in Gui's cartulary. This could explain why another famous chronicler of the construction of the Jacobins, Pelhisso, should have titled his treatise *De Empcione* . . . ('Regarding the Purchases . . .').[43] Far from making benefactions, the burghers in the quarter resisted even selling their property to the Dominicans, Pelhisso admits. But he has a ready explanation for this contrariness: 'Many were heretics,' he observes.[44] If what he meant was that they were anti-Dominican, his observation was far from wrong.

'Heretic' or 'Cathar' were scare-words equivalent to 'red' or 'subversive' in our times. Evidently they were used with the same indiscriminate recklessness and served the same intimidating purpose. An American scholar, Austin P. Evans, has demonstrated a surprising parallel between the medieval campaign of terror and the one fostered by US Senator Joseph McCarthy in the 1950s: the broad use of guilt by association and punishment of cognates, failure to produce witnesses, use of informants and fabrication of evidence.[45]

There was one big difference between the two cases. This was in the breadth of resistance to the medieval persecutions. When the Inquisitors holding court at Toulouse in 1235 called several leading burghers to their first inquest, the reaction was tumultuous. The city authorities shut the Dominicans up in their convent and put them under quarantine. When sympathizers succeeded in getting help to them anyway, the consuls decided to drive the friars out of the city. The friars put up a passive resistance, 'lay down on the ground . . . [and had to be] carried by the feet and head outside the gate.' Other citizens invaded the episcopal palace and attacked canons in the cathedral itself. In exile, the bishop excommunicated the city but priests who posted the interdict were themselves expelled by the consuls.[46]

Even earlier, students at Toulouse University, sons of the rich bourgeoisie for the most part, had revolted against their Dominican professors. The school had been set up by the Peace of 1229 with the avowed purpose of shoring up the orthodoxy. Ultra-conservative masters, chiefly friars, were imported (mainly from Paris) but were almost immediately subjected to a guerrilla of harassment. This reached its peak in a great eruption, in 1232. One of the masters, Jean de Garlande, has left an unintentionally diverting account of these events, describing how he finally had to run for his life by taking passage on a river boat, where the sailors robbed and almost murdered him. But he lived to tell the tale, getting back at last to Paris where he founded the college that long bore his name.[47]

After Toulouse's revolt in 1235, the Inquisition was forced to retreat temporarily. But it rebounded with greater fury when Raymond Gros, a Catharist minister, was reconverted to Catholicism and implicated a number of prominent associates in heresy. Death, life imprisonment or flight resulted for large numbers. Many of Toulouse's most prominent people—consuls, rich burghers, nobles—were compromised.[48] There are countless anecdotes in the archives revealing the cruelty of the repression. One tells how Bishop Falgar himself posed as a Catharist prelate and betrayed the confession of a dying woman. When the latter refused to recant, she was carried off in her bed to the pyre, after which the bishop and the monks returned to the refectory and 'dined joyously'. It was the first anniversary of St Dominick's canonization.[49]

It is significant that almost all condemnations for 'heresy' were accompanied by confiscations of wealth.[50] This was particularly true in cases of life sentences, and most early penalties seem to have been of that nature. In 1246 alone, several dozen Toulousans, mainly burghers, often women, received life prison terms.[51] Overall figures of confiscations at Toulouse are lacking but we do know that they went on for years. It was not only money that was taken, but anything of value, including stocks of grain and wine.[52] We do not hear of any of the condemned having their penalties changed to donations to church-building projects, however, such as occurred in other places.[53]

Behind the inquisitorial terror, church reaction rode high. Decrees of the papal legates added to the repressive measures against parishioners. Attendance at mass was rigorously enforced and lists were posted of those going to confession. Presence of a priest at the drawing up of wills was made obligatory on pain of refusal of burial in hallowed ground. A church council held at Toulouse in 1229 forbade the possession by laymen of either the Old or the New Testament, reflecting a tendency to individual worship which had to be suppressed.[54]

These actions, which strengthened the authority of the church, resulted in financial benefit to it as well. Pressure was intensified to force the return of tithes and other church revenue sources still in lay hands, while the clerics' favoured position with regard to taxation and justice was enhanced.[55] Churchmen abused their greatly expanded authority by exploiting their parishioners mercilessly through exorbitant charges for sacraments and other exactions. The result of these many abuses, a modern church historian, Abbé Julien, has concluded, was that 'good relations between priests and the faithful practically ceased at Toulouse's parishes in the second half of the thirteenth century'.[56]

We already know that Toulouse's cathedral was not getting built during the thirteenth century. Did the parish churches, in view of the widespread coercion, fare any better? A recent American author, John H. Mundy, has minimized the repression's negative effect in this regard, holding that the damage of the war and conquest has itself been exaggerated. Toulouse quickly repaired its wounds, he says, and its 'citizens were richer, more numerous, better serviced by charitable agencies and better educated by the mid-thirteenth century than they had been in 1200'.[57] This opinion is contrary to the one that many historians had previously held, which was that the Languedoc was ruined by the northern conquest, permanently retarded in its development.

A preliminary point must be made, however: that thirteenth-century prosperity was a widespread phenomenon stemming from a variety of economic, political, technological and other factors, which could have helped Toulouse to effect a partial recovery from the war and conquest. But this would merely have masked their harmful consequences, not helped us to measure them. To what could we relate Toulouse's claimed recovery? The present state of our information allows for no critical comparison of its general situation with that of other cities during the period in question or even with its own earlier condition.[58]

None of all this, in any case, enters the orbit of Professor Mundy's study, though its interest is very pertinent to us. His argument is confined to Toulouse's record of 'charitable and social work' and to its 'building of many new churches and mendicant convents'. Unfortunately, his evidence for the 'churches' is very scant. However, he does list a great number of hospitals, hospices, leper-houses, hermit-dwellings and schools that were founded at Toulouse up to 1250. But the big majority (sixteen of twenty-two) of these date from the twelfth century and the early years of the thirteenth.[59] Hence, they cannot be attributed to any postulated great recovery after the Albigensian war which ended in 1229! But since the Catharist heresy was endemic in the south already in the twelfth century, Professor Mundy applies the strong early record of auxiliary building toward making a sweeping disclaimer of the harmful effects of Catharism on orthodoxy for that period also: 'If charitable and social work is part of the church, the Toulousan church was blooming before the Albigensian war.'[60]

It seems that this conclusion does not necessarily follow from the premise. If, for example, donations by Toulousans to hospitals and other social welfare institutions were made at the cost of their patronage to churches, the fact might well have concealed an antagonism to the latter. We can see this kind of substitution of philanthropic goal repeatedly occurring in the Middle Ages.[61] Moreover, the premise itself is faulty since the contributions of citizens to hospitals cannot so categorically be assimilated 'to the church'. They certainly were as much a social manifestation, even a sign of the development of civic consciousness, as we saw at Amiens. And the burghers' foundation of schools cannot be seen as unalloyed proof of church attachment either. They would seem as much a demonstration of respect for learning!

Subjective motivation, admittedly an enormously difficult matter to probe for so distant an epoch, cannot be ignored even for church patronage itself. We have already referred to some examples of 'heretics' being forced to make donations to church-building funds. How many others remain unknown? How many 'voluntary' gifts were made by suspected people eager to divert accusation? A recent author who studied this question concluded that 'it is often those most compromised as heretics that are the most generous donors'. She tells of two 'notorious heretics' whose important gifts to an abbey were later challenged on this very ground by their 'orthodox' heirs.[62]

Finally, if we are going to judge orthodoxy by quantitative data, as Professor Mundy does, the establishment of a medieval hospital or hermit's enclosure or even a school can hardly be equated with the building of a church. An early 'hospital', as the author himself points out, most often designated a simple hospice without medical installation, a house harbouring about a dozen inmates.[63] And as for the hermit's dwelling, it was indeed a very minor object of philanthropy! Even most schools represented no important building enterprise unless a fine chapel was added to them, which was rare.

There is one outstanding exception to this qualification. This was the Collège de St-Bernard, a benefaction of Pons de Capdenier, Toulouse's leading capitalist, and the recipient of the greater part of his vast fortune. It was, in fact, the finest of all the city's philanthropies. It seems almost ungracious to point out, however, that the college was only the second-choice beneficiary of this treasure, contingent on the childless decease of Pons's only child and heiress, his daughter Stephana. Since this occurred but three years after the father's own death, the princely foundation became a reality.[64]

We come, then, to what is the central question for us: How were citizens' contributions to the construction and embellishment of churches at Toulouse affected by the repression? Did the period following the Albigensian war actually result in the building of 'many new parish churches'?[65] Professor Mundy gives us no evidence in support of this assertion, setting it outside the scope of his work.[66] The answer to the question, however, as far as it has been possible to determine, is emphatically in the negative. Though information is in some cases sparse or entirely lacking, what is available indicates that the building of secular churches at Toulouse all but ceased during the thirteenth century.

Aside from the new mendicant orders, which we shall consider separately, of the twenty churches for whose dating we have some pertinent data, which includes all the most important edifices of Toulouse, the overwhelming number were built either in the twelfth century or earlier.[67] True, some of them were subsequently rebuilt or at least importantly restored. But, aside from the cathedral, there is only one case of this kind that we know of that occurred in the thirteenth century. This was St-Sernin, which by the visible evidence of its partly rebuilt upper nave and graceless incomplete façade was done with steadily increasing economy until the effort petered out completely. All the other reconstruction projects came later, some much later. Emile Mâle was struck by the austerity of Gothic churches in this region, built during the earlier period. The south had a 'genius for simplicity', he observed. Was it not a case of making a virtue of necessity?[68]

Slackening of church-building in the often so highly productive thirteenth century was a phenomenon that also appears in other episcopal cities of France. At Amiens, it will be recalled, the parish churches were scantily endowed during this century but there was a good reason for it: the voluntary concentration of all financial resources on the cathedral. Nothing like that happened at Toulouse, of course. Poor St-Etienne remained for decade after decade abandoned and bereft.

Not only was there a dearth of church-building at Toulouse during the thirteenth century but pious foundations of other kinds were similarly sparse. Unfortunately, good cartularies for the thirteenth century are lacking for even the important churches. But the later-gathered repertories of the best of the city's early archivists, Claude Cresty, reveal very few burgher foundations.[69] There is a single striking exception, his inventory of the Knights Templars, which contains a great number of very substantial pious offerings from citizens during this century.[70] And the Hospitallers, though not inventoried by Cresty, apparently benefited in a similar manner.[71]

The thirteenth century, it should be noted, was a period when the popularity of the military orders was generally very much on the wane. Noteworthy, also, is the fact that a large proportion of the donations to the Knights were relatively important, a house, a vineyard, or other property. These gifts were not meant for building purposes, as far as we know. When the object of the gift was recorded, it was almost always in payment of masses or a burial. If big enough, it might have been intended in exchange for the donor's acceptance as an oblate, or permanent inmate. Was there a sudden stampede toward the protective armour of the Knights by individuals terrified of the Inquisition?

People had to be buried somewhere and they were far more concerned about where it should be during the Middle Ages than many of us are today. With numbers of individuals being accused posthumously of heresy, dug out of their graves and literally cast to the dogs,[72] Toulousans may have felt that they would rest more securely with the Knights than at the cathedral or even at famed St-Sernin with its dozens of holy relics. As for the new and supposedly more virtuous mendicant orders, which in so many other cities became peoples' favoured eternal resting-places, they were for the most part shunned by thirteenth-century Toulousans.

A circumstance appears to be inescapable in the way of explaining the Knights' popularity: the fact that neither the Hospitallers nor the Templars displayed much ardour for the Albigensian crusade, both of them remaining loyal to the cause of the south throughout.[73] The former, for example, went out of their way to prove their staunch friendship for the accused Catharist sympathizer, Raymond VI. They accepted him into the knighthood toward the end of his life in a patently sheltering gesture and harboured his body loyally (for centuries) while, gnawed by rats, it awaited a final entombment.[74]

And what was it that the Templars did or failed to do, in 1216, which so incensed the chief of the Albigensian repression, Simon de Montfort, that when he captured

Toulouse for the last time he burnt down their establishment?[75] All of these circumstances appear to illustrate an attitude which distinguished the Knights from other religious groups and which Toulousans evidently appreciated, judging from the extraordinary number of their benefactions to them.

The only considerable church-building that took place at Toulouse in the 'post-Albigensian' period was among the mendicant orders. But why should this occasion surprise? The same thing took place throughout France and all of Europe, for that matter, during the thirteenth century. The idea of monks shunning the pitfalls of lucre and living by begging fired people's religious sentiments. Dozens of such orders sprang up, so that the church was forced to abolish all but the most viable in the end.

In Toulouse itself, a number of these units proved highly ephemeral, the most substantial foundations being the Dominicans, Franciscans, Carmelites, Augustins and Trinitarians.[76] Of these five, the last two did not receive their definitive establishment inside the city until the fourteenth century, a period when, as we shall see, the worst of the Inquisition was past and a general reconciliation under way.

In fact, the accommodation with the friars began, at least with a part of the population, as early as the latter decades of the thirteenth century. The great wrath of Toulousans, moreover, had been turned against the Dominicans, who were in charge of the Inquisition and thus ultimately responsible for its excesses. Other mendicants were usually far less involved. Noteworthy was the case of the Franciscans, whose church, the Cordeliers, received some important burgher aid, including two endowments of chapels. Significant, too, was the fact that a leading bourgeois, Guillaume Saurin, was named head of the church's building fabric, around 1268.[77]

The case of the Carmelites would be even more impressive except that, like the Dominicans, their establishment patently benefited from confiscations. However, these were not directed against 'heretics' but, in the logic of the time, their equivalent—the Jews. Toulousan Jews had since Charlemagne's reign enjoyed a comparatively tolerable existence,[78] which besides religious freedom guaranteed them social rights such as the ownership of land and other property, including purchase, sale, rental and assignment in feudal fief, the tenants of one piece that belonged to a Jew being none other than the Templars.

This situation deteriorated rapidly in the second half of the thirteenth century, with the triumph of the Inquisition, and particularly after Alphonse de Poitiers, brother of St Louis, took over the Languedoc and launched that king's programme of anti-Jewish discrimination and expropriation in the province. At Toulouse, the campaign became intimately linked with the establishment of the Carmelites. Wedged into the heart of the Jewish quarter, the installation got the pope's blessings, in 1264. The founding group of prominent Toulousans had assured the pontiff that henceforth the Virgin would be 'honoured, loved and devoutly praised in the very place where the perfidious Jews had long blasphemed her'[79]—a reference to the Toulousan synagogue, no doubt. The Jews were likewise forced to sell their homes, unquestionably at sacrificial prices, in the valuable Joutz-Aigues ('Jews'-Water') quarter, where they had lived for centuries.[80]

This expropriation of the Jews in heretofore relatively permissive Toulouse was not the most striking feature of the Carmelite case, however. More pertinent historically was the indication it gave of the onset of a massive return of Toulousans to orthodoxy, by mediation of the Virgin Mary. In fact, the reconciliation was evidently too soon and too large to have seemed normal to the leaders of the repression. When the 'Confraternity of Carmel' had attained a membership of 5,000 men and women, Alphonse de Poitiers himself became worried, writing on two occasions to his vicar at Toulouse to get the help of Sicard Alaman, his man of confidence, and to determine whether, 'under the guise of good', it actually constituted a danger to authority. He demanded, in any case, that its numbers be sharply reduced.[81]

Alphonse may have been overly suspicious. There appears to be an inexorable tendency, following a lengthy period of even the most rancorous conflict, toward accommodation. By this time, moreover, most of the leading 'troublemakers' at Toulouse had either been burnt, died in prison or run off into exile.[82] Those remaining were certainly the more timid, the more conformist. Perhaps they were the 'silent majority' of that distant time, who had just been standing by, waiting for the bold ones, the outspoken ones, to be reduced to impotence.

By the fourteenth century, this trend had been confirmed. Three generations had passed since the days of greatest stress. The grandsons and granddaughters of the *faidits* had probably never even heard of their ancestors' dark unorthodoxies. The accumulation of great wealth by many families, particularly in rural properties and feudal fiefs, often resulting in ennoblement by the French king himself—all this had its normalizing influence also. Toulousan patricians in their lives and conduct were indistinguishable from their homologues in any great northern city.[83]

And on every hand, meanwhile, ardent new ties with the church were consolidated. Confraternities multiplied.[84] Relations even with the once-repulsed mendicant groups became more cordial.

A spectacular case was that of the mercers guild and the Trinitarians, whose relationship started before the latter moved into the city, in 1362. The tradesmen had their own chapel dedicated to the Holy Trinity at the original church, and when it was destroyed by the English in 1355 the rich guild and confraternity took over virtual responsibility for rebuilding it within the walls. In gratitude, the Trinitarians rewarded the mercers with unique privileges tantamount to admitting the whole mass of their members into the order.[85]

By all odds, however, the most significant reconciliation that took place in the fourteenth century was with the Dominicans, the chief instigators of the earlier conflicts and the target of sharpest hostility. It is impossible to determine to what extent the alteration was an opportunistic adjustment with triumphant previous antagonists, whose authority now spread throughout the Christian world. But the actuality of the concord can hardly be doubted.

From the evidence of recorded endowments in the new century, no other religious group at Toulouse comes close to the Jacobins as a burgher beneficiary.[86] Among the many very important foundations in their favour, there were no fewer than sixteen chaplaincies, three chapels and two Dominican nunneries.[87] But the most striking proof of the new attitude toward the Jacobins was no doubt the fact that many Toulousans now chose to be buried in their church. Few people would be inclined to do that while riven by animosity toward the friars. Indeed, the Dominicans had by now replaced the Knights as the city's leading funerary host.[88]

Two of the chapels at the Jacobins church were foundations of artisan guilds, the carpenters and silversmiths.[89] A third chapel, for which the burgher Jean Rostagni had left the important sum of 270 francs sometime before 1362, never got built. The money was consigned instead to the construction of the new chevet that was built to receive the body of St Thomas Aquinas in what was described by a contemporary as 'the most beautiful among all [the churches] of the Preaching Friars'.[90]

Though Jean Rostagni's family manifestly gave their approval to the transference of the endowment and its use for a more glorious purpose,[91] it was nevertheless a serious lapse against a solemnly consented burial vow. This cavalier treatment of a pious bequest reveals perhaps better than anything the Dominicans' overweening ascendancy. The broken confidence beyond-the-tomb would hardly endanger the steady flow of benefactions, it must have been felt. In fact, we can see the Jacobins church at this very moment being enlarged and elevated and refulgently embellished, with the aid of much bourgeois munificence.[92]

Such, alas, was not the fate of that nominal cathedral of Toulouse, St-Etienne. There had been, however, it must be recorded, one brief period of genuinely exciting promise at the end of the thirteenth century, when the cathedral seemed destined to be rebuilt, after all, on a magnificent scale. The mammoth project was undertaken by Bishop Bertrand de l'Isle-Jourdain, a man of splendid dreams, great drive, and, most important of all, seemingly inexhaustible wealth. To him, moreover, in contrast with his Dominican predecessors, it was clearly the cathedral that must constitute the diocese's leading edifice.

Pride would seem to permit no less to this scion of one of the province's most princely families. Though Bertrand held the see for only fourteen years (1272–86), he was able to push his great new choir (twice the size in itself of Raymond VI's much-vaunted nave) well along the way to completion, together with its splendid diadem of chapels. Abandoning the thrifty habits of the past, the opulent prelate chose to use a large quantity of stone (in lieu of brick) for his new edifice, which had to be hauled from the Roquefort quarries in the Landes, over a hundred miles away, by a costly, hazardous land-and-water route.[93]

It is one of the rare, happy episodes of the Toulouse cathedral story that this extraordinary man got the inspired idea that no one since Bishop Izarn had conceived and which no one after Bertrand would again seek to implement.[94] It was doubtless his intention to carry his project through to its logical goal, sweeping the Raymond VI nave away in its wake and ending with a monument of a splendour to challenge that of any other Gothic church. And, indeed, if he had lived long enough to carry the fabric past the transept and into the nave, the momentum might have forced its completion along the lines already attained.

Since money was the entire matter underlying this fate, one wonders why Bertrand did not make better arrangements for the continuation of the project in his will, which for the sum of its bequests could almost have sufficed for its successful termination. In breaking up his fortune into hundreds of grants, instead, he doomed his dream to lasting nonfulfilment. Though the gifts to his own cathedral included some

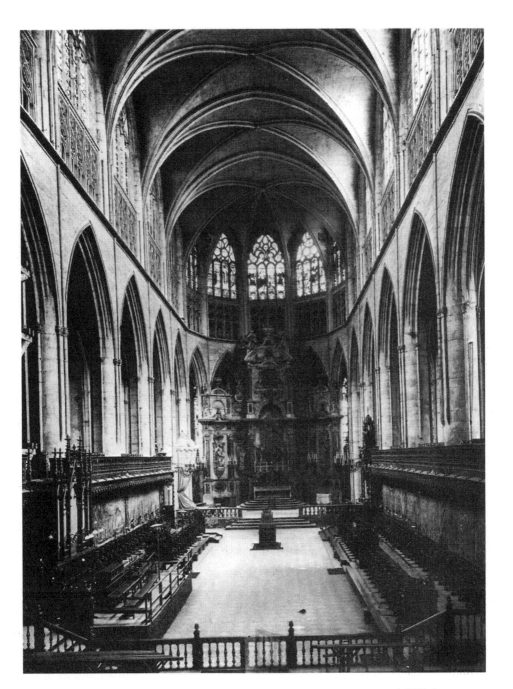

15. Bishop Bertrand's choir: a belated dream that was never fulfilled

splendid ones, for the fabric itself he left only 1,000 livres, about enough for only one year's building.[95]

There is much that is unaccounted for and even contradictory about Bertrand's will. It was prepared a number of years before his death, when the bishop asked papal confirmation for it, as though fearful that skulduggery in high places might violate its intentions. Had not Alphonse de Poitiers, pious brother of a most devout king, high-handedly annulled the great religious bequests of Count Raymond VII, his father-in-law, and appropriated most of the money to the royal exchequer?[96] Though Bertrand seemed eventually to regret his lack of foresight and prepared a second will, years later, which greatly increased his allowance to the fabric, that parchment disappeared, perhaps filched by those who would have lost by the alterations. The resplendent bishop was strangely abandoned in the end. His servants are said to have stripped the very robe off his corpse.[97]

Bertrand's grandiose project was never completed.[98] Indulgent historians have blamed this on the loss of revenues due to two split-offs from the diocese within the three decades after Bertrand's death.[99] The reductions were unquestionably impor-tant but the fact remains that even after the cuts there was still revenue enough to keep the enterprise going, if the will had been there. Besides, it was the misuse of the vast original income that was Rome's declared reason for breaking up the diocese. This, surely, would have been less likely to occur if the great construction project had been sedulously pursued.

Instead, the church became riddled by financial malfeasance.[100] During his epis-copacy, Bertrand had greatly increased the number of canons and made the necessary revenues available for thirty-eight prebends. But the chapter allowed many of these posts to lapse, splitting their incomes among themselves. The matter set off a great scandal when the chapter refused to seat a canon whom the pope nominated, alleging lack of funds.[101] The excuse was transparent, as John XXII well knew, maintaining on the contrary that the chapter's income was excessive and demanding that the sur-plus be used to increase its numbers as became so important a diocese. Fearing that the pope himself would announce such an increase, while naming a number of his own appointees, the chapter forestalled him in a machiavellian manoeuvre which only has been recently unravelled.[102]

Previously, historians had accepted at face value the chapter's declared reason for augmenting the number of its officiants as an eagerness to add to the church's 'splen-

16. Cathedral St-Etienne: looking towards the apse and choir from 'Raymond VI's Nave', showing the incongruity of the church's two halves which only the completion of Bishop Bertrand's project could have corrected

dour'. These authors thus not only disregarded the churchmen's previous neglect of the cathedral ritual but also the circumstance that all but two of the twenty-two canons named were relations of chapter members.[103] The pope, now installed at Avignon, hardly dared to annul their appointments, however, chosen as they were from among Languedoc's leading noble families,[104] even though almost half were of so tender an age as to be still studying their catechism![105]

There is a tricky little sentence in the document in which the church canons justified their selections. In it they pointed out that because of their high derivation, quality and wealth, the appointees would bring 'fruits to our church . . . by which (it) will be forever adorned'.[106] Probably intentionally, the meaning could be taken in both the metaphoric and literal, the spiritual and material (financial!) sense. Giving the canons the benefit of the doubt, we can almost see them for one florid moment expressing a desire to press the great Bertrand project through to its end.

Even if the surmise is correct, nothing was ever to come of it. Not this 'dream' or any other. Difficulties, real or imagined, always overwhelmed resolution. Time and again, with shame whipping up purpose, meetings were called, fund-raising plans laid out, drawings pencilled. But poor St-Etienne never profited the least bit from all these good intentions. In all the period following Bertrand de l'Isle-Jourdain's death, only minor additions were made to the cathedral's fabric. This included four chapels in the great builder's choir, each done by a different bishop, the relatively shallow effort requiring a full century. The choir itself was left vaulted in timber for three centuries until a fire in 1609 burnt out the wood, after which the stone vaulting was too quickly and too squatly built. To have had to wait for over three hundred years to do two years' work![107]

And thus St-Etienne still stands today, much as Bertrand left it seven hundred years ago, an unfinished dream-turned-nightmare, an architectural monstrosity. At best, it can be seen to serve man's historical knowledge in a symbolic way not intended for an aesthetic monument, reminding us by its disharmonious form of the cruel differences that rent this tragic province during the century of its making.

4

LYON

The Bridge to France

LYON CATHEDRAL CHRONOLOGY

c.1160	City invaded and devastated by Comte de Forez-et-Lyon. Romanesque church suffers serious damage.
1167	Rebuilding of the cathedral is launched at apse and choir on the Romanesque foundation, after basic agreement between church and count brings peace to Lyon.
1200–50	Lower windows of the choir are glazed during the first two decades (one still dating from twelfth century) but upper choir is not completed until c.1240, glazing of its windows extending past 1250. Transept is begun.
1245–69	Work on nave is started and continues at lively rate for two decades, when it is interrupted by protracted disturbances between church and burghers.
1270–1300	Little accomplished during this period. Nave proceeds very slowly toward the west, its vault begun only at the end of the century.
c.1313	Highly productive period follows after Lyon is absorbed into France in 1313. Last bay of nave is begun and at about the same time work on the lower façade with its rich portal sculpture, most of it unfortunately destroyed in 1562 by the Huguenots.
1350–1400	Work is interrupted by Hundred Years War. Nave vaulting and the upper windows (including the western rose) are not finished until the end of the century or early in the next.
15C	Upper façade is slowly built during this century.
14C–17C	Lateral chapels of nave are built between the abutments of the flying buttresses.

THE RELATIONSHIP OF CHURCH AND BURGHERS WAS NO MORE CORDIAL AT LYON than it had been at Toulouse though the antagonism was played out on different planes. Failure of the church of Lyon to understand the aspirations of its citizens had disastrous consequences for its own political fate and, incidentally, seriously hampered the construction of its cathedral. Its loss was France's gain, its miscalculations and prejudices eminently serving the expansionist sweep of the Capetians into the south-east.

This was hardly yet discernible in the middle of the twelfth century, when a high phase of the church's struggle for sovereignty over the important province took place. Germany and France were mere phantom contestants in the matter. But the church of Lyon's steady growth in political power had ended by throwing its chief rival, the count of Lyon, into an alliance with France. Frederick Barbarossa, the church's feudal seignior, countered by bestowing on it what has been called the 'golden bull', a grant of princely status. Actually, it was scarcely more than a magnificent swatch of parchment, since the emperor was too preoccupied with his own difficulties to be of any help to his church vassal.[1]

And the church of Lyon sorely needed help soon after this, around 1160, when the count invaded its lands, probably in retort to the 'golden bull'. His mercenaries penetrated into Lyon itself, where along with other desolation they gravely damaged the church of St-Jean, not yet Lyon's cathedral but which would attain that dignity when rebuilt. The further course of the war is obscure but the church of Lyon was able to extricate itself from its predicament, possibly with the aid of the citizens of the capital.[2] A peace was patched up in 1167, with count and archbishop agreeing to share the seigniory of Lyon. It proved an unworkable arrangement, but a more viable solution was found, in 1173, when by an exchange of finances and domains the church became sole sovereign of the great province and its capital.

A key feature of the accommodation was the acceptance of two of the count's sons into leading positions of the ecclesiastic family.[3] One of them, Renaud de Forez, was destined to become archbishop in 1193. He is often referred to as Lyon's outstanding prelate. There is no doubt that his accomplishment was pre-eminent in building up the temporal possessions of his church and in providing them with bristling defences.[4] This consisted in a widespread system of fortified castles and bourgs, the cathedral obituary crediting him with no fewer than fourteen such units.[5] And associated with these defensive measures went a programme of buying the vassaldom of bellicose feudals of the region with great baronial pensions.[6]

These massive expenditures had to be covered by borrowing. Already in 1173 the church had gone into debt to pay the count the money called for by the agreement establishing its sovereignty. It was obtained from two rich abbeys, to which the canons were obliged to pledge their own persons, possibly because all the church treasure had already been engaged.[7] The burghers were likewise a source of help. The terms of the sort of permanent loan that Renaud negotiated with them, in 1193, for 20,000 sous were in fact to prove fateful in the sequel. In return for the money, the citizens were to be relieved of certain taxes on consumers' goods, especially wine, which were to be reinstated when and if the money was paid back.[8]

The church of Lyon's income, though substantial, was not enormous[9] and something was bound to suffer because of these extraordinary disbursements. The evidence is that the cathedral was the prime loser. Its reconstruction had been undertaken soon after the first settlement in 1167, when the political auguries were for a swift and unencumbered building history. Indeed, a brilliant metropolitan church would have been an appropriate monument to a triumphant theocratic seigniory. But St-Jean's construction proved slow and leisurely from the start.

Commonly, the career of cathedrals follows a different course. Starting with a burst of enthusiasm, it will slow down only later, when the initial funds, gathered by zeal and promise, give out and are not renewed. In some privileged cases, the slackening-off may not ever occur, at least not for long. At Notre-Dame de Paris, the foundation stone was laid down at almost exactly the same time as at Lyon. Seventy years later, when the eastern sector of St-Jean was only just being completed,[10] the basic vessel of Notre-Dame had been accomplished and work on its façade was nearing completion.

Lyon's cathedral would not be getting to that advanced stage for almost another century. Nor was there any architectural complexity or decorative luxuriance at St-Jean that might have contributed to the delay. Handsome though it is in its quiet, dignified, old-fashioned way, Lyon's chevet is very modestly, even chastely built, without chapels or ambulatory, its old stained-glass filtering the morning light from across the Saône onto the church's spartan choir-space.

One of these windows, in the lower register, put in early in the thirteenth century, bears the inscribed name of 'Rainald' (Renaud). It is the only one that the archbishop could have paid for, we can be sure, since St-Jean's great obituary, which is remarkably (and rather exceptionally) informative about benefactors to its fabric, lists all the

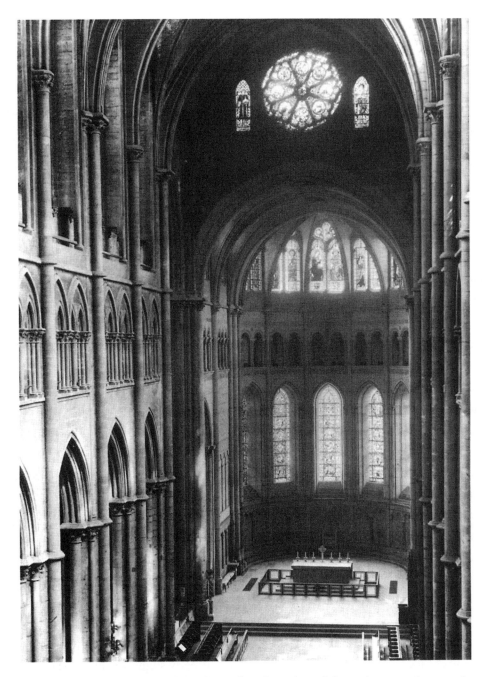

17. Cathedral St-Jean: view of the chevet ('modest, chaste') from the nave, showing the absence of choir, ambulatory, radiating chapels

donors of the choir lancets. They include a monk, two priests, a sub-deacon, the sacristan of the collegiate church of St-Paul, two deans of St-Jean, a canon, Duke Eudes III of Burgundy and a chamberlain.[11] Curiously, Renaud's name does not figure in this roster and it is conjecturable that his window was paid for by the fabric fund and credited to him out of a sense of propriety. Actually, he is recorded as having left but a single bequest to the cathedral-building fund—100 marks (80 livres)—enough to pay for the hire of eight masons for a single year.

Nevertheless, we know that Renaud made lavish contributions to his church. As listed in his obituary, they go on for page after page.[12] But they all went for building up worldly power and riches. This one-sided distribution defines perfectly the prevailing options during Renaud's long office (1193–1226). The new cathedral was only a vague second thought for Lyon's churchmen, often left out of their wills by the dignitaries, however lavish they might be on occasion in other bequests, particularly for their own anniversaries.[13] Altogether only thirty-three canons gave as much as one livre to the fabric during the seven decades when the choir was slowly going up, the sum of their benefactions averaging 10 livres a year. It was just enough to pay for one lonely worker.[14]

Knowing something about the character of Lyon's canons, we are not surprised by their lack of enthusiasm for the cathedral's building fate. For the greater part younger sons of nobles, scions of many of the province's greatest families, they were not even required to take priestly orders and had to be in residence for only sixty days a year. As churchmen, their interests remained basically secular. Renaud de Forez was a man of the same pattern. Before assuming the archbishopric, he served under Jean Bellesmains, a peace-loving man who patently could not cope with Renaud's ambitions. When Jean surrendered the office to him at last to go into monastic retirement, he left a touching letter explaining his horror for the life required of the Archbishop of Lyon, whose duties had often to be carried out *armata manu*, with weapon in hand.[15]

That Lyon's burghers did not make up for the churchmen's lack of enthusiasm about their new cathedral follows the rule that we have already suggested about the initiative for this tremendous project having to come from the church. There was no dearth of wealthy citizens at Lyon, whose population, variously estimated from 20,000 to 50,000, gave it the status of a veritable metropolis in the medieval period. One opulent merchant, for example, Pierre de Vaux, was the founder, around 1180, of the Waldensian heterodoxy, often called the 'Poor Ones of Lyon'. But Pierre, who gave his great fortune to the city's destitute, was by definition antagonistic to church splendour.[16]

Yet there were other burghers of great substance who were not ruled by such ascetic principles. One of these, Ponce de Chaponay, became early in the thirteenth century a familiar of prelates and princes and did business in the Holy Land for Pope Innocent III, who called him a 'noble man', though he was only a burgher.[17] Still, Ponce's donation to the cathedral fabric was far from notable: 10 livres for the hire of one mason for one year. His wife was somewhat more generous, paying for the 'rebuilding' of the altar of the Virgin and donating a mark toward the glazing of the 'great window' of that chapel.

Poncie Limanda, another bourgeoise, paid a larger part of the cost of the same window, 4 livres, while also contributing a year's wages for an artisan. Her husband's gift was less than modest, 20 sous.[18] And so it continues, the unimpressive register of burgher gifts to St-Jean, adding up to exactly 130 livres in a century and a half.[19] How little this would have advanced the cathedral's structure can be gathered from the fact that in a productive year at least 1,000 livres were needed for materials and labour.

Nor did the churchmen's social attitude toward even the wealthiest burghers help to elicit their patronage. Few churches have had a more snobbish chapter than this one of Lyon, which had the strictest requirements of high descent for membership. That the matter rankled is proved by the burghers' repeated requests for a relaxation of the canons' restrictions. On one critical occasion, after a sharp conflict of the kind in which Lyon's citizens and the church were often involved, the former proposed in the interests of peace that the chapter be increased to one hundred canons so that ample room would be made for commoners on the cathedral's directing body. Such a democratization could only have been wholesome and its effect on the church's construction might have been vivifying. But the chapter, in a typical arrogant act, took exactly the opposite course, cutting its numbers to thirty-two.[20]

Starting in the early thirteenth century, the political relations of Lyon's citizens with their church seigniors deteriorated steadily. What the burghers had gained from their 'loan' in 1193 of 20,000 sous to Archbishop Renaud was little enough—a release from some taxes and tolls. This was a time, besides, when many other towns, some even in neighbouring areas, were winning extensive privileges.[21] But far from conceding its Lyonnais subjects additional rights, the church of Lyon violated at every occasion even the sparse terms of the 1193 charter that had been duly paid for. A first, inevitable outburst came in 1208, when the heretofore timorous citizens went to the length of setting up a council and erecting a tower overlooking the bridge that linked their commercial quarter across the Saône with the great cathedral *cité* on the river's western bank.

Archbishop Renaud's reaction was savage, his troops demolishing and setting fire to the homes of a number of burghers and drowning their owners in the river.[22] Following a bristling rebuke by the pope, from which we learn about Renaud's many breaches of the 1193 pact, the prelate was constrained to accept arbitration of the dispute. The choice of moderators, two high churchmen and Duke Eudes of Burgundy, constituted no threat to the archbishop's authority, but the burghers may have had some illusions about Eudes, who had been quite liberal with his own subjects at Dijon.[23]

What Lyon won was once more relatively minor, such as the right to establish guilds and recognition of the traditional *coutumes*, which consisted mainly of common-law provisions regarding the inviolability of persons and property, assurances that many lesser places had long since enjoyed. In return, the burghers had to recognize formally the church's exclusive rights of justice and political hegemony, *tam citra Ararim quam ultra*, on both sides of the Saône. This would include the burghers' commercial quarter on the eastern peninsula between Saône and Rhône, where the church's crushing authority was thwarting economic progress. Ultimate outrage: the commoners had to pledge to abstain from forming any 'conspiracy or sworn commune or consulate' or to make mutual vows 'other than the legitimate oaths used in mercantile associations'.[24]

Lyon's citizens could hardly have been rapturous about this settlement and nothing suggests that it sweetened their attitude toward the church. No more did it increase burgher benefactions toward the cathedral's fabric. None the less, around 1245, the building campaign surprisingly took on a considerable spurt that lasted for some years, financed mainly by gifts from the churchmen themselves.[25] The reason for their sudden, untypical assiduity is not hard to conjecture since it coincided with the period of Pope Innocent IV's prolonged stay at Lyon (1245–51), after his 'deposition' by the German emperor, Frederick II.

Shamed, browbeaten or encouraged into paying more attention to their languishing cathedral, the Lyon churchmen displayed a more active concern about its fate during the following quarter of a century than in all its protracted building history. Almost all of St-Jean's nave was completed in this period.[26] Only the last double-bay was still left to do and the vaulting remained in suspension when the onset of a new series of violent clashes put the cap on the long-developing antagonism between church and burghers. And work on the cathedral halted for almost half a century. The great ecumenical council that met at Lyon in 1274, which sought to knit the long-severed eastern and western branches of the Catholic church, had to take place in the truncated vessel.[27]

As we look back on the 1269–70 revolt of Lyon's citizens, we almost feel that it could have been predicted. Certainly, its most immediate cause, Lyon's system of justice, was so patently inequitable that it is difficult to understand how it could have been tolerated for so long. The underlying evil was the existing duplication of jurisdiction by virtue of which independent temporal courts of the archbishop and the chapter operated competitively. To be sure, the medieval world was accustomed to a patchwork of tribunals, each seignior operating his own. But his powers were normally sharply circumscribed by the boundaries of his seigniory. The flaw at Lyon was that the city's two major church authorities both made general and over-riding claims.

What this meant in practice was incisively described by Pope Gregory X, who was called on to arbitrate the dispute in 1274. The pontiff sketched out an abrasive picture of the wilful acts and procedures which had finally brought on the great revolt. In the aggregate, he explained, they 'not only blocked the course of justice but caused grave annoyance to the people, multiplying their costs by requiring their appearance before different tribunals in cases involving the very same contract, violation or crime . . .'. This, the pope concluded, brought on 'such exacerbations as cause scandals, wars, seditions, murders and other similar perils'.[28]

The purely fortuitous incident that set the spark to the powder-barrel was the arrest and imprisonment by the chapter's police of an important citizen, Nicolas Amadour, and six other men, in two separate cases. The chapter had been taking advantage of a prolonged vacancy in the archbishop's post to expand its jurisdiction, in which the citizens could only see added penalties for themselves. When their demand for the release of the prisoners was rejected, they stormed the cathedral cloister and freed them themselves. This first violent act seems to have released the torrent of their stored-up wrath and the canons had to flee for their lives, scuttling up the bluff to the citadel of the Abbey of St-Just.[29]

Thereafter, events spiralled from violence to greater violence. Large numbers of troops were brought in by both sides, most of them mercenaries. Those fighting in the church's ranks were led by the Comte de Forez (formerly de Lyon), who was promised as his stipend one-third of the indemnity the church asserted it would extract from its rebellious subjects.[30] The citizens' forces, other than the armed burghers themselves, were, anomalously, supplied by a powerful seignior of the area, brother of a cathedral dignitary, Hugues de la Tour-du-Pin, whose support of the popular cause was the result of intra-chapter strife that was fuelled by feudal rivalries.[31]

The succeeding film of events can almost be described in acts of church destruction and profanation. Not only was the cloister of the cathedral of St-Jean attacked, it was also thoroughly pillaged, even to the removal of doors and windows. The church and bourg of St-Just up on the cliff overlooking the Saône's western front were under continuous siege, its subsidiaries outside its great walls wrecked. The city used the nearby oratory of Marie-Madeleine to quarter its troops, with the damage that can be imagined. The latter also occupied the neighbouring Notre-Dame-de-la-Fourvière, then only a small chapter residentiary and burial church, which likewise serviced the few vineyard keepers on the slope.

In the course of the struggle, the citizens set up all the apparatus of a self-governing body. They met in general assembly at the church of St-Nizier, which was located in the heart of the new commercial area on the peninsula. Here, though under constant excommunication, they continued to enjoy sacramental and other church rites with the help of sympathetic priests.[32] The burghers never forgot the role that St-Nizier played during these eventful days. As late as 1458, when its clocktower had to be rebuilt, the consulate in making its contribution declared pointedly that 'it had used this church more than any others' and that its great bell had warned the city 'in times of fire and fright'.[33]

On occasion, the church's mercenaries descended into the populous St-Nizier quarter to spread death and destruction. The burghers' forces struck back at the church's vulnerable possessions in the outlying regions. Witnesses at subsequent hearings told how one attack was made on suburban Ecully, a possession of the Abbey of St-Just, the high, impregnable citadel which harboured the church's marauding forces. Ecully's church was set ablaze, with the priest and many parishioners inside. This was followed by assaults on other church-owned villages, where the guild banners of Lyon's butchers and shoemakers were seen leading the attackers. And from all throats came the citizens' battlecry:

'*Avant! Avant! Lion le melhor!*'—'Forward! Forward! Lyon the best!'[34]

These violent events ended in a kind of armed truce that was like the pause of exhausted contestants resting up before resuming the conflict. An ostensible settlement was arranged by the arbitral award of Pope Gregory X in 1274, a provision of which called for the payment by the burghers of 7,000 livres for damage done to church property.[35] More important, the pontiff decreed the abolition of the dual-justice system, with the grant of basic jurisdiction to the archbishop.[36]

But the chapter refused to accept the pope's decision, launching a costly campaign to overturn it. The canons are estimated to have spent 40,000 livres toward this goal between 1274 and 1290.[37] Since the money was largely borrowed from Italian bankers, the inference is that it was used for bribes at Rome. The extravagance of the outlay indicates how remunerative the conduct of justice must have been at Lyon. Even at 5 per cent—and the Italian moneylenders certainly got much more than that—the interest alone would have cost the canons 2,000 livres a year. It was enough to bring the long inactive cathedral fabric into vibrant life and to a swift termination.

But even if money were available, building activities would have been out of the question at the time, for the chapter challenged the papal decision by violent acts at home as well as bribes at Rome. Aided by powerful barons of the region, the canons seized the archbishop's courts by force and even shut the doors of the cathedral to the prelate. The latter replied by sending his armed bands out to ravage the chapter's lands. The church's civil war went on for years until it was so weakened as to invite invasion by its own minor vassals.[38]

It was only a transcendent authority that could have brought peace to so torn and chaotic a situation. And that power had, in effect, already begun to shoulder its way into the region some time back by a series of not quite legitimate acts which ended nevertheless in fully established sovereignty. This power was royal France, which at the beginning of the century or a bit earlier had already started to move into the Lyonnais by way of its neighbouring possessions. By 1239, control over the adjoining Mâconnais was negotiated and thereafter the crown bailiff from that county found numerous excuses for making probative incursions.[39]

Final attachment of the great province to the royal domain was incalculably facilitated by the support of an important internal ally, Lyon's bourgeoisie. Exasperated
by their endless struggle for legitimate rights that even some towns belonging to the
church of Lyon had already been granted,[40] the burghers decided that their only hope
lay in a change of sovereignty. Accordingly, when Philippe III (son of St Louis) came
to the city in 1271 on return from the eighth Crusade, bearing his father's coffin,
despite the solemn circumstances, the burghers found an opportune moment to cast
themselves at the new monarch's feet, imploring him to place them under his 'special
custody'. Their pledge of fealty was without bounds in time or fortune:

> We obligate ourselves, our heirs and their heirs as well as all our worldly goods,
> present and future.[41]

When the switch of allegiance was formally accepted a few years later, the king
received the first payment of a never-ceasing flow of gold, arranged in the form of a
yearly graduated poll-tax of 12 deniers to 10 sous. The church of Lyon responded with
understandable wrath, blasting its disloyal subjects in every church of the city. They
remained in excommunication for eleven years. But the royal agents continued to press
their advantage, now seizing the church's temporal possessions, now taking over its
courts, now instituting some important request of the citizens. And each move on behalf
of his 'beloved and loyal Lyonnais people' brought the French king closer to his goal.[42]

According to feudal ordinance, the legality of the citizens' shift of allegiance was
more than dubious. In fact, France's takeover of the province would in the end
unavoidably require the consent of its legitimate sovereign, the archbishop of Lyon.
Since this was not forthcoming, it had to be accomplished by force. This act was conveniently triggered by a last flourish of resistance by a new prelate, Pierre de Savoie
(1308–32), scion of a great princely house, who no doubt counted on its high prestige to fend off a retort by the French. When the latter, hardly intimidated, sent an
army to Lyon, the burghers greeted it with enthusiasm and joined the short siege of
their prelate in his rocky redoubt above the Saône, the castle of Pierre-Scize.[43]

After a chastening imprisonment, Archbishop Pierre de Savoie, joined by his
chapter, acceded to the inevitable in 1313 by formally acknowledging France's suzerainty. A few years later, in 1320, the prelate, with great fanfare, granted a charter to
the city. The preamble echoes strangely stemming from this source:

Liberty is a natural right. For the honour of God, for the peace and tranquillity of our church, our city and the entire country . . . we recognize and wish to maintain inviolable in the future the customs, franchises and liberties of the city of Lyon . . .[44]

Recognized in the charter were the people's right to assemble, to raise taxes for the city's immediate needs and especially for its defences, to arm in face of danger, to possess the keys to the gates and to be allowed to guard them at night. But the basic political powers, including justice, continued in the archbishop's hands.[45]

The fact that the church of Lyon had been forced to surrender its temporal sovereignty, a calamity in feudal terms, was salutary in other respects. Most important, its

18. The archbishop's redoubt of Pierre-Scize. Here Pierre de Savoie was held in siege by the French troops, joined by Lyon's burghers. When the prelate surrendered, suzerainty over the province passed permanently to France

officials could, if they desired, turn their attention to their long-neglected cathedral, which after over a hundred and fifty years still lacked its façade and part of its upper nave. And this was exactly what Archbishop Pierre, who evidently was not one to brood over his losses, did. He sent the Confraternity of the Fabric of St-Jean out on quest all over the archdiocese. He assigned the revenues of all vacant benefices to the building fund for three years, then renewed the grant. For the first time in fifty-four years he asked for and got a papal indulgence for the fabric—and what an indulgence it was! John XXII added seven years and seven quarantines (forty-day periods) to all the years of grace already granted, then got twenty-three members of the Curia each to add one year and forty days.[46]

There resulted a burst of creative activity such as St-Jean saw but two other times in its prolonged building history. The magnificent lower façade was the beneficiary, justly decorated with arms of the House of Savoy and enriched by a mass of lovely sculpture. The large statues have been lost, destroyed by the Huguenots in 1562. But enough remains of the smaller work to indicate that the effort inspired by Archbishop Pierre produced what must have been the cathedral's most splendid area, its carving among the finest created in France during the first half of the fourteenth century.

After this productive effort, inspired by Pierre de Savoie, progress on the cathedral fell off sharply for the remainder of the century. True, the intervening period witnessed the coming of the Great Plague in 1348 and the English invasion, the latter particularly proving enormously costly to the church of Lyon.[47] There is nothing in the record to indicate that Lyon's citizens played a significant role as cathedral-building patrons during this entire century. Quite the contrary, as we can judge from their wills, which for the first time appear in the archives during this period.[48]

Indeed, nothing had happened in the interim to cause the burghers to be better disposed toward the hierarchy. The cathedral chapter's policy of exclusion had, in fact, undergone a further tightening, in 1337, which was directly aimed at commoners. Thereafter, choice of canons was restricted to those possessing sixteen 'quarters' of nobility on both parental sides. This prescript continued to be rigidly exacted over succeeding centuries, one ludicrous display being the chapter's refusal of an honorary canonicate to Louis XIV because of his 'bourgeois' grandmother, Maria de' Medici.

St-Jean's policy of barring commoners not only covered membership in its chapter, it even extended to their enjoyment of the sacraments at the cathedral. The

19. Berthet Fillatros's will. His request to the archbishop and his *official* begins at top of next page

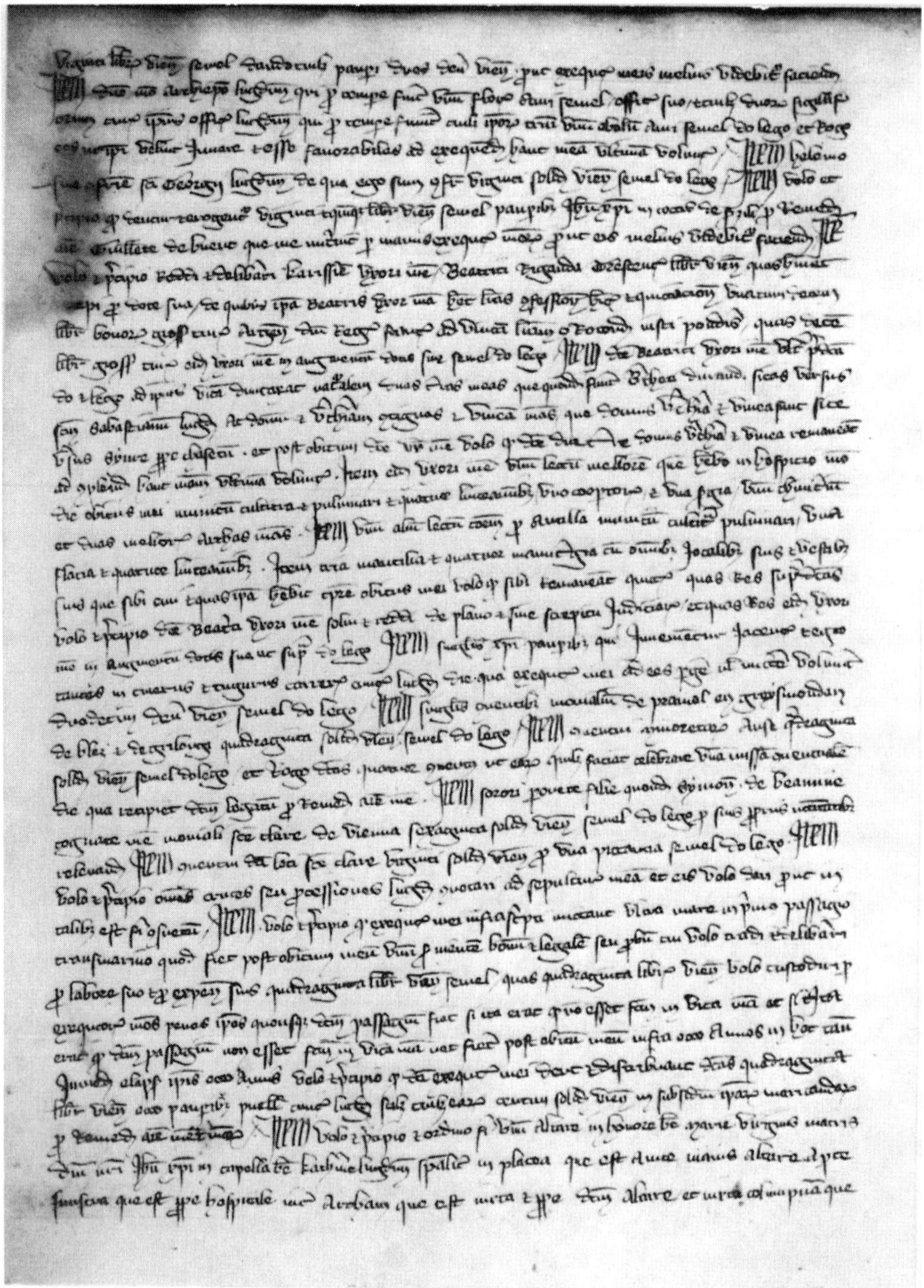

canons would not permit burgher burials or anniversaries to take place at St-Jean, shunting them off to the auxiliary churches of St-Etienne and Ste-Croix, which were located within the cathedral compound. Even at these units a policy was maintained of sifting out the most patrician of citizens and keeping the hoi-polloi at a distance. This is apparent from the great sums that were demanded for the commemorative masses at St-Etienne, where as high as 150 livres were obtained. This would have been more than enough to found a daily mass at Amiens cathedral. There can be no doubt that St-Jean was rigorously reserved for pontifical and capitular ceremonial.[49]

Curiously, reading Lyon's magnificent collection of burgher wills could almost lead to the opposite conclusion, indicating a strong burgher attachment to the church, or at least to its prelate. This appears from the frequent gifts that commoners left to the archbishop, which occur in as high as 30 per cent of the testaments.[50] The impression is fortified by the tender terms in which the churchman is addressed by the testators, which sometimes border on the mawkish. Thus, Jean de la Mure directs his gift of 20 florins to 'my reverent lord, pious in Christ, most beloved lord, the Archbishop of Lyon'.[51]

But the fervour was pure formalistic or notarial humbug and concealed a shrewd motive, besides. The true significance of these gifts is revealed by the fact that they were often accompanied by supplementary bequests to the prelate's 'official', the man in charge of his judiciary system and hence the registry of wills, which was under the archbishop's jurisdiction. Indeed, the wills themselves might baldly specify what was expected in return for these pious bribes.

A particularly disenchanted example of this underlying motivation is given in the will of Berthet Fillatros. It dispenses with all endearing appellations when announcing that this affluent burgher was bequeathing the archbishop a gold florin 'for his services' and to his 'official' a gold 'obole' for the two seals he was to affix to the parchment. And with what cynicism did the testator add the reminder that the recipients were fully expected in return to be 'favourable to my testamentary executioners if not to my own last wishes!'[52]

The evidence seems formal: Lyon's citizens continued as they had in the past to play a very minor role in the cathedral's construction history. As we have already noted, however, strained relations between the faithful and the hierarchy did not totally alienate the former from the church but merely forced them to find their indispensable devout attachments elsewhere than at the cathedral. This might be in the parish churches, often among the new mendicant orders. It was the pattern followed at Lyon.

Of all its churches, the one to which the burghers were most closely attached was St-Nizier, which was their assembly hall in the stirring days of 1269–70 and long after. It may seem strange that the intense burgher presence at St-Nizier in the thirteenth century is unmarked by any building reference. This is particularly surprising when one thinks that the church must have been in bad need of repair after a mysterious attempt around the mid-century to burn it down.[53] But the latter half of the century was altogether too disturbed a period for the burghers to have applied themselves to church building.

One can never say it too often, that even in the devout medieval epoch, the construction of churches was not the primary concern of the people. Not even of most churchmen! At Lyon, the building record during the thirteenth century is sparse.[54] In the two dozen or so churches for which we have some information, the examples of work of any importance that were done during that century are rare. Lyon's friars began prospering only in the fourteenth century. Though the Franciscans and Dominicans had churches there by the thirteenth, they were unimportant, the latter being actually restricted by the terms of their establishment not to acquire property of any kind whether by gift or purchase!

There was one remarkable exception to this negative building record, the church-citadel of St-Just, which was largely rebuilt in the second half of the thirteenth century. But this, unquestionably, was due to the extraordinary impulsion given it by Innocent IV during his long stay at Lyon, when he made this abbey-on-the-bluff his headquarters. The pope, it must be noted, actually considered pursuit by his mortal enemy, Frederick II, imminent. Did he also think of St-Just as a permanent papal emergency retreat, as Avignon was to become a half-century later? Innocent turned over to the abbey two great domanial properties, bought with his own 'pennies'. And he gave its fabric an unending battery of dispensations, which brought such a flush of donations that that body was soon investing the excess. Meanwhile, the church went up rapidly, to become what has been rated Lyon's second most splendid edifice (now totally rebuilt).[55]

It was only in the fourteenth century, in 1303, that the job of repairing St-Nizier was seriously thought of for the first time. It is hardly unexpected that the work was initiated by a burgher, Jean de Marines. However, it was not completed at the time,

20. The magnificent burgher-built church of St-Nizier

for the citizens were still preoccupied with many functional matters which left them few extra funds for donations to church-building projects. On the other hand, its reconstruction was not much more advanced several decades later, when the Black Death, which came to Lyon in 1348, paradoxically enriched the church's building fund with 1,000 florins that were turned over to it from the poor fund. The archbishop explained this decision in a pathetic topical remark: 'since hardly any poor people remain due to the mortal pestilence that everywhere prevails'.[56]

St-Nizier was not finally completed until the fifteenth and sixteenth centuries, when burgher aid was determinant. But the church's clergy also played an important part, which is understandable in the light of the excellent relations that had always existed between them and the parishioners. This situation had been consolidated in 1305, when St-Nizier was given collegiate status with a chapter of canons, four of whose posts were explicitly reserved for sons of ordinary citizens, 'who would enjoy the same privileges, immunity and liberty' as any other members.[57] What a difference from the attitude of the haughty cathedral canons!

Indeed, whatever we find in the way of improvidence or political error as factors hampering the expeditious building of St-Jean Cathedral, it is hardly of greater importance than the waste due to pride. In addition to what has already been cited under that heading, moreover, was the extraordinary outlay, shared by all the city's churches, for ceremonial and mortuary display. The fundamental motivation was undoubtedly the demands on a city claiming to be the seat of the primatial church of Gaul. The fact that the price of this affirmation might slow progress on its metropolitan church seemed to hold little weight. The construction process was never-ending, during which the great monumental goal was obscured by mounds of litter and scaffolding. The shine and glitter of ceremony were more immediately impressive.

One important feature of the cathedral's ritual was its liturgical chant which was so renowned that distant churches sent their cantors there to study its choral work, whose high repute has carried on into modern times.[58] But far more dispersive were the mortuary manifestations, by much the costliest that we have found anywhere, and it is hardly surprising that coercive measures had to be used at times to impose them on the parishioners. The canons of St-Jean on one occasion expressed indignation that the people should balk at having fine funerals, 'in contempt of the churches'.[59] But in this respect the parish clerics were hardly more reasonable.

Thus, the canons of the collegiate church of St-Paul, where the middle class was very active, would not permit mass to be sung for a dead man unless a foundation for his anniversary had previously been arranged for or if his body was accompanied by a 'quantity of wax candles in excess of those paid for in the price of the funeral'.[60] Here, too, as even at the strictly bourgeois church of St-Nizier, commoners' corpses were not allowed into the sanctuary unless garbed in a special woven cloth of a value of at least 10 florins, which the church got after the burial. These were then loaned out to impecunious parishioners, bringing an important income, as did also the extra wax that was required, which was periodically melted down and sold.[61]

While from the viewpoint of church-building, Lyon's pervading cult of death no doubt diminished the total accomplishment, in other ways it served an aesthetic goal itself. The fourteenth century was the time when the people of Lyon—as all over France, in fact—became conscious of the tomb. The chapels and altars that were paid for by the burghers at St-Nizier, which was the city's leading interment church,[62] were often conceived of as part of an elaborate arrangement that included tomb, chaplaincy and sacerdotal gear.[63] At times the wills told in detail how the tombs were to be built.

Etienne de Plastre, for instance, specified that his sepulchre was to be approached by a subterranean arcade borne by stone pillars and closed in by a plaque whose inscription would be devised by a clerical friend.[64] Clara Martinero did not even leave the inscription to another hand in the richly detailed setting that she ordered for her and her husband's grave. It was to be adorned with

> a cross made from handsome stone on which will be carved figures of Christ on the Cross and of the Blessed Virgin Mary and there [I wish] to be carved the following words: *Ceste cruys a fait fere Clara relicta de Johan Torneon, citoyen de Lion, saye[n]arruier.*[65]

Artistic objects ordered by the parishioners often accompanied the tomb foundation. The small waxen image of the Virgin that Martin de Molendinis bequeathed to the famous Mary Chapel of St-Nizier may have been a kind of *ex voto* that was prepared in quantity.[66] But this could hardly have been the case with the wax carving of the Virgin ordered for the same chapel by Jacquemette d'Ambérieu, which by her specification was to weigh no less than 126 pounds![67]

This was, to be sure, the era when the cult of Mary was at its pinnacle, when even a simple street image of the Virgin in the parish of St-Nizier won important bequests in people's wills for 'perpetual lights'.[68] In fact, there was such a flood of cash offerings to this particular street shrine that a permanent chaplaincy dedicated to it was established at the church itself, grandiloquently named 'Notre-Dame-de-la-Rue-Neuve'.[69]

That St-Nizier should also lead all churches in burgher-founded chaplaincies is no more than might have been expected.[70] But other churches of Lyon had considerable numbers of these daily mass foundations also and vast quantities of anniversaries, which were of course much less expensive than the chaplaincies and hence available to a far greater portion of the population. The church of St-Paul was particularly active in this field, with over 150 lay anniversaries established there in the early decades of the thirteenth century alone.[71] The way these foundations could build up a church's wealth is shown by the property investments recorded in St-Paul's cartularies, which totalled over 1,500 livres during the first half of that century. St-Paul also received noteworthy patronage from the burghers to its fabric, some of it going back to the twelfth century.[72]

One of the most amazing features of the mortuary cult was the family chapel-mausoleum, which in effect abstracted important sections of God's house from the mass of faithful for the exclusive use of the wealthiest patricians. An example was the arrangement made by Jean Ogier, a civic leader, who in 1327 bequeathed the great sum of 2,300 livres to the newly founded Franciscan church, St-Bonaventure, with which he bought 'eternal' rights for his family to the Chapel of the Virgin, where his carved coat-of-arms can still be seen today.[73] Other chapels at this church were paid for by a number of guilds: tavern-keepers, painters, curriers, cloth-shearers, 'the merchants of Troyes', etc., though not for exclusive use.

How a family assured itself of sole possession of the church-segment which it purchased is fully illustrated by the case of Etienne de Villeneuve, first compiler of Lyon's archives, who in 1343 bought permanent ownership of the Chapel of St-Pierre at the abbey church of St-Martin-D'Ainay.[74] For 300 florins, Etienne's family were granted the 'rights to close [the chapel] off with key' and to have private daily masses there, celebrated by one of their three salaried chaplains. Actually four keys were made, one going to each of the three chaplains, and the fourth—not to the church, by any means—but into the hands of the recognized chapel-owners, the Villeneuve family.[75]

Most commoners, who could not afford such extravagant private arrangements, had to content themselves with a single day of glory, that of their death. At Lyon, a funeral was not considered complete unless accompanied by a procession. In its simplest form this would call for a little parade in the parish cemetery, led by as many priests as could be paid for.[76] For the rich, these parades became veritable processionals through the city, swollen by numbers of 'mourners' who got a penny or two for their participation. The importance that Lyon's citizens attached to their posthumous dignity is revealed by the great sums that they often allotted for this purpose. Giraud Leblanc not only left for it the annual revenue on 300 livres, which would have paid for hundreds of mourners, but added 100 livres to clothe a number of them suitably, in serge.[77]

Henri Moissard asked that his coffin be carried in the procession by nine poor men, dressed in white and holding torches.[78] Thus appears in a documented bequest this image that has become so familiar to us in mortuary art. Laurent Garin's will calls forth another symbol of funerary imagery when he specifies that a group of priests was to watch the night through beside his body, around which was to blaze a constellation of candles.[79] Many of the city's priests and particularly the mendicants became specialists in these mortuary functions. It may explain the meaning of those mysterious, sad-faced monks that can be seen on both sides of St-Bonaventure's inner façade looking like an illustrated advertisement of an available service.

Most highly appreciated of all processionals at Lyon, no doubt, were those performed by the snobbish nuns of St-Pierre Abbey, to whose spectacular displays may possibly be attributed their ability to remain entrenched for centuries in the heart of an artisans' and tradesmen's quarter. They would not hear of a daughter of the bourgeoisie entering their ranks and it is a mystery how one of them, Bernarde du Fuers, stemming though she did from a high patrician family, was able to slip through St-Pierre's silken defences. However, she seems to have remained the sole exception. After the upheaval of 1269, the burghers pleaded for a democratization of the nunnery's ranks, as they did for the cathedral chapter's, with as little success.[80]

But the nuns did not mind being *looked at* by commoners, making available a closed-off space in their church nave from which the faithful could watch their magnificent offices, which were performed with sparkling ornaments ('the richest of

Lyon') and accompanied by the city's finest chimes.[81] For their own masses and sacraments, however, the parishioners were confined to the auxiliary church of St-Saturnin nearby, which has been described as being 'very small and badly built'.[82] Otherwise, the *nonains* lived as self-indulgently as any noblewomen 'in the century', each in her own 'hôtel', attended by private domestics, who served her meals on silver plate.

Above all else, however, the nuns of St-Pierre were renowned for their frequent parades, their art of display reaching its apogee on Corpus Christi Day. Flanked by her gentleman-esquire and the other officers of her 'court', the regal, crosier-bearing abbess led an elegant train of thirty-two nuns and many *fillettes* and novices, as young as four or five, daughters of the best houses of the province. None of the participants attracted more attention than the garlanded choirboys who, in the costume of angels, swung silver censers and scattered roses from woven baskets. On Pentecost, a popular holiday and time for revelry, the nuns even knew how to unbend for a moment of gracious 'condescension', the abbess inaugurating the festivities by dancing a bourrée with the parish curé in the square outside the church.[83]

Lyon's most extravagant procession of all was reserved by the ecclesiastics of St-Jean for the festival day of their patron saint, John-the-Baptist. Since the celebration was likewise associated with the local saints of the early centuries, the solemnity came to be called in their honour the 'Festival of Miracles'. The most imposing part of this famous jubilee was conducted on water, in reference too, no doubt, to 'John as baptizer'. Every major guild and church was expected to have its barge, richly decked out and manned by paid oarsmen. The cathedral's craft, seconded by the boats of the four other leading churches, filed ceremoniously down the Saône to the point where it joined the Rhône. Here a circuit of obeisance was executed about the church quintet by the guild launches.[84]

It was a portentous sign of the breaking up of the church's hold on the commoners when the latter began, sometime in the thirteenth century, to balk at the pompous manifestation.[85] Its enormous cost was the reason given. One does not hear of the churchmen having ever suggested a worthy substitute: like contributions to the cathedral-building campaign! But apparently both archbishop and canons considered the transitory glamour of processions more important than completion of their church.

However, besides the costliness of the Festival of Miracles, could there have been some unspoken objection to it that the citizens shared, something almost ideological? The Guigues, Lyonnais historians, have suggested that the symbolism of the ceremony began to irk the burghers. People of the Middle Ages were deeply sensitive to such clouded meanings and some of those contained in this Festival may have affronted the commoners' increasing disavowal of the church's political mastery as well as their own passionate desire for emancipation.

Opposition to the Festival of Miracles intensified in the fourteenth century and with the coming of the Hundred Years War the burghers' contention that the money spent on the extravaganza could be put to better use for the city's defences won it yearly postponements by king's decree, always over bitter church protests. Toward the end of the century, when the threat of attack had subsided, Lyon's citizens were faced with the prospect of a resumption of the costly and objectionable ceremony in honour of arrogant hierarchs whom they despised. But once again they found a substitute project of unquestionable merit to propose.

Not the still unterminated cathedral of St-Jean, alas. No, it was the great bridge over the Rhône. Actually, this formidable project had challenged the city's ingenuity since the twelfth century and intermittently much fortune had been lavished on it.[86] The great economic and strategic importance of the bridge had sustained the people in this effort despite repeated failure. Lyon, which had no important industry, owed its prosperity largely to its marvellous geographic position. At the confluence of two major rivers, it was at the crux too of the overland route between the North and Italy, where goods and travellers had to be transported by a toilsome and sometimes dangerous ferry system.

After the success of the famed Pont d'Avignon, Lyon had brightened with the same idea and was probably aided in its effort by men brought up from the south who belonged to a lay brotherhood, which in the medieval manner took on the punning name of Frères Pontifes. But the Rhône at Lyon was not the same river as at Avignon, where it was gentler, slower.[87] At Lyon, the great river would sweep the banks at springtide with a turbulence that could carry a great mound of stone and mortar away with it, to say nothing of wood, with which its first bridge was made. Triumphantly completed in time for the crusading troops of Philippe-Auguste and Richard the Lion Heart to make the crossover, tradition holds that it was this heavy usage that caused it to founder, in 1190, with much loss of life.[88]

But the task was taken up briskly again, probably at a new location,[89] funds being gathered by a Confraternity of the Holy Spirit, a burgher group. The bridge became for a time what must have been the most active construction site in town. It was certainly more animated than the cathedral fabric! Auxiliaries sprang up at every hand: an almonry for receiving and storing donations, often in kind, two chapels, a hospice for tired pilgrims, a cemetery for those who would never resume their journey, even houses, built from donated funds, that were rented out for the income that would be put into the construction of the bridge![90]

The Pont du Rhône has left no cartulary, and burgher testaments are lacking before the fourteenth century. But there can be little doubt that Lyon's citizens were very liberal in donations to their bridge. In fact, the scarcity of church building in the city during the thirteenth century may not have been due to burgher-hierarchic animosities alone. In any case, their raging antagonism could only have encouraged the citizens to favour this worthwhile project with their benevolence.[91] By the fourteenth century we have documents about the great sums that the burghers spent on the bridge. This outlay would certainly have interfered with an active cathedral-building programme, if such were going on.

The tragedy of the vast exertions on the bridge was that prevailing technical resources were patently not equal to the proposed goal. Time after time, years of effort would be swept away by the floods. It is astonishing with what courage the task was repeatedly taken up again. Toward the mid-thirteenth century, the bridge's abutments began to be changed to stone.[92] But the great turmoil that churned the city after 1269 must have slowed its favourite project for many years, just as it did the cathedral-construction programme, with which the burghers were so little concerned. The prolonged pause in work on the bridge served Archbishop Pierre de Savoie as an excuse for taking the task away from the city, in 1308, alleging 'just and reasonable motives'.[93]

Two Cistercian groups, in rapid succession, tried their luck with the ungrateful job and as swiftly abandoned it, though the latter of the two, the Abbey of Chassagne, held on to the remunerative auxiliaries. Misappropriation of bridge property by the monastic custodians and misuse of its revenues, as well as the halting of all pretence of building finally forced the return of the project to the burghers, in 1338.[94] Soon after, according to the evidence of the testaments, donations, which had fallen off for several decades, took a great spurt.[95] A number of these were very substantial, running to 20 florins and more, far exceeding anything the burghers ever gave to the cathedral fabric. But the wary testators often added a little phrase to their bequests: 'To pay the men who are working there and not otherwise'.[96]

The great plague and the war came soon after and once more work on the Pont du Rhône had to be abandoned for several decades. When, toward the end of the century, Lyon was freed from these great blights as well as from the pretentious waste of the Festival of Miracles, its citizens set to the task of completing their bridge with euphoric zeal. An altogether unique idea for gathering funds was put into execution, with all papal blessings. A reinvigorated Confraternity of the Holy Spirit opened its ranks to 1,000 members, who on payment of a fee of 5 florins (4 livres) would be confessed and duly declared competent of receiving 'at the article of death full remission for [their] sins'.[97]

The thousand were swiftly enrolled and the list expanded. By the end of the century, at Lyon alone, 4,178 confrères had been registered and the receiver of the bridge fabric was able to report by 1403 that a total of 36,610 livres had been collected by this method.[98] Simultaneously, other money-raising techniques were used. Questors were sent out all over the country, the same as for any major church-building project. Royal permission for shifting funds marked for the Festival of Miracles was renewed for six years, as always over sharp church opposition.[99] But the people of Lyon were in no mood to return to that extravagant symbol of the cult of death. The Pont du Rhône was, in a profound sense, their cult of life.

They considered the bridge of such importance that one woman, Anceline, widow of Ennemond de Lausanne, bequeathed all her worldly goods to its fabric.[100] Another burgher had a chaplaincy established at the confraternity's bridge chapel of St-Esprit.[101] But while the effort benefited from this universal goodwill, it continued to be plagued by insuperable technical difficulties. Several new stone arches were added and two-thirds of the great river had been spanned when, in 1407, a torrential flood ripped away a large part of the construction.[102]

Amazingly, these accidents did not permanently dampen the people's determination to see their bridge through to the end. All through the fifteenth century we hear of work going on. Each time the gap caused by a flood would again be arched in wood and the stone replacement work would be once more begun. Again it would be torn loose, new funds once more gathered, work again begun. Relentlessly, unyieldingly, the task was pressed toward its eventual termination—late in the sixteenth century.[103]

Strangely like the drawn-out story of Lyon's cathedral, which it so closely paralleled over the centuries, was this saga of the Pont du Rhône. But it was also utterly different. Not only were the technical odds greater, but so much of the work was a

21. Lyon: the city seal. It was attached to the charter of May 1271, in which the citizens of Lyon placed themselves under the 'special custody' of Philippe III, king of France (see p. 94). The seal features the Pont-du-Rhône and the French fleur-de-lys, which surmounts it prominently

repeated thrust into the unknown. The enthusiasm and sense of participation inspired by the Pont du Rhône exceeded anything that the cathedral had ever called forth, certainly from Lyon's citizens. To them, in fact, the bridge had, in a manner of speaking, become their cathedral, what the metropolitan church of St-Jean had never been. It is hardly a coincidence that early city seals should depict a bridge with a great stream pouring through its stone arches, in contrast with the cachet of so many other towns, where the cathedral was featured by the burghers.[104]

As we look back over the centuries this attachment of the Lyonnais people becomes easy to comprehend. Discouraged by the unfriendliness and even animosity of their prelates, shouldered off by the overweening canons, the citizens lost all interest in the cathedral and in the end found what was almost a substitute for it in this bridge, whose construction, beyond the utilitarian goal, became a kind of permanent object of pious dedication.

All the more meaningful, therefore, that their gifts to it should have been enveloped by divine sanction, as would be any other religious act. They themselves clearly felt that their contribution to the Pont du Rhône was a devotional gesture. It was the way Hugues de Vaux, a parishioner of St-Nizier, expressed it in his will of November 1360 when bequeathing a yearly stipend of 5 florins for ten years to the bridge's fabric and asking that it be put into the erection of a pier with 'great and powerful stones'. Then he added, in perfect faith of efficacy, that this bequest was being made 'for the remedy of my soul, and of those of my ancestors, and for my own salvation'.[105]

One can find no such glowing testimonial expressed by a citizen-patron to the cathedral of St-Jean, whose prolonged building period and relative simplicity of style were very much the result of this lack of popular attachment, which we shall find extraordinarily displayed at Strasbourg.

5

STRASBOURG

The Burgher-Builders

STRASBOURG MÜNSTER CHRONOLOGY

1015 Romanesque church launched by Bishop Werner.

c.1176 After a fire, rebuilding of apse is undertaken in Romanesque style, into which parts of the early fabric are incorporated.

c.1190–c.1220 Work on transept proceeds slowly as Alsace is embroiled in the struggle for succession following Frederick Barbarossa's death.

1200 Romanesque windows are reglazed, indicating a continuing hesitation to rebuild the church in new style.

c.1225 Decision reached to reconstruct transept in Gothic, accompanied by importation of sculptors from Chartres. Following period is featured by some of Münster's finest carving: 'Pillar of Angels', Church and Synagogue and other work in south portal, now lost.

c.1240 Work on new nave begun. Previous period marked by entrance of burghers onto the building fabric.

1250 Famous stained-glass series in north aisle of 'Gallery of Kings' is glazed, originally matched by Apostles and Prophets on the south side.

c.1252 Roodscreen is built, containing the city's 'Morning Altar'.

1275 After Battle of Hausbergen (1263), building takes big spurt under burgher impulsion and nave is rapidly finished (by 1275). Work moves without pause to the great façade, whose foundation stone is set in 1277.

1280–98 Work on façade proceeding swiftly, its sculptured portals are completed during this period. Fabric administration is taken over by the city in 1282 or a bit later.

1284–1316 Erwin von Steinbach is master-of-works, concentrating on the façade but is also responsible for other work.

1291 Statues of Clovis, Dagobert and Rudolf von Habsburg are mounted on façade at rose level.

1331–49 Ste-Catherine Chapel built off south nave-aisle.

1332 South aisle windows reglazed in popular style while the 'Gallery of Kings' is retained.

1365 After the Black Death (1349), work on façade is resumed but is slowed by several recurrences of the plague. Work is animated by extraordinary burgher benevolence, however: 1365, towers built to platform level; 1382–8, belfry built between towers; 1399–1419, north tower octagon is completed.

1439 North tower spire is terminated.

MEDIEVAL STRASBOURG'S MOST FAMOUS EVENT, THE BATTLE OF HAUSBERGEN, where in 1262 the city militia crushed the bishop's troops in an epochal encounter, has tended to falsify its history. At first flush it appears to illustrate the proverbial antagonism of the church to the burgher commune. This prejudice did adversely affect middle-class patronage of cathedral-building programmes in various cities where the bishop held the seigniory. The case of Lyon was hardly exceptional. In fact, a kind of historical law seemed to operate under these circumstances: the dearth of burgher support appearing as an inevitable response to the hostility of the ecclesiastic power to the commoners' aspirations.

The episcopal city of Strasbourg seemed to fit neatly into this pattern. The slow progress of its Münster during three-quarters of a century was exactly what might have been predicted from the traditional class antagonism, to which Hausbergen would be the dramatic climax. But a closer study of the city's history proved this assumption to be utterly without foundation. The expected animosity simply did not exist at Strasbourg. Everything reveals, on the contrary, that churchmen and burghers there attained a very high degree of collaboration in most respects, including that of building the cathedral. Hausbergen, far from being typical, was an aberration. This discovery was a sobering footnote to a bewitching theory.

Central to this anomalous situation at Strasbourg was the grim conflict in which the papacy and the German empire were long engaged. The Rhine city's prelates, like most others in Germany, had from an early period almost always sided with their anti-papal sovereigns. Typical was Bishop Werner II (1065–77), who accompanied Heinrich IV to Canossa in January 1077. He was imprisoned soon after by Pope Gregory VII and died in disgrace that same year while on campaign against the papal anti-Caesar.[1]

Strasbourg's bishops did not switch loyalties in the succeeding hundred years. Bishop Rudolf (1163/64–79), for example, who was Frederick Barbarossa's chaplain, joined that monarch on his march into Italy to chase Pope Alexander III from the throne. He fought in the disastrous battle of Lugano, in 1176, and was still far from home when he heard that a fire had ravaged his cathedral. In 1177, the prelate pronounced his *mea culpa,* but he was deposed anyway, two years later, by the pope.[2]

It was only toward the end of the twelfth century that Strasbourg's prelates abruptly (and still quite exceptionally among German churchmen) veered to an anti-empire position.[3] They seem to have suddenly become aware of a dangerous development that had actually been going on for a considerable time, the quiet, powerful build-up by the ruling Hohenstaufens of their possessions in Alsace.[4] This not only imperilled the Strasbourg church's temporal position but also that of the bishops' own families, who stemmed almost exclusively from leading Alsatian houses during this period.[5] Thereafter, Strasbourg's prelates were chronically at war with the crown. It was the time also, as fate ordained, that the episcopal church demanded a major reconstruction effort.

The rebuilding was begun around 1176. And for the following seventy-five years, when one would have expected to find them occupied with this task, one can see Strasbourg's bishops in an endless series of military campaigns against supporters of the Swabian kings.[6] A study of their registers will, on the other hand, reveal only a rare gesture on behalf of the cathedral fabric during this entire period. But this examination also discloses another very curious thing that was going on: the frequent participation of the burghers, to the extent of hundreds of men, behind their battling bishops![7]

This unwonted activity of commoners, even of artisans and tradesmen, or their sons, was, it is safe to conjecture, the reason for the extremely cordial relationship between the Strasbourg church and the bourgeoisie, to which we have alluded. Indeed, the burghers won significant privileges in return for their invaluable voluntary military service, which culminated about 1220 in what is called the 'second' *Stradtrecht* (city charter), in which their virtual self-rule was established.[8] And meanwhile, their repeated combat duty produced a great body of militarily sophisticated citizens who would play a fateful role in the city's subsequent history.

But progress in the cathedral's reconstruction lagged after the 1176 fire. A significant part of the old Romanesque apse, which had been built in 1015, was preserved, and work on the transept, launched around 1190, went on for thirty years or more.[9] This inertia can without doubt be explained by the troubled times that set in with the death of Frederick Barbarossa that same year, and the prolonged struggle for the succession, in which Strasbourg's prelate was deeply involved through 'family interests'. It was a period when Alsace was frequently invaded and Strasbourg itself put under siege, its suburbs ruined.[10] This sequence of disasters may have annulled any existing plan to rebuild the cathedral at that time. As a scholar has shown, new lancets were glazed around 1200 for the nave's Romanesque windows, which would hardly have been done if the plan was to reconstruct the church a few decades later in the Gothic style, as actually occurred.[11]

Strasbourg's bishops had neither the means nor the patience for so vast a build-ing programme, their engrossing military exploits exhausting both. The first half of the century saw them engaged in fifteen or more campaigns.[12] Art historians have suggested that the slowness of the Münster's progress was due to the competitive demands of the canons' new communal dwelling[13] or their contributions to the reconstruction of the collegiate church of Jung St Peter.[14] It is as though only some other church-building operation could prevent concentration on the cathedral, which should at any event have taken precedence over all other similar tasks. Neither of these projects, however, would have cost nearly as much as keeping hundreds of armed men in the field for several months, as Strasbourg's bishops kept doing, year after year.

Since erecting a new cathedral seemed unlikely, plans to adapt the old Romanesque church were apparently set in motion. Though dating from the beginning of the elev-enth century, the early structure must still have been quite impressive, being at the time one of the most ample edifices in Christendom.[15] But it was unquestionably old-style and it is difficult to see how the great capital of Alsace could have made a permanent accommodation with such a church at a time when numerous lesser cities were building great structures in the bright new Gothic mode.

Strasbourg's burghers were very much in the picture when the decision was reached, shortly after 1220, to press the reconstruction forward by proceeding with a new transept, for which a group of sculptors was brought in from Chartres.[16] The citizens were, in fact, almost certainly responsible for the south arm's richly sculp-tured portal, which was the seat of their justice, as has been shown in a remarkable study.[17] The 'court' itself, long since effaced, can be seen in the background of a famous painting by Mathis Grünewald, the Stuppacher Madonna: a platform shel-tered by a canopy and set off by a stone balustrade at the top of a flight of stairs.[18]

This brilliant period around 1220, when Strasbourg's municipality attained its full maturity, was marked by other important middle-class patronage besides their cathedral contribution. Most interesting, no doubt, was an amazing series of ten or more nunneries, which was mainly due to burgher financing.[19] These institutions, which were devoted almost entirely to daughters of the rich bourgeoisie, suggest that an extraordinary cause of male mortality in this class may have deprived many young women of eligible husbands.[20] Could not the reason have been their frequent partici-pation in the bishop's battles? A matching manifestation appeared for the lower classes, for whose unmarried girls lay sisterhoods (*béguines*) were set up as early as 1244.[21] Thus were many hundreds of women taken out of the marriage market, though at least one of the nunneries did permit on occasion a votary to break her vows if an eligible mate presented himself.[22]

With the death in 1250 of Frederick II, last of the Hohenstaufens and arch-enemy of Rome, the attitude of Strasbourg's bishops toward their subjects took on a dramatic change. The military aid of the burghers had momentarily lost its importance and Bishop Heinrich von Stahleck (1244–60) reacted with abrupt animosity.[23] Swiftly the drift of his unfriendly acts became clear: to recapture privileges that the city had acquired over the previous decades, some of them perhaps by usurpation.[24]

One point of contention was the great city common, which the Rat (city council) had administered by mutual consent for many years and which Heinrich now reclaimed for the church.[25] More serious still was the violation of a privilege Strasbourg had enjoyed for over a hundred years and which bishops and kings had confirmed: that its citizens would never be required to answer a plea outside their city.[26] Bishop Heinrich likewise removed leading burghers from their appointive posts of Schulteiss (a city judge hearing cases of robbery, vice, debts), which they had filled for years. And he joined to these grave reversals a blast at the city for its 'evil and detestable' efforts to challenge the church's rights of justice.[27]

This violent change of attitude in their prelate must have seemed sinister to Strasbourg's citizens, after a hundred years of amity pledged in blood. But it was only introductory to an even sharper hostility, that of Heinrich's successor.[28] The appearance of Walther von Geroldseck (1260–63) seems one of those fateful choices called forth by the historic process. He was only 29 when he was granted simultaneously the episcopal consecration and priestly orders. But he was never intended to perform a religious function. Bellicose son of a powerful noble house, Walther's actions seem to have been inspired by an ambitious father through whose influence at Rome he had been rapidly pushed up the hierarchic ladder.[29]

The young prelate came to Strasbourg to deliver his inaugural mass accompanied by over a thousand mounted knights in the suite of his uncle, the Abbot of St-Gall, and other high-ranking members of the family.[30] Whether they were brought for protection or monition, Bishop Walther had decided in any case not to live at the diocesan capital, retiring instead to his castle at Dachstein soon after the ceremony.[31]

From here began to emanate a battery of accusations and demands addressed to Strasbourg's municipal officials.

They were charged with increasing the cost of living by putting high duties on imports, of misusing the common for private gains, of taking illegal exactions from 'our Jews', of abusing the asylum privileges of the city's altar at the cathedral, which had been established in the newly completed roodscreen, with papal blessings, around 1252. The city council, Walther contended, had made a haven of this so-called *Frühaltar* ('Morning Altar') for 'criminal' and exiled people, 'enemies of the bishop'.[32] One or two of the bishop's accusations had a certain demagogic appeal, aimed at exploiting real grievances that the commoners harboured toward the bourgeois oligarchy. But 1261 was not the proper year for such a divisive effort and the unity of Strasbourg's citizens was preserved for the critical events that were in preparation.

The city's reply showed confidence and determination: an armed sortie in strength and destruction of the important episcopal citadel of Haldenburg, which commanded the roads to Hagenau, Zabern and other key towns.[33] Walther struck back by ordering Strasbourg's united clergy to leave the city, which he put under a sweeping interdict.[34] It was at this point that the cathedral's precentor, Heinrich von Geroldseck (no relation of the bishop), broke ranks, refusing to abandon the citizens, thus preparing a shining destiny for himself.[35]

An even more important ally that the burghers won was Count Rudolf von Habsburg, who took over a number of the bishop's cities in Upper Alsace. Rudolf's acts were no doubt motivated primarily by self-interest but they provided precious help to the city by protecting its southern flank.[36] The pact that Strasbourg's burghers and this prince had sworn the year before in a great ceremony at the cathedral's new south porch was declared to hold 'against all men'.[37] But Bishop Walther and his expected belligerency were clearly aimed at.

As a series of skirmishes and sneak attacks on the church's outlying possessions kept the burghers' bellicose spirit keyed up, serious fighting was put off for many months by factitious offers of peace, by an autumn truce to permit the gathering in of the harvest and other such curious medieval gestures.[38] Finally, on 8 March 1262, the bishop set his force—consisting of about 300 horsemen and 5,000 foot soldiers—into motion from his redoubt at Dachstein.[39] The mounted troops arrived far in advance at their destination, Hausbergen, located just three miles outside of Strasbourg, and took up positions on a high point, no doubt to await the coming of the ground fighters.

The city had realized that an attack was imminent when an attempt had earlier been made by an enemy force to breach the St Aurelia gate 'during lunchtime'. But the alert defenders, chiefly bakers under their leader 'Lanky Reimbolt', put sixty steeds out of commission without losing a man.[40] Then all the church bells of Strasbourg began clanging the alarm and men seized their weapons and ran to their prearranged stations on walls and towers. But Strasbourg's citizens had no intention of waiting out a siege. By the hundreds and thousands they began pouring through the gates beneath their guild banners, their mass soon blanketing the broad field on the way to Hausbergen.[41]

Details of this momentous event have been preserved in a priceless chronicle prepared only two decades later by Ellenhard 'the Great', so named because of his size and not for any dynastic importance.[42] But the man was by any standards a most worthy citizen, who later served as the administrator of the cathedral fabric during a highly creative period. His account of the battle illustrates the burghers' superb grasp of military science, telling, for example, how a reserve force of cavalry was kept inside the city, awaiting the onset of the combat, while on the field another reserve, of

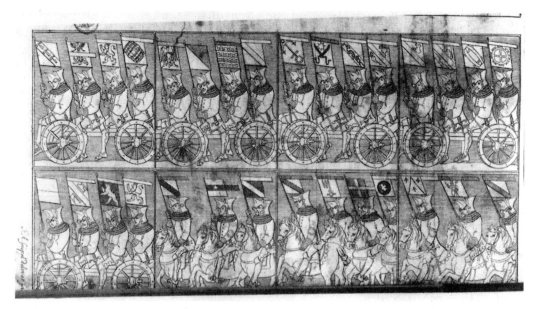

22. Strasbourg's city militia: this old engraving of a stained-glass painting from the city's former Pfennigturm (Treasury) shows the burghers going to battle, in 1336. The bourgeois 'knights' are on horseback. The guildsmen, under their individual craft banners, ride on horse-drawn wagons

bowmen and arquebusiers, was set aside. Posted on the route of the bishop's foot soldiers, their role was to keep the latter out of the fighting for as long as possible by a rain of missiles.[43]

A further directive, given to the rest of the foot soldiers by the city's commander, Reimbold Liebenzeller, reveals a trait of the new plebian fighting tactics that were destined to revolutionize feudal warfare.[44] While addressing his men before the battle, Reimbold asked rhetorically, no doubt echoing a question in the minds of many: when the opposing groups of horsemen had mingled, how would the bowmen know in all the confusion which mounts to aim at? To which he gave the singular reply:

'Kill all the horses, no matter if they are ours or those of the enemy!'

Which plainly meant: Don't stop to think or waste time in doubt! The main job was to send the enemy's mounted men tumbling to the ground in their ponderous armour, where Strasbourg's butchers and other huskies could get at them with their mail-crushing battle-axes.[45] In closer contact, the city's horsemen would be recognized, and in any case the critical fighting would be done on the ground.

At a particular moment during these preliminaries, the city forces moved to improve their position by outflanking a declivity that could have hampered the mobility of their troops. In the manoeuvre they had to turn their banners and lances back toward Strasbourg, which caused the over-eager young Bishop Walther to make a fatal miscalculation.

'They're running away!' he shouted and called for an immediate attack by his cavalry.

The bishop's commanders strongly opposed this, arguing that it would be dangerous to start the battle before their foot soldiers had arrived.

'Cowards!' the choleric prelate retorted. Let anyone who was afraid of fighting remain in the rear. And promising his knights *multa et magna* in spoils, he bade them get ready. And the wiser heads were forced to give in, 'for honour's sake but with death in their hearts'.

Seeing these preparations, Liebenzeller got his own troops in order, addressing them in memorable words: 'You will be fighting today, strong in spirit and fearless, for the great honour of our city and for our liberty and that of our children and our children's children in all eternity!' It might have been 1776 or 1789. Meanwhile, the signal was given for the reserve of horsemen, led by Nicolas Zorn, to storm out of the city and join the main force.

'Welcome, beloved Sir Zorn', Liebenzeller greeted him, adding with a wink of popular humour: 'Never before have I been so eager to see you!'

And so the battle was joined, the foolhardy young bishop attacking a force far superior to his own, his foot soldiers still far out of range. The burghers' shrewd precautions preordained the course of the combat, which could not have lasted very long. Half of the bishop's knights were killed or captured (*debellati*, in the pretty Latin word), the remainder lucky to get away. This included Walther himself, who fought intrepidly, the chronicle concedes, losing two horses beneath him before fleeing on his third mount.

Amid exultant joy and renewed ringing of bells the victorious citizens returned to Strasbourg, trailing their dozens of noble captives. In wry defiance, they locked them up in the cathedral cloister,[46] from which they were released in the following weeks and months as large command ransoms were paid to the triumphant burghers.[47]

They were the least of their gains, whose true value must be measured on an historical scale. Strasbourg became in effect, through Hausbergen, an independent city-state (owing not even an oath of allegiance to the emperor), whose seigniory would be elaborated in the following decades.[48] Certain of its broad lines were laid down in the peace which was forced on Bishop Walther, who died two weeks later—of a broken heart, it is always said.[49] His successor, Heinrich von Geroldseck, the cathedral precentor who had opted for the city during the crisis, was an automatic choice. Since 1241, Heinrich had been waiting for the fulfilment of his papal provision to a bishopric.[50] He was in his fifties when it was realized at last (an old man by medieval reckoning), and he had only the city to thank for it.

Still the wary and power-conscious burghers did not formally accept Heinrich as the new prelate until he and the city's three great chapters (those of the cathedral itself and of the collegiate churches of St Thomas and Jung St Peter) had engaged themselves to honour all their rights and privileges. Specifically listed in the 'agreement' were those items that had been in controversy: justice, the toll and the common. We are hardly surprised to learn, besides, that the city's Great Hospital 'sol ouch in irre gewalt sin' ('shall also be under its control') since the archives had shown a strong burgher presence there from early in the twelfth century.[51]

Pertinent to the city's relationship with the cathedral and hence with its continuing interest in the building programme was the pact's formal recognition of the Rat's rights to the Münster's 'Morning Altar'. This included the privilege of starting the sacerdotal day off with the first mass and, more important, its right of asylum.[52] Consecrated by papal decree, this prerogative was more than a mere formality. As it was used by the city, the 'Morning Altar' was transformed into an area of divinely protected civil sovereignty in the very heart of the bishop-and-chapter's church.

In a manner, it seems strange that this official recognition of the city's implantation within the Münster was not accompanied by the candid grant of control of its building committee, the fabric, which was to take place anyway two decades later. But appearances had to be preserved. At any event, decisive participation by burghers on the fabric had already begun a bit earlier.[53] This was consolidated in 1264 by the establishment by the fabric's dynamic burgher administrator, Heinrich Wehelin, of a second citizens' altar, which quickly became the site of the committee's activities and was frankly dubbed the 'Fabric Altar'.[54]

Because of the delay in the city's acquisition of formal authority over the building fabric, historians have tended to separate this extraordinary event from Hausbergen. As one recent authority, Peter Wiek, has insisted, the memorable accomplishment was the result of an evolutionary process that had started several decades earlier, when burghers had begun to serve on the fabric's three-man committee. They were then, and continued to be, acting as individuals, the author asserts, being appointed to their posts by the church.[55] Certainly it would have been impossible for the city to take command of the fabric without the church's consent. But to seek to depoliticize this unique development is to strip it of reality.

As Wiek himself points out, the eventual assumption of this privilege by Strasbourg's Rat in 1286 was unmatched in all of Germany. The only other German city that acquired a similar prerogative was Vienna, but this did not happen until half a century later.[56] It seems illogical, therefore, to deny the relationship of this unparalleled realization with the city's tremendous surge of power resulting from the famous battle. It is highly significant, besides, that right after the peace settlement, the fabric was taken out of the bishop's hands and turned over to the chapter.[57] That this was merely a transitional step, awaiting its eventual grant to the municipality, emerges from the fact that almost immediately thereafter, important legal questions in which the fabric became involved were brought before the city's Ratgericht, its court of justice.[58]

In any event, the city's control over the fabric was soon enough regularized. One result was that recorded donations by burghers took a big spurt.[59] These gifts were deposited on the new 'Fabric Altar',[60] eventually to the accompaniment of a remarkable ceremony. This took place every Sunday, after high mass, when the names of donors during the previous week were read and then written down in the *Liber Donationum*. It was all done in joy and general approbation, as the protocol puts it: *mit singen*. Then a paternoster followed by an Ave Maria were intoned by the mass of communicants.[61]

These years turned out to be the most vibrant in all the Münster's building history. The nave was completed in a splendid burst of energy, by 1275, and the sheer momentum of accomplishment pushed the effort on without delay to the new façade. Still standing here was the last remaining element of the early Romanesque edifice, built 250 years before. It was a fine front, too, by all accounts, surmounted by monumental towers, and might easily have been preserved, as was done at Chartres and Le Mans. But the new masters of Strasbourg's fabric could hardly have been satisfied with so unambitious a plan. They clearly wanted their own façade and especially their own great tower.

Their enthusiasm seems even to have swept up—for a while anyway—the bishops themselves. It is surely fitting that the great spurt which terminated the nave in record time should have occurred during the office of Heinrich von Geroldseck, who was so closely linked with the city's rise to power. And his successor, Konrad von Lichtenberg (1273–99), eager to impress the citizens favourably, no doubt, started off his episcopacy with auspicious zeal. Greeting the completion of the nave with fervid felicitations, he launched the work on the new façade with a broadside of splendid indulgences.

Though indulgences cost nothing but the parchment on which they were written,[62] prelates have often been extravagantly praised for issuing them. Those granted by Konrad did, however, call for a special effort of the imagination as well as a certain amount of organization. They were also memorable in that they were the last to be published by the church for over seventy-five years,[63] proving either the ecclesiastics' flagging interest, the success of the city's efforts, or both. Konrad's appeal was couched in poetic language. The cathedral, he opined, reminded him of the flowers of May (actually it was still January), pushing upward in variegated splendour, nourishing sweet delight. 'And thus comes the thought into my heart that we must by every possible means bring this work faithfully to an end.'[64]

One of the prelate's ideas we hear of elsewhere: that of turning over treasure obtained by rapine or theft—after a search, no doubt perfunctory, for the legitimate owners—to the building fund.[65] Familiar, too, was the provision of special burial rights to those pledging a yearly donation.[66] A charming if rather noisy fund-raising innovation, and a very popular one since we continue to hear of its being used for many years, was the grant of remission of sins to those who paid for ringing the cathedral's big bell, either for the living or the dead. The same reprieve was won by the saying of special prayers before the church's miracle-working great cross.[67]

And the bishop also added some practical suggestions to his clerics that are revealingly disenchanted. One was to remind them to take advantage of the confession stool to pressure parishioners for gifts. Then, too, he indicated that he did not exactly trust all his subordinates to carry out this task with proper zeal or even honesty since he provided for a court of three church dignitaries to punish those who did not co-operate. A still more useful measure of ensuring collection, we can be sure, was the committee of two laymen he called for in each parish who would be in charge of the fund.[68]

This important list of fund-raising manoeuvres, which seemed to herald at long last a great church-building prelate at Strasbourg, virtually ended Konrad's personal participation in the effort. Like so many of his predecessors, he proved to be less dedicated to his church than to his clan, one of the most powerful lineages of Lower Alsace. The very year that he had assumed the episcopacy, he and his brother Friedrich were taken prisoners by the Count of Lorraine while fighting a purely feudal quarrel, a ransom having to be paid for their release.[69] As prelate, the registers show Konrad as well as his brother, now the cathedral provost, as hardly leaving their saddles.[70] And on occasion the bishop was still accompanied by 'a strong troop of Strasbourg burghers'.[71] They were with Konrad in 1299, outside Freiburg, when a spear cast by one of the rebellious burghers there struck the prelate, causing a fatal wound.[72]

Bishop Konrad's shirking of his cathedral-building responsibility was past damaging its success, at any event. For Strasbourg's burghers were now in complete charge and doing a blazing business on the site. When Ellenhard 'the Great' took on his post as the city's first *procurator fabrice*, in 1284, the Münster's most famous builder, Erwin von Steinbach, also became associated with its destiny. Until his death, in 1316, he occupied himself with various tasks but worked chiefly on the great front.[73] And as this remarkable pile mounted steadily, Strasbourg's citizens became fully

23. After Hausbergen, the Münster's most dynamic building period begins. The nave, glitteringly adorned with stained glass, is built largely under bourgeois impulsion

identified with this cathedral, which, they boasted, 'shines more magnificently than all others across the breadth of Germany'.[74]

The assumption of political power by Strasbourg's burghers resulted in radical changes of viewpoint of the kind we have already seen occurring at Amiens. Here too the sharpest confrontations were with the Dominicans. The city had warmly welcomed these friars on their arrival in Strasbourg several decades earlier, refusing to join the local clergy's opposition to their establishment.[75] When the Dominicans acquired an important property in the centre of town intended for their convent, for example, the Rat quickly gave the transaction their blessing.[76]

But Hausbergen and the subsequent developments altered the texture of the city's judgment.[77] Representing henceforth a new seigniory, the burghers now became eager to keep the land-gobbling convents outside the walls. As early as 1265,[78] and again in 1285,[79] the Strasbourg Rat succeeded in preventing two of the Dominican nunneries, St Katherine and St Elizabeth, from moving into the city.

At about this same time, when the city took control of the cathedral fabric, another highly objectionable feature of the Dominicans' activities struck its administrators most forcefully. This was the powerful competition that the friars were setting up to the Münster's donor collections. Although the municipal *Urkundenbuch* (cartulary) shows a sudden leap in substantial burgher gifts to the cathedral's building fund at that time,[80] the fabric managers could hardly have been unaware of the fact that the Dominicans and their seven nunneries were receiving at least as many donations, often important ones, which were, as they claimed, 'sneakily' obtained, hence probably snatched away from the Münster.[81]

Avowedly consigned to poverty, the Dominicans had swiftly adapted themselves to the ways of the world after their short early ascetic period, showing an especial talent for extracting bequests from dying people, sometimes over the loud protests of would-be heirs.[82] Continuing grants of city real estate to the friars now struck Strasbourg's burghers as particularly ominous since this property was permanently lost to secular control.[83] This endangered the very basis of communal seigniory, as the Rat later declared in a circular letter to other towns explaining why it had put an end to this process:

'Our city would have shortly become entirely theirs!'[84]

In 1283, the city fathers reached a drastic decision: to halt the profusion of bequests to the friars by several forthright regulations.[85] One was meant to check what was picturesquely termed 'inheritance trickery' at people's deathbeds by requiring four members of a testator's family to be present at the preparation of his will. Another called for all donations by bequest to churches to pass before the Rat. Also, convents were forbidden to receive novices under 18 without permission of their parents, a measure aimed at discouraging the practice of recruiting children of the rich for their expected heritage.

The various mendicant orders were asked to swear to observe these edicts. The Franciscans immediately complied, 'out of friendship for the city'.[86] But the Dominicans refused, arguing obliquely that it was against their vows to take an oath.[87] The Rat proposed that the friars give them a letter instead to the same purpose, but this too was turned down.[88] The city showed considerable patience but in 1286 it decided to close down the Dominican convent.

A certain amount of popular support, particularly feminine, for the friars manifested itself at this point, as was later frankly admitted by the Rat: 'Our women came running, striking our guards with *bengeln* and *schufelen* (rolling pins and wooden clogs) so that one of them lay dead of his wounds.'[89] The city mayor, the famed Nicolas Zorn, had to go in person with his officers to lock the convent's doors. The papal legate excommunicated the city and took other steps to isolate it. Strasbourg replied by ordering the Dominicans to leave, threatening otherwise to tear their convent down.[90]

A not entirely surprising feature of this conflict, which lasted three years, was the almost unanimous support given the burghers by the secular clergy, who keenly resented the friars' competition.[91] Their most militant advocate was a canon-jurist of the collegiate church of St Stephan, Mattias by name, who broadcast the city's cause in bristling letters.[92] The papal legate, the cardinal of Tusculum, acting from a safe distance, fired volley after volley of fulminations at the city, finally calling on the secular powers of all Germany to send their armies against it.[93] There was not the slightest chance of compliance with this fantastic demand. At that very moment, indeed, the city was signing a defence pact with its great friend and ally, King Rudolf von Habsburg. Many other towns showed their unabashed friendliness for Strasbourg while even churches posted the pronouncements of the Rat or of their clerical confederates.[94]

By 1290, the Dominicans were sick of the contention. They were also broke, as can be seen from the permission granted them in exile to sell their books and even their kitchen utensils.[95] Finally, by mutual consent, the quarrel was put into Bishop Konrad's hands for arbitration. The latter displayed neither valour nor ingenuity, issuing a perfunctory judgment in favour of the friars, who were still solidly sustained by the pope. The city refused to accept the prelate's ruling, insisting that it would hold the friars to its regulations on heritages. Nevertheless, they were allowed to return, and, to underline the city's authority, Mayor Nicolas Zorn and a cluster of Rat leaders headed their procession back to their now weed-grown, destitute convent.[96]

No further obstacle seemed to stand in the path of the cathedral builders. Every augury indicated that it would be completed within two or three decades at most. That this did not happen cannot be blamed on the Black Death, which was still almost half a century away. And it cannot be attributed to any great war, invasion or other national disaster. True, progress was slowed for a while by one of those fires so common in the medieval period. Occurring in 1298, it destroyed 355 houses, according to the sixteenth-century chronicler, Daniel Specklin, and at the Münster consumed 'the belltower base, the organ, the entire roof and much of the beautiful ornamental work; all the lead of the vault was melted by the great heat until it ran into the river and much of the stonework burst from the great heat . . .'.[97]

But the slackening of the cathedral's pace that is noticeable in the new century cannot be ascribed to this fire despite the delay caused in patching up the damage.[98] Far more to the point, certainly, were the great responsibilities acquired by the city's all-embracing seigniory which inevitably limited the financial help available for the Münster.[99] Strasbourg's external relations were multiplied and the costly militia was probably put on a permanent basis.

There was, besides, a great amount of functional building that the city had to undertake. This included a new city hall and what was called the *Pfennigturm* ('penny tower'), a kind of combined treasury, archival depository and storehouse for weapons and banners.[100] The city hall was a first-class structure (see Fig. 1), for which the officials with overweening self-importance appropriated the name of the bishop's palace, *der Pfalz*, which had now become an anachronism, in any case, since the prelate no longer lived at Strasbourg. The political fact of the city's far-reaching powers was simultaneously consecrated in a new constitution that the burghers offered themselves. It spelled out in inexhaustible detail every least right and privilege of the sovereign city. Adopted without anyone's let or allowance, it was none the less formally acknowledged by the king, Ludwig of Bavaria, in 1328.[101]

Despite its extraordinary outlays, the city might yet have found the funds to help continue the cathedral-building campaign at a high pitch if the church itself had been willing to carry its share. However prosperous, Strasbourg's burghers still could not match the resources of a great episcopacy, with its vast properties, its thousands of subjects and hundreds of parishes, to say nothing of the huge institutional revenue: the tithe. By church law, one-fourth of all income was supposed to be devoted to building. This rule was not always observed, but it could serve a conscientious bishop as the basis for taxing benefices and prebends.[102] The Strasbourg fabric also had some property in its own name, which brought in a substantial, though insufficient, income.[103]

While its bourgeois administrators tried steadily to increase this base by encouraging the establishment of annuities in its favour by burghers,[104] the major source of funds which should have been forthcoming from the church all but disappeared. The city's assumption of the fabric gave the ecclesiastics a welcome opportunity to divest themselves completely of this burden. Gifts to it thereafter by canons and dignitaries were almost non-existent.[105] The archives list one grand donation of 200 livres by the cathedral chapter in 1305. It shines by its isolation.[106] The bishops were constantly borrowing great sums, but never with their cathedral in mind.[107] They even taxed prebends and parish churches—but it was to help pay their debts incurred in battle![108]

It was violence of another kind—within the bourgeoisie itself—that was, finally, perhaps the most important impediment to the city's cathedral-building effort. For the early fourteenth century witnessed the shattering of the burghers' unity as revolts erupted against the powerful oligarchy. Challenges came from two groups essentially. One was made up of prosperous burghers whose wealth was more recent than that of the dominant patriciate and who were, as a result, excluded from the Rat. Posts in the Rat had become virtually hereditary, passing from father to son by co-optation. The second disturbing element was the mass of guildsmen, who had no formal political status at all.[109]

The oligarchy were in the main associated with the mint.[110] This gave them a monopoly of money-exchange whose profits permitted a few of them to become important financiers.[111] Other families had grown rich in the great Rhine river commerce in grain, wine, wood, leather and silver, and some had invested their profits in land and forest as well as in urban property that commanded high rents.[112] And social division, inevitably sharpened by the accumulation of great wealth, was often congealed by ennoblement.[113]

As for the commoners, their chief grievances, aside from the taxation inequities that were fostered by the oligarchy, were unquestionably economic. The cost of living at the end of the thirteenth century took a great leap at Strasbourg, part of a Europe-wide phenomenon.[114] Discontent broke out in 1308 in a serious revolt, when members of the city's guilds tried to force their entry onto the Rat. It was put down with bloodshed by the leadership.[115] A kind of gangland terror was imposed on the artisans and small tradesmen by the rich burghers.[116] Strasbourg's commoners were momentarily cowed, but their experience in warfare made their submission less than certain—they remained a latent threat that seemed merely to be waiting for a favourable opportunity. That Strasbourg's guildsmen were still militarily active in the early fourteenth century was remarkably illustrated by a great stained-glass painting that was glazed for the city's Pfennigturm (now vanished), showing the city's foot soldiers going to battle on horse-drawn wagons (see fig. 22).[117]

That chance came in 1332, a consequence of the fatal weakness that the patriciate had for swordplay. For some time, the city's two most powerful families, the Zorns and the Müllenheims, had been embroiled in a feud, whose characteristics call forth the quarrels of the Montagues and the Capulets. The Strasbourg vendetta, as it comes down to us, was more complex than the Shakespearean animosity, for the two contending houses are seen here frequently intermarrying,[118] purchasing shares of the mint in partnership[119] or joining to help build an important church. The handsome Jung St Peter benefited from this type of collaboration, both clans founding great chapels in it. It may be significant, all the same, that they were located at widely separated parts of the edifice.[120]

The events of 1332 alluded to were touched off at a typical establishment of German *Gemütlichkeit*, a *Trinkstube*, which as in modern times played an important role in the political and social life of that period. The Strasbourg pubs were segregated by class and clan and often by guild.[121] We even find one group of rich burghers donating their clubhouse to the cathedral fabric. No one seems to have been affronted by its malodorous name, Der dringstube züm drecke im Criegsgasze ('At the Sign of the Muck-Heap in Battle-Alley'). The act of donorship did, however, contain a firm order that the club should be taken out of the bibbing business.[122]

It was evidently a Zorn tavern where the fighting began. But it spread quickly into the Rossmarkt (Horse-Market) square outside, where it was viewed by a great crowd,[123] until most of the contestants were killed or wounded. Among the dead were a number of the city's leading patricians, including seven Zorns and two Müllenheims. Still the feudsmen counted on continuing the fray the following day and those who were still mobile went out into the countryside searching for reinforcements.

When they returned to Strasbourg in the morning, they were stunned to find the city in arms. They themselves were quickly seized. A quiet revolution had occurred during their short absence. Leaders of the 'new bourgeoisie', of the guilds and a few lesser nobles had formed a common front, taking over the city seal, its banner and the keys to the gates, which constituted the insignia of authority.[124] Thus, without a blow, the power of the oligarchs was destroyed.

It was basically the same new alliance that took control of the renovated Rat that was promptly elected on the wave of indignation that followed the riotous night. The guilds got half the members of the city council, their first formal representation on this leading body. A new officer in charge of the guilds, the Ammeister, was designated. Significantly, however, he was not an artisan himself but a merchant, as were all the other top officials. Together with the representatives of the wealthy guilds like the furriers and drapers, these men managed to secure a continuation of control by the propertied citizens. Power was far from being turned over to the masses! What actually happened was a broadening of the bourgeois base, a democratization of the ruling council.[125]

This significant social and political change almost seems to have been deliberately illustrated in an important work at the Münster that was produced at this time (1332) and fortunately has been preserved. It is the famous stained-glass cycle in the south nave-aisle windows. Sometimes misnamed the 'Bible of the Poor', actually the great series was an aesthetic product of the bourgeoisie that had come to power in 1262, but did not free itself from the oligarchic grasp until seventy years later. While depicting entirely conventional scriptural themes from the public life of Christ, the Passion and post-Passion events, the style and especially the personality of the actors were completely renovated: rendered human, popular, unmistakably middle class. An Italian influence of the new humanist style of Giotto and his followers is also distinctly recognizable.

It is particularly when this cycle is contrasted with the work on the opposite side of the nave (executed around 1250), that the reality of the change becomes persuasive. There we see the striking gallery of the kings and emperors of the German Reich, presented in all their feudal glaciality.[126] The contrast takes on added meaning when one learns that the south-nave lancets themselves originally presented the same type of figures as those on the facing side. Apostles and prophets, they were patently meant to portray the theocratic side of feudal authority, whom the burghers had the temerity now to abolish and replace with their own glorified doubles.[127]

While the guilds were neatly outmanoeuvred during the 1332 events, due no doubt to their political inexperience, they learned their lesson quickly. In 1349, a new rising by

24. Judgment Day: a group of the elect. In this stained-glass series of the south nave-aisle, done around 1332 and replacing lancets of the previous century, the actors take on a distinctly bourgeois character

25. Gallery of kings and emperors: Otto III Rex. In contrast with the stained-glass series of the south-aisle, the figures of the north-aisle, dating from c.1250, before the city had taken over control of the cathedral fabric, reflect the austere style of feudalism

the commoners was released by the great Black Death, the disturbances becoming enmeshed in an anti-semitic drive of genocidal proportions that spread through the Rhineland. For various reasons, some opportunistic, some purely humane, perhaps, Strasbourg's officials resisted the anti-Jewish hysteria, as did the leaders of several other cities, notably Cologne, who after a conscientious investigation rejected as 'unproved rumours' the widespread charges that the Plague had been caused by Jewish poisoning of the wells.[128]

Strasbourg's commoners, backed by their bishop, were in contrast rabid on the subject, their hatred whetted by greed since many of them were pawned out to the moneylenders who were often Jews. Accordingly, one evening in 1349, the city's guildsmen gathered in a dense mass before the scaffolding-enclosed Münster façade, shouting angry accusations that their officials had been 'bought off by Jewish gold'. But the presence of their fighting banners under which they marched in the city militia designated a broader meaning for their demonstration, other grievances than their leaders' sparing of Jewish lives.[129]

Led by the militant butchers, the guildsmen held the city officials in grip all night long until they had agreed to their demands. The Ammeister was forced to resign and his post, appropriately, was handed over to a butcher, the first member of a craft to hold this commanding office. Yearly elections of other officers, which had been suspended, were restored. The new Rat that was chosen further consolidated the guilds' power. However, voting was still restricted to property-owners, thus assuring the preponderant choice of solid members of the citizenry.[130] Small wonder that this new set-up lasted substantially unchanged until the Revolution. (Strasbourg was taken over by Louis XIV in 1681.)

As the contemporary chronicler, Jacob von Königshoven, smugly comments, the 1349 convulsion took place 'without loss of blood'. He meant Christian blood. For the day after the new Rat was sworn in, the city's Jews were rounded up and without trial or other formality thrown onto a great pyre. It was a Saturday. Contemporary reports tally the victims at 2,000. There were a great number, in any case. The site of their execution today bears the gruesome name of 'rue Brulée' ('Street of the Burning'). The Jews' liquid assets were distributed among the guildsmen, some of whom, in an access of conscience or piety, gave their share—to the cathedral fabric![131]

The settlement of 1349 seems to have pacified the situation at Strasbourg for a considerable period. The brawling feudists agreed to keep their swords sheathed and were rapidly readmitted into the city's political life. Strasbourg's prestige became such that the king is seen in the archives sending an apology to the city for passing nearby without dropping in to pay his respects. Another time, he petitioned the powerful city-state for the aid of its militia.[132] But in the main, Strasbourg's citizen army was now used to serve neither king nor bishop but rather its own interests: to protect distant property owned by the commune or private citizens, to keep the highways—and particularly that most important highway of them all, the Rhine—clear of illegal tolls or other blocks.

Meanwhile, the wealth of its privileged citizens multiplied and with it, together with the elements of purely personal ostentation, their patronage of church architecture and art. Leading recipients were the great collegiate units of St Thomas and Jung St Peter and the parish church of St-Nicholas, which was appropriately nicknamed *Leutkirche*, or 'people's church'. The archives show burghers endowing these and other churches with a huge quantity of chapels, altars and chaplaincies while also extending themselves in the foundation of private pious establishments of every kind.[133]

St Thomas and Jung St Peter played the important additional role of providing canonic posts to sons of the aspiring bourgeoisie, who were banned from the cathedral chapter by the usual hereditary nobiliary requirements.[134] But even at the Münster an arrangement had early been made (*c.*1229) to take burgher sons into an auxiliary group of prebendaries called the Great Choir, another evidence of the cordial burgher-church relations subsisting at Strasbourg.[135] The Great Choir was more than just a substitute unit for bourgeois placements. Since the regular canons were chronically non-residential, the other group ended by absorbing all the cathedral's major activities, thus assuming effective church control.

And the great cathedral itself benefited significantly from the establishment of a stable communal regime at Strasbourg. Though the Black Death hobbled the building programme for a time due to the loss of skilled workmen, nevertheless by 1365 the great façade had reached the platform level, just above the rose-window.[136] Then all at once a great outpouring of effort was released, as if by common accord it was decreed that the cathedral must be terminated. And the final campaign was under way.

Fuelled by a huge mass of donations, almost exclusively from burghers, the wide area of the front above the platform was completed and crowned by the famous Gallery of Apostles (unfortunately destroyed during the French Revolution). And work went on from there. Nothing could impede its verve. Damages from another fire, in 1384, were repaired within a year, after which work on the gallery proceeded without let-up. During much of this productive period, the closest collaboration with the city administration was assured by admission to membership on the city Rat of the cathedral's 'master-of-works' (architect).[137]

Ironically, in the very midst of this great building spurt, like a harsh voice rising out of the distant past, came the demand of the bishop of Strasbourg for the return of the fabric into his hands, which the church had surrendered over a hundred years ago![138] By 1350, in fact, church representatives were no longer even allowed to sit in on fabric meetings, so alien had they grown to its activities.[139] Bishop Friedrich von Blankenheim castigated the administrators for wasting money, charging that they spent 3,000 gulden (1,650 livres) a year of the fund's revenues on private banquets. The accusation, however fantastic, does in any case indicate that there must have been a lot of money around.[140]

More pertinent, no doubt, to the prelate's actual intention was his final reproach. The very cathedral itself, he contended, had been taken over by the burghers. Thus, he said, names of clerics who accepted the rule of municipal justice were read from the top of the roodscreen (where the city's chapel was located). City officials held meetings at the Münster, the bishop added, and their decisions were proclaimed from that same vantage point. Services were even halted for these announcements.[141]

How much like Walther von Geroldseck do these fulminations sound! And Friedrich rounded out the parallel by mounting an armed vendetta of the surrounding barons (in which even the king got somewhat involved) against the sovereign city. It was almost with a kind of joy that Strasbourg's 'War Council of Seven' prepared for its defence, with 1,500 guildsmen alone seizing their weapons and banners.[142] When his offensive fizzled out miserably, Bishop Friedrich lost his post.[143] His successor, Wilhelm von Diest (1394–1439), was more than willing to acknowledge formally the city's full rights to the fabric, thus permitting work on the great tower to proceed in peace. It was completed during his episcopate.[144]

This accomplishment was facilitated by the powerful Rat's final success in bringing its old antagonists, the Dominicans, to heel, issuing a decree, in 1383, forbidding gifts of any kind to these friars.[145] This amazing measure was implemented, in 1386, by the placing of 'caretakers' over all convents, empowered to examine their books and even their correspondence. Any sales or purchases of property were declared illegal without city approval.[146] There is evidence that the city authorities were able to enforce these sensational restrictions, aided, it is true, by a great scandal involving some nuns and the Dominican monks who had spiritual charge of them.[147]

The bridling of the friars was all the more important in that it occurred during what was called the *grosser sterbot* ('the big dying'), recurrences of the Black Death, which at least twice during these decades seem to have been as lethal at Strasbourg as the 1349 epidemic. Testamentary bequests everywhere took a great surge in this period, making possible the rebuilding of several of the city's churches.[148] Alone the Dominicans were forgotten, cut down to two minor anniversary announcements during the ten years following the Rat's ban of 1383.[149]

Far and away beyond all other pious outlets, however, the cathedral became the most favoured recipient of bourgeois largess. In the two decades of 1370–89 alone, it was named 117 times by Strasbourg donors listed in the city's *Urkundenbuch*, often in enormous gifts running as high as 200 livres and more.[150] Memorable, besides, is the fact that one-third of these benefactors were women, whose donations frequently consisted of their entire share of a married couple's communal property.[151]

And, most remarkable of all was the persistence with which the talismanic phrase—*omnia bona sua*—recurred in the testamentary bequests of burghers or burgher couples to the cathedral fabric, appearing no less than sixty-eight times![152]

This mass eagerness to bequeath all one's worldly goods to the cathedral's building-fund was the secret of the success of the last campaign that permitted the termination of the church. The unprecedented phenomenon is all the more amazing when compared to the record of other cities that we have studied. At Toulouse, at Lyon, even at Amiens, those burghers who made any church their universal heir were rare. Those giving their all to a church's *fabric* were almost non-existent. Even if they made a substantial bequest to its building-fund, the greater part of their fortune would either go to their heirs or be portioned out for prayers and masses.

The great flood of *total* gifts to the Münster fabric during those two decades indicates that this act had somehow taken on a unique spiritual connotation for the testators, promising, more than did any other pious work, eternal salvation. There is nothing to explain how or by whom this astonishing belief was inculcated. The constant repetition in the bequeathing act of the phrase—*in remedium*—merely underscores the fact of faith, without further accounting for it. We are left with the inescapable impression, nevertheless, that the decision was hardly accidental but was fostered by a simultaneous and vast upswelling of appreciation and love for the beautiful cathedral.

This amazing consecration in the people's hearts was the Strasbourg Münster's final destiny. It is not surprising that its marvellous tower, completed under this enchantment and added eventually to the communal seal, should have come to have the very special place that it still enjoys in this city's thoughts. True, a cathedral tower has traditionally been the burghers' particular attachment, often containing areas connected with their activities.[153] At Strasbourg, besides, the aesthetic features of the tower match in complexity and richness the total content of many another fine church. Indeed, the rest of the Münster compared to its tower almost shrinks off into a kind of subdimensional appendage.

But, over and above aesthetics, there must have been the feeling at Strasbourg that can be called forth only by something in whose making one has shared. And this tower of the Münster was in the fullest sense built by all the people of the city. So were, to be sure, other important parts of the cathedral, to the extent that the burghers' total responsibility for its creation exceeds that of any other group, including the ecclesiastics. Such a role has been rarely matched in the Middle Ages.

That it was possible at Strasbourg was the result admittedly of a combination of most unusual circumstances. Elsewhere, the citizens might have been equally excited by such a task and as willing to undertake it, but other requisites would have been lacking. The fact that they were all present at Strasbourg has, in the end, furnished us with a remarkable historical phenomenon, as exceptional as it is adventitious, as exciting as it is instructive.

6

YORK

Pride, Greed and Charity

YORK MINSTER CHRONOLOGY

1220   New south transept begun by Archbishop Walter Gray, probably meant to enclose St William's shrine of same period. Work completed in about two decades.

*c.*1230–50   Central crossing, central tower and north transept are built, being terminated before the death, in 1255, of Treasurer John le Romeyn, their chief animator.

1250   Five Sisters, grisaille lancets at north transept, done at about the same time as the architecture of this area.

1280s   The chapter-house, begun as independent structure soon after termination of the north transept, is completed, encased in splendid glass lancets.

1285–90   Remarkable suspended wooden dome of chapter-house installed.

1290   L-formed, stained-glass-decorated vestibule joining chapter-house to north transept is built.

1291–1322   Major part of nave is completed.

Pre-1310   Easternmost nave-aisle lower windows on the two sides (north and south) are glazed. The others are continued in sequence.

1338   Great west window is painted.

1345–60   Nave is wood-vaulted, in imitation of masonry.

1350   Zouche chapel is added at the east side of the south transept.

1361–73   Four easternmost bays of John Thoresby's new choir are completed before his death.

1385–1400   Western bays of the choir and the eastern sections of the transepts are terminated.

1405–8   Great east window painted. The sixteen other choir windows follow in succession, under Archbishop Henry Bowet (1407–23).

1407   Central tower falls after futile attempts to build up its underpinning.

1443–55   Roodscreen is carved under Dean Richard Andrew.

1472   After foundations are strengthened, central tower is rebuilt though not raised to planned height; the lantern is vaulted, glazed. The façade and front towers had been built in previous decades. The Minster is completed.

PRIDE, FIRST OF THE SEVEN DEADLY SINS, WAS THE MAJOR SOURCE OF YORK Minster's troubles, draining away a large part of its fortune and dragging out inordinately its construction. Begun at the south transept by Archbishop Walter Gray around 1220, its terminal element, the lantern of the central tower, was not completed until two-and-a-half centuries later, under Archbishop George Neville. We are fairly well informed about York's important building periods. The gaps in accomplishment were far more frequent and often more protracted.

Though the chapter had formal control of the fabric, York's prelates were its energizing force. Their difficulties, accordingly, reflected inevitably on its progress. Among these, the most damaging and persistent was the struggle with Canterbury for the primacy of the English church. The conflict between England's two archbishoprics stemmed back to the tenth century but became particularly acute after the Conquest. An example was Archbishop Thurstan's (1114–40) refusal to make the required profession of obeisance to the Archbishop of Canterbury while receiving consecration from his hands. King William II, furious, drove Thurstan into exile, where he obtained his investiture from the pope. But the king would not permit his return until Calixtus threatened to put all of England under interdict.[1]

That quarrel was adjusted but the pattern was set and lasted throughout almost the entire construction period of York Minster. Among the many important men who got embroiled in the Thurstan wrangle, Bishop Ivo of Chartres, a friend of the archbishop, had sought to introduce a pacifying note, offering advice that was as sensible as it was disenchanted. Ivo argued that

> it mattered little how investiture was given, by a staff, a ring, a hand, a loaf, or in any way . . . because both the giver and the receiver of the investiture understood that what was given and received was not a sacrament or anything sacramental, but manors, farms, and rents. . . .[2]

Unfortunately, the York prelates could not adopt this commonsense approach.

Shortly thereafter, Thurstan's successor, Archbishop Roger de Pont-l'Evêque (1154–81), became even more deeply enmeshed in the Byzantine maze. An anomalous feature of his role was that he started as a Canterbury man, having been archdeacon of that see. It was doubtless a great coup when Canterbury's Archbishop Theobald was able to get him into the rival church, though the York chapter resisted stubbornly

26. York Minster: note the south transept where Archbishop Walter Gray began the new building in 1220, the great stretch at the right of Archbishop John Thoresby's 'new choir' which was begun in 1361, and the central tower, the final element built, in 1472

before giving its consent.[3] But Roger's shift of loyalty thereafter was very fast, particularly after the death of Theobald and the election of Thomas à Becket as his successor. When the latter became involved in his own reverberant struggle with King Henry II, Roger saw it as a splendid opportunity to advance York's quest for the primacy.

Becket was understandably furious that the second most important ecclesiastic of England should introduce a divisive element into the hierarchy at so critical a time, which of course the monarch promptly exploited. When he sent a delegation to Rome to argue his case, he put Archbishop Roger at its head. The York prelate got his reward by being allowed to crown Henry II's oldest son, hapless Prince Henry, king of England, and helped organize a powerful group of English churchmen 'to pull down the arrogance of Becket'.[4] Roger was even accused of complicity in the assassination of Thomas and, though a papal investigation absolved him, the taint stuck. Was it a sense of guilt that led him to include in his will a great bequest of £500 to the Archbishop of Canterbury and his suffragans?[5]

The York-Canterbury controversy was often marked by undignified, even violent incidents. The prelates themselves were not hesitant about getting personally into the fray. Thus, when Roger on one occasion entered the Royal Council at Westminster only to find Canterbury's Richard already occupying the leading seat, he walked straight over to that prelate and plopped into his lap. Richard's supporters seized Roger and dragged him by his robe along the floor before casting him out of the hall, shouting: 'Away, away, betrayer of St Thomas, his blood is still upon thy hands!'[6] On another occasion, it was again the Archbishop of York, William Wickwane (1279–85), this time, who got the worst of it. After being consecrated by the pope at Rome, the plucky churchman sent word ahead that he would land at Dover bearing his cross erect, a position that had a peculiarly mutinous connotation to the medieval ecclesiastic mind.

Canterbury's prelate prepared to meet the challenge in a carefully planned campaign whose outlines are known to us.[7] Led by the justice of his court, Adam de Hales, a greeting party took Wickwane in hand, smashing his crosier and pummelling his companions before allowing the party to go on toward London. The clergy all along the route had been instructed to shun the intruders like the pest and to see to it that no one sold them 'bread, wine, beer, meat, fish or hay and oats'. Unfortunately, Wickwane could not avoid going to the capital since he had to put in an appearance to reclaim his temporalities, which the king seized for their revenues during every vacancy (the so-called 'right of regalia'). As the archbishop's party neared London it made a prudent change of route, circling the city widely to enter at another gate, thus escaping a gang of hired mobsters who were waiting at the southern entrance.

The procedure by which York's prelates avoided confirmation by Canterbury was permanently resolved into the trip to Rome, which the latter soon established as obligatory, even when conditions rendered it perilous. This was the case with Henry of Newark (1298–9), who pleaded with the pope for an indulgence from travelling on the continent because of the war then raging between England and France. Boniface VIII delayed for well over a year before consenting to a substitute consecration by a group of Henry's bishops, alleging that it was only done to please the king. Knowing this greedy pope as we do, it was more likely the raising of 5,500 marks (£3,667) by

Henry's proctors and the promise of numerous Yorkshire dignities and prebends that brought on this relaxing decision. Unhappily, Archbishop Henry lived only one year after the arrival of his pall.[8]

It would seem that papal blessings to a newly elected prelate could be taken for granted. Problems did arise, at times honest enough, like the opposition of the king or the claims of a rival candidate, which caused delay. In the end, however, the obstacles raised were usually as factitious as they were inescapable. Artificial problems were drummed up and the new archbishop would have to spend as long as two years waiting humbly on the Curia, bribing and rebribing influential members. The money was chiefly borrowed from Italian merchants and bankers, whose names are often known to us (Bardi, Spini, Frescobaldi . . .) as patrons of some of medieval Italy's celebrated monuments, for which the English today would be warranted in claiming a part of the glory!

York Minster was the primary victim of this transferred splendour. Before its archbishop could leave Rome, he was usually so deep in debt that unless his tenure was moderately long he never succeeded in regaining solvency. The extraordinary archiepiscopal registers of York, which begin with Walter Gray (1215–45), are laden with this kind of information. Archbishop Gray, for example, reportedly paid £10,000 (a modern equivalent of about $10,000,000 or £5,500,000, assuming a value for the early-thirteenth-century English pound of 1.25 French livres) for his consecration.[9] This could account for the delay of a number of years in the launching of his great project of rebuilding the Minster.

The key feature about Gray's term was its length, which enabled him to see the south transept, where he initiated the rebuilding programme, through to the end. He was also responsible for getting the north transept (completed about 1250) well along the way, with the help of his treasurer, John le Romeyn, one of the small number of Roman beneficiaries of a York dignity who actually came up to assume its responsibilities in person.[10] Medieval cathedrals were almost always rebuilt in a series of piecemeal substitutions, which allowed for their continued functioning during lengthy building periods. At York, the Gothic edifice we know replaced a less spacious Norman church. Gray's transept was so expansive that, once finished, the incongruity of its size compared to the rest must have been painful to the aesthetic sense, fairly shouting to be carried forward.

But little could be undertaken by the next four archbishops, none of whom succeeded in extricating himself from the morass of debt.[11] Sewall de Bovill (1256–8) held his post for too short a span to accomplish anything on the Minster. But it was long enough for him to become embroiled with Rome over claimed prebends, and he was in the end excommunicated on this account. On his deathbed, he is quoted as writing a bitter, warning letter to the pope reminding him that 'the Lord said to Peter, feed my sheep, and not shear them, skin them, tear out their entrails, or eat them up'.[12]

About Godfrey de Ludham (1258–65) little is known since his register has disappeared. But his sojourn in Rome is reported to have been very costly and his successor complained that he had saddled him with a great debt of £4,000.[13] Indeed, Walter Giffard (1266–79) never seems to have come out from under this burden.[14] By 1275, he was still heavily in debt, despite the endless payments to his creditors recorded in his register.[15] His instructions to his Roman proctors are often accompanied by wry observations, as when he ordered them to pay Cardinal Ancher of Santa Prassede 300 marks, adding 'lest he obtain satisfaction from the pope [who was his uncle] against us, which would be easy nowadays. Accordingly, to make a virtue of necessity . . .'.[16] And like Giffard, William Wickwane (1279–85) never freed himself from payments 'for our dealings with the Roman Curia'.[17]

That the long pause of a third of a century in the Minster's building activities should have finally been broken under Archbishop John le Romeyn (1286–96) is surprising since this man was burdened by all his predecessors' afflictions plus some peculiar to himself. The fact that he was an illegitimate child of a churchman, Walter Gray's treasurer of the same name, doubtless entered into the great sums that were exacted of him at Rome.[18] The 2,000 marks he had to turn over to the king, besides, officially termed a loan, were probably meant to serve the same laving purpose.[19] Romeyn also had to promise the pope that he would do everything he asked for in the way of benefices for his favourites,[20] a terribly imprudent pledge when addressed to a man like Boniface VIII.

Archbishop Romeyn must have inherited his father's building zest, and he is credited with starting work on the new nave in 1291. The chapter-house, one of England's handsomest, was also completed during his office and was joined to the Minster by the glass-adorned vestibule about this time. However, in the end he succumbed to an accumulation of woes and died so destitute that the expense of his very plain funeral had to be borne by 'strangers'.[21] It is not known how much he contributed to the Minster building funds but if it had totalled the amount he had to pay in Roman bribes (£3,604 in twenty-five listed operations[22]) it would have sufficed to finance several years of activity at the most intensive rate recorded in the fabric rolls.

And so the pathetic story continues, through short-termed Henry of Newark (1298–99) and Thomas of Corbridge (1300–04) and longer-termed William of Greenfield (1306–16), and beyond.[23] The last-named prelate had hardly acceded to his office when Pope Clement V threatened him with excommunication if he did not promptly pay the Spini house of Florence the 6,000 marks (£4,000) he had received from it 'in order to expedite his affairs in Rome'.[24] Desperately, Greenfield borrowed from everyone he knew, as his pathetic register shows, from bishops, priors, abbots, canons, friends. He even touched his valet for £40.[25] Small wonder that work on the new nave languished, meanwhile.

Since the archbishops were so hampered in their capacity to contribute to the Minster's fabric, one wonders about the other sources of aid that are normally available. What, for example, was the role of the rich bourgeoisie, particularly the famous woolmen of York? The archbishop, unlike his homologue at Lyon, lived in relative harmony with his burghers. If the latter were virtually excluded from the Minster, a circumstance that we shall examine later, it was for other reasons than a clash of economic or political interests.

That the canons and dignitaries were deficient in fabric contributions had no valid excuse, on the other hand, though this failure can to a degree also be traced back to the quarrel with Canterbury and the Roman exactions that resulted from it. A large part of York's payment for the consecration of its prelates was demanded in the form of canonic prebends, to which the archbishop had the right of nomination. There were thirty-six of these benefices at the Minster, each based on some heavily endowed church of the archdiocese, whose annual earnings ran as high as 250 marks (the equivalent of about $168,000 or £92,400 today).[26]

The most attractive feature of such a prebend was that the beneficiary was not expected to perform the priestly functions to draw its income. Personal service would in fact have been impossible to fulfil in most cases since the recipients usually held a number of prebends simultaneously, often in several countries. They were allowed to hire a poor priest to carry out the sacred duties, paying him the customary rate of

5–10 marks in annual wages, the remainder or a large part of it going into their own pockets.

The neglect of churches that resulted from this widespread abuse was only one of its harmful effects. More serious, no doubt, was the financial loss to the country, which was recognized even in those early days. John Wycliff (1324–84), the great contemporary church reformer, observed shrewdly about this: 'When a lord hath the gold for presenting [that is, when a prebend was in the hands of an English layman], the gold dwelleth still in the land. But when the pope hath the first-fruits the gold goeth out and cometh never again.' Wycliff alleged that £100,000 (£55 million today) were lost to England every year in this way.[27]

It was actually 'white gold' that Wycliff was talking about. For a large part of the payments on 'alien prebends' was in the form of wool, picked up by Italian merchants doubling as papal proctors and carried off to the great drapery centres of north Italy. Yorkshire was simultaneously one of the country's great wool producers and a leading possessor of abbeys, priories and nunneries, most of which were engaged in the grazing industry.[28] The practice of assigning many of York's canonries to foreigners was at its height during most of the thirteenth and fourteenth centuries, in other words, throughout the Minster's major construction period.[29]

This was the pattern. Archbishop Giffard complained that half his canonries were in the hands of aliens.[30] In Corbridge's brief pontificate, of fourteen admissions only three were Englishmen, whereas of fifty-one admissions in William Melton's register (1317–40), just over half, twenty-six, were foreign.[31] Similarly, of the thirty-six canons listed under Greenfield, just under half, sixteen, can be recognized as non-English by their names.[32] Among the latter was one cardinal, Napoleone Orsini, who held his prebend from c. 1286 to 1342.[33] No wonder the chapter became suspicious on occasion of such longevity, sequestrating the prebend of Giovanni Landulphi Colonna in 1314 until his proctor could prove that he was alive.[34]

One can find in the 'enjoyment' of York's benefices by foreigners instances of the kind of cynicism which two centuries later helped to fragment the Roman church. When, for example, Cardinal Matteo Rubeo Orsini turned his prebend over to his Hospital of Santo Spirito di Sassia at Rome, it caused a premonitory furor among the English, who thought that their money should be used for their own sick and infirm. But Matteo staved off the attack for almost twenty years, ceding at last for 'compensation'.[35] And Cardinal Ancher Panthéléon, a native of the French town of

Troyes like his uncle, Pope Urban IV, used two lush York prebends to complete the beautiful church of St-Urbain in that city, which his uncle had begun as a personal memorial.[36]

Even more serious than the assignment of prebends to absentee foreigners (or royal clerks) was their common occupation of the most important (and most remunerative) Minster dignities. The two leading posts, those of dean and treasurer, were particularly vulnerable and both were held in the pope's provision over lengthy periods. The result was a grave neglect of their vital functions.[37] Thus, in the critical years when Archbishop John Thoresby (1352–73) was building the Minster's great choir, the chapter was nominally leaderless. As for the treasury, of the fourteen holders of this post from 1200 to 1328, only four were in residence, though fortunately one of them was John le Romeyn, who figures so prominently in the creation of Walter Gray's transept.[38]

An incident occurring in the middle of the thirteenth century illustrates Rome's hold on the church of York. It was soon after the accession of Archbishop Sewall de Bovill (1256–8) that three strangers appeared in the Minster choir, asking which was the dean's stall. One of them took the seat indicated while the other two, holding a paper in their hands, went through a mock ceremony, ending: 'Brother, we install you by the authority of the pope!'[39] The man receiving this caricature investment was, in fact, the proctor of Cardinal Giordano Orsini, recently assigned to the York deanery by Pope Alexander IV, whose signed 'provision' was the sole sanction for the august solemnization.[40]

It is an ironic twist that the English kings, on occasion so sternly opposed to the pope's claims on investiture, should have at other times blandly played into his hands. The Edwards were particularly guilty of such collusion, a reflection of their dependence on Italian moneylenders, who financed their wars with France.[41] Finance was, likewise, the entire motive for a king's keeping a prelate's post vacant for months and even years, during which he enjoyed the fruits of its temporalities.[42] Meanwhile, he could make all appointments in the archbishop's nomination, thus furnishing his favourite clerks with prebends, which they would hold *in absentia*, free to do the king's business.

The kings also used these posts for what might be termed political bribes to powerful families, allies or their own relations, like members of the House of Savoy. One of these Savoyards, Aymon, bastard son of the count, was, at the age of 17, a multiple pluralist, holding canonries at Reims, Lyon and Paris as well as the Archdeaconry of York, which proctors serviced for many years while he was supposed to be 'studying'.[43] An even more notorious case was that of a son of the powerful Earl of Gloucester, Bogo de Clare, who held as many as eighteen prebends at one time besides the Treasury at York, which he probably never visited. His deputy likewise neglected his duties, leaving 'the vestments unrepaired, the censers broken, the bells ill-hung and the clock . . . out of order' while he 'used the best silken altar cushions for his bed'.[44]

If the leading dignitaries of York chapter were so frequently absentees, how could it be expected that ordinary canons would be more dutiful? Even the most important chapter meetings drew only a small minority.[45] This could be particularly harmful to building operations since the chapter chose the master of the fabric and supervised the gathering and distribution of its funds. Its decisions, usually adopted by a small fraction of residentiaries, were often hampered in the execution, as a result. And how could it be otherwise? Why, indeed, should a canon who rarely if ever came to York care anything about the appearance of its church? And why should he volunteer to spend money for it out of his own pocket when nothing bade him to consider his post as an object of consecration or even glory, but only as a source of income?

The huge exactions to which York's ecclesiastics were subjected could easily be considered an all-sufficient reason for the Minster's slow progress. But the record shows that many of them might still have done far more for it than they did, so ample were their revenues. Walter Giffard's 'household expenses' totalled £735 in 1268 (£167 for wine alone) and £951 in 1270.[46] But he is not listed as giving a single penny to the fabric. Walter Gray was also very spendthrift, disbursing 4,000 marks on a single banquet when he was host to the marriage of Alexander III of Scotland and Margaret, Henry III's daughter.[47] Still, Gray was able to find sufficient funds to build the Minster transept. True, he was reputed to be very rich, but not even opulence was an assurance against neglect of York Minster by its prelates.

Excuses are never lacking for failure of accomplishment. At York, the perennial Scottish invasions are often blamed and are said to have cut William de Melton's (1317–40) revenues by half during a certain period.[48] He had hardly assumed his office, when, in 1319, fulsome Edward II ordered him to stop the Scots. The 3,000 men—monks, priests, artisans and tradesmen, chiefly—that he hastily gathered, were cut to pieces by their seasoned opponents at Myton, just a few miles from York. Melton was there in person and wrote a pitiful letter after the battle pleading for financial help from abbeys and convents to make up for his personal losses. Among the things he listed were his *carriagia*, in which apparently he had gone out to fight, and 'our plate, silver as well as brass'.[49]

Anomalously, the Scottish wars were not a total loss to York. England's second city became for a number of years its political and even administrative centre and local tradesmen and artisans enjoyed spates of great prosperity.[50] The Minster fabric itself benefited. Work on the nave and chapter-house vestibule was under way at various periods of the wars and the donations of titled fighters who had come up for the campaigns were emblazoned on the latter's windows and in the spandrels of the high nave arches.[51] One could hardly think of more worthy *ex voto* offerings for their safe return.[52]

An indulgent historian could assume that William Melton's calamities in the Scottish wars were the reason that the only fabric donations listed in his register come near the end of his long pontificate, when supposedly his situation had sufficiently recovered to permit him to turn to the building of the Minster. But one also finds in those same archives a long series of loans made by the prelate, starting as early as 1319 (his third year in office)[53] and continuing all throughout his tenure. There were loans to kings and barons, bishops and priors, but also to smaller fry, often running to a total of several thousand marks a year.[54] Whatever their motivation, the archbishop fully expected to be repaid. He took pledges of their plate from lesser nobles[55] and dunned the executors of those who had died in debt to him or even sequestered their possessions.[56]

We must conclude from these loans that Archbishop Melton was even in the worst of times hardly destitute. It is the more difficult, therefore, for us to be grateful for his two gifts to the fabric of 500 marks and 100 marks, made in 1338 and 1339, the latter to help pay for the great west window, a famous dating point in the Minster's building history.[57] These £400 have merited Melton the qualification of 'munificent benefactor' by the best known of the church's historians, Canon James Raine. Averaged over Melton's twenty-three years, they would have sufficed to pay for the hire of three or four workmen.

William Melton's register tells us in the most unmistakable terms that his ruling priorities did not include the Minster. In 1330, eight years before his first fabric contribution, he made a gift of £1,000 to William de Melton, eldest son of his brother Henry, and £100 more to each of William's siblings, Thomas, John and Joan. The following year, the archbishop found another £1,000 'as a mark of our affection' for his nephew and namesake,[58] through whom he evidently had the vicarious sense of founding his own lineage, particularly after his brother's death. Though the Meltons had begun in a relatively humble state they were not meant to remain so, for the archbishop pursued a relentless policy of buying up great domains from his huge church revenues, all of which he engrossed in his own name. He bequeathed ten manors in several counties to his nephews, who thus became one of the most richly propertied clans of Yorkshire.[59]

At Melton's death, in 1340, the 'new' nave was still not vaulted, though it was fifty years after its inception. By 1345, the Minster's condition was critical, as a famous passage in the fabric rolls of that year reveals. Due to negligence and lack of proper authority, materials were stolen, workers overpaid while others disobeyed instructions of the architect. Meanwhile, much of what had been accomplished was in decay. The outside buttresses had 'for the most part perished for defective covering' and the lack of lead roofing had resulted in the accumulation of 'such a quantity of water that lately a lad had almost been drowned. . . .'[60]

Only a miracle would seem capable of saving the Minster.

The astonishing presence of the great cathedrals tends to lift them above all circumstance. This has led to the acceptance of all kinds of fables regarding their construction, which have survived into our own supposedly disenchanted age. Actually, when one studies their histories, one learns that there was often more to hamper their creation than to help it. It was of course the stupendous role that the church played in medieval life that furnished the dynamics for cathedral-building. But there was nothing inevitable about it. A cathedral had to be wanted and this one at York was more often than not a waif.

Fortunately, this situation was changed with the coming to office of Archbishop John Thoresby (1352–73).

The role of a zealous, strong-willed, resourceful individual (sometimes of two or three such individuals) is salient in the story of almost all cathedrals. Toulouse had its Bertrand de l'Isle-Jourdain, Amiens its Geoffrey d'Eu and Paris its Maurice de Sully, to cite a few examples. While he was still waiting at Rome for his pall, how impatiently one can imagine, John Thoresby acted to fertilize the fabric fund with an indulgence.[61] Since the first gesture of this nature at a change of prelacy was almost always the chapter's, this act seems to have meant that the new archbishop was serving notice that he himself intended to lead an active, aggressive building programme.

John Thoresby had evidently set his heart on erecting a new choir and thus eliminating the last important section of the old Norman structure, which more than ever must have appeared disproportionate compared to the imposing dimensions of the Gothic construction. But the choir had to wait until the long-neglected nave had been completed, a task that was no doubt hampered by the loss of trained workmen in the Great Plague, which struck England in 1349. Thus, in the end only about half of Thoresby's precious term was left for the tremendous task he had set himself.

He is listed as being present at the chapter session of 20 July 1361, and the dean 'in foreign parts', when that body consented to his grandiose plan. Accepting his aesthetic vision that the Minster 'ought in all respects to be of the same uniformity and proportion', the canons

> unanimously agreed and consented to begin the new work of the quire which then if compared with the new erected nave was very rude and disorderly, and so resolved that the old quire should forthwith be taken down and re-edified.[62]

As one reads the full wording of this historic decision, one has the sense that the forceful archbishop had to use all his persuasive powers to get the chapter's approval. Even so it was obtained only with a stipulation rigidly limiting the canons' responsibility:

> they not consenting, but expressly protesting to the contrary, that . . . the canons of the said church, or any of them, their heirs or executors or their goods or chattels whatsoever . . . shall be anywise bound . . . beyond what they shall be willing to contribute to the fabric of the said work, from motives of charity and devotion. . . .[63]

Thoresby's name was also associated with this demurrer, but since in his case it turned out to be a pure formality one imagines it as a concession meant to quiet the chapter's fears of exorbitant deductions from their revenues. His own intentions were shown soon after when he ordered the old hall from the archbishop's manor at

Shirburne to be pulled down, its stone to be used for the proposed choir. It may have been one of these blocks which, ten days later, he posed as the cornerstone of the new structure outside the old chevet, accompanying the act with a donation of 100 marks. It was the first of a large number of recorded gifts, spaced at £200 a year and totalling £2,600 by the time of his death. In addition, he unquestionably made other contributions in the form of bills paid on the spot, one example of this kind, which found its way into the prelate's *Register*, telling of his having paid for two dozen great logs for the use of the Minster fabric.[64]

Urged on by Thoresby, without a doubt, the chapter made some effort to match his bounty by taxing all benefices. But receipts must have been unsatisfactory, since the archbishop called the entire diocesan clergy together in October 1365 to get them to agree to put an additional levy on their earnings. There was, plainly, resistance since a year later Thoresby empowered his receiver 'to compel and coerce' the recalcitrant clergymen 'by all manner of church censures'.[65] His appeals to the parishes must have been meeting with sufficient success, on the other hand, to tempt fake questors to go around making collections with forged documents. These dastards Thoresby cursed in every act of their existence and vowed that they would be 'blotted out of the Book of the Living' if they did not bring their ill-gotten contributions promptly over to the fabric fund.[66]

Despite his consuming preoccupation with the Minster choir, Thoresby found time and finance to encourage many other building projects. He was also an energetic administrator and a peacemaker of strong persuasiveness, finally settling the ludicrous, centuries-old controversy with Canterbury as well as a long-enduring jurisdictional squabble between the municipality and the powerful St Mary's Abbey over claims to the rich suburb of Bootham, a frequent cause of disorders. In both cases, he took what must be regarded as the anomalous side, granting primacy to York's old rival and Bootham's rights to the burghers.[67]

His most notable accomplishments as administrator were associated with the Great Plague. With great numbers of his churches left rectorless, the rapid training of hundreds of new priests was the most urgent task. To aid them in their work, the archbishop arranged for the preparation of what has been called the 'Lay Folks' Catechism'.[68] It is a document of historic moment, translated into the English vernacular in simple, mnemonic verses aimed as much at the ignorant new clergy, one imagines, as at the neglected flock.

27. John Thoresby's new choir: greater than the nave, it was more than half-completed in a dozen years

Archbishop Thoresby's most glowing monument, however, was his choir and the great chevet that enclosed it. Entailing nine capacious bays, one more than the nave, about half of them were finished before his death. It is hardly surprising that Thoresby died a relatively poor man. His will contained forty-four bequests, the highest for 40 marks and many as low as 5. Several members of his family were named but never for more than 40 marks.[69]

Great as were the archbishop's revenues at York, they could not patently serve two major goals: those of self-enrichment and building the Minster. William de Melton and John Thoresby: each of these celebrated archbishops of York made the choice in keeping with his fundamental character. It is only sad that the fate of the Minster should have turned on this accidental personal difference.

After Thoresby's death, work on the chevet languished for several decades once again, four archbishops adding little or nothing to it.[70] The last of the group, Richard le Scrope (1398–1405), did make an important contribution, as it turned out, permitting the completion of the new choir. But that happened inadvertently—through his death! The occasion was the Yorkshire disturbances that followed the execution of Richard II, for whom York felt a strong sentimental attachment which the archbishop shared. When some royal troops were in the vicinity, Scrope headed a small army and went out to 'reason' with them. The captain of the royal troops disarmed the prelate by trickery, then summarily tried and executed him. This unhappy end had the features of a martyrdom and Scrope's tomb at the Minster swiftly began drawing throngs of the faithful, accomplishing many miracles.

Oblations left at his shrine were soon far and away the most lucrative of all those at the cathedral and continued to be amazingly productive year after year, bringing as high as £150 annually. Henry IV, Richard's executioner, raged at this veneration of a patent traitor and royal officials demanded that the tomb be shut off by a high stone wall 'in order to stop the false fools from coming there under the colour of devotion'. But the chapter had no intention of smothering this unexpected windfall. Instead, the Scrope oblations were deftly shunted to the tomb of St William and the money assigned to the fabric fund.[71]

York had always lacked a popular local saint who could attract the farthings and now at last it had one—let Rome refuse to sanctify him if it would![72] As it fell out, also, there now came to the archbishop's throne another builder, Henry Bowet

(1407–23), the last of the rare and precious series, who, with the aid of the unhaloed Scrope and his own powers of actualizing the deniers, pressed the great Minster toward its completion. In particular, he was able to get important noble families and rich ecclesiastics to pay for the glazing of the vast windows of the choir, his pontificate being credited with fully seventeen of these, one during each year.[73]

Most of this stupendous quantity of medieval glass prepared for the Minster choir can still be seen there. From the coats-of-arms and inscriptions that have been painted on to these numerous stained-glass windows one can determine to a considerable degree their donors. They include some of the great county lineages like the Rooses and the De Mauleys as well as some of the most powerful churchmen of the archdiocese. The shields of 'England' and 'France' are also to be found in these lancets.[74] Only the burghers are missing from York's choir, the area of preference for patronage of the middle class in so many French cathedrals.

28. The Bellfounder's window. Donated by Richard Tunnoc, burgher, the donor panels describe the bell he founded for the Minster. LEFT TO RIGHT: He pours the molten metal; he is blessed by St William (a banner bears his name); he buffs the finished bell

Indeed, York's citizens are almost totally missing as donors of the Minster's great mass of 109 medieval windows still extant (though much of the earlier glass is effaced), which a modern specialist catalogued.[75] One firmly established exception to this surprising absence is the so-called Bellfounder's window, paid for around 1330 by Richard Tunnoc, who 'took his freedom' (a kind of required civil registration) as a goldsmith. But he also founded bells and must have made one for the Minster, which is the subject of his window. The lancet's 'signature' panels are inscribed with his name and show him, aided by a journeyman, casting and buffing a great bell, which he then presents to St William. And all around the borders and strewn over the field and even hanging from Tunnoc's pouch are countless tiny golden bells which the late afternoon sun causes to glow with an almost audible lustre.[76]

There are, besides, a few glass fragments remaining that probably refer to burgher donors. One famous panel depicts what looks like the sale of three casks, with the price inscribed above: 'P(o)ur Cink Mar(k)s' ('for five marks'). Also, in the will of Agnes de Holme, dated 1361, there is provision for the payment for another window, which is couched in the most curious terms:

> I also bequeath to the new fabric [of Thoresby's choir, she doubtless meant] . . . such a sum of money, to be levied on my goods, as would be sufficient wherewith a competent person would be wont and could be hired to make a pilgrimage for another person to [the shrine of] the Apostle of St James, *for the construction of one glass window.* And I desire that in one light [lancet] of the said glass window be placed an image of St James the Apostle, and in the other light thereof an image of St Katherine the Virgin.[77]

This strange bequest reveals not only the wonderful adaptability of the medieval church in the matter of oblations but also the subtle hand of Archbishop John Thoresby. Finding that this woman had set her heart on sending a vicarious pilgrim (a common enough practice) to Santiago de Compostela, a voyage she herself was incapable or unwilling to undertake, the prelate appears to have been able to convince her that St James would be just as pleased and responsive if she put up a lancet to his honour at the Minster. The glass itself, wherever it was originally placed, has unfortunately disappeared.

And the scarceness of burgher donations of glass lancets to the Minster was not compensated by other types of patronage, as far as it has been possible to determine.[78] Only sixteen gifts (plus five chaplaincies[79]) from the middle class were gathered by me from a wide variety of sources covering a spread of 172 years. What, then, was one to make of the contrary opinion expressed by the well-known York historian, Canon James Raine, that was bolstered by seemingly incontrovertible proof, to the effect that: 'Indeed, so widely diffused was . . . the wish to decorate one of the noblest of God's temples, that there were few wills in which there was no bequest to the fabric . . . ?'[80] Since this claim was in sharp conflict with my own findings, it appeared that nothing but a complete reading of the original middle-class wills could resolve the discrepancy.

Filed in either the archbishop's or the dean-and-chapter's temporal court, the 356 burgher wills of the fourteenth century (the earliest is dated 1321) produced ninety bequests to the Minster fabric, or almost exactly 25 per cent.[81] In the case of the dean-and-chapter group of 140 wills, moreover, an important qualification has to be allowed for, stemming from the fact that these testators had the privilege of asking for burial in the Minster compound. If granted, a fee was paid—*to the fabric*—which could not be regarded as a donation to the building-fund, accordingly. Over and over the wills say as much: 'pro consuetudine sepulture mee'—'for my burial, as customary'.[82] When allowances for such requests are made, the rate of unqualified donors to the building-fund in the dean-and-chapter registry is cut to 14.3 per cent, or one in seven![83]

There is evidence, however, that requests for burial at the Minster were often turned down. The proof that there was no obligation on the canons to honour them is that the words 'if possible' or 'if acceptable' accompanied these requests in many cases. Besides, the testators knew that they would have to pay a higher price for the honour, as did Matilda de Alnewyk, who left 20 shillings for a resting place at the cathedral, which was to be reduced to 13s. 4d., she specified, if she must be satisfied with a spot at her parish nearby, St Michael-le-Belfrey. The fact that she would be lying at her husband's side there suggests that she was prepared to accept an even greater sacrifice for the privilege of a Minster burial.[84] As it turned out, Matilda (or Maud) was spared this renunciation since she is listed as having been interred at St Michael's, after all.[85]

That the Minster chapter was selective in its grants of the burial privilege is most strikingly illustrated in the case of Robert de Holme, wool merchant (d.1396), who scattered his benefactions with a lavish hand unequalled by any other York patri-

29. Holy Trinity, Goodramgate: one of the modest parish churches which York's wealthy patricians are supposed to have preferred to the Minster

cian.[86] Included among his dozens of pious bequests which have been estimated to total £1,400,[87] there was one for £400 establishing a chantry (private chaplaincy) at the Minster. This sum, which could be expected to bring an income of at least £20, would have left over, after payment of the chaplain's modest salary, almost enough to hire two masons for the fabric, in perpetuity. The chapter turned down this attractive gift and the chantry was established at St Anne's Chapel on Fossbridge instead.[88]

Everything indicates that York's churchmen, like those at Lyon, were determined to keep the Minster as the untroubled stage of ecclesiastic dignity and ritual. This is certainly understandable at York, when one considers the touchiness of its hierarchic position (as illustrated chiefly by its searing conflict with Canterbury), as well as its importance in the royal galaxy. The virtual freezing out of commoners from the Minster's orbit that resulted was not accompanied by the profound political antagonism that prevailed at Lyon between citizens and churchmen, however. For York's archbishop was not its seignior. York was a royal city whose rights were sharply limited by the crown. The powerful centrism imposed on England by the Conquest would not allow for the kind of chronic civil strife found so often on the continent and of which Lyon was only one of many examples.[89]

The loss of burgher patronage by the Minster as a result of its policy of exclusion had an exhilarating effect on the parish churches, almost half the original forty-four or forty-five of which are still standing. There is a touching image of the sturdy York 'merchants and tradespeople' that purports to explain their avoidance of the Minster as purely voluntary and due to their preference for their own modest parish churches. Here, 'with their wives, their children, their workmen, and their serving maids, they knelt each Sunday.' Here too they expressed their 'desire to be buried rather than in the more aristocratic atmosphere of the cathedral'.[90]

Granted that a dyer with his tinctured hands, or a fuller or a skinner, might feel out of their element in the snobbish Minster. But it is difficult to believe that the same would apply to those members of the patriciate that the quoted author lists as examples of social humility: Sir Richard Yorke, twice Lord Mayor of York and Mayor of the Staple (England's wool export monopoly) at Calais, or Nicholas Blackburn, Lord Mayor and Admiral of the Fleet.[91]

These men's portraits and those of their families (Yorke with his six sons and four daughters, the latter all arrayed in their embroidered gowns) can still be seen in the windows that they endowed, at St John the Evangelist, Micklegate, and at All Saints, North Street. But were they truly in these parishes by choice, after supposedly spurning an invitation of the cathedral canons? It is hard to imagine that these wealthy gentry would not have preferred to have their memorial lancet shining away in the pre-eminent Minster. It seems more reasonable to assume that York's affluent burghers, shown unmistakably that they were unwanted at the archbishop's church, learned to make do with their parishes.

And there is every evidence that they were lavish benefactors on their behalf. Indeed, the great body of York's commoners demonstrably shared this role with them, though the poorer ones found the extravagant Corpus Christi plays in which the city's ninety-five guilds were obligated to participate, often against their wills, a drain on their pennies that were available for charity.[92] Lack of early parish registers obscures the extent of burgher donorship. Nevertheless, the great number of remaining parish churches, often splendid, bear eloquent witness of its munificence. These neighbourhood churches still contain a quite considerable amount of old stained-glass, for instance, frequently accompanied by their donor panels.[93] But by all odds, the most impressive record of the benevolent presence of the burghers at the parish churches is the extraordinary number of chaplaincies that were founded by them there, over a hundred of them having been collated by me.[94]

Though basically a *quid pro quo* arrangement, the chantry, as has been said, had other advantages for a church, sealing a family's loyalty to it and drawing supplementary donations to the foundation altar. The attitude of the York burghers to their chantry priests was a very special one. The mayor and council had administrative authority over them as a group and often had the 'presentation' of the successor at the time of vacancy. In many cases, the parishioners (or as it might be written, 'six of the best parishioners') were empowered to make the choice. So as to add assurance that the chaplain would take his task seriously and scrupulously supervise the property of the foundation, city officials would often be asked to participate at his induction services.[95] But the firmest security, it seems, came from putting the property directly into the city's hands and empowering it to oversee (usually for a fee) the chaplain's functions and morals.

So strongly did the idea of a daily personal mass appeal to the medieval mind that many people bequeathed the larger part of their fortunes—often to the detriment of legitimate heirs—to establish one. In some cases, special arrangements would be made to give the chantry a firm financial foundation, as when the baker, Robert de Sallay, undertook in 1332 to build some houses in the churchyard of St Michael, Spurriergate, the rent from which would furnish the called-for revenue.[96] More often, the parishioners as a whole made similar arrangements, as happened at Holy Trinity, Goodramgate, in 1316,[97] or at the prosperous merchants' church of St Martin, Coney Street, in 1335. The faithful at All Saints, Pavement, the following year, were also allowed to erect their houses in the parish cemetery, 'where the dead were not interred'.[98]

Those citizens who were wealthy enough to erect a private chapel usually preferred to do so in their own town house or country manor.[99] But joint projects, with shared costs, were naturally far more numerous. Bridge chapels which guarded spiritually the most important lifelines of a medieval city, were very popular. St William's

30. All Saints, North Street: Nicholas Blackburn, Jr, and his wife kneeling at the bottom of the lancet that they donated

Chapel on Ouse-bridge, which boasted seven chaplains, was actually a fully-fledged church, built and administered by the city.

As everywhere else in the Middle Ages, York burghers also founded many small hospices for the poor and infirm, phonetically written 'mesondews' (*Maisons-Dieu*).[100] Some of these were established by guilds, the richest of which also built their own halls, with attached chapels. Two of them—the Merchant Taylors Hall and Merchant Adventurers Hall—are still standing, the latter one of York's most interesting medieval structures.[101] It was the city as a whole, on the other hand, that supported St Leonard's Hospital, which has been called the most important medical establishment in North England. Its annual income in 1280 has been evaluated at £1,062, close to $715,000 or £393,000 today.[102]

As for burgher benevolence to the regular clergy, distance from York did not diminish the possible interest of the city's inhabitants, who frequently had rural origins, or of the wool-men who sometimes developed devotional attachments to their monastic suppliers. Among the beneficiaries, famous Fountains Abbey and Whitby Priory were particularly favoured, the latter possessing so much property at York that it had to keep a rent-collector there.[103] Great St Mary's Abbey, on the other hand, which was located at York, did not fare quite as well at the hands of its citizens, with whom it was often in conflict over tolls and jurisdictional matters.[104] Yet the abbey, fabulously endowed, was able to build a great Gothic church (371 by 60 feet) in the astonishing span of thirty years, *c.* 1270–1300, its magnificent ruins being there to attest to this miracle,[105] as well as to the inherent wealth of York's clerical community.

Following the normal pattern, bequests left to the mendicant orders of York by the burghers exceeded in frequency those to any other group.[106] This became particularly marked during the Black Death, when people frantically sought an untarnished intercessor in all the clamour of the dying to carry their name to God's ear. As at Lyon, paupers and other unfortunates were also considered to have a special claim to Jesus' attention and often received alms for prayers on a man's burial day. Prayers were, indeed, the constant burden of testamentary grants to the friars, the fees being set according to the number requested. The most desirable arrangement was permanent placement on the friars' bede rolls.[107]

While the 356 burgher wills represent but a small proportion of the people who lived—and died—at York during the fourteenth century (estimates of its population range from 15,000 to 45,000!), they still remain an extraordinary source for under-standing the life-style and thinking of its inhabitants and particularly the underlying motives that occasioned their enormous contributions to pious objectives, including art. For, though the testator was basically concerned with his passage to the other life and with his status there, the conditions that he sought to arrange for it by his foun-dations often bore an aesthetic facet.

Even though the place of burial, the parish church, was in the great majority of cases prescribed,[108] a preferred spot in it was at times allowed, particularly to pros-perous parishioners. In fact, the testator was on occasion very insistent on the matter, emphasizing that 'the place was assigned me by oath'.[109] When one's mate was already interred, it almost went without saying that the survivor would be permitted to lie beside him or her. At times, the tombstone would be designated and even located, as it was once charmingly described, 'under a blew marble'.[110]

Those married a second or a third time would seem to have had a problem. But they usually were quite decided about which of their mates they wished to lie beside. Thus, Emma de Stayngate chose her first husband, Thomas le Sadeler, underlining emphatically: 'I do not wish my body to be put in any other place.'[111] Often the selec-tion of the burial site calls to life some now obscure corner of a church: 'beneath the stone arch' or 'before the painting of the glorious Virgin Mary'[112] or beside a statue of St Christopher.[113] One will, which asks for burial at the Minster—'beneath the path taken by processions'[114]—seems to fill the great church with a rumble of van-ished ceremonial pomp.

All the more surprising, therefore, when a testator marked his contempt for his mortal remains by suggesting offhandedly that they be interred 'wherever God dis-poses'.[115] Such an arrangement was of course unavoidable when a travelling wool-man was in a foreign land when stricken down, one such instance being recorded in far-off Danzig.[116] The frequency of requests for burial in a person's native town,[117] on the other hand, shows that people's ties with 'the place where I originated'[118] were still strong in fourteenth-century York.

In the main, donations to the parishes for building or decoration are not listed in the wills.[119] One reason is that many such contributions were arranged for during a person's lifetime, an example being the considerable number of known donations of stained-glass lancets which never appear in the testaments.[120] Yet now and then some work-in-progress was benefited, as for instance the Preachers' (Dominicans') belltower to which Margaret de Aldborough bequeathed two cloaks, 'bloodred and green, both furred with miniver', with other gifts going to the infirmary fabric.[121] Women's bequests often included clothes, though rarely so fairytale-like an object as Alice de Ripon's 'pair of silver slippers'.[122] At times they had a whole collection of belts to leave,[123] at others a quantity of beads ('bedys'), or jewellery, with which they might ask that some favourite image of the Virgin or a female saint should be adorned.[124]

That Margaret de Knaresborough, a seamstress, should have a large wardrobe overturns the proverb of the unshod shoemaker.[125] But the *longam gonnam* that Peter de Barleburgh, tailor, bequeathed must have been part of his leftover stock, as were 'my otter skins and twenty-four arrows plumed with peacock feathers' which he left to the Priory of Bridlington.[126] The wills show us that the average medieval shopkeeper was sparsely supplied. The list of Constantine del Dame, apothecary, is quickly covered, including a mortar, a balance and the 'droges' in the window.[127] However, every artisan treasured each one of his tools and when Alan de Alnewyk, goldsmith, consigned a few of them, including his 'wyrkyngborde', to his apprentice, William, a relation, he asked that his executors withhold the rest until the lad was 20 and had proved to be of good morals and comportment, particularly 'not arguing with my wife or contradicting her'.[128]

The frequent cropping up of terms like 'wyrkyngborde' proves that the English language was a lusty reality in fourteenth-century York. The wills were almost always written in Latin, with a rare reversion to the Conqueror's tongue,[129] as when William Mowbray asks burial 'a lez meson de les freres menores del cite de Euwyk [York] en le quer' del dit meson ioust ma dame ma mer' ('. . . in the house of the Franciscan Friars of the city of York, in the choir of the said house next to madame my mother').[130] A will written in English is equally uncommon, an example being John de Croxton's parchment which identifies a vanished corner when giving 'my body to my graven in the mynster garth be for the buttres in the charnell by side my childer'.[131]

Even though the parish clerk's Latin might be equal to the higher hurdles, it was with the everyday things that it sometimes stumbled, out of ignorance of the ancient equivalents, as with the *optimum bortcloth cum touellis* ('best broadcloth and towels') listed by John de Carlele.[132] The parish dominie had a particularly hard time listing the bequests of Richard de Dalton, barber, as shown by such items as *unum potelpot et unum quartpott* or his six *qyshyns* ('cushions') or, especially, his favourite *razor* with its *manubrium de ebore* (razor with ivory handle).[133]

Long-vanished eras often take on a poetic resonance in their routine elements, as when one testamentary donor reminds her beneficiary that the property given owed the yearly payment to the area seignior of 'a rose in the time of roses' (*unam rosam tempore rosarum*).[134] Though the remittance was only a token and the qualifier could be taken for granted, the entire weft of medieval life seems to blossom from this lovely phrase. The secret is the continuity of man's social being and particularly of his aesthetic sense. It is the same basic phenomenon which permits the anthropologist to reconstruct an ancient race from a single bone or artifact of pregnant content.

York's medieval burgher wills are full of this kind of charmed detail, revealing (in addition to their aesthetic data) touches of simple humanity that bring the testators instantaneously close. What difference if we no longer share the spiritual sanctions of those times? The elementary impulses remain virtually unchanged, echoing in the voice of Isabell de Wele when she places £10 in the hands of her husband, Roger, to keep for their son until he comes of age. She reminds him that he must do this faithfully since he would have to appear one day before God and give account.[135] Isabell also left small sums for the city's destitute, as important in her modest circumstances as the grandiose gifts of York's greatest plutocrat and church patron, Robert de Holme.[136]

And still, humanity vibrated in this man also, as witness his testamentary provisions for alms to prisoners, shoes for the poor, and aid, too, for those 'who once were powerful and have come to great poverty'. He felt particular concern for the fathers of indigent families, 'especially those from whom my servants have bought wool for my trade'. The poor inmates of the hospice he founded on Monkbridge were to get a penny every day of their lives, not a negligible pension. And his eight employees were magnificently remembered, two of them getting 40 marks apiece, enough to set up a young man for an independent career.

Such acts of individual charity were as characteristic of medieval man as were his institutional and artistic grants, of which Robert de Holme himself was responsible for an endless number. He left £20 to the Minster fabric; 100 shillings to the fabric of his parish, Holy Trinity, Goodramgate; 10 marks more to it for 'forgotten tithes' and £20 to be distributed among its poor parishioners on the day of his funeral. The four mendicant orders got a total of £70 and St Leonard's Hospital 100 marks, while every nunnery in the province received 100 shillings. Nor was his native village, Holme-on-the-Wolds, forgotten, 100 shillings going to its church and 40 shillings to its altar.

All these bequests were made by the millionaire wool-man in glittering gold and silver coin[137] and were, we can imagine, gratefully received. Only the largest grant of all was turned down: the £400 he assigned to the Minster fabric, a part of whose earnings were to be used for the singing of a daily mass at the cathedral in his name. No doubt the haughty dignitaries had their special reasons for refusing this truly princely foundation, as has already been surmised.

Nevertheless, such a self-denial was a luxury that the Minster's building fabric could ill afford. It exemplified an incalculable number of similar losses that were due to the permanent gap that was wilfully maintained between the mass of York's citizens and the hierarchy. The ultimate effect of this alienation was to add one more serious impediment to the others: the churchmen's neglect of their church, their self-serving impulses and especially their misplaced pride—all contributing to the Minster's inordinately drawn-out building history.

7

~

POITIERS

Old Style versus New

Poitiers Cathedral Chronology

1162   New building begun at apse.

1199   Date of consecration of high altar, probably meaning that apse has been completed by this time. Two of its three bays have Romanesque arches, the third being ogival. The choir is without upper windows.

12C–13C   The eight apsidal lancets, including those of the famous Crucifixion window at the axis, are glazed at the end of the twelfth or beginning of the thirteenth century. The window arches are rounded.

Early 13C   There being no proper transept, the north and south terminals of the nave's easternmost bay, which was probably done in the twelfth century, are built in the form of two rectangular chapels early in the thirteenth.

13C   The remaining four of the nave's five bays are erected all through the century, the last two dating from its very end.

   The nave windows, like those in the apse, are cut out only on the lower level since the domed vaulting falls too low to permit clerestory apertures. The first windows are given rounded Romanesque form, the later ones pointed arches.

   Curiously, however, the blind arcade that runs the full length of the two aisles, is entirely round-arched, as though all had been done in a single sweep.

   The arcade cornices are supplied with charming modillions, carved in popular iconography.

End of 13C   The lower two registers of the façade, including the three portals, are completed, all richly sculptured, the higher levels being done at a leisurely pace thereafter.

13C–16C   Construction of the two towers, which are merely joined to the nave at one angle, is strung out over several centuries.

POITIERS, THE 'CAPITAL OF THE ROMANESQUE', SEEMS TO OWE ITS INDIVIDUALITY to some fortunate hazard that has preserved its monuments of that style. The roll-call summons up a memorable procession: Notre-Dame-la-Grande, St-Hilaire, Montierneuf, important parts of Ste-Radegonde and St-Porchaire, to say nothing of that fascinating relic of an even earlier epoch, the Baptistry of St-Jean, some of whose elements lapse over into the Romanesque, nevertheless.

It is only when one goes outside Poitiers and finds the same preponderance in architectural style for many miles around that one realizes that accident could hardly have extended that far.[1] What we have learnt about the great variety of socio-historical factors that have affected cathedral and other church building makes us wonder whether influences of the same order may have been involved here. Up to the present we have had demonstrations of such an impact on what might be conveniently called quantitative matters, like construction time, size, number of subsidiaries and other supplementary elements, while stylistic influence has been illustrated much more rarely and is doubtless more difficult to prove. Does the art of Poitiers present an interesting exception to that rule?

Regional art historians appear to endorse this conjecture, telling us that the existence of the great patrimony of Romanesque architecture at Poitiers was the result of a concerted determination to preserve it. And, associated with this resolution, was what they call a 'resistance' to the Gothic.[2] It is true enough that the movement from the earlier mode to its successor has often been accompanied by an obliteration of the first. But the contemporaries themselves were customarily little troubled by such substitutions. Hence, their presumed failure in this instance to show the same indifference is surprising.

Exactly how was this rejection of the Gothic—that brilliant, breathtaking form which swept Europe in a vast creative wave—supposed to have taken place at Poitiers?[3] The reply of the local authors is arresting. The resistance was, we are told, in response to political conquest. We recall that French military power drove the Plantagenets out of most of the western provinces shortly after 1200 and several decades later consummated its victory by subduing the local barons. Refusal of the Gothic, the Capetian style *par excellence*, is said to have lasted all through this period of forceful domination and ended 'abruptly when the beneficent . . . administration of the brother of St Louis, Alphonse de Poitiers, restored prosperity to the land'.[4] Alphonse took over the appanage of the western regions in 1242.

This attractive argument runs into several difficulties, among which is a flaw in dating. Long decades prior to the subjugation of 1204, the royal French style had already been realized in a series of lustrous monuments which could have been copied by the west without patriotic umbrage. Moreover, one wonders why, if the Gothic was not acceptable coming from the French, it had not been more widely welcomed at the hands of the Plantagenets. When the latter had married into Aquitaine in 1152, the vast domains that they had brought to the twelfth century's most spectacular alliance included the great dukedom of Normandy. And here, as has been said, Gothic architecture had flowered 'in all its perfection' and so early, besides, that it was an open question as to which had the priority in the new style, that northern province or the Île-de-France.[5]

That Normandy was unable, during the thirteenth century, to uphold its pioneer position in the evolution of the Gothic style, certainly not at a pace with the dazzling accomplishments of royal France, could hardly have been due to a bristling reaction to an enemy's aesthetic imposition, accordingly. Yet, the same as Poitou, it too was subjugated by the French, though this process met with considerably less resistance in the Norman duchy, a fact that had its influence on the building of the cathedral of Rouen, as will be seen.

Finally, the claim of aesthetic irredentism that was supposed to have resulted in Poitou's retention of the Romanesque fails to take into account other factors of a socio-historical nature that would have had much the same consequence, that is, in stifling the expression of a new and very costly architectural style. Primary among them was the enormous loss of resources suffered by the province from confiscations which the French exacted for the better part of the thirteenth century. While the period of pacification of the absorbed western regions is often vaunted by French historians for its affluence and concord[6] (familiar claims in the modern colonial era), the truth is that a large portion of their substance was either destroyed in the process of their domination or siphoned off by the conquerors.

In Poitou, indeed, the waste of war started a good half-century prior to the coming of the French. It featured in much of the reign of Henry II, who after his marriage with Eleanor of Aquitaine was engaged in an unrelenting struggle to unify his enormous empire. This translated itself largely into the need of subjugating powerful, self-willed vassals.[7] That his own wife and sons should have added to the magnitude of this task by frequent breaches of family loyalty (so different from the closeknit

31. Poitiers, the 'capital of Romanesque'—Notre-Dame-la-Grande

Capetians of this period) was probably only a complicating but not a decisive factor. For the task itself, of holding together all of England and half of France, was doubtless an impossible one at this juncture in history.

Henry II is said to have fallen behind his predecessors among the counts of Poitiers as a donor to churches. An analysis of the printed volumes of his papers reveals a total of seventy-five such gifts in all his continental possessions, or about two a year during his long reign (1150–89).[8] They constituted only a tiny percentage of the king's great revenues. This is hardly surprising, however, considering the breadth of his imperial design, with its perennial necessity of arms. His wars, radically different from the brief sorties of traditional feudal practice, were often protracted, characterized by his use of mercenaries on a vast scale.

His professional army not only helped to revolutionize military strategy and tactics but also called forth a complete revision of the taxation system. This was required by the unprecedented cost of his great permanent fighting force: more than 6,000 livres a year.[9] In addition, there were the expenses of the new 'machines' of war, of the great buckler of châteaux needed to rivet down the king's huge domain and the price of buying up the loyalty of vassals, never durable, moreover.[10] Small wonder that there was comparatively little left for munificence to churches.

Nevertheless, the fable that Henry II 'built' Poitiers's cathedral has led a hardy life. The claim is based chiefly on the presence of the king's portrait with those of his wife and children in a panel of the great central Crucifixion window before its modern 'restoration'. But this could have simply designated the royal couple as donors of that lancet.[11] Authors have also claimed Alphonse de Poitiers as the builder, with even less evidence or likelihood. The cathedral, it is said, 'took on new life under Alphonse', but it is difficult to figure out where that could have occurred. Long before his accession, the choir and transept and part of the first two of the nave's four bays had been completed, while at his death, three decades later, the last two bays were still not built![12] As a matter of fact, the cathedral's archives are totally silent on this score and are very sparse altogether, as are those of other important Poitiers churches, a result of the Huguenot pillage of 1562.[13]

It is far more likely, in any case, that the major initial impulse for St-Pierre was given, around 1162, by its bishop, Jean Bellesmains. The rebuilding was required not by war damage or fire but by the prestige needs of this prelate, one of the foremost churchmen of his day, who was to move on eventually to the most exalted post of the Gallic church, the archbishopric of Lyon.[14] The episcopal edifice that Jean found at Poitiers when he took office had been dedicated back in 1025. Even if it was not in a bad state of repair by the second half of the twelfth century, it may have been considered far too modest for so important a capital. The cathedral had, besides, been greatly surpassed by at least two other local edifices, St-Hilaire and Montierneuf, which even after modern amputations still overawe by their proportions.

Called the 'Chapter of the Rich', St-Hilaire especially, as much by its possessions as by the massiveness of its church, could challenge the pride of a great prelate. The count of Poitiers was its *ex-officio* abbot, while four of its canonicates were reserved for Poitou's leading baronial families.[15] The treasurer, who was the collegiate church's active head, was appointed by the prince, and the chapter's revenues were immense, financing a group of prebends almost twice as numerous as the cathedral's, which had fewer benefices than canons, half of whom were forced to make do with a semi-prebend each.[16]

Possessing vast domains, waterways, whole towns and a swarm of subsidiary churches, the abbey owed this opulence mainly to the original grants of the counts. Its eleventh-century church, important parts of which are still standing, was built chiefly by two countesses, one of whom brought down a renowned English architect, Gautier Coorland, for the task.[17] When the church underwent important reconstruction in the twelfth century, it seemed to have little difficulty in finding the necessary funds.[18]

This is certainly more than can be said for the cathedral, whose resources seem to have been exhausted by the building of the three-bay choir, which must have been terminated by 1199, when the high altar was consecrated. In 1198, indeed, Bishop Maurice de Boson found the episcopacy so loaded down with debts that he could not arrange a modest loan without the chapter's guarantee. The asked-for advance was, as it happened, for the refounding of the cathedral's cracked bells. At Poitiers, this was the bishop's responsibility, and the chapter, no doubt wary of establishing a costly precedent, hesitated before signing the loan papers. Yet the bishop's financial straits must have been truly as he described them in his imploring letter—'borne down by numerous debts and other heavy charges'—for he was able to convince the tight-fisted canons to stand him good—for all of three years! As it turned out, it took fifteen to repair the cathedral's bells.[19]

The revenues of Poitiers's bishop were never brilliant and the active cathedral-building campaign that had been conducted for almost four decades could well have left them in an embarrassing state.[20] Judging from stylistic evidence, a substantial amount of construction had in fact been accomplished during the initial period. It included the entire chevet (as well as the gigantic apsidal eastern wall); the choir; the rectangular chapels that shut off the north and south 'transept' terminals; the carved modillions of the aisle-wall cornices and the stained-glass windows pertaining to these areas.[21] As one examines the church today, one realizes that, the western façade and towers apart, considerably more than half of the new cathedral was built in this short 'Plantagenet period'. It would never do as well under the Capetians.

As surprising as this observation may sound, considering the acknowledged benevolence of the French monarchs, the underlying reason is not far to seek. France's royal family, however devout, consistently acted out their role as sovereigns, whose posture in Poitou was that of conquerors. One would have to be blind, prejudiced or sycophantic not to see the evidence of this.[22] The process began in 1204, when Philippe-Auguste, taking advantage of the ignominious abandonment of Normandy by King John, overran most of the rest of his great continental realm and placed it under French suzerainty.[23]

The latter part of this conquest was largely a symbolic act that had to be repeated several times in the following decades. Meanwhile, confiscations began early and the possessions that Philippe stripped from supporters of the English rulers were in part added to the crown, in part used to buy up vassals who could help him dominate the newly acquired provinces.[24] For Poitou was a distant and alien land to the French, 'too remote to visit or send [representatives] to', as a French official said in a letter to a great western seignior to whom he offered the leading post of king's seneschal.[25]

While the direct link between this political situation and the cathedral-construction programme can hardly be demonstrated as on a chart, the signs of delay and economy are inescapable, noticeable especially in the re-use of decoration and even 'entire wall-surfaces' from the earlier, Romanesque edifice.[26] The meagre four bays of its attenuated nave took almost all of the thirteenth century to build.[27] This is about two-and-a-half times the duration of the entirely equivalent accomplishment of the apse and transept. Nor could one argue a significant increase in the complexity of structure or design. St-Pierre retained throughout a placid simplicity, lacking the daring venturesomeness of the greater Gothic monuments.

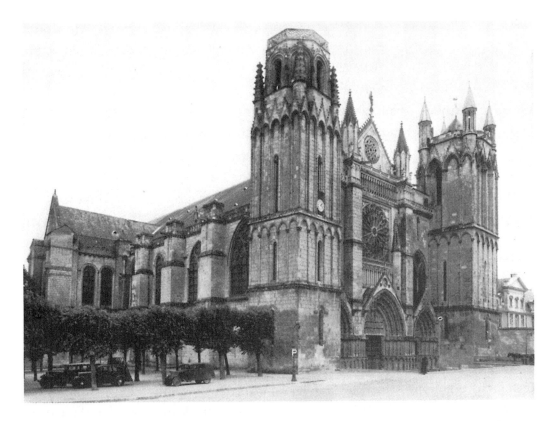

32. Poitiers, cathedral of St-Pierre, with its abbreviated nave of only four bays and very low vaulting which eliminated the possibility of high windows

Much of Poitiers cathedral's architecture is marked stylistically by what have been loosely called 'Romanesque survivals'.[28] Most characteristic are the dome-like (*bombées*) vaults, which descend so low as to abolish window spaces in the upper nave. Obviated, too, was the need for flying buttresses, the vaulting being shouldered by high aisles rising almost to the level of the central vessel. All of these features could, of course, be argued as demonstrations that Poitiers's builders were turning deliberately away from leading features of the royal French style.

Whether this was due to anti-French animus or to the simple desire to remain attached to the region's traditional architectural mode, it seems far-fetched to generalize either of these supposed intentions on the strength of Poitiers's only totally built new church, the cathedral. More significant, it would appear, is the fact that so many Romanesque churches in that city and in the general area were basically preserved, while any alterations that they did receive were largely done in an austere Gothic style. There is only one explanation we can think of that covers both these circumstances: the great impoverishment of the region due to the vast and long-lasting French extortions. This factor, when it did not prevent new building altogether, would certainly have tended to inhibit costly experiments with unfamiliar and daring forms and to encourage instead the use of conventional and more economical methods.

It is curious that those who argue an antagonism in Poitou to the French architectural modes should find no contradiction in the fact that there was not the same opposition to styles in the plastic arts stemming from that source.[29] It is quite certain, for instance, that glaziers from Chartres, Bourges and Poitiers shared their technical knowhow. One recent authority has demonstrated that some of St-Pierre's Gothic lancets actually antedated those of Bourges and offered evidence that a master-artisan from Poitiers went to work in the latter city and later returned to continue his operations at St-Pierre, where its workshop, after 1225, 'was subjected ever more strongly to the influence of the Île-de-France'.[30] The cathedral's sculpture has likewise been shown to have a strong affinity to the French style.

The drawn-out building time of the nave at Poitiers included one complete halt in operations beginning before the middle of the thirteenth century and continuing for at least thirty years.[31] Significantly, a simultaneous break took place in the partial reconstruction of the neighbouring church of Ste-Radegonde, whose nave was built in a kind of mimetic exercise to that of St-Pierre.[32] Ste-Radegonde was a dependency of the cathedral and some of the same workers were probably used there, as one can infer from the great similarity of various details.[33]

At St-Pierre the prolonged break in productivity appears to have halted the very attempt to gather funds for the fabric. It would be difficult otherwise to account for an enormous endowment made in 1279 by a leading cathedral dignitary to a flock of pious causes while completely excluding his own church's building fund. Guillaume Gabet's benefactions chiefly aided non-religious projects of the municipality, in whose name he established annuities totalling 300 livres. The grants, partly for the maintenance of bridges and roads, partly for dowering poor unmarried girls and for aid to the destitute, represented an initial investment of 6,000 livres ($4,800,000 or £2,640,000 today).[34]

There is no evidence that these extraordinary gifts to the city rather than to his church's building fund were due to a reflex of animosity to the churchman's colleagues, as we have sometimes seen occurring in other places.[35] Gabet was on the best of terms with the cathedral's clerical family, to whom he left a number of handsome bequests in his will.[36] The dignitary appears rather to have decided to place his fortune where it would really be put to use. As long-serving cathedral provost, or chief administrative officer, he had had close business relations with Poitiers's citizens, and doubtless came to share their primary urgencies, which his large bequests for roads and bridges seem to illustrate.[37]

Together with his city endowments, Guillaume Gabet's bequests attained the stupendous revenue of 500 livres a year, half enough to keep the cathedral-building programme going at a lively clip. It would of course have been very unusual for any ecclesiastic, except a most dedicated 'builder' like John Thoresby of York or Bertrand de l'Isle-Jourdain of Toulouse, to be that concerned about a cathedral as to apportion even a goodly fraction of his fortune to it. Nevertheless, the fact that Gabet did not leave a single sou to St-Pierre's building fund when it was still far from terminated indicates the lack of urgency in the long-suspended construction programme. One could almost conclude that a resumption of work was no longer even contemplated.

That this great halt in production should have coincided with the permanent takeover of Poitou by the French in 1242, and to have lasted at least through the thirty-year appanage of Alphonse de Poitiers, confirms the indifference of that prince to the cathedral's fate. As a matter of fact, the building campaign had dawdled through the first four decades of the century as well, starting with Philippe-Auguste's conquest and during which Poitiers itself was steadily held by the French.

In that same interval, the rest of Poitou and the other western provinces were prey to a bitter and very costly struggle that has been described shrewdly as a 'contest between English pounds and French livres', tens of thousands of both having been documented as being spent on it. This troubled period reached its apex in 1242 with the revolt of the united barons that seemed to doom the French occupancy.[38] But the nobles, execrated by an often pillaged and violated people, proved astonishingly weak in the field and were quickly subdued by the royal forces under St Louis and his brother, Alphonse de Poitiers.[39]

The defeat was a lasting one this time and its bitter price was extorted systematically thereafter by the victorious French. All that can be said in mitigation of these enormous exactions is that a heavy portion was borne by the ravaging barons. But they

were not the only ones to pay. The penalties were quite general and in any case, who-
ever footed the bill, the provinces as a whole were impoverished. The documentary
sources regarding the treasure that left the west to enter French coffers are contained
in three main archival collections: Alphonse's correspondence with his seneschals; the
accounts of his revenues; and most pertinently in the reports of the great investigations
that were conducted at his behest (following his brother's example) into complaints of
injustices suffered at the hands of royal officials during the occupation.[40]

The last category—called *Enquêtes*—has won the Capetians deserved praise.
Inspired by their desire to prepare their souls before setting off on their two Crusades,
in 1248 and 1270, each of which was likewise accompanied by a great mass of foundations for prayers to the same purpose,[41] these broad inquests were undoubtedly conceived as acts of Christian charity. But to the historian they have the added significance
of furnishing copious proofs of antecedent expropriations. Many of the recorded complaints go back to Philippe-Auguste's earliest seizures, in 1204, and to the confiscations
practised by his short-lived dauphin (Louis VIII), in 1214 and 1224.[42]

Accordingly, even if some restitutions were made as a result of the investigations,
it was often only the heirs of the principals who benefited, after the undue exactions
had gone on for thirty years or more. The number of expropriations was swollen by
the war of 1242 and in the years that followed they became so widespread once again
that inquests had to be continued throughout Alphonse's appanage.[43] The royal bailiffs who bought the 'farm' of a certain area (that is, the right to collect royal taxes
and impositions in it) had a strong personal reason to squeeze as hard as they could,
while Alphonse, avid for his Crusade fund, constantly added to the pressure.

How often was one of the claimants asked why he had not put his petition in earlier, only to reply that he feared that things would have gone even worse for him if he
had.[44] Many others never found the courage to ask, or died without heirs, or moved
out of the country when their house and land were expropriated.[45] There were,
besides, a great number of claims that were turned down—*nichil habebit* ('he shall
get nothing')—where the father or brother was found to have fought too doggedly
against France or had run off to England, or for no given reason.[46] This was true
especially of the more important cases (and hence those involving the most wealth),
which Alphonse often reserved for his own judgment or that of his Paris council.[47]

Thousands of expropriations were effected in the west during the six or seven
decades for which we have some records.[48] There were to begin with the big penalties

exacted of the great seigniors in the form of repurchase fees (*grossa racheta* or *redemptiones*), which did not include the vast properties that were confiscated outright. Great feudal landowners like Raoul de Mauléon, Geoffroy de Rochefort, Hugues de Lusignan or Archbishop Hugues of Bordeaux each paid fines running into thousands of livres.[49] The smaller fry, whose *terre forefacte* ('forfeited lands') were less important, paid up to 100 livres each, nevertheless.[50]

Even these formally established ransoms might not bring the payers back into full grace, moreover, since they continued often to be mercilessly extorted. This appears, for example, in a plaintive plea made by Countess Yolanda of La Marche and Lusignan in 1257, years after all indemnity settlements had supposedly been accomplished. The countess gave a long account of continued pillaging of her own domains and those of her vassals, seizures of taxes due her, usurpation of her rights of justice, confiscation of the property of 'her' burghers or the carrying off of the financial resources of 'her' Jews. Yolanda's complaints patently produced little improvement, since twelve years later much the same grievances were repeated by Count Hugues XII of Lusignan.[51]

Many of the complainants were people of the most modest circumstances, victims of unscrupulous men who took advantage of their unchecked sway and the troubled times. One listing alone of the 'Enquêtes' contains five hundred such entries.[52] An official ordered a man's wife to go to bed with him; repulsed, he fined the husband 9 livres.[53] A fisherman's nets were 'confiscated', loaded with fish.[54] A man, accused of heresy, lost his house; after his death, his son and daughter begged for the return of their mother's half, swearing that she was 'orthodox'.[55]

The most personal possessions were not exempt. One cleric had his clothes taken.[56] Other cases were almost humorous, as when a woman demanded the return of a fine imposed on her husband for adultery: the one he had lain with was nothing but a prostitute, she protested.[57] One bailiff, seeking to shift blame for extortions to his seneschal, charged that the latter or his wife always exacted a big cut of what he got: four silver cups on one occasion, a palfrey worth 13 livres on another.[58] No question but that many royal officers were enriched by their exactions. One bailiff was reported to have married his son off to a wealthy heiress, whose own fortune stemmed from—a confiscation.[59]

A large number of the listed extortions occurred at Poitiers itself. Burghers and churchmen were both habitual victims.[60] The most prominent establishments were not safe from lawless acts of agents of the crown. Notre-Dame-la-Grande was partly wrecked by royal officers come to seize some men who had taken asylum there.[61] Another time, its important Rogations collections were violently confiscated.[62] Even the *rente* for an anniversary at this church was seized, as was a forest supplying the income of a prebend at Ste-Radegonde.[63] The bishop himself was a frequent victim, filing twelve complaints on one occasion.[64] As late as 1278, the 'grave invasions' of his rights by royal officials continued to be so frequent that Pope Nicholas III had to grant the prelate special powers of excommunication against the violators.[65]

Surely the most paradoxical feature of this vast extortionate programme was the way it was spurred by Alphonse's hectic drive for Crusade funds. The prince's seneschals could hardly have remained indifferent to his clamorous and repeated admonitions that the time of departure was 'drawing closer every day' or to his demands that they 'put pains and study into the pursuit of deniers for us in the greatest quantity that you can. . . .'.[66]

The enormous anticipated cost of the Crusades was the goad that blurred all other considerations.[67] A knight's yearly salary was 15 livres (about the price of a stained-glass lancet), a crossbowman's half that amount, to say nothing of the cost of their equipment. And there were hundreds of each that Alphonse had to hire. One seignior, who contracted to supply ten chevaliers, got an hereditary annuity of 80 livres as compensation (enough to pay the annual wages of ten or twelve sculptors or masons).[68] True, only a part of Alphonse's fund came from direct confiscations, a goodly portion being the result of sales of forests and lands from his western domains.[69] But these had all been expropriated in the first place and in any case the money from their alienation permanently left the country.

An ethical low in Alphonse's fund-raising efforts was his pledge to the burghers of Poitiers, made shortly before his departure for the 1248 Crusade, to expel the city's important colony of Jews. The citizens undoubtedly expected to benefit by a cancellation of their debts and agreed to pay Alphonse a permanent fee of 4 sous per 'hearth' to compensate him for his important loss of revenue stemming from the expellees. The Jews managed to buy off their eviction for a large sum, reportedly 1,000 livres. But Alphonse continued to collect the hearth tax, nevertheless.[70]

Results of these various expedients can be followed year by year in Alphonse's steadily mounting balance at the great Templars' bank in Paris. At low ebb on his return from his first Crusade in 1251, the account read 37,421 livres. It was already doubled by 1263 and shot up steeply thereafter: to 104,566 livres in 1265 and attained 385,592 livres by 1268. Historians venture that by the time Alphonse left France in mid-1270, he carried with him close to 500,000 livres.[71] This fantastic sum would have been adequate to build half a dozen great cathedrals from chevet to façade. It is certain that Poitou's share of lost treasure would have sufficed to terminate expeditiously and splendidly its episcopal church. Instead, St-Pierre's construction continued to drag on, broken by lengthy pauses and marked by cramping economy. After its sculptured portals were done, the façade's upper areas assumed a spartan form and the unadorned and unfinished towers went on a-building forever.

It was not the cathedral alone that suffered. There was very little church-building done in Poitiers altogether in the thirteenth century,[72] aside from two mendicant structures of lesser importance. The modest accomplishment of the friars here was confined to churches of the Dominicans and Franciscans. The former were given an already built chapel by the cathedral chapter, to which the bishop added a house for the monks to live in. In 1249, these friars were permitted to change their chapel into a refectory and to erect a new church in its place. It probably was not very impressive since it was very quickly built.[73] The Franciscans' story is even less noteworthy since they did not obtain a permanent site until 1295.[74]

An extraordinary number of Poitiers's other churches that were in use in the thirteenth and fourteenth centuries had been built in the eleventh or even earlier. This was true of fully twenty of the twenty-seven church units for which we have found some documentation. Five of the others were built in the eleventh century with some subsequent changes and one entirely in the twelfth century.[75] Local art historians do not seem to have recognized this preponderantly early building record of Poitiers's churches and one of them has even suggested that it was their late construction that made it unnecessary for them to be rebuilt in the thirteenth or fourteenth centuries![76] Unnecessary or impossible? For if the cathedral suffered from Poitiers's systematic impoverishment, how much more would this be true of the lesser churches?

Erection in the eleventh century or earlier of almost the totality of Poitiers's important abbey or collegiate churches confirms this trend.[77] The only exception is the Abbey of Fontaine-le-Comte, which lay in the city's outskirts and was established in the first third of the twelfth century.[78] Substantiation of the early dating of these edifices can be found in the record of the patronage that made their building possible.

This is supplied, largely, by the remarkable, voluminous transcriptions of an excellent eighteenth-century archivist, Dom Fonteneau, which show that more than two-and-a-half times as many pious donations occurred in the tenth and eleventh centuries as in the twelfth and thirteenth.[79]

That the vast majority of these very early donors were non-burghers is not surprising. And even in the thirteenth century, we know of only two middle-class foundations of any importance, both of them modest hospices, one of which was established in the name of the city aldermancy.[80] And the fourteenth century was memorable solely for a series of donations to the Augustins by the Berland family, one of the city's richest, which has merited it the name of *fundator* of this monastery.[81] Two laymen, Jean Chandos and Guillaume de Felton, are likewise listed as founders of the Carmelite convent, in 1361–9. But neither of them was a burgher, nor even a citizen of Poitiers.

The first man was an English general, in fact, and seneschal of Poitou during that country's reoccupancy of the province in 1360–72. In making his important gift, Chandos designated it as 'an act of grace for the victory of Maupertuis'.[82] The reference was to the famous early battle of the Hundred Years War that took place near Poitiers in 1356. Here the French army was ignominiously routed, King Jean taken prisoner and the country's most disastrous era opened.

While documented burgher benevolence to the cathedral and other Poitiers churches is sparse, the wanton destruction of archives by the Huguenots in 1562 must assume a considerable part of the blame for this. Responsible Poitiers archivists like Dom Fonteneau and René Crozet allude to lay patronage at St-Pierre as an indubitable fact while giving hardly any solid proof for it. After a good deal of searching, I found a few chaplaincies, anniversaries and other gifts by laymen to the cathedral but they are too meagre to constitute a credible record. One would almost think that the Protestant iconoclasts had deliberately sought to obscure the sources of patronage at the cathedral by smashing the lower panels of its glass lancets (they were easily accessible to a club-swinging zealot), in which donor 'signatures' or other revealing emblems are often contained.[83]

Nor can the lack of burgher donorship at Poitiers be attributed to a basic economic deficiency in the city. Hardly a first-rate commercial centre, Poitiers's position as the capital of the great western provinces did nevertheless bring much wealth to it, proofs of the enrichment of a few of its citizens being available.[84] However, data of this kind alone, as we have already seen, do not give a trustworthy picture of a city's economic state and that of Poitiers unquestionably suffered greatly from the systematic extortions of the French conquerors. The notorious weakness of the city government at Poitiers, a demonstrable consequence of the occupation, would inevitably be translated into economic loss. Its municipal charter, which was won very late— 1222—was a grant of Philippe-Auguste, meant to tie the city to France. It was tainted from the beginning by important shortcomings.[85] One of these, the military obligation, made the city's militia actually an adjunct of the crown rather than, as in the proud instance of Strasbourg, an independent arm of the powerful bourgeoisie.[86]

Poitiers's charter likewise established a built-in weakness in the city's rights of jurisdiction, with high justice reserved to the crown, thus shunting the most important cases away from burgher control.[87] The city's courts were also limited to causes occurring within the walls and were categorically denied jurisdiction over the rich ecclesiastic suburbs.[88] This failure of Poitiers's justice to extend beyond the city limits meant, moreover, that it was incapable of protecting its out-of-town property or that of its citizens. The former contingency arose repeatedly in connection with the great Guillaume Gabet endowment, for example, payments on its rural components often being halted on the flimsiest of pretences.[89]

The lack of pith in Poitiers's municipality was reflected in various other damaging ways. An example was the exclusive, hereditary right enjoyed by a single family, the Berlands, to establish a fair. Granted in 1187 by Richard the Lion Heart for unknown reasons, this seigniorial privilege went on for centuries, winning its possessors the title of 'Lords of the Market'.[90] Another typifying case was that of the city's inability to buy off until the end of the thirteenth century the tax rights that a nobleman enjoyed over all sales of wine, salt and bread. The price demanded for the abolition of this privilege was 650 livres, which the burghers could not raise. It was only after the death of Guillaume Gabet that this became possible when the city channelled off part of the churchman's magnificent bequest for that purpose.[91]

Analogous prerogatives enjoyed at the cost of the feeble municipality were never shaken. One of these was the tax on wheat which the Abbey Du Pin possessed, likewise by gift of Richard I and which was upheld by the French crown as late as 1307, after Philippe-le-Bel had shrewdly acquired half the benefits.[92] Both curious and amazing, too, was the city's obligation to turn over the keys to the town gates every year to Notre-Dame-la-Grande for the three days of Rogations, with all the tax privileges that went with this possession.[93] This blemish on the city's dignity and drain on its income lasted far into the later centuries, though the surrender of the keys was eventually cloaked in a solemn ceremonial.[94]

Emancipation from such feudal economic trammels being the overriding concern of burghers, their continued subjection to them at Poitiers was almost *prima facie* proof of financial incapacity, which prejudiced inevitably their church donorship as well.

Was Poitiers, finally, inherently attached to archaic forms? For this is a phenomenon that we do meet up with in the medieval period. While trying to answer this question we must not lose sight of the fact that so very little church-building (only the abbreviated naves of the cathedral and of Ste-Radegonde) took place there altogether all through the thirteenth century and that this in itself would have tended to limit the evolution of new architectural forms. But even so, there is plenty of evidence that, far from systematically rejecting innovation, Poitiers's builders were from early times open to stylistic change.

At Notre-Dame-la-Grande, for example, a discovery in the last century brought to light a great twelfth-century fresco in the choir vault presenting Christ in Majesty, the Virgin and Child and the twelve Apostles, together with flights of angels and groups of the Elect. This painting has been qualified as one of the most 'gracious' compositions of Romanesque art, though this is impossible to verify today because of the unsightly nineteenth-century restoration. And yet, already in the thirteenth century, it was covered over with whitewash and some other—presumably more 'modern'—decoration substituted.[95]

Even earlier, the willingness of the church authorities at Poitiers to undertake architectural transformations on a grandiose scale had been demonstrated, of all places, at the great collegiate church of St-Hilaire. Built by the famed Gautier Coorland and completed around 1080, the edifice was only a few decades later subjected to far-ranging alterations—vaulting, choir, ambulatory, *absidioles*—which fairly transfigured it. Part of this large-scale project called for the construction of crossing ogives in the clock-tower vaulting, a work that has been qualified as 'the timid beginnings of Gothic architecture in Poitou'.[96]

Whatever else thirteenth-century Poitiers may have been, it was not 'anti-Gothic' either since the only major building that did take place in this century was done in

33. North wall of Ste-Radegonde's 'new' nave: the windows of the first two bays still retain the narrow, Romanesque form inside the Gothic upper arches

that style, even if to an extent still in the 'Angevin-Gothic' mode. While hardly as ambitious as the Île-de-France variety, it nevertheless strove to attain the same effects that normally typify this great form: spaciousness, luminosity. During the century that it took to put up the very short naves of the cathedral and Ste-Radegonde, we find significant technical changes tending to 'Gothicize' these churches. This is most evident in the window-forms, though other features reveal a similar trend.

At Ste-Radegonde particularly, the transition in window-styling can be studied very graphically. In its first two bays, probably begun in the late twelfth century and continuing on into the thirteenth, the nave windows were still given the narrow Romanesque form, probably because of a lingering fear of weakening the carrying capacity of the walls by opening them more widely. Since Ste-Radegonde with its single vessel was to get neither supporting aisles nor flying buttresses, this timidity was at least theoretically understandable.

In the church's last two bays, however, in the latter part of the century, after the prolonged halt in work already mentioned,[97] the entire upper wall space was laid bare by windows created in the full cry of the current Gothic technique. Clearly, the builders no longer lacked audacity. Their adaptation to the great new style would also seem to have been complete.

It must have been considerations of economy that prompted the abandonment of an even more ambitious project at Ste-Radegonde: that of tearing down the beautiful eleventh-century choir and substituting a new one for it.[98] With our present penchant for the early Romanesque we can only breathe a sigh of gratitude that this plan was not carried out.

But there are reasons to believe that the important renovating programme was indeed seriously weighed by the church authorities after the new nave had been completed. This can be conjectured from the remaining fragments of what must have been intended to be the first bay of the new choir. These remnants can be seen at the cut-off ends of the nave-walls at the beginning of the choir, including especially the cornice sculptures (modillions) that must have been meant to continue the series that runs the entire length of the nave on both north and south sides. These initiating forms seem clearly to illustrate a firm decision that for whatever reasons could not be fulfilled.

Nothing, however, permits us to conclude that the failure to continue the project was due to second thoughts about wanting to spare the lovely old choir.

34. A bay of the north wall of Ste-Radegonde's 'new' nave: the windows of the final two bays were done in advanced Gothic. Note in contrast the Romanesque form of the blind arcade beneath

Ste-Radegonde's canons of that period were probably no more attached to its charms than were their successors of the fifteenth century who provided the early Romanesque front porch with a flamboyant portal!

During the first half of the fourteenth century, as had been the case throughout the thirteenth, money for church-building at Poitiers was hardly plentiful. And thereafter, we must make allowances for the Hundred Years War. Not only were resources exhausted in its pursuit but the western capital was itself occupied and pillaged, the entire province laid bare. This drastically reduced earnings of church groups from their landed holdings, ruling out architectural undertakings of almost any kind.[99]

It is not until the fifteenth century that one begins to see important work done on a number of churches at Poitiers. This was, for instance, the period when the vaults of the brief three-bay nave and north collateral were built at the church of St-Germain[100] and when the choir was rebuilt and most of the burgher-endowed chapels at Notre-Dame-la-Grande were added.[101] It was not until the sixteenth century that the parish church of St-Paul was totally rebuilt[102] and the new nave of St-Porchaire done, while fortunately conserving the handsome Romanesque porch-belltower.[103]

It was during a lull in the hostilities in the last quarter of the fourteenth century, after the great Du Guesclin had cleared the English out of Poitou, that the Palais des Comtes was partially rebuilt in splendid flamboyant style by that renowned patron of the arts, Duke Jean de Berry.[104] And around the same time, the only other major project of the latter half of this century was undertaken when the magnificent abbey church of Montierneuf had its upper choir redone in lofty, majestic Gothic with seven great double windows opening the sanctuary to a vast periphery.[105]

One is struck, nevertheless, by the strangeness of this soaring structure set down on the Romanesque base. This impression is reinforced when one passes to the exterior and notes the incongruous fit between the new upper choir and the old, low-lying nave, whose roof seems to be several metres beneath the former's aspiring canopy. No doubt the choir had to be cut off short because the nave vaulting could not have been raised to a more harmonious elevation without a mammoth reconstruction of the whole gigantic edifice.[106] Or was such a project actually contemplated and later abandoned because it was found to be beyond the capacity of even this richly-endowed abbey?

Whatever the case, this curious amalgam at Montierneuf seems a fitting symbol of Poitiers's architectural history. Most of its edifices were built early, often largely

35. Montierneuf: showing how the high Gothic choir with its flying buttresses was inserted into a totally Romanesque ensemble. Concealed by the transept to the right is the long nave, dropping far below the choir

funded by the benevolence of its counts. Their preponderant monumental style—the Romanesque—has in the main been preserved, though all have sustained important changes. The maintenance of the early form was not, we have suggested, due to resistance to new stylistic modes but rather to more basic circumstances, notably economic ones.

These aesthetic consequences were a part of the great socio-political complex surrounding the conquest of the west and its absorption into France, which can amply explain the extraordinary retention of old structures in the Poitou on a basis other than artistic taste. Choice was in any case hardly free. It was largely imposed by the prevailing conditions which spelled out a stylistic destiny which may only give the impression of being willed.

8

ROUEN

The Wages of Submission

Rouen Cathedral Chronology

1155	Rebuilding of the Romanesque church, which had been consecrated in 1063, is begun.
Pre-1165	North-west Tower of St-Romain is built.
1170–80	West façade is erected but portal sculpture is not done until after 1250.
End of 12C	Four or five bays of the new nave are completed.
1200	A fire does serious damage but evidently spares the new work. After repairs, reconstruction resumes in 1206.
1225–50	Remainder of nave and new choir (begun 1214) are completed.
1250–75	Tympanum sculpture of façade portals is carved. The transept is completed.
End of 13C	Its north and south façades, with brilliantly sculptured portals (*Libraires* and *Calendes*), are done by the end of thirteenth century and beginning of the fourteenth.
*c.*1300	Nave-aisle chapels built between vertical buttresses, part of the pre-1250 glass being re-employed in new windows.
14C	Much reconstruction undertaken, notably on façade. Also, high windows of nave and choir are enlarged at the end of the century. Some glass of apse also is reglazed.
*c.*1406	New central portal of west façade is begun when flaw in foundation is discovered.
1430	Lower apse windows are enlarged.
1457–69	The choir-stalls, largely devoted to scenes of Rouen's workaday world, are carved.
1468–78	Last storey added to Tower of St-Romain.
1485–1506	New 'Tour de Beurre' is built at south end of western façade.
1509–14	Great central portal of façade, evidently threatening to fall after a fire, is totally rebuilt, featuring the tympanum representation of the 'Jesse Tree'. During about the same period, the high interior façade is built.

IT IS HISTORICALLY ANOMALOUS THAT THE GREAT DUKEDOM OF NORMANDY, from which the predatory hordes had so long terrorized France, should have been spared the worst effects of the Capetian turnabout. Rouen went over to the French in 1204 without a fight and was, accordingly, spared those forty years of bitter retribution that were the lot of Poitou and the other western provinces and which ended in the crushing débâcle of 1242.

Was this difference in historic background reflected in the building history of Rouen's cathedral? Its early course, before the French conquest, was close enough to that of Poitiers's church. Notre-Dame was begun somewhat in advance of St-Pierre, around 1155, starting from the west, and its pace was fairly steady, the façade (built 1170–80) and north tower and four or five bays of the new nave being erected by the century's end.[1] Meanwhile, St-Pierre, built in the opposite direction, could show an equivalent accomplishment. When, in 1200, a bad fire occurred at Rouen, one might expect it to have fallen behind its rival. But the new work was evidently spared and swift repairs rendered the damaged parts serviceable by about 1206.

Where the two churches parted company was in style. That of Rouen was more advanced throughout. And when work was resumed on its nave after the fire, this progressive character was accentuated.[2] No one is likely to credit this development to the influence of the French king, Philippe-Auguste, who seems to have paid scant attention to Rouen's cathedral. He was much more interested, clearly, in the swift erection of his great citadel that would vigilantly overlook the conquered capital.

Nevertheless, in contrast to St-Pierre, the construction of Notre-Dame proceeded without known pauses. Its vessel was completed by the second quarter of the thirteenth century and, at the end of that century, its two great transept portals—the celebrated *Calendes* and *Libraires*—richer than the embellished arms of Paris's cathedral were done.[3] Funds were likewise available to fit out the church's great window spaces with stained-glass, most of it glazed before 1250.[4]

This pace, though not matching the speed of Amiens, Paris or Chartres, was very creditable and certainly surpassed the achievement of Poitiers's episcopal church. Where did the money come from? Not from the conquering dynasty, it is positive, for whose endowments we have fairly complete documentation. This applies particularly to St Louis, who is not mentioned in a single gratification to Rouen cathedral's building fund. And surely if Philippe-Auguste had been responsible for any important gift to it, his elegist, Guillaume Le Breton, would have blown it up extravagantly.[5]

In the earlier period, as at Poitiers, the Plantagenets had proved far more liberal as cathedral patrons than the Capetians were to be. But this is hardly surprising since Normandy was home to them, still more a home than England at the end of the twelfth century. Henry II is not credited with any gift to the cathedral fabric itself but we do find him making important donations to the archbishop and the chapter.[6] Furthermore, several huge gifts by Henry to the building programmes of other Rouen churches are catalogued, largely financed from his taxes on the river commerce at Rouen, gathered by the so-called Vicomté de l'Eau. The most notable case was the *ex voto* church that he dedicated to his illustrious victim, Thomas à Becket, to whom he had prayed, patently with success, to lift the siege of Rouen in 1174, during his war with the revolting barons.[7]

Henry's successor, Richard, was a documented donor of a very important grant to the cathedral, a *rente* of 300 measures of wine, worth annually 300 livres, a third going to the chapter and two-thirds to the archbishop. The latter post was held at the time by Gauthier de Coutances, a famous English churchman and close associate of the sovereign.[8]

King John's gifts, finally, were offered directly to the cathedral fabric and were the most considerable of all, perhaps, which is surprising in a man who was far from devout.[9] His great donation of 2,000 livres, made in 1202, which permitted the swift repair of damage after the fire of 1200, was the more memorable in that it came at a time when his own money needs were desperate. On one occasion, shortly before his expulsion from the continent, when the royal exchequer failed to send in the fabric's yearly quota, the king intervened personally to see that this was promptly done.[10]

But the aid of the Plantagenets was all too soon ended and Capetian gifts did not make up for the loss. The cathedral cartulary is almost devoid of pertinent information[11] but there are other data indicating that Rouen's churchmen and the commoners were the chief sources of the cathedral's building finances. The well-known seventeenth-century local historian, François Farin, for example, reports that the chapter had 'put aside funds for the purpose and named a master of the fabric to be in charge of their administration'. This arrangement lasted until the middle of the thirteenth century,[12] he adds, and we can only take him at his word since whatever evidence he had is now gone.

We have, on the other hand, visible proofs of the Rouen burghers' lively participation in the cathedral's building programme. In a letter written in 1198 in which

36. Rouen cathedral's Gothic nave. The metropolitan church, built more swiftly and on a grander dimension than Poitiers's cathedral, no doubt benefited by Normandy's early and peaceful absorption into France

Innocent III urges the chapter to energize the work, the pope alludes to the possible role of the mayor and councilmen.[13] In lieu of documents, we have other evidence that when the appeal was made it met with singular success. This appears in that most trustworthy of records—stained-glass lancets—where work-scene donor 'signatures' have been identified for the fishmongers, cloth-shearers, carpenters, leather-dressers, masons and church-builders (twice), all contributions of the first half of the thirteenth century.[14]

It is hardly surprising that this list of guild donors should include the city's two most important handworking industries, leather and cloth. As for river commerce, far and away Rouen's most remunerative occupation, it too had its place in the cathedral's illustrative glass though we no longer know its amount or character. All that remains of it now are a pair of donor panels at the Musée des Antiquités. Dated stylistically as post-1250,[15] these magnificent pieces depict a group of longshoremen who are lifting heavily loaded bags from the hull of a boat and carrying them up a ladder. It is in all likelihood grain that has been moved up the Seine from the great wheat-producing regions of central France and is in the process of being reloaded onto larger, ocean-going ships.

The existence of so many burgher-endowed lancets at the cathedral (and how many others have disappeared?) calls forth visions of the active guild and confraternity life that is known to have existed there. Nine of these organizations are documented at Notre-Dame,[16] all of which had their festival days, weekly masses and funerary observations, to say nothing of the anniversaries and chaplaincies that individual members arranged for themselves.[17]

37. Rouen's Seine-River longshoremen: donor panels from a vanished stained-glass window lancet of the cathedral, representing work scenes from the city's leading activity, ocean-bound commerce

It is markworthy, moreover, that when the cathedral's chantry chapels were built late in the thirteenth century or early in the fourteenth to house more conveniently all this active altar-life, an operation which called for the cutting out of greater window spaces to avoid darkening of the church's interior, the guildsmen's lancets, at least those we know of, were retained, sliced to fit into the new window-framing.[18] It is probable that this was done at the insistence of these organizations, which may mean that we owe to the early guilds of Rouen the preservation of some of the most precious storied glass of the thirteenth century.

Included in this treasure, for example, is the sole lancet of this period that we know which is signed by the artist: *Clemens vitrearius carnotensis m(e fecit)*— 'Clement, glassmaker of Chartres, made me'. It furnishes us with a further proof, moreover, of the free commerce of artistic creativity that existed at that time and to which we adverted in the previous chapter. Another set of the 'signature' panels, that of the cloth-shearers, who donated the lancet dedicated to Joseph, possessor of the 'coat of many colours', adds incidentally to our information of the kind of ritualistic activity that surrounded these organizations.

Different from the typical presentation of some appropriate operation of the trade, the three great shears depicted in the donor panels are not shown in the process, say, of clipping the nap of the wool-cloth surface. Rather, the tools are held erect in formal stances while a mysterious pattern of activity takes place around them, involving especially the pouring and drinking of wine. It is almost inescapable that what is occurring here is a kind of blessing of the instruments of the cloth-shearers' trade, talismanic gestures that reflect the medieval world's devout attitude toward work.

Most important of all such celebrations by the cathedral's fraternal groups was one enjoyed by the Confrérie de Notre-Dame, which was made up of the wealthiest merchants and their wives. It was attached to the cathedral's leading chapel, dedicated to the Virgin, which occupied the treasured central space of the apse ambulatory, directly behind the choir.[19] Since the twelfth century, this group had been the primary actors in what was called the 'Privilege of St Romain',[20] probably the great church's most spectacular annual ceremony.

Of unknown origin, it called for a sumptuous procession to the ducal prison, where a condemned criminal was delivered into the care of the confraternity. The lucky man or woman was then accompanied back to the cathedral, where he was received in the Chapel of the Virgin by a leading member of the group, who, symbolizing the eternal forgiveness that all men hoped to win at the hands of God, liberally endowed the sinner for his return to normal life.[21] This central position of a burgher group in so stellar a sacerdotal function strongly suggests a key role in any important undertaking such as the rebuilding of the cathedral.

Given the poor condition of Notre-Dame's archives, it is not surprising to find that there are few important gifts documented for individual burghers to the cathedral's building fund since the same is true of representatives of all other social groups.[22] All the more satisfying, therefore, is the evidence of such gifts in two further donor panels, both in the Chapel of St-John-the-Baptist-near-the-Fonts. One of them depicts an unidentified woman kneeling before the Christ of the Baptism, while the other actually names the donor in an inscription. It is Ace (or Azon) le Tort, a well-known burgher of great wealth, who left a testament, dated 1266, in which he provided bequests for a number of local churches.[23]

Among his numerous foundations, one finds an arrangement for a cathedral chaplaincy, which surely was celebrated in this Chapel of St-John-the-Baptist, before the lancet which he had donated.[24] Actually, this provision for a daily mass in the name of Azon le Tort was only one of a long list of similar foundations established by commoners at Notre-Dame.[25] They give one more indication—an important one, to be sure—of the strong interest that Rouen's bourgeoisie manifested in their cathedral and which goes far to explain the favourable course of its construction.

This impressive record of middle-class patronage would seem to denote a cordial relationship between Rouen's burghers and the cathedral hierarchy. Though this was true in the main, there was one early period of acute conflict between the two groups, whose consequences might have been seriously aggravated if the power of both had not been sharply limited. Especially toward the end of the Plantagenet regime did the situation become embroiled, a result no doubt of the progressive breakdown in authority. It was during Richard's prolonged absence at the 1190 Crusade and his subsequent captivity that burgher-church differences erupted into violence.

As so often occurred in such situations, the trouble was touched off by an arbitrary act. In this case, it was the unilateral decision of the canons to build a high wall about the cathedral compound, inside which they established shops for artisans and tradesmen. Since the latter were exempt from the charges and regulations required of other members of these trades, the reaction of the municipality was immediate: they tore down the enclosure. The chapter retorted by putting the entire city under excommunication, extending themselves in melodramatic detail by ordering the snuffing out of church torches, the removal of crosses from altars and the veiling of statues, in addition to the halting of all offices.

This first interdict lasted six months while the bodies of the dead gathered in the public squares. At Easter, their patience at an end, the city authorities decided to open the churches by force and with sympathetic priests brought in from the outside conducted mass and provided communion. The chapter responded by excommunicating the illicit officiants. At this point, the enraged burghers broke into the cathedral cloister, killing some canons and cutting off the genitalia of others.[26] The intercession of the archbishop and two popes did not succeed in resolving the controversy.[27]

This was hardly surprising in the light of the 'settlement' that was imposed by the arbiters, the city being ordered to pay reparations and rebuild the wall. It staved off doing so for half a century, finally acceding to St Louis's conciliation. But the enclosure that resulted was a mere token, only four feet high. In return, the city's supervisory authority over the trade activity that went on inside the enclosed area was tacitly recognized by the church.[28]

That the bitterness had by this time long gone out of the contention is proved by the fact that in the intervening period a large proportion of the known burgher contributions to the cathedral-building programme occurred. The establishment of a firm authority after France's takeover of Rouen certainly had something to do with mitigating the sharpness of the conflict. What the incident illustrates, besides, is that the church did not have the power to impose its will on the bourgeoisie. Rouen was not Lyon, where the archbishop was the sovereign and an autocrat. The political chance that curbed the sway of Rouen's chief ecclesiastic greatly benefited the building fate of its cathedral.

On the other hand, Rouen was not Toulouse either during that city's great 'age of liberty'. Still the Norman capital did possess a body of rights of considerable importance, indispensable to so active a commercial centre. Their acquisition had begun in the early part of the twelfth century, at the latest, and under Geoffrey, the first Plantagenet duke of Normandy (1144–52), Rouen had gained franchises of indisputable significance.[29] Confirmed by his son, Henry II, the charter covered trade advantages, particularly, on the Seine and especially in England and Ireland.[30] These grants fell far short of giving Rouen the status of a commune on the Amiens or Strasbourg model, however, since basic rights of justice and political power were lacking.[31] The Plantagenets, inheriting William the Conqueror's authoritarian methods, kept their cities under strict control.

A significant advance in the municipality's position came around 1174, none the less, after Rouen's burghers courageously defended their city against Henry II's enemies at a critical point of his war with the barons.[32] The famed *Établissements de Rouen*, probably granted then, served as a model in the entire western region for many decades and was wisely confirmed by Philippe-Auguste after his victory.[33] This confirmation was, in fact, part of the agreement of 1204 whereby Rouen went over peacefully to France. The burghers, who were joined by the knights and other elements of the population in the capitulation, received additional pledges from the French that their continental trading rights would be honoured.[34]

The middle class has often been ironically treated by authors for being prone to put business interests above patriotism. The records are eloquent, on the contrary, as to how the barons of the west repeatedly huckstered their fealty to the highest bidder whereas it was often the commoners who remained loyal.[35] The burghers of La Rochelle, for example, suffered grievous aggressions by the count of Lusignan and other great seigniors of the western regions, yet they maintained their attachment to the Plantagenets for many years. They went over to the French only when it was clear that the English were incapable of preserving peace.[36]

It was this need for peace and security in their trading pursuits which above all else determined the political judgments of the bourgeoisie. In 1204, when the burghers of Rouen made the hard decision to surrender their city to Philippe-Auguste, they knew that by so doing they would be sacrificing their favoured position in the commercial structure of England. Yet the realization must have grown inexorably that the Plantagenets could thereafter bring them nothing but continued war, devastation and ruin of trade, in a contest that was plainly doomed.[37]

Normandy was financially exhausted in the end. Indeed, this condition had been long evolving. In 1184, already, after Henry II had spent many thousands of livres to build his defences against Philippe-Auguste's increasingly dangerous thrusts, his bailiff's summary report read: *In thesauro nichil* ('Nothing left in the treasury'). And Richard's reign, besides continuing such military extravagances, had its own ruinous specialties like the Holy Land adventure of 1190, the king's ransom of 150,000 marks that ended it and the nearly 50,000 livres required for the building of Château-Gaillard, which did not save Normandy from the French, after all.[38] In his feeble attempt to stave off the final débâcle, after having mulcted Normandy 'dry', John had to run back to England to refill his coffers so that he might continue the war, bringing to the continent 48,320 livres in 1203 alone.[39]

There was never any doubt that the Capetians regarded the absorption of Normandy as an alien conquest, however. After 1204, Philippe-Auguste proceeded systematically to hand over great parcels of his newly acquired domains to court favourites, seigniors, churchmen, burghers, even to ordinary soldiers and archers or personal servitors like his barber.[40] The top royal officers who administered the invested province were exclusively French throughout the century.[41]

Only the lower echelons were filled by local men, who, buying up the 'farms' of royal exploitation, served their own interests more aggressively than seneschals or bailiffs served those of the crown.[42] The result of these concerted efforts can be read in the royal accounts, with Rouen alone bringing the king over 7,000 livres in 1230. And other Norman towns mined out equivalent sums.[43] The churches too were made to pay their share, in the way of 'defence' subsidies, which were rigorously collected by Eudes Rigaud, St Louis's close friend and finance minister, whom that king had designated archbishop of the conquered province.[44] In the end, Normandy's contributions to the royal treasury were, as a modern historian has declared, 'far larger than other regions of equal size'.[45]

As in the western provinces, the explicit proofs of exploitation that speak most limpidly are the 'inquests' that the virtuous grandson of Philippe-Auguste launched into the multiple injustices that had resulted from the occupation. St Louis's great investigation of 1247–8, first of the famous series, was given the poetic-sounding name of *Querimoniae Normannorum*—'Norman Complaints'.[46] Though somewhat less extensive than those of Poitou or Languedoc, many a tragedy is revealed by their contents, the aggregate of which constituted an enormous and long-lasting drain on the wealth of Normandy.[47]

It is one of the ironies of this vast extraction that the haloed king's pieties were responsible for an important part of it. His charities, no less than the brutally extorted fines and ransoms, dispossessed the land from which their endowment funds were withdrawn. Some of St Louis's most famous foundations were beneficiaries, notably the Abbey of Royaumont, a celebrated favourite of the king's benevolence, whose major revenue came from lands and forests of Normandy which had fallen into the royal domain.[48] Part of this money was drawn from over 2,000 acres of land which had been colonized by peasants, in the form of the yearly rent of 500 livres that they paid to the king for the right to till the soil.[49]

The extortionate measures suffered by Rouen's middle class at the hands of the French were somewhat balanced by the peace it won under them, almost a century's worth, a rare and appreciated guerdon.[50] But the burghers lost more than they had expected in their economic status, over and above the anticipated cancellation of their English advantages.[51] It was inevitable that Paris, traditionally Rouen's greatest rival, should now be the chief gainer through its decline, all the more so that by their geographic position the two cities were inevitably competitive, both being inland ports on the great Seine waterway, for whom free access to and from the sea was of preponderant importance.

Rouen's advantageous position had been assured under the Norman dukes and Plantagenet kings, both in the control of the Seine's outlet and upriver as well, almost to the outskirts of Paris.[52] Very soon after the conquest of Normandy, however, Rouen's prerogatives began to be gnawed away. One of the French crown's earliest acts of an economic nature was to forbid the passage of wine from the Poitou-Aquitaine region by way of the Seine into central France.[53] The measure was a serious blow for Rouen, whose greatest revenues came from the toll on this commerce.

Philippe-Auguste matched this order by the almost equally damaging decree that wine exported from Burgundy was thereafter to enjoy free passage down the Seine, past Rouen.[54] A further blow, in the mid-century, was the decision of the parliament of Paris in banning the free use of the port of Mantes, a key calling-place on the way to the capital, by Rouen's boat-owners.[55] In striking contrast, Paris's position on the Seine was strengthened when its boatmen were permitted to go the full length of the river out to the Channel while paying toll only to the king.[56] The drastic effect of these measures is revealed by the sharp drop in the fee that could be charged for the farm of the king's tax-collections at Rouen, which went down from 6,000 livres in 1180 to less than one-third that amount by 1298.[57]

That Rouen's steadily worsening economic situation did not disrupt the cathedral's building programme is largely due to the fact that the decline was gradual and the worst effects of the regression were not felt until late in the thirteenth century, after the major part of the edifice was completed. Even so, Notre-Dame took a century and a half to build.[58] A better performance could have been expected from what still remained for some time after the conquest the second most important city on the territory of France. Economically notable as a producer of leather, shoes and drapery, Rouen was a commercial port without a peer. It was also the great archdiocesan capital of 1,388 parish churches.[59]

But it was not the cathedral that suffered most from the effects of the French conquest and the occupation of Normandy. Despite the relative slowness of its construction, Notre-Dame made up for it in magnitude and decorative richness. But this accomplishment was just about the full extent of independent church-building that took place in the affluent Norman capital during the thirteenth century. The rest of Rouen's many churches paid the price of the city's subjugation.

Construction work on the parish churches or even on wealthy abbeys or priories virtually halted during the entire century or was confined at best to indispensable post-incendiary reparation.[60] General church-building at Rouen was not fully resumed until the fifteenth century or later, though it must be said that the subsequent destruction of the great majority of its parishes has left us without categorical proof of the extent of the cessation of building enterprise which stylistic study alone could supply.[61]

Only a few convents of the new mendicant orders enjoyed a lively building experience during the thirteenth century. But this to an overwhelming degree was due to the benefactions of St Louis, which, as has already been noted, were largely based on earnings of his Norman acquisitions. Most richly subsidized by the king were the so-called *Emmurées* ('Walled-in Sisters'), a group of Dominican nuns. Louis not only paid for their conventual buildings but also put to their account an annuity of no less than 400 livres.[62] This was almost half enough to have financed all the cathedral's yearly construction needs.

St Louis also made bountiful assignments of funds from the royal revenues of Normandy to other mendicant groups, helping the Dominicans and Franciscans to establish important colonies throughout the north-western province.[63] His partiality for these orders fed the blazing animosity of Rouen's entire clerical family against them, which displayed itself most violently after the death of St Louis's custodian of the archdiocese, Eudes Rigaud.[64]

In the overall, however, funds for church-building at Rouen were so scarce during the thirteenth century that they were often lacking for badly needed repairs. Many of its churches, besides having been erected early, were often also deprived of stone vaulting. This made them particularly vulnerable to fires, for which Rouen, a city of serried wooden houses and high winds, was notorious, experiencing no fewer than eight conflagrations during this century that were so ruinous as to be chronicled.[65] None of the fire-damaged churches could be rebuilt. Merely patched up, their basic reconstruction is not heard of until the fifteenth century or later.

Several of these church units were hardly poor[66] and it is no less than astonishing to find the extraordinarily opulent Abbey of St-Ouen, Rouen's second most important religious establishment, experiencing difficulty in mustering the funds for rebuilding its church after what must have been very serious damage from the great fire of 1248, one of the worst in the city's annals.[67] The ravages were so extensive that the monks had to leave the abbey and live outside for a lengthy period[68] (in the partial rebuilding, the dormitory and refectory were done first), while abbots could not be buried in the church choir for several decades.[69] St-Ouen was so short in finances, it had to raise 500 marks on its benefices for use of the reparation fund.[70]

Some time prior to 1318, the patched-up chevet of St-Ouen's church collapsed and a total reconstruction became necessary. There followed what was Rouen's most impressive building accomplishment in the entire post-conquest period. Of broad historical importance, besides, is the evidence that this great project furnishes of the liquidation of the conquest and the assimilation of Normandy into France.[71] Not only is this reflected in the oft-vaunted 'pure French' style of the new edifice but also by the very significant role that French royalty played in its funding. This took the form mainly of great cuts of timber that the abbey was allowed to take from the king's Norman forests. Topping off these favourable circumstances was one of those fortunate accidents that occurred very intermittently in the history of a great church: the assumption of its responsibilities by an impassioned builder.

Jean Roussel's nickname could not have been more appropriate—'Marc-d'Argent' ('Silver-Mark')—which seemed to honour his great talent for raising money. Money, indeed a fabulous amount: 63,000 livres of recorded treasure. Even with the livre being pared and slivered by the ever money-needy last Capetians, the sums that Silver-Mark gathered were utterly unprecedented, averaging over 3,000 livres a year. The

38. St-Ouen: a section of the upper choir. Erected by the great builder, Abbot 'Silver-Mark', with strong financial assistance from the French crown. Done in 'pure French' style, St-Ouen seems symbolic of Normandy's full assimilation into France

documents are there to show it: 14,448 livres from the sale of abbey properties; 23,569 livres 'and more' from several cuts of forest; and the rest presumably obtained from the 'faithful'.[72]

These huge sums were, during the two decades of Silver-Mark's abbacy, translated into a building record of almost unsurpassed scope that matches the accomplishment of John Thoresby at York. Completed were the church's great apse, its choir and most of its transept, all of which was fitted out with towering ogives and handsome stained-glass lancets.[73] Also, the adjacent subsidiary church of Ste-Croix-St-Ouen had to be rebuilt when it was found that excavations required by the abbey's new foundations had endangered its stability.[74] The exceptional nature of the achievement stands out the more clearly since it ended abruptly at the death of Silver-Mark. The church was not completed then for almost two hundred years.[75]

We know the reasons for this 'pause'. After Silver-Mark's successor paid the king 2,103 livres for repossession of his temporalities,[76] he was told to proceed to Avignon for the pope's approval. This cost him no less than 15,768 livres and 4 deniers for papal gratifications, scarlet robes for the cardinals 'and other things',[77] which, the St-Ouen *Chronique* reports, blandly, left the new abbey church 'heavily indebted'.[78] The situation grew worse in 1355 when the crown imposed a great fine of 10,000 écus for 'excessive' use of royal timber during Marc-d'Argent's building campaign. To avoid ruin St-Ouen had to sell all its gold and silver vessels and even pawn its relics.[79]

We cannot conclude that this act was peculiarly vindictive or that it reflected on the reality of Normandy's assimilation into France. Not long after, another French king atoned with a huge gift to St-Ouen's fabric.[80] Also, 1355 had been a desperate year for France and 1356 was even worse, bringing the frightful defeat near Poitiers and the capture of King Jean. After that, France's deepest tragic time set in. For almost a century, it appeared to have permanently reversed the great historic trend, begun in 1204, which had carried the country to the acme of power, consolidated by a vast territorial expansion that brought it close to its modern boundaries.

Normandy entered a period of genuine prosperity following the Hundred Years War. The conflict itself seems to have contributed indirectly to this outcome by increasing France's maritime interests from which the northern province's geographic position was bound to profit. Rouen became an important shipbuilding centre dating from

TOMBE DE LAURENT LEBAS ET DE JEANNE SA FEMME.

39. A bourgeois couple taking a boat to heaven: fifteenth-century tombal plaque of Laurent and Jeanne Lebas of Harfleur, Rouen's Channel port, a probably unconscious reflection of the rising importance to France of oceanic exploration and commerce

this period that just preceded Europe's great exploratory epoch. The now extinct parish church, St-Etienne-des-Tonneliers, magnificently rebuilt after the war by its wealthy shipbuilder parishioners, was long a lively symbol of this development.[81] By the evidence of church construction, much of it burgher-sponsored, there can, moreover, be little doubt about a resurgence in the city's economic vitality. What had been impossible to accomplish in the thirteenth century and very difficult in the fourteenth became entirely practicable in the fifteenth. St-Ouen was one of the churches that profited, its huge nave being completed in one sweep starting in 1459.[82]

At least two-thirds of the city's numerous churches—over thirty of them—were entirely or in great part rebuilt during this surge.[83] The most impressive of these projects was the reconstruction of St-Maclou.[84] Originally only a chapel, it had been badly hurt by at least two fires in the early thirteenth century but in both cases had found the means only for summary repair. In the fifteenth century, however, its parishioners, who had greatly increased in numbers and wealth, set to rebuilding their church with unstinting generosity: meshed monumental stonework, dense statuary, thirteen chapels, great lancets above and below. Most of this is gone now and the church itself was reduced to half its original size by the last war. But the sense of splendour is miraculously preserved and St-Maclou remains one of the most attractive medieval edifices of Rouen.

The cathedral itself shared richly in the great renovating wave of the fifteenth and sixteenth centuries. This was when its lofty Tour de Beurre was built, paid for as its name suggests by Lenten indulgences bought by bourgeois gourmands.[85] An even more ambitious programme was that entailed by the remaking of the entire central section of the west front, evidently required, besides, by a fault in the foundation.[86] The major project eventually included double rows of larger-than-life statues in the upper registers, a complete refashioning of the central rose-window and a great sculptured tympanum over the portal with richly figured enfolding arches.

Many of the church's lancets were also reglazed at this time. All of these operations apparently occasioned no financial difficulty. One can, in fact, find in the fabric cartulary, which is gratifyingly informative for this period, great numbers of foundations established by the co-operative bourgeoisie. Especially relished as a reward for their gifts were arrangements for bell-ringing in their name, for which a complicated programme of varying combinations of tinkling and booming sounds could be scheduled, *in perpetuum*, by the week, the day, at the very hour desired.[87]

Notre-Dame's imagery done in the new period has a strongly popular accent. The art of the new central portal seems, in particular, to echo the throb of joy that must have gone up when the long-sighed-for peace was at last attained. How appropriate that the great tree of life rising from Jesse's fecund loins should replace the terror-ridden eschatological scenes of previous centuries.

Even the vulgarity of the period strikes one as imaginative. Who other than the burghers could have thought up that extraordinary scene at the top of St-André's tower nearby, where Adam and Eve after their sin are shown busily unrolling the bolsters of cloth that will be used to cover their nakedness, thus incidentally advertising Rouen's boasted drapery!

It is a similar vein of popular inspiration that animates the great number of little figures in the splayed arches of the cathedral's central portal and in the upper section of the interior façade. The same kind of 'life-of-the-time' carving can be found in the cathedral's choir-stalls, which were done in the mid-fifteenth century. These have

40. A bootmaker and his client: woodcarving of a misericord, c.1460, from the cathedral's choir-stalls, illustrating one of Rouen's two major industries

been much diminished by neglect and war's destruction, one-fourth of them disappearing as late as 1944, from a single bombing. Fortunately, the sketches of a devoted nineteenth-century art historian help us to reconstitute this particular loss.[88]

But there were earlier amputations that have deprived us of the entire upper-stall structure, about which our knowledge is mainly confined to the written word of the original fabric records.[89] They resurrect the figures of apostles and angels and saints with which Philippot Viart, Pol Mosselmen and other woodcarvers peopled the great enclosure. Fate has dealt more tenderly with the stall seats and in particular with their misericords that were carved beneath them. An almost purely secular and bourgeois art, it is nowhere more enchantingly illustrated than here. In a rich variety of domestic scenes and social settings and especially in the trade and artisan tasks performed, the city's vivacious life of five hundred years ago is stirringly recalled.

It is a long way further back from these men and women of mid-fifteenth-century Rouen to that clouded epoch of their early ancestors, whom we have vaguely skirted in our exposition. But these modest underseat carvings help us somewhat to bridge the gap, bringing us closer to the astonishing race from whom these people sprung, whose extraordinary vitality they still display for us through the medium of art. Established in this very place by conquest, the Normans were themselves conquered and absorbed by their erstwhile victims. Thus, in the end, they added one more rich ingredient to the vibrant, creative Gallic strain and helped set France upon its brilliant modern course.

Glossary

THIS GLOSSARY IS NOT A UNIVERSAL MEDIEVAL LEXICON. IT IS A SELECTED LIST OF terms that the reader will meet with in this book, as well as some useful background material. Rare occurrences are excluded, as are commonplace terms, except for those having an uncustomary medieval usage. Arrangement is not in strict alphabetical order but by related subject-groups.

1. The Cost of Building

THE EIGHT CATHEDRALS: Despite the wealth of financial data available, systematic budgeting figures are virtually non-existent; a few exceptions:

Strasbourg: Donations to the fabric fund listed in the city's archives (*Urkundenbuch*) are impossible to calculate accurately since a big majority are in the form of property or *omnia bona* (all the worldly goods). The Münster's *Liber Donationum* lists 1,237 donors for 1257–1324, mostly small gifts, the annual total averaging well under 200 livres. Since the fabric committee's income on property and other investments totalled 550 livres (figure for 1338) and the cathedral chapter's last gift to it was in 1305, it can be assumed that the building fund did not much exceed 1,000 livres a year during most of the fourteenth century. An exception must be made for the last three decades, when recurrences of the Black Death brought a great surge of patronage, the fabric's revenues for 1386 totalling 1,797 livres (usually abbreviated as l.).

Amiens: The single year with extant fabric accounts in the medieval period (1357–8) comes long after the major construction was ended. Hence, its figures could have little meaning for us.

York: Its fabric rolls start only around 1350 but fortunately include the very active building period under Archbishop Thoresby, expenditures for his highest year (1371) being listed as £622. We must, however, make allowance for bills paid on the spot and even more for donations not listed in the rolls' summary *elemosinae et legata*. The pound sterling was, moreover, a strong currency compared to the livre. All in all, expenditures in 1371 certainly exceeded 1,000 l. (French).

SOME OTHER CHURCHES: Though mostly deriving from churches not studied in this book, the following data are all related to the contemporary period:

St-Ouen, Rouen: During an extraordinary reconstruction campaign on Rouen's second-most-important church, the apse, choir and transept were built in two decades (1319–38), at an expenditure of 63,000 livres, or an average of 3,000 l. per year. This would be the top figure in our records but for the fact that the French livre in the fourteenth century was much devalued over that of the thirteenth.

St-Nicaise, Reims: Expenditures at this splendid collegiate church (destroyed), for 1232–58, totalled 28,191 l., the record going on brokenly thereafter until 1282. For the first twenty-seven years, the average spent was about 1,000 l., varying from 620 l. to 2,480 l., the spread being attributed to differences in the costliness of the work done.

Milan Cathedral: It furnishes one of the most complete records of fund-raising available. In a galvanic campaign in which the entire population entered, donations for the first five years (starting in 1387) probably averaged as much as 5,000 l. a year.

Chartres Cathedral: Comprehensive budgetary records are unavailable for this refulgent and marvellously preserved church. But the building campaigns are well documented for 1194–1223, when the cathedral was almost totally rebuilt after the disastrous fire. Based on this construction record, John James, an Australian architect, recently undertook an interesting project at Chartres: 'to cost a medieval cathedral as if we were building it today'. Using the same materials, but modern cranes, scaffolding, mechanical tools and diesel-driven trucks, he arrived at a figure of about $50 million (American). This seems low, one reason probably being that the average Australian yearly earnings in 1972 used by James were only $5,000, well below those of the USA or several other advanced industrial countries.

Further, James estimates that an average work force of 270 men (perhaps 300 with auxiliaries) would be needed to rebuild Chartres today. It is certain that at least that many would have been required in medieval times, working on the site, at the quarry face, for transport, etc. With our own partial findings from several churches hovering around an expenditure of 1,000 l. during an 'active' year, and using James's calculation of labour costs at 80 per cent of the total, we obtain a work force of 80 men. This is based on documented yearly wages of 10 livres tournois for the early thirteenth century. Given Chartres's fantastic speed of construction and the opulence of its fabric, however, a work force several times as great would certainly have been needed there. Even using James's low figure of $50 million spent in thirty years, the equivalent in 1200 (see this Glossary under 'Money') would have been about 82,500 livres or 2,750 l. a year. Of this sum, 2,200 l. would have gone to labour for the hire of 245 men. Amiens and Paris, the 'richest' of our eight cathedrals, took about twice as long as Chartres to build and probably averaged half its yearly outlay.

2. Building Personnel and Funding

FABRIC COMMITTEE: While the cathedral chapter was formally in charge of construction, active authority was in the hands of two men, the procurator and the master-of-works.

The Procurator Fabrice: He was usually a member of the chapter, the man in charge of funds. In Strasbourg, he became a layman when the commune took over control of construction of the *Münster*.

The Master-of-Works: The man in charge of building operations, that is, the architect. He was almost always a layman. He was also called a *master mason* and was 'capable of drawing plans and details for others to work from' (L. F. Salzman, *Building in England down to 1540*, 1952).

The Mason: General term for the skilled building worker. He worked from dawn to dark, six days a week, earning less during the short winter days and totalling about 10 livres tournois a year in France of the thirteenth century. The architect's earnings were somewhat higher, but he also received various perquisites like living quarters, use of a horse, a yearly bonus and a robe. Apparent earnings increased sharply in France in later centuries as the value of the livre continued to decline. In England, wages remained fairly constant from 1370–1530, a mason making 3 shillings per week or £7.80 per year during that entire period (E. A. Gee, *The Archaeological Journal*, 1952).

THE BUILDING FUND: The finances that were assigned by the cathedral chapter for construction. They were derived from a variety of sources:

Fixed Proportion of Church's Earnings: Often stated as one-fourth of its income, which was supposed to be put aside for building. Since this was certainly not done consistently, extraordinary assessments were often levied on all clerical benefices during an active building campaign, as at Strasbourg, York, Lyon and other places.

Oblations: Collection boxes were posted throughout the diocese and fund drives were constantly renewed. Questors were sent out, at times carrying an important relic. Forced donations are not often heard of but they are sometimes cited, as at Rouen, in the eleventh century. At York, in 1370, John Thoresby *suggested* that every man and woman put a penny on the high altar every year for the building fund.

Fabric's Independent Income: Occasionally mentioned as based on property owned by it. At Strasbourg this income was 550 l. in 1338, an important sum, and campaigns were put on to establish additional annuities of one livre each in the fabric's name.

Patronage by Individuals or Groups:

> *Chantry Chapel*: Founded by an individual, a confraternity or a guild in whose behalf special, periodic masses were held.

> *Donor's altar*: Built and outfitted by an individual or group, the altar at which masses in their name were conducted.

> *Patron*: Saint to whom an altar or a chapel was consecrated. Was usually the patron saint of the donor as well.

> *Donor lancet*: A stained-glass lancet paid for by an individual or group, often containing the legend of the donor's patron saint.

Donor panels: Lancet panels, usually at the bottom, which refer in some manner to the donor.

Donor 'signature': A work scene referring to the donor guild or confraternity.

Bequest: A common type of aesthetic patronage, made either in a simple mention of the fabric or for a specified objective.

Indulgence: The recompense for certain donations to a named objective, offering relief from required observances (like Lenten abstinence from meat) or reduction of the time the donor would have to serve in purgatory. One of the major methods of financing church-building, it usually bore the sanction of the pope or other high churchmen.

3. Church Sections

Orientation: The church façade very generally faces toward the west. Hence, it is customary to specify locations by directional ordinates: north, south, east, west.

Façade: The church front, where the main portals are usually located. It most often contains the finest sculptural decoration of the church exterior.

Nave: Central section of the church, extending from the west front to the choir or transept. The section in which the congregation usually assembles.

Nave-aisles: One or two lateral units flanking the nave, usually on both north and south sides.

Vault: The arched upper cover of the nave, apse or other section. Term is habitually applied to both the inner ceiling and the outer roof.

Bay: A vertical division of the nave, apse, aisles, etc., contained between two major points of support (pillars, transverse ribs . . .).

Tribune: Wide gallery built above the nave-aisle and often continuing into the choir. Used as an element buttressing the vault, it eventually disappeared from Gothic churches.

Triforium: A kind of narrow tribune consisting of a passageway with arched window-like openings overlooking the nave. No longer a supporting unit, it was basically aesthetic.

Transept: Transverse arm (sometimes absent) between the nave and apse. The point of juncture is called the *crossing*. The transept usually extends outward beyond the nave wall, terminating in one or more portals.

Porch: A covered transept terminal but also sometimes found at the west front, especially in Romanesque churches. The south porch was often a point of assembly of the burghers, the site of their court of justice.

Apse: English usage: 'A semicircular or polygonal recess . . . at the end of the choir, aisles or nave of a church' (*Oxford Dictionary*), French usage: In general, equivalent to the *chevet*.

Chevet: 'The French name of the apsidal termination (semicircular or polygonal) of the east end of a church . . . sometimes surrounded by apsidal chapels' (*Oxford Dictionary*). The French often expand this area to include the choir.

Choir: Central section of the chevet (or apse), containing the high altar and often shut in by a *choir enclosure* at the sides and back and by a *roodscreen* at the front. Sometimes projects into the transept or even the nave.

Ambulatory: Curved aisle separating the choir from the outer section of the apse, that is, the part containing the radiating chapels.

Chapel: Enclosed area usually built against the church's outer wall, containing minor altars and used for accessory offices. Those in the nave-aisles are called *lateral chapels,* those in the apse *radiating chapels,* the one directly behind the altar, the *axis chapel*.

Chapter-house: Structure, attached to or entirely separate from the church, used for meetings of the cathedral chapter or other important assemblies.

Cloister: Section outside a cathedral or monastery, formed by covered galleries surrounding a quadrilateral court or garden. Often contains much art, including immured tombstones, sculptured columnar capitals, roof bosses, frescoes and at times communicating chapels.

4. TECHNICAL TERMS

Buttress: A supporting element in an architectural ensemble of which two commonly occurring types are:

Flying Buttress: Curved or angular horizontal arm (sometimes double) leading from the vault exterior to a strongly-rooted vertical pier.

Vertical Buttress: Support applied against a terminal pillar of the vault rib.

Capital: The top of a column or pilaster, usually covered by a floral, geometric or figured carving.

Clerestory: Upper-nave wall extending above the aisle vaults with apertures meant to allow light into the central vessel.

Flamboyant: A late Gothic form characterized by the flame-like tops of its window design and the decorative complexity of its vault-ribbing.

Gothic Style: Building style originating some years before 1150 and continuing into the fifteenth century. Characterized by the lightness of its structure compared to the Romanesque as well as by certain associated details such as the high, cross-ribbed vault, the broken arch, the flying buttress and large window spaces.

Lantern: Top section of a tower over the transept crossing containing open spaces to allow light down into the church centre.

Lintel: A horizontal band decorated with sculpture, located beneath the tympanum of a portal.

Misericord: A carving on the underside of a choir-stall seat, usually secular in subject matter.

Modillion: Carving on the supporting stone of the wall cornice of a nave-aisle.

Ogive: The diagonal rib of a Gothic vault. It is actually a separate member beneath the vault, to which it was supposed to give support.

Register: Horizontal building division of a church-section, as the nave, the façade, a tower, etc.

Romanesque Style: Building style prevailing in the eleventh and twelfth centuries, of distinctly heavier composition than its successor, the Gothic, and typified by the rounded arch (sometimes slightly broken), small windows, high aisles and generally narrower and lower vaulting.

Spandrel: Triangular space above the meeting point of two arches, as in the upper nave wall, sometimes decorated.

Stained-Glass Window: A form of painted decoration on glass that required a highly complicated technique of colouring, drawing, baking, cutting and assemblage. Following are associated terms occurring in this book:

Glazing: The general term applied to the preparation of stained- glass.

Grisaille: Glass stained in monochrome, usually of a light translucent colour.

Lancet: A tall narrow window of painted glass made up of a number of individual panels and topped by a pointed arch.

Light: A lancet (English usage).

Rose-window: A great circular stained-glass window located at the top of the west and the transept terminal walls.

Roundel: Circular painted panel at the top of a lancet.

Stalls: Ensemble of the seats arranged in the choir used by the clergy for their offices. Usually elegantly built in wood and richly provided with sculpture.

Tympanum: The great panel of a portal in ogival or semi-circular form between the arch and the lintel. Usually heavily sculptured.

Vaulting: The reference here is to the ceiling of a single bay. There are a number of different kinds of vaulting, most of which are amply described by their names. Those occurring most frequently in this book are the *cross-ribbed vault* and the *domed vault*.

5. The Medieval City

City Charter: Body of rules on the basis of which a city operated. Could vary from a few paragraphs to a great volume though many unrecorded privileges could be enjoyed by tradition.

City Officials: The basic medieval posts of *mayor* and *council* (in Toulouse, *consulat* or *capitoulat*) have come down to us, however altered, while for others, like the French *échevins*, a small number of important assistants to the mayor, we have no equivalent. While the officials were answerable to a group of citizens, their number was usually very restricted, and the great mass of people remained without a political voice.

City's Responsibilities: In an active municipality, these would cover the building and maintenance of walls, roads, waterways, bridges, quays, control of markets and the slaughterhouse and regulation of quality in consumers' goods and of weights and measures. While sharing with the church the conduct of hospitals (often called Hôtel-Dieu or Maison-Dieu) and hospices, the administrators and most of the funds usually came from the citizens. Some of the richest cities also maintained a standing *militia*. The medieval tax system never sufficed for these and other activities and cities tried to make up for the difference by borrowing, going deeper and deeper into debt.

City Seal: Highly esteemed symbol of municipal power. Its iconography often reflected strong local attachments, like Strasbourg Münster's tower and Lyon's Pont du Rhône.

City's Seigniory: The medieval commune's chief aim was to be accepted as a representative group within the feudal system. A basic feature of this status was seigniory. As warrant of all subsidiary privileges, it was essentially a proprietary right and was pursued determinedly by the commune through purchase of city property and quitrents as well as buying off feudal taxes and charges stemming from serfdom. The quest sometimes resulted in conflicts, particularly with church groups who claimed that property occupied by them was exempt from various city taxes and regulations (the so-called privilege of *main-morte* or mortmain).

Commune: The most advanced form of the medieval city government. Often (though not always) peacefully established, sealed by vow and granted the formal consent of king, count, bishop or other seignior, its powers varied but usually covered taxation, control of industry and commerce, defence, police, some legislation and especially justice. Many cities, including Paris, never had a commune. A weak city not only enjoyed fewer powers but was often subjected to a variety of extraordinary charges (like Poitiers), collectable by a sovereign, a church or even a rich burgher.

Coutumes: The evolved commonlaw customs and practices concerning such matters as the inviolability of persons and property.

Free City: Spoken of a municipality like Strasbourg which enjoyed complete independence, not even owing a vow of allegiance to the emperor.

Guild: An organization of merchants or artisans practising the same trade. Each guild had its own charter, which was made up more of responsibilities than rights. A famous collection of such charters was Paris's thirteenth-century *Livre des métiers*. Not all trades had guilds and some of the latter were hardly democratic, being 'owned' by a sovereign or one of his favourites.

Italian City-State: An extreme type of the 'free city', which ruled an extensive surrounding area. Sometimes cited in reference to Toulouse early in the thirteenth century.

Middle Class: Often loosely used as an inclusive term, extending from the rich merchant to the labourer. But aside from his social disadvantage, the latter was excluded from all political rights by the oligarchy, whose evolution as a separate class was already under way by the twelfth century, ending in ennoblement for many by the fourteenth. Wealth was the basis for this differentiation. It cost money *to take one's freedom* (a kind of registration by tradesmen and skilled artisans), to buy a place on the city mint or to acquire the fief or the prince's accolade that made a man a 'seignior'.

Paris Hanse: A small group of merchants monopolizing commerce on the Seine, who established a fragmentary 'municipality' in the twelfth century. Though somewhat expanded in the thirteenth and acquiring a *Provost of Merchants*, it remained very limited in power and participation.

6. FEUDALISM

CLASSES AND CLASS RELATIONS

Lord; Seignior: In the feudal sense, the owner of an estate or domain.

Vassal: Person attached to a sovereign or seignior by oath and homage and owing him certain personal services, such as the military obligation.

Serf: Person attached to land belonging to a seignior. Distinguished from a slave by the possession of certain rights like the ownership of personal belongings and a permanent claim, even hereditary, to the land he farmed, from which he could not be removed except by manumission.

Manumission: Freedom from serfdom obtained by grant or (far more often) by purchase. Occurred in a great wave in France of the thirteenth century.

Fief; Noble Fief: The domain which a vassal held from his seignior under obligation of homage and a rent.

Ennoblement: Starting in the thirteenth century, a wealthy commoner could buy a noble fief; in the fourteenth he could be ennobled for owning it, though this dignity could also come from a prince's accolade.

TAXES AND OTHER CHARGES

Taille: The chief tax in France, levied on commoners by a seignior. Based on income in a city, it was imposed annually. In Paris, in 1292, it was rated at 2 per cent.

Quitrent or 'Cens': A small rent paid by a freeholder to the seignior in lieu of certain feudal services. It was by no means the sole financial benefit received by the seignior, who collected a fee for any change of tenure in addition to his earnings from his rights of justice and other feudal privileges attached to the land.

Sur-Cens: A kind of permanent mortgage on land widely used in the thirteenth century. Based on the great increase in property values at the time, it allowed the peasant to improve his holdings while for the moneyed classes it constituted an excellent form of investment that evaded the church's ban on usury.

Aide: Royal tax levied on important occasions like the coming to age of the dauphin, the marriage of a princess or on behalf of a military campaign.

Amortization: Fee collected by the sovereign on any property bought or otherwise acquired, even by a church.

Scutage: Tax collected in lieu of feudal military service required, which was limited to about six weeks a year. The tax was widely used by Henry II (Plantagenet), for example, to help him establish a permanent army.

Other Taxes: There was a wide variety, often peculiarly feudal, like the required use of the lord's oven to bake bread in, for a fee.

Tax Farmer: Agent who purchased a sovereign's 'right' to collect various taxes, a frequent source of enrichment in the Middle Ages.

FEUDAL USAGES

Right of Asylum: Privilege extended to some altar, church or even an entire city providing protection against seizure of an accused criminal. The Strasbourg commune had such an altar in the Münster, granted by the pope.

Right of Regalia: King's right to seize a prelate's temporalities during a vacancy, meanwhile enjoying its income and other privileges.

Jurisdiction: Feudal justice was conducted by a bewildering patchwork of courts, each seignior operating his own. It was considered primarily a source of income. Most municipalities had a court, the extent of its jurisdiction (*high, middle and low justice*, in the extreme case) and hence its earnings depending on the city's overall political strength.

Usury: In the feudal sense, the lending of money at interest, however small. Banned by the church, it was practised by sufferance by Jews, Italian bankers and others, who paid huge fees to permissive sovereigns.

7. MONEY

Comparative Medieval and Modern Values: Many attempts have been made to establish a slide-rule, but they have all run into the problem of the great number of variables involved. Otto von Simson (*Gothic Cathedral*, 1956) and an associate devised the simple method of comparing earnings of an unskilled worker in early thirteenth-century France and in the United States of *c.* 1950, obtaining the ratio of 1:320 for the *livre tournois* against the dollar. With obvious reservations, this ratio has been used in the present book. However, the American dollar has been enormously devalued since 1950 due to inflation and other causes, requiring a corresponding adjustment in this ratio. From US Government statistics, the cost-of-living index has gone up from 72.1 for 1950 (based on 1967 = 100) to 180 for 1977. In other words, the 1950 dollar would be worth very nearly $2.50 today. This would raise the above livre-dollar ratio to approximately 1:800. To express this in English pounds of November 1977, when the pound was quoted on the exchange market as about $1.81, we obtain a French livre–English pound ratio of approximately 1:440.

Comparative Values of Different Currencies: In the absence of a central mint, money values varied greatly even in different sections of the same country, no doubt a function of the quantity of metal contained. Systematic coin-debasement, as by the French kings starting in the late thirteenth century, further complicated the matter to the point of chaos.

Strong and Weak Currencies: In the thirteenth century, there was a considerable spread in value of the French livre in different parts of the territory. The livre of Toulouse for example was strong; that of Paris of medium value; those of Tours and Angers weak, the livre tournois being worth a quarter less than the livre parisis (usually written tour. and par.).

OTHER CURRENCIES:

Pound Sterling: A strong currency compared to the French livre.

Mark: Used in York, where it is cited as being worth two-thirds of a pound, and in Strasbourg, where its value is said to have been eight-tenths of the French livre.

Florin: Used in Lyon, where it is quoted as eight-tenths of the 'franc-d'or', which is considered equivalent to the French livre.

Gulden: Used in Strasbourg, where it is cited as 55 per cent of the livre.

Others: There is an utterly confusing mass of other units, often given as variants of better-known currencies, like the *livre fortium*, the *obole d'or*, the *gros d'argent*, etc.

20:12:1 Ratio: Our acquaintance with the (until recently) anachronistic English monetary system helps us to understand the medieval ratio of *livre-sou-denier*, or pound-shilling-penny. There were, in other words, 12 deniers to the sou and 20 sous to the livre. The French *obole* (equivalent to the half-penny) is often met up with in mentions of oblations, especially by the poor.

8. CHURCHES AND ORDERS

Abbey: Important monastery presided by abbot or abbess.

Basilica: Originally an early church of rectangular form; later applied to a church of special importance.

Cathedral: Leading church of a diocese, containing the bishop's *cathedra*. Contrary to often-held opinion, there is only one cathedral in each diocese. Some cathedrals in England are traditionally called minsters, though the term is also applied to a number of other important churches. The German equivalent is Münster.

Collegiate Church: Important secular church run by a group of canons who lived communally.

Diocese: Church area under a bishop's jurisdiction. Roughly based on population, it could vary greatly in size. An *archdiocese* was made up of a number of dioceses and was administered by an archbishop, who was also called a *metropolitan*. The *primate church* was the leading archbishopric of a country. Though often in conflict, Lyon was generally considered to have this position in France, Canterbury in England.

Mendicant Church or Convent: Unit of one of the orders of friars.

Metropolitan Church: Leading church of an archdiocese.

Parish Church: The basic church unit, topically distributed, to which all the people of a neighbourhood or village belonged and where they received their sacraments.

Pilgrimage Church: Goal of some special pilgrimage, usually possessing an esteemed relic; also a stopover point on such a route, as on the 'pilgrimage road' to Santiago de Compostela.

Primate Church: A country's leading church.

Priory: Monastery, ruled by a prior or prioress, often an offshoot or a dependency of an abbey. There have, however, been some famous priories, like Paris's St-Martin-des-Champs.

Religious Order: An organization of multiple units, usually international and answerable directly to the pope. Its members took a vow to observe strictly a prescribed set of rules. Among the best known:

Benedictines: Order founded by St Benedict in 529 at Mt Cassino, Italy.

Cluniacs: A reformed offshoot of the Benedictines founded in 910 at the Abbey of Cluny, France.

Cistercians: Another offshoot founded in 1098 at Citeaux, France, and known for its asceticism.

Friars: A term (deriving from *frater,* or brother) applied to a variety of groups founded mainly in the thirteenth century and consecrated (at least initially) to poverty and living by begging (hence also the name, *Mendicants*). Best known of the friars were: *Augustins; Carmelites; Celestines; Trinitarians;* and especially the *Dominicans* (also Preachers, Jacobins, Black Friars) and the *Franciscans* (also Cordeliers, Minorites).

Lay Orders: *Béguines,* sisterhoods often devoting themselves to social welfare work; *Frères Pontifes,* bridge-builders, hence their punning name.

Military Orders: Units founded early in the twelfth century during the first Crusades, the best known being the *Knights Templars* and the *Knights Hospitallers*.

9. Church Personnel

THE CATHEDRAL AND THE DIOCESE

Bishop. Head of the diocese. Elected by the chapter (though the choice was often imposed by the pope or sovereign) of which he was only nominally a member. Nevertheless, he engaged actively in some of the chapter's functions, in particular in fostering cathedral-building operations.

Chapter: Ruling body of the cathedral, made up of the dean and other dignitaries, which included the canons. The chapter had its own property and revenues, jurisdiction, courts, prisons, etc.

Dean: Chief dignitary of the cathedral chapter. Elected by the vote of the latter, he was installed by the bishop.

Canon: Member of the chapter's largest group, their number sometimes exceeding fifty persons (Paris had fifty-two). Usually nominated by the bishop but requiring the chapter's approval, especially with regard to the strict hereditary rules it often imposed. Priestly orders were not obligatory for canons nor regular residence beyond a minimum of about two months a year, generally.

CHAPTER DIGNITARIES: Their number and functions varied considerably. At Paris, there were eight dignitaries, including, besides the dean:

Precentor: The second dignitary of the chapter, he was in charge of liturgy and chant. He shared his duties with the *Assistant-Precentor,* who was likewise a dignitary.

Archdeacons: Of which there were three, each the overseer of an important division of the diocese. They were also the bishop's chief counsellors and stewards of his 'house'. In England, the archdeacon was strictly a diocesan official.

Chancellor: The chapter secretary, who had charge of its seal and the preparation and care of its documents. He was responsible also for the maintenance of the cathedral seminary.

Penitentiary: The officer dealing with matters of penance and absolution.

OTHER CHAPTER DIGNITARIES: Besides those used in reference to Notre-Dame-de-Paris, there are some additional dignitaries that are cited in this book, including:

Treasurer: Besides his conventional financial duties, he was in charge of valuable ornaments and relics. He was next to the dean in importance in the chapter at York Minster.

Sacristan: In some churches, he carried out the treasurer's functions, especially as concerning relics, jewels and ornaments, and supervised the chapter library.

OTHER CATHEDRAL OR DIOCESAN POSTS, FUNCTIONS

Provosts: Important administrative officers who handled the business affairs of the bishop and the chapter (always separate individuals, however). Besides the Provost of Paris, there were fourteen episcopal provosts in the diocese exclusive of the capital, all functioning under the bishop's *Bailli*.

Official: Judge of an ecclesiastical court. At Paris, he was a canon of Notre-Dame though not a dignitary of the chapter. Term was usually applied to head of bishop's justice, which covered not only clerics and monks but students, crusaders, widows, orphans, and all cases in some manner concerned with religion.

Prebendary: Cleric enjoying a *prebend*, that is, an income based on property or other investment. Prebends were attached to the posts of most cathedral dignitaries (including canons) and were usually highly remunerative. Thus, at York the Masham prebend paid 250 marks a year, the equivalent of $168,000 or £92,400 in modern money. The York archbishop and dean earned two or more times as much as that from their prebends and 'preferments' alone.

Residentiary: Member of the chapter in permanent residence; usually a minority of the total number. All dignitaries received a daily *distribution* in food and drink but more usually in money, in addition to their income, while in residence. It was a measure designed to combat chronic absenteeism. At Paris, the dignitaries received 84 *livres parisis* for the 'general' assemblies and 6 deniers a day for the 'ordinary' ones.

Vicar: Substitute for a dignitary when not in residence. Often obligatory as at York, where the canonic vicars were permanently organized into the *Vicars-Choral*, who administered the Minster's sacerdotal functions. A similar arrangement obtained at Strasbourg, with its *Great Choir*. In modern English usage, the vicar is a priest in charge of a parish, appointed by a bishop.

Vidame: Official of the bishop concerned chiefly with his secular affairs, such as management of church property, exercise of his temporal jurisdiction, etc. At times a very important personage.

ADDITIONAL CHURCH POSITIONS

Chaplain: Priest, privately endowed, who conducted commemorative masses in a chapel of a church or in a private oratory.

Churchwarden: Lay administrator of a parish church, often in charge of building operations. At a cathedral, a secular or clerical functionary (of which there were four each at Paris), who took care of lights, dressing altars, maintaining reliquaries, as well as the cleaning and guarding of the church.

Curé: Priest in charge of the spiritual direction of a parish. English equivalents: vicar; rector.

Papal Legate: Cardinal charged with a special, temporary mission.

Proctor: Representative, often of the pope or a cardinal; could also be a vicar filling some post held *in absentia*.

Provincial: Head of a group of units of an order, as the Dominicans.

Regular Clergy: Clerics belonging to a religious order, following a 'rule'.

Roman Curia: The papal court of officials, including cardinals, aiding the pope to administer the business of the church.

Secular Clergy: Non-affiliated clerics.

10. Church Usages and Revenues

Alien Prebend: Prebend granted as a bribe or gift to a member of the hierarchy (often the Roman Curia) and enjoyed *in absentia*.

Benefice: Income attached to a cleric's post.

Clerical Prison: Prison in which clerics (and students) were jailed for crimes punished in the ecclesiastic court with jurisdiction over them.

Excommunication: Expulsion from the communion of the church with denial of sacraments and other rights. Used against cities and countries as well as individuals and for various reasons other than religious ones.

Fees for Sacraments: Collected by the medieval church according to a prescribed schedule, for baptism and burial (as well as the non-sacramental blessing of the nuptial bed, fee in lieu of partaking of wedding dinner, etc.).

Interdict: Exclusion from church offices, sacraments or privileges.

Offices: Prayers and liturgical ceremonies engaged in by the clerics at prescribed hours of the day and night.

Pallium: Circular white wool band worn over shoulders by archbishops. A large fee to Rome was customary for the pallium but the archbishopric of York became peculiarly vulnerable to this extortion.

Papal Provision: Refers to posts for which the pope had the right of appointment.

Presentation: The right to nominate a successor to a vacant clerical post, often held by a layman.

Priestly Orders: Sacrament endowing right to practise a priest's functions.

Relic: Part of a saint's body or object associated with him or her; considered to have miraculous properties and usually displayed in the church sanctuary for adoration.

Temporal Justice: Jurisdiction over lay subjects possessed by clerics.

Temporal Possessions: As of a bishopric, often stemming from early gifts, spreading throughout a diocese and bringing great revenues.

Tithe: Though the major institutional revenue of the church, the right to its collection had often fallen into lay hands during the deep Middle Ages, requiring centuries to be reclaimed.

Visitation: Right of supervisory (usually annual) visits of subordinate churches by a superior church official. Illustrated in the 'Journal' of Archbishop Eudes Rigaud of Rouen.

11. Foundations and Donations

Anniversary: Foundation providing the yearly citation of the person on the day of his death. Could merely call for reading his name or a full commemorative mass, depending on the importance of the initial funding.

Bede Rolls: Records kept by a convent, particularly of a mendicant order, of persons to be cited at periods of prayer or commemorative masses.

Chaplaincy: Very costly foundation calling for a daily mass in founder's name, usually also providing for private chaplain 'in perpetuity'.

Ex Voto Foundation: Established by virtue of a vow made at some time of danger or stress.

Forgotten Tithes: A conscience bequest often appearing in wills, strongly implying the person's having skimped his earnings when paying his tithes.

Foundation: The general term for a quid-pro-quo arrangement, funded by some property that brought an expected income.

Indulgence: While many indulgences served an aesthetic goal, others were used to stimulate ordinary oblations to the church.

Mortuary Celebration: Rite usually involving a procession with lighted candles, etc. following a person's death.

Obit: Short for obituary; also used in sense of an anniversary.

Omnia Bona Sua: Bequest of all one's worldly goods.

Perpetual Lamp: Foundation providing income to pay for a lamp that would be kept constantly burning in the church.

Prayers and Masses: Foundation calling for a certain number of either or both, often in the days and weeks following a person's death.

Quid-Pro-Quo Foundation: The most common type of donation for which some return service was expected.

Rente or Annuity: The yearly income earned by a foundation.

12. Heresy

Cathar Heresy: A Manichean type of doctrine that polarized the world into dual powers of Good and Evil, denied the divinity of Christ and other Catholic dogmas. Widespread in Europe, it had several foci in France.

Cathars on Usury: They were permissive on the subject, which was a major attraction of this heresy for merchants, who found the church's ban on borrowing and lending at interest a serious restraint on economic development.

Albigensian Crusade: A destructive, bloody war conducted by northern French forces, supported by the church, against the Languedoc, 1209–29. Ostensibly a fight against Catharism, it ended with the absorption of the great province into France.

Anti-Cathar Inquisition: Established under the Dominicans in 1233 to help rout out strong Catharist remnants, it resulted in the execution and expropriation of many people at Toulouse, among other places, and seriously prejudiced the building history of its cathedral.

Waldensian Heresy: Sect founded c.1180 by Pierre de Vaux, rich merchant of Lyon, who preached the need of returning the church to its primitive austerity.

13. MEDIEVAL RECORDS

Cartulary: Collection of documents of a church, city, etc. Early cartularies are in manuscript but often continue so into later times. Those published by modern archivists were generally collated from a variety of sources and cover a broad range of subjects.

Délibérations Capitulaires: Minutes kept by a chapter of its meetings. *Actes Capitulaires* refer more precisely to a compilation of a chapter's documents.

Fabric Records: Building and decorating procedures kept by the fabric committee of a church, including expenditures, receipts and (less often) donors.

Inventaires-Sommaires: An important series of printed inventories prepared by modern French archivists, of documents, cartularies, etc. to be found in the departmental and communal archives. Individual documents are usually dated and often given in considerable detail.

Obituary: Record of names and days of death of members of a church who arranged for anniversaries; often extended for important people to leading acts of their lives, including gifts to the fabric of the church.

Papal Bull: Official papal document bearing pope's seal (bull). Carefully preserved, they are largely available in printed form.

Pouillé: Catalogue of church benefices in a diocese or province. Often contains sources of income, original founders and other important data on individual prebends.

Register: Record of activities, events, correspondence, etc., kept by or for an official, particularly a bishop or archbishop.

Repertory: A manuscript record copied from early sources, many of which may have later disappeared.

Roll: Continuous parchment register rolled into a cylinder for convenience and better preservation. Most famous examples are the English *Rolls Series* of early royal records.

Testament: Since its preparation was generally the church's responsibility and it was probated in the ecclesiastic court, a considerable number of these documents have been preserved, dating from the thirteenth century on. They furnish a precious source of otherwise largely neglected information regarding aesthetic church patronage by commoners as well as various other matters. There are especially fine collections at York and Lyon.

Notes

Abbreviations of Often-Appearing Titles of Magazines,
Journals, Reviews, etc.

AASRP Associated Architectural Societies' Reports and Papers

AHP Archives Historiques de Poitou

Annales Annales du Midi

BEC Bibliothèque de l'Ecole Nationale des Chartes

BSACS Bulletin de la Société des Amis de la Cathédrale de Strasbourg

BSAL Bulletin de la Société Littéraire, Historique et Archéologique de Lyon

BSAM Bulletin de la Société Archéologique du Midi de la France

BSAO Bulletin de la Société des Antiquaires de l'Ouest

BSAP Bulletin de la Société des Antiquaires de Picardie

BSHP Bulletin de la Société de l'Histoire de Paris et de l'Île-de-France

Cartulaire municipal M.-C. Guigue, *Cartulaire municipal de la ville de Lyon . . . formé au 14e siècle par Etienne de Villeneuve,* 1876

Inventaire-Sommaire *Inventaire-Sommaire des Archives Départementales antérieures à 1790*

MAST Mémoires de l'Académie des Sciences, Inscriptions et Belles-Lettres de Toulouse

MSAM Mémoires de la Société Archéologique du Midi de la France

MSAN Mémoires de la Société des Antiquaires de Normandie

MSAO Mémoires de la Société des Antiquaires de l'Ouest

MSAP Mémoires de la Société des Antiquaires de Picardie

MSHP Mémoires de la Société de l'Histoire de Paris et de l'Île-de-France

Positions de thèses Positions de thèses de l'Ecole Nationale des Chartes

Recueil des monuments Augustin Thierry, *Recueil des monuments inédits de l'histoire du tiers état . . .* Tome Premier: *Les pièces relatives à l'histoire de la ville d'Amiens,* 1850

Regesten der Bischöfe Regesten der Bischöfe von Strassburg bis zum Jahre 1202

Urkundenbuch; UB Urkundenbuch der Stadt Strassburg

Victoria History The Victoria History of the Counties of England

YAS, Record Series Yorkshire Archaeological Society, Record Series

York Memo Book York Memorandum Book

ZGOR Zeitschrift für die Geschichte des Oberrheins

The reader will find the notes divided into three major categories: (1) printed and archival sources; (2) background material; (3) lists of donations, endowments and foundations, particularly by commoners.

The author has taken considerable pains in collating burgher chaplaincies, monetarily the most important of foundations. They called for a daily mass in a designated chapel and at a particular altar, often conducted by a private chaplain, for whom a yearly income was established 'in perpetuity'. As a matter of fact, a number of chaplaincies continued in the same family's possession until the Revolution of 1789.

Payment for the building or decoration of the chapel is less frequently recorded. One reason is that such arrangements were usually made during the lifetime of the founders and hence were not cited in their wills. Also, the church had less interest in recording this patronage since when the work was done the funds were exhausted, whereas a chaplaincy continued to earn money from the property initially deposited to its credit. It also kept the family of the original donor attached to the church, often bringing in supplementary endowments. Many chapels were eventually taken over entirely by the family, becoming in effect areas of private property within the church.

Data regarding burgher chaplaincies, even for the leading cathedrals, have rarely been gathered by scholars. The author makes no claim to completeness for his own work in this field. But the places where it was done more thoroughly will illustrate the usefulness of this information.

The author has frequently assembled material on donations of burghers to other churches besides the cathedrals. This task was hampered by the sparseness of parish documents prior to the fourteenth century. The archives of important monastic and collegiate churches are somewhat better supplied. It must not be forgotten, however, that a great proportion of the primary documents of churches has been lost or destroyed during wars or social and religious upheavals. Some of the data were copied into manuscript inventories by early archivists (of the seventeenth and eighteenth centuries, especially) before the sources vanished and furnish a partial replacement.

INTRODUCTION

1 For a discussion of the 'cost of building' the cathedrals, see the Glossary.

2 The enormous loss of early documents has been particularly costly to the financial records of church-building; property papers were more carefully kept. For the cathedrals studied in this book, scholarship has by no means exhausted the subject.

Notre-Dame de Paris has left no fabric accounts. Donations for construction or decoration have had to be culled from cartularies, obituaries and independent archives. Marcel Aubert (*Notre-Dame de Paris, sa place dans l'architecture du 12e au 14e siècle*, 1920, pp. 138–48) gathered material for the dating and patronage of a number of the chantry chapels, a late feature of the church's construction, to which I furnished some additional data ('New Documents for Notre-Dame's Early Chapels', *Gazette des Beaux-Arts*, 6e période, tome 74, Sept. 1969, pp. 121–34).

Amiens cathedral evidently lost its thirteenth-century chapter records in a fire in 1258. Individual documents concerning fabric resources that have been found are post-1240, which was after the larger part of the cathedral was already up. The earliest available systematic fabric accounts are for 1357–8. The most precious records that we have are for a part of the thirteenth century stained-glass windows, whose donors' inscriptions were recorded in 1667 by the archivist, Charles Du Cange; the glass itself was destroyed during or shortly after the Revolution. The Du Cange recording is reproduced in the 'Appendices' of George Durand, *Monographie de l'église Notre-Dame, cathédrale d'Amiens*, 1901. The *Monographie* gives a detailed account of the cathedral's construction, analysing the pertinent existing documents, including some that cite financial data.

Toulouse cathedral has left a very spotty record of the contributors to its construction, which indeed has not yet had the benefit of an exhaustive scholarly study. Typically, we are better informed about the Jacobins, the Dominican church, as for example: *Bernardus Guidonis, De Fundatione Conventus Tholosani,*

Bibliothèque de Toulouse, ms. 490; Guilelmus Pelisso, *De Empcione et adquizicione secundi loci Fratrum Predictorum Tholose*, 1263; J. Contrasty, 'Travaux de Jean Maurin aux Jacobins, etc.', *Revue Historique de Toulouse*, t. 9 (1922), pp. 11–15; Archives Départementales, ms. 112 H, No. 26; Elie Lambert, 'L'église et le couvent des Jacobins, etc.', *Bulletin Monumental*, t. 104 (1946); etc.

What we know about the building record of Lyon cathedral is largely contained in M.-C. Guigue's 'Notice historique', which introduces the Lucien Bégule *Monographie de la cathédrale de Lyon*, 1880. The footnotes of Guigue's account contain references to financial data, including an occasional listing of the donor of a window or a pillar. Guigue's chief sources were the *Actes Capitulaires* and especially the printed *Obituarium lugdunensis ecclesiae*, 1867, edited by Guigue himself, available in the more recent edition of Jacques Laurent, *Obituaires de la province de Lyon,* I, 1951. Some cathedral patronage information drawn from Lyon's collection of early wills is available in the inventory cards of the nineteenth-century archivist, Vital de Valous, which are at the Archives Départementales.

The richest source of information on the financing of Strasbourg *Münster* are the printed volumes of the city's *Urkundenbuch* (book of archives), which I collated very carefully. More especially concerned with finances is the excellent, though incomplete, *Liber Donationum*, which was prepared between 1318 and 1328. It contains a large number of donors from 1257 to 1324 and has been analysed in detail by several scholars, including H. Woltmann, 'Das Wohltäterbuch des Frauenwerks in Strassburg', *Reportorium für Kunstwissenschaft*, I, 1876; Louis Pfleger, 'Das Schenkungsbuch des Strassburger Münsters', *Elsassland Lothringer Heimat*, 1935; and especially Antoinette Joulia, *Étude sur le Livre des Donations de la Cathédrale de Strasbourg*, 1960.

There is no systematic listing of York Minster's financial records. Much of what we know about them has been drawn from two original sources: the Archbishops' *Registers* and the testaments of York. A considerable part of the former has been published in volumes of the Surtees Society. The latter has been unsatisfactorily published by James Raine (*Testamenta Eboracensis*, 1836), who also did the minster's fabric rolls (*The Fabric Rolls of York Minster*, 1859). Unfortunately, the latter start very late, between 1350 and 1360. The author has inserted into them incomplete entries of donations and bequests from the wills, as can be attested from a reading of the latter. Good supplementary material on financing and donorship can be found in John Browne's two books, *The History of the Metropolitan Church of St. Peter, York*, 1847; and *Fabric Rolls and Documents of York Minster*, 1863, the latter being a polemical reply to James Raine's work and not a complete record.

A large part of Poitiers cathedral's archives was destroyed by the Huguenots in 1562 and those of Rouen's episcopal church are hardly more copious. Only the accounts of the latter's choir-stalls are complete: *Comptes de la fabrique*, Archives Départementales, G. 2492–2503; *Délibérations Capitulaires*, G. 2135; and the excellent printed summary by E. H. Langlois, *Stalles de la cathédrale de Rouen*, 1838.

There are a number of other authors who give some attention to the financing of churches other than those considered in this book, notably:

Rose Graham, 'An Essay on English Monasteries', *Historical Association Pamphlet*, CXII, 1939.

Pierre du Colombier, 'Les chantiers des cathédrales', *Art Bulletin*, t. 37 (1955).

Abbé Suger, *De rebus in administratione sua gestis* and *De consecratione*, both put into English with commentary by Erwin Panofsky, *Abbot Suger on the Abbey Church of St-Denis and its Art Treasures*, 1946.

A. Deville (ed.), *Comptes de dépenses de la construction du château de Gaillon*, 1850, which contains expenditure accounts of the building and decoration of the château's chapel.

Otto von Simson, *The Gothic Cathedral*, 1956, which has a section on the financing of

Chartres cathedral (pp. 170–82); the same subject is treated in John James, 'What Price the Cathedrals', *Transactions of the Ancient Monuments Society*, XIX (1972), pp. 47–65, but in more detail as to cost, his findings being considered more fully in the Glossary.

Edmund Bishop, 'How a Cathedral was built in the 14th century', *Liturgica Historica*, 1918, pp. 411–21, which gives a synopsis of the first five years of money-raising methods used at Milan Cathedral, 1387–92, drawn from the church's complete series of account books published shortly before. The essay shows literally the entire population swept into the campaign and by fervour, imagination and persistence raising an extraordinary amount of money, as well as furnishing short periods of unskilled labour.

Robert Branner, 'Historical Aspects of the Reconstruction of Reims Cathedral, 1210–1241', *Speculum*, XXXVI (1961), pp. 23–37. While the author gives few examples of funds actually donated for building purposes, he furnishes inferences on several occasions when such money may have been supplied by the cathedral chapter. Of great interest is the detailing of a violent conflict between the burghers and the hierarchy, which halted operations for several years. Curiously, the author quotes a complete record of expenditures during the building of another important contemporary Reims church, St-Nicaise, now vanished, during 1232–58.

3 It has been estimated that France alone built 700 churches in each of the twelfth and thirteenth centuries, or seven units a year for 200 years!

4 The idea came from Professor Meyer Schapiro of Columbia University, who, struck by the novel findings at Strasbourg, suggested that a study of an English cathedral be included as well.

I PARIS

1 At the end of the twelfth century, the royal domain of France took in a narrow oblong of territory centring on Paris, reaching up to Amiens and down to Bourges. In 1204, Philippe-Auguste added by conquest Normandy, the Maine, Anjou, the Touraine, Poitou and the rest of the Plantagenet provinces down to Bordeaux. Much of this was only loosely held at the time and had to be reconquered by St Louis and Alphonse de Poitiers in 1242. Previously, in 1229, the great province of Languedoc had been ceded by the count of Toulouse through the Treaty of Paris. In 1285, Champagne was brought into France by purchase and, toward the end of the century, Lyon and the Lyonnais were conquered, though they did not formally pass under the crown until 1312.

2 For the dating of Notre-Dame, I will use chiefly the works of Marcel Aubert, especially *La cathédrale de Notre-Dame de Paris* (Paris: Firmin-Didot, 1950) and *Notre-Dame de Paris, sa place dans l'architecture du douzième au quatorzième siècle* (Paris: H. Laurens, 1920). The cathedral was begun at the choir *c.*1163, which was completed, including its two aisles though not its vault, by 1177. By 1196, the year of Bishop Maurice de Sully's death, the entire nave except one bay was finished. The Ste-Anne portal of the façade was made partly in the twelfth century and partly altered in the interval of *c.*1225–35. The rest of the façade, including the lower registers of the towers, was built around the same time, as was the gallery of the interior. By 1245, the church as planned by Maurice was completed. However, this initial edifice was already undergoing fundamental changes, a major purpose being to bring more light into the dark interior; another was to expand the space available for sacerdotal activity. Around 1220–30, the internal vaulting of choir and nave was redone. About the same time, window spaces were greatly enlarged in all parts of the structure, choir, nave, transepts, tribune. Also, the flying buttresses of the nave were doubled. In 1235, the great perimeter of chapels was begun at the western extremity of the church, reaching the transepts by 1250. These latter were reconstructed in their present splendid style, starting at the north around 1250, at the south around 1257. About the same time, the choir chapels were begun, their construction continuing into the second decade of the fourteenth century, when the church as seen today was completed. Also included in the reno-

vation was a great amount of decorative work, now mostly gone, such as the reglazing of the stained-glass windows, the roodscreen and the richly sculptured choir enclosure, as well as other statuary, both inside and outside.

3 See, among various others, especially Charles-Edmond Petit-Dutaillis, 'La prétendue commune de Toulouse', *Comptes Rendus, Académie des Inscriptions et Belles-Lettres* (1941), pp. 45–64; E. Levasseur, *Histoire des classes ouvrières et de l'industrie en France avant 1789*, t. I (Paris: Arthur Rousseau, 1900), p. 251; and Frédéric Lecaron, 'Les origines de la municipalité parisienne, première partie, la hanse ou marchandise de l'eau de Paris', *MSHP*, t. VII (1880), p. 109.

4 L. Dubech and P. D'Espezel, among others, discuss the identification of the city municipality with the Paris Hanse, which well into the thirteenth century was the *de facto* representative of the entire population (*Histoire de Paris*, Paris: Les Editions Pittoresques, 1931). Nevertheless, the powers of the Hanse were themselves extremely limited; they included juridical powers only after 1220 and these were confined to 'low' justice (pp. 96–8). The Hanse was a limited band of merchants who enjoyed monopoly privileges for their boats on the Seine as far downstream as the port of Mantes. They were the only ones allowed to unload merchandise at the port of Paris (Emile Picarda, *Les marchands de l'eau, hanse parisienne et compagnie française*, municipality Paris: Emile Bouillon, 1901, pp. 38–9). The actual emergence of the city municipality as an independent entity is not clearly defined. It is generally considered to have taken place after the post of prévôt de Paris ceased to be farmed out by the king to the highest bidder and became a salaried office. Soon after, in 1263, there is found cited for the first time in the documents a 'prévôt des marchands', as distinct from the first prévôt, who was the king's representative. Thereafter, a kind of municipal administrative apparatus began to evolve (Le Roux de Lincy, *Histoire de l'hôtel de ville de Paris, suivie d'un essai sur l'ancien gouvernement municipal de cette ville*, Paris: J. B. Dumoulin, 1846, pp. 153ff).

5 The city's administrative officers—the prévôt des marchands and his four échevins, or aldermen—were elected for two-year terms by about eighty of the 'most notable' citizens. The officers were assisted by a group of twenty-six counsellors (chosen from the king's parlement), lawyers, notaries, important merchants, who not only kept their posts for life but could, with approval, transmit them to their sons (Dubech and D'Espezel, 1931, pp. 63ff). The only involvement by the great mass of the city's working population was through their guilds, but these had a largely regulatory function and were without political or judicial authority. A number of the city's trades, besides, were not organized into guilds and others had been sold or given by different kings to private individuals, under whose control and exploitation they remained. See on this Alfred Franklin, *Dictionnaire historique des arts, métiers et professions exercés dans Paris depuis le 13e siècle* (Paris: H. Walter, 1906), pp. 188–9; also Etienne Martin Saint-Léon, *Histoire des corporations de métiers* (Paris: PUF, 1945), p. 68.

6 An example was Armand de Corbie, a close partisan of Marcel, who was so quickly graced by the king as to become councillor-clerk of the parlement by 1364, its president in 1373. Ennobled, he was awarded 1,000 gold francs by Charles V in 1375 and received many other royal gifts (*Testaments enregistrés au parlement de Paris sous le règne de Charles VI*, in *Mélanges Historiques*, Paris: Imprimerie Nationale, 1880, p. 285).

7 The king identified only one of these men by name, Pierre le Maréchal, the rest being cryptically designated by their initials: T.A.E.R.B.N. (Alexandre Vidier, 'Les origines de la municipalité parisienne', *MSHP*, t. 49, 1927, p. 266). The celebrated archivist, Léopold Delisle, worked out the riddle of the initials from the names of those signing royal documents during Philippe-Auguste's absence. See his *Catalogue des actes de Philippe-Auguste* (Paris: Auguste-Durand, 1856), p. lxiii.

8 Joseph R. Strayer, 'Normandy and Languedoc', *Speculum*, vol. 44, no. 1, pp. 1–12. The royal revenues from Normandy alone were 120,000 l., the author points out, 'or about as much as

all of the old domain'. At a later period of the thirteenth century, 'when the king's ordinary annual revenue was about 450,000 livres par.', he finds that 'Normandy and Languedoc were responsible for something like 200,000 livres par., or nearly half the total'.

9 A recent author, Marguerite David-Roy, in 'St. Louis, batisseur des monuments disparus', *Archeologia*, no. 31 (1969), pp. 14–21, lists twelve, and we could add the Carmelites, who were established in a house by the king, in 1256 (Emile Raunié, *Epitaphier du vieux Paris*, Paris: Imprimerie Nationale, 1890) as well as the Prieuré de Ste-Croix-de-la-Bretonnerie, toward whose foundation in 1259 St Louis contributed importantly (*ibid.*).

10 Aubin-Louis Millin, *Antiquités nationales, ou recueil de monuments, etc.*, t. IV (Paris: Drouhin, 1792), p. 8.

11 Paul et Marie-Louise Biver, *Abbayes, monastères et couvents de Paris dès origines à la fin du 18e siècle* (Paris: Editions d'Histoire d'Art, 1970), p. 76.

12 Léopold Delisle, 'Fragments de l'histoire de Gonesse principalement tirés des Archives Hospitalières de cette commune', *BEC*, 4e série, t. 5 (1859), pp. 115–16.

13 L. Delisle, 'Fragments de l'histoire de Gonesse', p. 125.

14 L. Delisle, *Recueil des historiens des Gaules et de la France* (Paris: Imprimerie Nationale, 1904), t. 24, p. 136. Acarin gratefully established an anniversary in Philippe-Auguste's honour at his church, acknowledging that 'I acquired much wealth in the service of the aforesaid king and of his illustrious sons'.

15 Fournier Bonnard, *Histoire de l'abbaye . . . de St-Victor de Paris* (Paris: Arthur Savaète, n.d.), pp.113–14.

16 L. Delisle, 'Fragments de l'histoire de Gonesse', p. 123. See also Adrien-Henri Théry, *Gonesse dans l'histoire* (Persan, Seine-et-Oise, 1960). The wall built to enclose the Hôtel-Dieu's many buildings alone cost Pierre de Thillay 200 livres.

17 Quoted by L. Delisle, p. 126.

18 For the best source of Jean Sarrazin's many pious bequests, see Borrelli de Serres, *Recherches sur divers services publics*, I, 1895, p. 123. He founded at least three other chaplaincies, two of them at Paris (churches of St-Gervais and St-Victor) and the third at the Abbaye de Chaalis. While he lived he had his own personal chaplain, Richard de Mellemmare, like any great seignior (Fournier Bonnard, pp. 322, n. 4, 324). Another important foundation by Jean Sarrazin was an annuity of 20.5 livres, in 1257, set up to furnish annual grants for four students at the Hôtel-Dieu: would they have been studying medicine? (Léon Brièle, *Archives de l'Hôtel-Dieu de Paris, 1157–1300*, Paris: Imprimerie Nationale, 1894, no. 991).

19 Auguste Molinier (and Auguste Longnon), *Obituaires de la province de Sens*, t. I, 1ère partie (Paris: Imprimerie Nationale, 1902), 'Abbaye de St-Victor', 26 November.

20 L. Delisle, *Catalogue des actes de Philippe-Auguste*, no. 2140 (1222).

21 Léon Le Grand, 'Les maisons-dieu et léproseries du diocèse de Paris au milieu du 14e siècle', *MSHP*, t. 25 (1898), p. 53.

22 Benjamin Guérard, *Cartulaire de l'église Notre-Dame de Paris* (Paris: Crapelet, 1850), *Chartularium Episcopi*, no. 168 (1202); also Jean Lebeuf, *Histoire de la ville et de tout le diocèse de Paris*, t. III (Paris: Féchoz et Letouzey, 1883), pp. 174–5; and Marcel Poëte, *Une vie de cité, Paris de sa naissance à nos jours*, t. I (Paris: Auguste Picard, 1924), p. 206. Escuacol was bailiff of Rouen for ten years (1208–17) and one bit of recorded royal guerdon was the grant of an important fief on the former site of the city's demolished château. Rennemoulin was about 25 kilometres west of Paris, near Versailles.

23 L. Delisle, *Catalogue des actes de Philippe-Auguste*, no. 1677 (1216); also L. Delisle, *Les enquêtes administratives du règne de St. Louis*, in *Recueil des historiens . . . de la France*, t. 24, p. 277.

24 Joseph R. Strayer, *The Administration of Normandy under St. Louis* (Cambridge, Mass.: The Mediaeval Academy of America, 1932), pp. 49–50. Arrode, who served also as king's storekeeper (*panetier*), received among his known rewards the fishing rights at several bridges in the Paris area (*Catalogue des actes de Philippe-Auguste*, no. 1709).

25 Martin Marrier, *Monasterii regalis S. Martini de Campis paris. historia* (Paris: Sebastien Cramoisy, 1636), pp. 573–5; also Jean Lebeuf, edited by Hippolyte Cocheris, t. II (Paris: Auguste Durand, 1864), pp. 331–2. Nicolas Arrode also invested in anniversary masses at a number of Paris churches, including Notre-Dame (Molinier-Longnon, *Obituaires*, 8 November); St-Germain-des-Prés (*ibid.*, 12 August); and St-Victor (*ibid.*, 11 August). In his obit at St-Martin (*ibid.*, 12 August), his chapel is cited but he is also credited with having given 'much more treasure' to the priory. There are other burgher agents that could be listed, who served the crown in the occupied lands and then returned to put part of their gains into pious foundations, but space does not allow it.

26 Archives Nationales, L. 474, no. 138 (1288); S. 87, no. 3 (May 1283); S. 87, no. 5 (September 1287).

27 Marquis de Belbeuf, *Notice sur le collège du trésorier* (Paris: Ch. Lahure, 1861), especially Appendice O, pp. 76–80. The two colleges founded by the Harcourt brothers were the Collège d'Harcourt and the Collège de Lisieux. For full details about this very interesting assimilated Norman family, see H. L. Bouquet, *L'Ancien collège d'Harcourt ...* (Paris, Delalain Frères, 1891).

28 The royal foundations at Notre-Dame were carefully recorded. I have collated the following, a majority of them from the cathedral's *Cartulaire*:

(1) *1175*, Henri, archbishop of Reims, brother of Louis VII, founded an anniversary with a gift of 9 arpents of vineyard, whose earnings were to be used for establishing twelve lamps at Notre-Dame (*Cartulaire*, IV, no. 322).

(2) *1180*, Louis VII gave 200 l. to the fabric and also made arrangements for adding to the meals of the Notre-Dame family on his anniversary (*Cartulaire*, IV, *Obituarium*, no. 263).

(3) c.*1186*, Philippe-Auguste founded four chaplaincies and added a *rente* of 100 sous at some other unspecified date, meant for distributions to the cathedral family (*ibid.*, no. 192).

(4) *1189*, Isabelle, wife of Philippe-Auguste, founded a chaplaincy at the Altar of St-Nicolas (Arch. Nat., LL. 247).

(5) *1206*, Queen Adèle, Louis VII's widow, donated 20 marks to the fabric (*Cartulaire*, IV, *Obituarium*, no. 164).

(6) Louis VIII and Blanche de Castille founded chaplaincy in the name of their deceased son, Philippe (*ibid.*, no. 335).

(7) *Pre-1271*, Alphonse de Poitiers founded chaplaincy in Chapel of Ste-Agnès (Bibliothèque Nationale, ms. latin 18361, fol. 174v°).

(8) *1296*, Philippe-le-Bel and his wife Jeanne donated a *rente* of 20 l. tournois, in return for which the chapter established a festival for St Eutrope for whom the royal couple had a special devotion; the canons arranged to celebrate one mass for the king, another for the queen (*Cartulaire*, IV, *Obituarium*, no. 314). May I add here that from the evidence supplied by Pierre Le Vieil, in *L'Art de la peinture sur verre et de la vitrerie*, Paris, 1774, as interpreted by me in the *Gazette des Beaux-Arts*, September 1966, pp. 131–48, the royal couple were probably also founders of the two apse chapels of St-Eutrope and the Décollation-de-St-Jean-Baptiste.

(9) *1302*, Marguerite de Provence, widow of St Louis, founded by testament a chaplaincy (Arch. Nat., S. 90B, no. 19).

(10) *1304*, Philippe-le-Bel founded a *rente* of 100 l. on behalf of Notre-Dame to commemorate the victory in Flanders at the battle of Mons (*Cartulaire*, t. II, pp. 147–51).

(11) *1313*, Philippe-le-Bel, after confiscating the property of the Templars at Paris, is said to have made a donation of part of the spoils to help erect the enclosure of the choir, on which a relief was reportedly carved showing the Templars in chains and the king and his wife kneeling nearby (T. B. Emeric-David, *Histoire de la sculpture française*, Paris, 1853, quotes the nineteenth-century archaeologist, Fernand de Guilhermy, on this).

29 Natalis de Wailly, *Dissertation sur les dépenses et les recettes ordinaires de St Louis*, in *Recueil des historiens ... de la France*, t. XXI (Paris:

Imprimerie Impériale, 1855). The author lists expenses for a period of only three years and twenty-five days of the first Crusade, totalling 793,728 l. The Crusade lasted five years.

30 C. A. Robson, *Maurice of Sully and the Medieval Vernacular Homily* (Oxford: Basil Blackwell, 1952), pp. 110–13.

31 Henry Kraus, 'Notre-Dame's vanished medieval glass', *Gazette des Beaux-Arts*, 6e période, t. 68 (September 1966), pp. 131–48, and t. 69 (February 1967), pp. 65–78. As for the guild that probably donated the stained-glass roundels, which have of course long since disappeared, there is a document showing that in 1379 Charles V gave his consent to the request, made five years earlier, by the journeymen shoemakers of Paris, that they be allowed to celebrate a mass every Monday in honour of their patron saints at their chapel in Notre-Dame (Gustave Fagniez, *Etudes sur l'industrie et la class industrielle à Paris au 13e et au 14e siècle*, Paris: F. Vieweg, 1877, appendice V; derived from the *Trésor des chartes*, reg. 118, pièce 456).

32 Adrien Friedmann, *Recherches sur les origines et l'évolution des circonscriptions paroissiales de Paris au moyen âge*, thèse de doctorat (Paris: Plon, 1959), p. 119.

33 Among the rare contributions by Notre-Dame's hierarchy for building purposes listed in its obituaries are two famous dating milestones. One was Maurice de Sully's bequest of 100 livres to buy lead for the nave roofing (*Obituarium*, no. 252), which informs us that at his death, in 1196, the church vessel was already nearing completion. The other is in the obit notice of Jean de Paris, who left a sum of money around 1270 'for work on the transepts recently begun' (*ibid.*, no. 214).

34 The present author has collated many examples from the *Cartulaire* of important donors among the clerical family for the period under discussion. For Maurice de Sully and Simon de Buci, see *Obituarium*, nos 252 and 173. Space does not allow a fuller listing.

35 One highly remunerative revenue, for example, was the bishop's one-third share of the crown's levy on every transaction taking place at Les Halles, which all tradesmen and artisans were required to attend three days a week while shutting down their own shops (Victor Mortet, *Maurice de Sully, évêque de Paris, 1160–1196. Etude sur l'administration épiscopale pendant la seconde moitié du 12e siècle*, Paris, 1890). Another great source of revenue was the bishop's share of temporal justice at Paris, which exceeded even that of the king, while the chapter also possessed a considerable jurisdiction. These rights stemmed mainly from the enormous stretches of property owned by the church at Paris, the prelate's holdings spreading over most of the Seine's right bank while those of the canons took in mainly the Île-de-la-Cité. And these properties were more than matched by those outside the city, the chapter especially owning many villages and domains throughout the diocese (Louis Tanon, *Histoire des justices des anciennes églises et communautés monastiques de Paris*, Paris, 1883, pp. 2, 130ff). Regarding the property holdings of the Paris church, this is summarized in the Préface of the *Cartulaire de Notre-Dame*, p. lxxxv. In addition, other church groups owned great amounts of property at Paris, the total for all such church holdings having been calculated as taking up two-thirds of the capital's soil (Adrien Friedmann, p. 41). There is, likewise, a good deal of documentary evidence that the Parisian ecclesiastics sold a considerable amount of its propertied wealth during Notre-Dame's building period. Thus, the *Cartulaire de Notre-Dame* shows the burgher Guillaume Barbette as having purchased fiefs from Bishop Eudes de Sully in 1208, 1228 and 1229 (t. I, pp. 11, 148, 149). The *Cartulaire* shows other Parisians making similar acquisitions later in the century, one of whom was a woman, Aveline, widow of Bertaud Arrode (pp. 204–5). Borrelli de Serres (*Recherches sur divers services publics*, I, p. 561), lists other commoners as holding some of the 'principal fiefs' at Paris under the bishop's jurisdiction early in the thirteenth century, including the important families of Pacy, Popin and Arrode.

36 Victor Mortet, *Etude historique et archéologique sur la cathédrale et le palais épiscopal de Paris, du 6e au 12e siècle* (Paris: Alphonse Picard, 1888), pp. 70, 74, 75, *passim*.

37 Marc Bloch, 'Blanche de Castille et les serfs du chapitre de Paris', *MSHP*, t. 38 (1911), pp. 224–72. Blanche died in 1252, whereas the chapter's serfs began to be freed only in 1263, when 636 of them bought their manumission (*ibid.*, p. 247).

38 *Ibid.*, pp. 226ff.

39 *Ibid.*, p. 247; also Pièces Justificatives, pp. 251, 254–5, 258, 259. The arbitral commission of bishops delayed two years before making known its decision, announcing it three days after Blanche's death. The serfs were no doubt in the wrong when they argued that only the king had ever imposed the *taille* on them. Among those who testified against this declaration were burghers from some of the villages involved in the controversy as well as from Paris itself.

40 *Ibid.*, pp. 240, n. 6; 242–3.

41 *Cartulaire de Notre-Dame*, Préface, p. cc. The cathedral was not the only important Paris church that used its serfs' emancipation payments for building purposes. The lovely Chapelle de la Vièrge of St-Germain-des-Prés, a victim in 1802 of official vandalism, was built largely from money obtained in this manner. See on this Jacques Bouillart, *Histoire de l'abbaye royale de Saint Germain des Prez, etc.* (Paris: Gregoire Dupuis, 1724), pp. 216–18; also Adolphe Berty et L.-M. Tisserand, *Topographie historique du vieux Paris. Région du Bourg St-Germain* (Paris: Imprimerie Nationale, 1876), p. 107.

42 Many of the church inventories of that period which I have examined are replete with such investments. They are fully discussed by Robert Genestal in his *Rôle des monastères comme établissements de crédit, étudié en Normandie du 11e à la fin du 13e siècle* (Paris: Arthur Rousseau, 1901). Based on the great increase in land values that occurred during this period, they were an allowed evasion of the church's ban on interest collection (usury) and became a major form of capital placement in the thirteenth century.

43 Raymond Gazelles, 'La rivalité commerciale de Paris et de Rouen au moyen âge', *BSHP*, t. 96 (1969), pp. 99–112.

44 Marcel Poëte, *Une vie de cité*, pp. 206–7, 208, 212, 213, 214, 223–4. Borrelli de Serres also contains much pertinent material on these subjects.

45 A. Lecoy de la Marche, *La France sous St. Louis et sous Philippe-le-Hardi* (Paris: Librairies-Imprimeries Réunies, 1893), pp. 167–8.

46 Jean Lebeuf, *Histoire de la ville et de tout le diocèse de Paris*, édition de H. Cocheris, t. I; also Emile Raunié, *Epitaphier*, etc., t. IV, p. 4, n. 3.

47 Henry Kraus, 'New Documents for Notre-Dame's Early Chapels', *Gazette des Beaux-Arts*, 6e période, t. 74 (September 1969), pp. 121–34.

48 The list of chaplaincies founded by burghers at Notre-Dame follows. It should be noted that those listed in nos 3, 5, 6, 9, 12 and 16 are all the earliest foundations for which documents have been discovered for the corresponding chapels, coinciding in fact with the probable dates when these chapels were built. This adds to the possibility that the chaplaincy founders also paid in part or entirely for the erection of their chapels. The information of the documents was rarely complete in this matter, one exception being the case of Odeline Coquillière, a bourgeois woman, who paid for the Chapel of St-Eustache in the north apse and established a chaplaincy there:

(1) *1217*, Agnès, first wife of Garin de Moncel, at Altar of Ste-Catherine, prior to the erection of the cathedral's chapels, which began only in 1235 (*Cartulaire de Notre-Dame*, t. I, p. 400).

(2) *1221*, Raoul Poquet (Arch. Nat., Salle des Inventaires, *Archevêchés et Evêchés*, L. 414, no. 16). Jean Lebeuf, based on Gerard Dubois, *Historia ecclesiae parisiensis*, t. II, p. 270, says that the chaplaincy was dedicated to St Léonard (t. III, p. 570).

(3) *1237*, Emeline de Chaumont, the first chaplaincy founded at the Chapel of Ste-Anne (*Parvum Pastorale*, Arch. Nat. LL. 77, no. 222, fols 333ff). The document does not actually name the chapel but it *is* named in the creation of a second chaplaincy which was founded there in 1265 by Emeline's third husband, Benoît de St-Victor (Marcel Aubert,

Notre-Dame de Paris, sa place, etc., p. 140, which gives the source).

(4) *1243*, Marie dite Allemande founded a chaplaincy at the episcopal palace, whose enjoyment she reserved for her son, a priest, if he desired to accept it (*Cartulaire*, t. I, p. 152).

(5) *c. 1246*, Aléaume Hécelin, at Chapel of St-Augustin (Arch. Nat., S. 92, which contains a summary sheet attributing the foundation 'towards 1246' of a chaplaincy by Hécelin le Voyer (inspector of roads), bourgeois de Paris, through his testamentary executioner, Guillaume de Varzy, canon; the document itself was even then missing).

(6) *1255*, Odeline Coquillière founded a chaplaincy at Chapel of St-Eustache (Arch. Nat., S. 87, nos 38, 39 and 41; also LL. 7–8, no. 95; see also *Cartulaire de Notre-Dame*, t. III, *Magnum Chartularium*, no. 63 and no. 95). Jean Lebeuf, t. V, pp. 137–8, is the one who identifies Odeline as the founder of the Chapel of St-Eustache as well. A 'coquille' was a kind of coiffure popular at the time, but Odeline evidently was not in the hairdressing business, as I once suggested, her name being merely the feminine form of her husband's, Coquillier.

(7 and 8) *1255*, Sancelina Hermande founded two chaplaincies at Chapel of St-Michel (Arch. Nat., L. 76, *Magnum Pastorale*, Liber 20, no. 92; or *Cartulaire*, t. II, p. 440).

(9) *1255*, Adam Bigue, a chaplaincy dedicated to St-Julien and Ste-Marie-l'Égyptienne (Arch. Nat., LL. 7–8, *Magnum Chartularium*, fol. xlvii rº; also *Cartulaire*, t. III, p. 47).

(10) *1263*, date when Agnès Le Roux, widow of Eudes Le Roux, paid an amortization to St Louis on a *rente* of 15 l. for the foundation of a chaplaincy (Arch. Nat., Salle des Inventaires, *Répertoires Numériques . . . par Lelong, Série S, Chapitre Notre-Dame de Paris*, t. 80, no. 9).

(11) *Pre-1265*, Benoît de St-Victor (see no. 3 above).

(12) *1267/70*, Marguerite Houdeard founded chaplaincy at Chapel of Sts-Pierre-et-Paul (Arch. Nat., S. 90B, nos 66 and 88).

(13) *1268*, Josse, *sergent* of the bishop, founded a 'second' chaplaincy at Altar of St-Eustache (Marcel Aubert, who gave as his source Arch. Nat. documents, L. 474, no. 98 and L. 535, no. 14, which have been checked).

(14) *1275*, by Marie, widow of Baudouin Maréchal (Arch. Nat., LL. 76, Liber 20, no. 223; also *Cartulaire*, t. II, p. 490).

(15) *1275*, Jean Sarrazin, at Ste-Agnès Chapel (Arch. Nat., LL. 247, Table).

(16) *1278*, Pierre Apothicaire, at Chapel of St-Gérard (Arch. Nat., S. 93, nos 7 and 55).

(17) *1296*, Gilles Arrode at Chapel of St-Rigobert (Marcel Aubert; his source, Arch. Nat., S. 92, has been checked).

(18) *1299*, Galerand Le Breton, at Chapel of St-Louis (M. Aubert, his source being Arch. Nat., L. 535, no. 19 and S. 87, no. 51. Another document in S. 87, no. 2, dates the foundation as March 1302).

(19) *1302*, Étienne and Jeanne Haudri (Arch. Nat., LL. 76, Liber 22, no. 49; also *Cartulaire*, t. II, p. 524).

(20) *1313*, Philippe le Pévrier (Arch. Nat., LL. 7–8, fol. 261, showing that Philippe founded the chaplaincy for his father, Jean; also in *Cartulaire*, t. III, *Magnum Chartularium*, no. 280).

(21) *1318*, Jacques Boucel, St-Pierre-Martyre (LL. 7–8, fol. 259 vº; also *Cartulaire, Magnum Chartularium*, no. 278).

(22 and 23) *1326*, Jean Haudri founded two chaplaincies by testament (*Cartulaire*, t. III, p. 228).

(24) *1329*, Pierre and Pernelle Mulet, St-Jean-Baptiste et Ste-Marie-Madeleine (S. 88B, no. 99).

(25) *1331*, André Giffart, at the Altar of Ste-Geneviève (Jean Lebeuf, t. IV, p. 438, who gives the name of Giffart and the altar name but not the date; the latter can be found at Arch. Nat., *Série L, Archevêchés et Evêchés*, L. 535, no. 30).

(26) *1332*, by Marie La Josequine, wife of Etienne Haudri (Jules Viard, *Documents parisiens du règne de Philippe VI de Valois*, t. I, 1328–38, under January 1332, where Philippe VI amortizes a *rente* of 20 l. for Marie La Josequine, to found a 'chaplaincy in the church of Paris, in honour of the Virgin Mary and of St Denis').

(27) *1336*, Dreue de la Charité, Philippe VI's clerk (*ibid.*, under May 1336).

(28) *1337*, Amaury de Gray, master of the mint, founded the chaplaincy of the Sts-Innocents at the Altar of Ste-Catherine; date of amortization by Philippe VI (Marcel Poëte, *Répertoire des sources manuscrites de l'histoire de Paris*, t. III, Paris: Ernest Leroux, 1916, giving source as Arch. Nat., S. 94B, no. 31).

(29) *1339*, Pierre Barrier (Jules Viard, no. 226, where the foundation is referred to as an 'anniversary', which is a patent error, considering the big annual *rente* of 30 livres par. that is provided).

(30) *1340*, Martin des Essars, Altar of St-Eutrope (*ibid*., no. 229).

(31) *1342*, Jeanne, widow of Jean d'Avranches (*ibid*., no. 294). The church is not named but the foundation is called 'a chaplaincy of Paris'.

(32) *Pre-1350*, Jean le Leu (*ibid*., no. 133). A chaplaincy is not mentioned but it is a chaplaincy equivalent, at least, entailing a big bequest of 13 l. of annual quitrents, donated for 'causing to sing the *Inviolata* every day and at processions of the Assumption and the Nativity'.

(33) *1351*, by Hugues Porcherit, called de Besançon, officer at the parlement (Arch. Nat., *Série L, Archevêchés et Evêchés*, L. 535, no. 37).

(34) *1360*, Ithier de Manhaco, professor of law (*ibid*., no. 39).

(35) *1361*, Gilbert Aymelin, king's physician (M. Poëte, t. II, under 'Notre-Dame'; the note specifies an anniversary but with so large a foundation, a *rente* of 18 livres, it is probably a chaplaincy).

(36) *1379*, date when Journeymen Shoemakers took over the Chapel of Sts-Crépin-et-Crépinien; they undoubtedly also had a chaplain here (see note 31).

(37) We add here a chaplaincy, founded in *1328* at the Chapel of Sts-Martin-et-Anne (Arch. Nat., LL. 247, *Capellaniae*), by Geoffroy de Plessis. This man was a cleric but he did not become a monk of the Abbey of Marmoutier until the end of his life, having been a notary in service of the church before that. He is also credited with having founded

a college with its chapel at Paris, which he turned over to Marmoutier.

49 Marcel Aubert, in *Notre-Dame de Paris, sa place, etc*., p. 156, remarks that 'Starting at the end of the twelfth century, the right of being buried in the cathedral, reserved at first to the clergy, to the founders and to the princes, was extended more and more to the entire bourgeoisie and foundations multiplied.' This is, from the available evidence, incorrect. In any case, I have been unable to find any record of a burgher being buried at Notre-Dame either in the twelfth century or long after. It was not until the fifteenth century, apparently, that this began to be allowed and then only in a few isolated cases. On the other hand, the prestigious Parisian Abbey of St-Victor did welcome commoners for burial. It received gifts from kings, barons and churchmen but its chief benefactors were wealthy burghers, who were received into the abbey's family of canons *ad succurrendum*, at the approach of death. Many of them were buried in the abbey cemetery, their tombs marked by splendidly carved headstones bearing their portraits, some of which were copied by an artist hired by Roger de Gaignières in the late seventeenth century, these drawings being now at the Bibliothèque Nationale and the Bodleian Library at Oxford. The abbey's extraordinary *Obituaire* of *c*.1360 contains approximately 1,200 anniversaries, for which very big sums were often paid, in addition to other gifts, including a number for aesthetic purposes. One finds many familiar names among those that the abbey 'remembered' gratefully after their death. Thus, king's chamberlain and burgher Jean Sarrazin was acclaimed for 'embracing our church in life and death with his special love' (*Obituaire*, 21 June). The gifts of his wife, Agnès Barbette, included a silver statuette of Mary Magdalene and were rewarded with a 'mass at the high altar with all vestments carefully prepared' (*ibid*., 3 November).

50 The information gathered on burgher chaplaincies founded in Parisian churches has required 10,000 words to detail, rendering their publication here impossible. In summary,

the total number of churches named (many no longer exist) is 56, in addition to 14 that are unnamed and 13 more outside Paris. Those with ten or more chaplaincies include: St-Jacques-aux-Pèlerins (49); Cathédrale Notre-Dame (37); Les Célestins (20); St-Sépulcre (14); St-Germain-l'Auxerroix (14); St-Gervais (13); Hôtel-Dieu (12); St-Eustache (12); St-Jean-en-Grève (11); St-Jacques-de-la-Boucherie (10). Seven of the 335 burgher chaplaincies collated were founded in the twelfth century, 63 in the thirteenth and 259 in the fourteenth; the others of unknown century.

51 A number of these churches are discussed individually in the text or in other notes. It should be pointed out that in the thirteenth century, Paris's leading parishes were almost exclusively centred on the Seine's right bank, especially north of the Île-de-la-Cité. In this area was concentrated the city's industrial and commercial life. Recent scholarship has greatly reduced the estimated population of Paris in the thirteenth and fourteenth centuries, bringing it down from the more than 200,000 previously calculated to something closer to half that amount. The new evaluation is based on comparative figures of other important cities and similar considerations (Ph. Dollinger, 'Le chiffre de population de Paris au 14e siècle: 210,000 ou 80,000 habitants?', *Revue Historique*, t. 216, July–September 1956, pp. 35–44). Most of these leading parish churches on the right bank are well known to us by name at least. Three of them each had more people paying the king's *taille* in 1296 than all the left-bank parishes taken together. These were St-Germain-l'Auxerrois, 912 taxpayers; St-Eustache, 624; St-Jacques-de-la-Boucherie, 665. The entire left bank had only 574 taxpayers that year (Karl Michaëlson, *Le livre de la taille de Paris l'an 1296*, Göteborg: Elanders Boktryckerie Aktiebolag, 1958, Appendice). As for the Île-de-la-Cité itself, it remained the clerical heart of Paris, whose many small churches (now all gone) served as auxiliaries of Notre-Dame or as parishes of the domestics, artisans and tradesmen that accommodated the clerics. The bells of these churches never ceased to sound the offices, from which the Cité came

to bear the name of 'sonorous island' (Adrien Friedmann, *Recherches sur les origines et l'évolution des circonscriptions paroissiales de Paris au moyen-âge . . .*, p. 58).

52 Jean Lebeuf, t. I, 1883, pp. 323–4.

53 Arch. Nat., LL. 387, *St-Germain-l'Auxerrois, Cartulaire du Chapitre*, August 1207, fol. 118v°; Emile Raunié, *Epitaphier du vieux Paris*, t. II, 1893, pp. 95–6; and Jean Lebeuf, t. I, pp. 38, 56. The rapid growth of the Chapel of St-Honoré is described in *Titres de la fondation et établissement de l'église et chapitre de St-Honoré de Paris*, n.d. I have assembled data on nine other colleges founded by Paris burghers, as well as a long list of chapels (nineteen of them as independent structures or as part of a hospital-plus-chapel unit). A few of the bourgeois-funded hospitals or hospices attained fame, such as Les Haudriettes, established by the Haudry family, one of Paris's most important medieval welfare establishments.

54 Emile Raunié, t. IV, pp. 1–4; Victor Calliat, *Histoire de l'église et de la paroisse St-Eustache* (Paris: Author, 1850), with an 'Essai historique' by Le Roux de Lincy, pp. 1–3; and Amédée Boinet, *Les églises parisiennes* (Paris, 1958).

55 The small church or chapel that was built here early in the twelfth century was largely due to the efforts of the butchers and tanners, who were located outside the walls, as was required by medieval regulations. When the church was rebuilt, the initiative was taken by the Confraternity of St-Jacques (Et.-Fr. Villain, *Essai d'une histoire de la paroisse de St-Jacques-de-la-Boucherie*, Paris: Prault père, 1758, pp. 5–6 and 14, note a).

56 *Ibid.*, pp. 29–31. For information about Nicolas Flamel's many aesthetic benefactions, see by the same author, *Histoire critique de Nicolas Flamel et de Pernelle sa femme . . .* (Paris: G. Desprez, 1761).

57 Et.-Fr. Villain, *Essai d'une histoire, etc.*, p. 54.

58 Adrien Friedmann, p. 286 and note 2.

59 When St-Jean-en-Grève was torn down in 1800, its 'name, traditions and parishioners' were inherited by the church of St-Jean-St-François, according to the placard put up on a front-nave pillar of this church by the 'Beaux-Arts de la Ville de Paris', bidding the visitor to study a

group of eight tapestries running the length of
the nave, 'relating to the scenes of the crime
of the Jew Jonathas, perpetrated on Easter
Sunday, 1290'. Outside the Virgin's Chapel in
the church's north aisle is the copy of an early
painting which has been set up like a shrine,
depicting the gruesome acts of Jonathas. Near
the entrance of the church, a sign, set down in
gleaming white letters on a black background,
asks the visitor 'to pray, adore, expiate, in reparation of the outrages done to the Living
Christ in the Host'.

60 Archives Nationales, L. 663, no. 1, 1290.

61 Le Roux de Lincy, *Histoire de l'hôtel de ville,
etc.*, pp. 64–5. As for the house of the Jew in
which the alleged acts took place, after its
demolition, a burgher, Ragnier Flaming, got
permission, in 1294, to build a chapel on the
site, which came to bear the name of 'Les
Billettes'. Monks of the Order of Charité
Notre-Dame were brought in to service the
large crowds that came to view the spot 'where
Our Lord was boiled' (J. Du Breul, *Le théâtre
des antiquitez de Paris*, 1639, pp. 729–30).
Many foundations were launched. One of the
most interesting endowments was that of a
Confraternity of Carpenters, who in 1368 did
all the woodwork in the church, including the
choir stalls, for which they were given a chapel
of their own, which the monks agreed to service with masses for a small annual *rente* (E.
Raunié, pp. 217ff).

62 Léon Brièle, *Archives de l'Hôtel-Dieu de
Paris, 1157–1300. Notice, Appendice et Table
par Ernest Coyecque* (Paris: Imprimerie
Nationale, 1894); and Ernest Coyecque,
L'Hôtel-Dieu de Paris au moyen-âge (Paris:
H. Champion, 1891) are the basic printed
sources which have been consulted. For the
thirteenth century alone there were 132 gifts
of some importance, including 43 houses and
39 other pieces of property; 20 *rentes* for an
annual total revenue of 159 l.; 14 quitrents; 2
tithes; 4 money gifts totalling 102 l.; and some
others of indeterminate value. One source for
Oudart de Mocreux's gift is Piganiol de la
Force, *Description de Paris, de Versailles, etc.*,
t. I, pp. 470–3.

63 Jules Boullé, 'Recherches historiques sur la

maison de St-Lazare de Paris . . .', *MSHP*, t. 3
(1876), pp. 126–91. St-Lazare's close relationship with commoners is symbolized by the
touching arrangement that gave priority of
entry to stricken bakers, a reward for the
loaves they furnished the lepers all through an
early famine (Léon Le Grand, 'Les maisons-
dieu et léproseries du diocèse de Paris au milieu
du 14e siècle, d'après le registre de visites du
délégué de l'évêque, 1351–1369', *MSHP*, t. 24
(1897), p. 315).

64 Léon Le Grand, 'Les Quinze-Vingts depuis
leur fondation jusqu'à leur translation au
Faubourg St-Antoine, 13e-18e siècle', *MSHP*,
t. 13 et 14 (1887), pp. 5ff. The author records
a number of important donations by burghers
to the Quinze-Vingts and summarizes them
up to 1550 as bringing in an annual revenue of
967 l. 17 s. 11 d., tour. (p. 59).

65 Et.-Fr. Villain, *Histoire critique*, etc.

66 Joseph Berthelé, article on 'St-Esprit-en-
Grève' in *L'Hôpital et l'Aide Sociale à Paris*,
January–February (1961), no. 7.

67 The goldsmiths, for example, operating
through their Confraternity of St-Eloi, established a *maison commune* in 1330 for indigent
goldsmiths (Jean Chuzeville, 'La première
chapelle des orfèvres de Paris', *Le centre de
Paris*, t. IV, no. 2, February, 1939, pp. 50–2).
Other similar examples can be found in
works on Paris guilds, confraternities and the
medieval working class, notably: René de
Lespinasse et François Bonnardot, *Les métiers
et corporations de la ville de Paris, 13e siècle.
Le Livre des métiers d'Etienne Boileau* (Paris:
Imprimerie Nationale, 1879–97); Gustave
Fagniez, *Etudes sur l'industrie et la classe
industrielle à Paris au 13e et au 14e siècle*
(Paris: F. Vieweg, 1877); Alfred Franklin,
*Dictionnaire historique des arts, métiers et
professions exercés dans Paris depuis le 13e
siècle* (Paris: H. Welter, 1906); Wilhelm
Gallion, *Der Ursprung der Zünfte in Paris*
(Berlin & Leipzig, 1910); F. B. Millet, *Craft-
Guilds of the 13th Century in Paris* (Kingston,
Canada, 1915); Etienne Martin Saint-Léon,
Histoire des corporations de métiers (Paris,
1941); and others. The *Livre des métiers* is the
best source on Paris confraternities, Lespinasse

and Bonnardot in particular having singled out all those formed by the guilds. Léon Le Grand's important study of the hospices and hospitals of Paris ('Les maisons-dieu et léproseries de Paris, etc.') includes a large number that were founded by artisans' and tradesmen's guilds as well as by individual burghers.

68 G. Faniez, p. 39 and Appendice, no, XII (1319).

69 This could be illustrated in various ways but perhaps in none as striking as the partial figures of chaplaincies founded by Paris burghers, as summarized in note 50.

70 Marcel Poëte, *Une vie de cité, etc.*, t. I (Paris: Auguste Picard, 1924), p. 450. The policy of ennobling citizens for meritorious service, usually fiduciary, was instituted by the crown around 1317 (*ibid.*, pp. 449–52). See also the following reference in which king's amortizations of a great number of pious foundations by wealthy burghers are listed, often with a mention of the services rendered by these individuals to the crown.

71 Jules Viard, *Documents parisiens du règne de Philippe VI de Valois*, t. II, *1339–1350* (Paris: H. Champion, 1900), no. 53, p. xix. The Vicomté de Maulevrier was located in Normandy.

72 C. Piton, *Les Lombards en France et à Paris* (Paris: Honoré Champion, 1892), p. 99. The *taille* of 1292 has been estimated to have been about 2 per cent of the individual's income (Et. Martin Saint-Léon, p. 160). Since Gandoufle paid 114 l. 10 s., he will have earned about 5,725 livres in 1292. But by then the early-thirteenth-century livre had been considerably devalued so that we have to use a multiple of 550 instead of 800 to obtain the approximate value of his income in dollars today, which would come close to $3,150,000 or £1,730,000. See also Anne Terroine's article on Gandoufle d'Arcelles in *Annales d'Histoire Sociale* (1945), nos I and II.

73 M. Poëte, pp. 442–3. Actually, these facts were recorded in the *taille* of 1292, which listed the servants of the wealthy prévôt de Paris as well as their master.

74 *Ibid.*– pp. 454–6

75 G. Fagniez, p. 51; also Bernard de Montfaucon,

Les monuments de la monarchie française, t. II (Paris, 1733), p. 203; and Le Roux de Lincy, *Histoire de l'hôtel de ville de Paris*, pp. 140, 141, 230–1, *passim*.

76 Pierre Vidal et Léon Daru, *Histoire de la corporation des marchands merciers, grossiers, jouailliers, le troisième des Six-Corps des marchands de la ville de Paris* (Paris: Honoré Champion, 1912), p. 377.

77 Jacques Du Breul, *Le théatre des antiquitez de Paris*, 1639, p. 737; also see B. Bernhard, 'Recherches sur l'histoire de la corporation des ménétriers et joueurs d'instruments de la ville de Paris', *BEC*, t. 3 (1841–2), pp. 377–404. Du Breul, who is responsible for the St-Julien story, is not always as critical of his informants as modern historical science demands. But he has nevertheless been found to be a largely trustworthy and, in view of the great loss of archives since his time, an often invaluable and irreplaceable source.

78 Archives Nationales, T. 1492, *Titres de propriétés, inventaire de titres . . . de l'hopital et confrérie St-Julien-des-Ménétriers, quatorzième-dix-huitième siècle*. It is a document of 10 July 1331.

79 A.-L. Millin, *Antiquités Nationales*, t. IV (Paris: Drouhin, 1792), pp. 10–11, 16. Millin is another precious source of early art as well as inscriptions since he inserted many engravings in his volumes of art works that subsequently disappeared, his illustrations often proving the sole visual record that we have of them.

80 J. Greult, *Boulogne: son histoire et ses institutions* (Paris: Charles Schiller, 1869); also Abbé Duchaine, *Le mémorial du Chrétien, suivi d'une notice sur la fondation de l'église de Notre-Dame de Boulogne-sur-Seine* (Paris: Leroi, 1833).

81 Emile Chénon, 'Les origines de la paroisse de Boulogne-sur-Seine', *Bulletin de la Société Nationale des Antiquaires de France*, 8e série, t. 7 (1926), pp. 126–30; also J. Du Breul, pp. 1040–1; and Lebeuf-Cocheris, t. IV, pp. 237–40.

82 Léon Brièle, *Inventaire-Sommaire des archives hospitalières antérieures à 1790*, t. III (Paris: Grandremy et Henon, 1886), *Rotule de 1319–1324*.

83 *Ibid.* As detailed as its information is, the St-Jacques building record does not in these early figures differentiate clearly at all times between expenditures for the church and those for the hospice and accessory accommodations, which were quite extensive, since St-Jacques was built to take care of fifty guests a night.

84 Of this sum of 162 l. 13 s., the king donated a *rente* of 20 l., or one-eighth of the total, the rest being given by listed citizens, whose donations have been collated by Henri Bordier, in a two-volume manuscript, D 124: t. II, 1859–60, for 1323, at the Archives de l'Assistance Publique, entitled *Inventaire des archives générales des établissements de bienfaisance du département de la Seine.*

85 Archives de l'Assistance Publique, *St-Jacques-aux-Pèlerins*, liasse 73, *Rotule en parchemin, no. 231, Cote 2248, 1319–1324*: 'Charpentiers en taache et a journeez . . . Richart de Bailleul . . . Item pour faire xxviii sieges des chaieres du cuer . . . a besteléstes . . . Item pour faire iii chaieres pour les iii prestres toutes plaines . . .' The fact that three seats, meant for the priests, were to be left undecorated raises the possibility that the others were reserved for prominent confrères or even members of the nobility, who were likewise members of the confraternity.

86 While it might appear from these foundations that there would be over fifty priests and chaplains at St-Jacques eventually, to say nothing of choir-boys and clerks, we learn from the Confraternity's later *Registres* that the foundation of a chaplaincy by an individual did not necessarily mean his right to the exclusive employment of the chaplain's services. In any case, the twenty-eight stalls plus three were needed and used, since by 1347 the rolls show that four more stalls were ordered (Henri Bordier, no. 2271).

87 Brièle, no. 2143.

88 *Ibid., passim.* The Compostela pilgrim died in Spain but a man from Navarre brought a letter to Paris with the news that the pilgrim had left half his fortune to St-Jacques (no. 1361: 1343–4).

89 *Ibid.*, no. 1346: 1327–8.

90 *Ibid.*, no. 1346: 1327–8. The *vidimus* of William's legacy can be seen in *ibid.*, no. 11 (1327), making St-Jacques his sole heir.

91 *Ibid.*, no. 10 (1328).

92 *Ibid.*, liasse 74, *Rotule de 1324–1325.*

93 Henri L. Bordier, *Les statues de St-Jacques-l'Hôpital au Musée du Cluny. Extrait du 28e volume des Mémoires de la Société Impériale des Antiquaires de France*, pp. 18–19.

94 Brièle, liasse 76, *Rotule de 1326–1327.*

95 *Ibid.*

96 Françoise Baron, 'Enlumineurs, peintres et sculpteurs parisiens des 14e et 15e siècles d'après les archives de l'Hôpital St-Jacques-aux-Pèlerins', extract of *Bulletin Archéologique du Comité des Travaux Historiques et Scientifiques*, nouv. série, no. 6, pp. 77–115: *Raoul de Heudicourt.* Henri Bordier, in 'La confrérie de St-Jacques-aux-Pèlerins', MSHP, t. II (1876), pt 2, p. 344, tells of the great relief described in the text: 'a vast sculpture where all the personages of the inauguration ceremony were represented', done by Raoul Heudicourt.

97 Henri Bordier, *Inventaire des archives générales . . . Archéologique Comptes de 1319–1324*, p. 199.

98 F. Baron, under Robert de Launay. This man was perhaps the most important artist participating in the church's decoration, furnishing both sculptures and paintings, especially the former. He was responsible for ten of the twelve great Apostles; a St Christopher; a St Michael; four reliefs carved on two stones set at the entrance; four angels and four doves; a Christ on the Cross with Mary and John; and various other jobs. His name appears on the pay lists from 1319 until 1348 and it is known that he lived on until 1360.

99 Philippe-le-Bel's three sons who succeeded him were: Louis-le-Hutin, 1314–16, who died at age of 27; Philippe-le-Long, 1316–22, who died at 28; and Charles-le-Bel, 1322–8, who lived to be 34.

100 Henri Bordier, under Guillaume de Noutriche, sculptor: 'Item for cutting the stone to be placed on the side of the portal, which was to be made in such a manner that the queen could set the first stone and the confreres [theirs] beside it, 4 livres . . .'.

101 Brièle, *Comptes de 1326–1327*: 'receipt of gifts that the queen gave on Saturday, May 2 ... when she offered the gold and silver jewel containing a bone from the arm of Monsieur Saint Jaques; first, 2 gold cloths which Estienne Chevalier sold to Lende Belhome, 28 l. tour., worth at Paris, 22 l. 8 s.'

102 Henri Bordier, *MSHP*, t. II, 1876, Pt 2, p. 396.

103 Brièle, *Comptes de 1329–1330*: 'For straw when Queen Jeanne was brought to the hospice, 5 sous ... for one tumbrel for removing the mud when the queen was carried back to Paris, 6 sous; etc.'

104 Henri Bordier.

105 According to the Confrérie Notre-Dame's statutes, the membership was to be evenly divided between clerics and laymen. The latter could be kings, princes and seigniors but especially 'honest bourgeois, well-reputed, courageous and strong, well-revenued and living in Paris' (Le Roux de Lincy, *Recherches sur la Grande Confrérie Notre-Dame aux Prêtres et Bourgeois de la ville de Paris*, Paris: E. Duverger, 1844, p. 22).

106 Henri Bordier, 'La confrérie des pèlerins de St-Jacques et ses archives', *MSHP*, t. II (1876), p. 363, n. 2. The confrères celebrated with gargantuan meals, consuming on this occasion eight cows and thirty-two pigs. A penny was given away to all beggars presenting themselves at the door, recipients totalling 3,000 in 1324 (M. Poëte, *Une vie de cité*, t. I, p. 413). The number of St-Jacques confrères is all the more remarkable in that members were either supposed to have already done the Compostela pilgrimage or to be solemnly pledged to do so.

107 According to an early inventorist, writing in 1724, Paris possessed at the time over two hundred 'old' churches. Today there are but twenty-one remaining, most of them largely rebuilt in more modern styles.

108 MM. de Lavillegille, de Longpérier et Gilbert, rapporteur, 'Rapport sur les statues découvertes dans une maison située au coin des rues St-Denis et Mauconseil', *Mémoires et Dissertations sur les Antiquités Nationales et Etrangères*, nouv. série, t. 5 (1840), pp. 370–3. The commission reported that at the time St-Jacques had been torn down, one portal had been left standing for a while and was done away with later. It had been decorated by three statues, two of which represented bishops. The two were moved to a house when the portal was itself obliterated, where they occupied for a time the incongruous position for such dignitaries of guards of the coach-gate (*Porte-cochère*)!

109 Henri L. Bordier, *Les statues de St-Jacques-l'Hôpital au Musée du Cluny*, 1864.

2 AMIENS

1 See Glossary under 'the Medieval City' for the definition of commune.

2 Colonel Borrelli de Serres, *La réunion des provinces septentrionales à la couronne par Philippe-Auguste* (Paris: Alphonse Picard & Fils, 1899), pp. xxv–xxvi.

3 Baron Albéric de Calonne, *Histoire de la ville d'Amiens*, t. I (Amiens: Piteux-Frères, 1899), pp. 137ff.

4 Jean Massiet du Biest, 'Géographie historique de la ville et du comté d'Amiens ...', *Premier Congrès-International de Géographie Historique*, t. I (1930): 'Compte-rendu des travaux du congrès', pp. 80–1. Also see by the same author, 'Les origines de la commune d'Amiens', *Positions de thèses* (1919), pp. 15–26, where he points out that the possessions of the *châtelains* in Amiens and its suburbs were broken up in the thirteenth century by gifts especially to the Abbey of St-Jean but also to the cathedral chapter and to the Hôtel-Dieu, as well as by sales to the royal *prévôté* (or eventually the city). Further gifts of local property to St-Jean came from the *vidames* of the House of Picquigny. In general, the *vidame* was the bishop's steward and the *châtelain* the lord of a château. But in the Amiens region both had early assumed far greater importance, the former post especially being held by the powerful House of Picquigny.

5 J. Roux and A. Soyez, *Cartulaire du chapitre de la cathédrale d'Amiens*, t. II (Amiens: Yvert & Tellier, 1905–12). The accords would begin with something like: 'Lettera de concordia facta inter capitulum et villam Ambianensem super pluribus articulis.'

6 Edouard Maugis, *Recherches sur les transformations du régime politique et social de la ville*

d'Amiens . . . (Paris: Alphonse Picard et Fils, 1906), p. 5. In 1185, Philippe-Auguste granted the commune of Amiens the 'eswardise' (right of inspection) over woad, 'under pain of total confiscation by the king's treasury of all goods of those challenging this right', which was equivalent to a monopoly.

7 Edouard Perroy, *Le travail dans les régions du Nord du 11e au début du 14e siècle* (Paris: Centre de Documentation Universitaire, 1961), p. 64.

8 Am. de Francqueville, in 'Les vieux moulins de Picardie', *BSAP*, t. 23 (1907–8), pp. 27–115, made a collation of these mills out of documentary sources. A recent author, who made an exhaustive study of the documentary sources of the history of Picardy, found twelve old texts citing woad-mills, all dating from after 1240 (Robert Fossier, *La terre et les hommes en Picardie jusqu'à la fin du 13e siècle*, Paris-Louvain: Béatrice-Nauwelaerts, 1968, p. 383, n. 84).

9 As expressed in the charming Picard spelling *une queville et 1 anel* (*Inventaire-Sommaire des Archives Communales*, IV, Série CC: CC 7, fol. III).

10 J. B. M. De Sachy, *Histoire des évêques d'Amiens* (Abbeville: Veuve de Vérité, 1770), pp. 103–7.

11 The legend is narrated by Georges Durand in his *Monographie de l'église Notre-Dame, cathédrale d'Amiens*, t. I: *Histoire et description de l'édifice* (Amiens: Yvert et Tellier— Paris: A. Picard et Fils, 1901), p. 10. The breviary is at the Bibliothèque Municipale d'Amiens, ms 112, fol. 290.

12 Jean Massiet du Biest, 'Les origines de la population et du patriciat urbain à Amiens (1109–14e siècle)', *Revue du Nord*, t. 30 (1948), p. 129.

13 Augustin Thierry, *Recueil des monuments inédits de l'histoire du tiers état . . .*, t. I: *Les pièces relatives à l'histoire de la ville d'Amiens, depuis l'an 1057 . . . jusqu'au 15e siècle* (Paris: Firmin Didot Frères, 1850), pp. 56 and 61. The document of 1151 is concerned with the donation of Jean de Cruce. Actually, Nicolas donated twelve *hospites* (hosts), whose status was somewhat higher than serfs.

14 One of the earlier cathedral's twelve chapels also seems to have been the gift of a burgher, who was identified merely as 'Sara, veuve' (Maurice Leroy, 'Histoire des chapelains de la cathédrale Notre-Dame d'Amiens', *MSAP*, t. 35, 1908, 253).

15 Albéric de Calonne, *Histoire de la ville d'Amiens*. He quotes the letter from Aug. Molinier and A. Longnon, *Recueil des historiens . . . de France*, t. XV, p. 492, Lettre 25.

16 Georges Durand (ed.), in the *Inventaire-Sommaire des Archives Ecclésiastiques*, t. V, Série G (nos 1–1169), 1902: G. 1157, *Comptes de la fabrique de la cathédrale, 1357–1358*. It records the only fabric accounts extant at Amiens before the eighteenth century.

17 Charles Du Cange's memorandum is quoted in full in the Appendices of Georges Durand's *Monographie*, t. II, pp. 632–4.

18 The destruction of the stained glass at Notre-Dame de Paris in the seventeenth and eighteenth centuries, for example, has been almost completely documented, partly in the chapter's registers but especially by the man who did most of the vandalism, Pierre Le Vieil, in his *L'art de la peinture sur verre et de la vitrerie*, Paris, 1774.

19 Du Cange's notations are at times difficult to read but they seem to add up to the following: André Malherbe's name occurs once and his coat-of-arms five times (twice with that of the commune; twice with the arms of Thomas Renieu and of the St-Fuscien family; and once with the joint arms of the Conty family, the St-Fuscien family, both burghers, and a bishop). There are three inscriptions specifying the heads (*maieurs*) of the guild of woad-men as donors. In one window the mayors' names are given: Hugues Liénart Le Secq and Robert de St-Fuscien; and in two others, the inscriptions are accompanied by the city's arms. In two other window inscriptions woad-men are named in a probable reference to their guild. Finally, in the twelfth window given by burghers, Du Cange reports an inscription marking the city alone as donor. The eighteenth-century historian, L. F. Daire, in his *Histoire de la ville d'Amiens, depuis son origine jusqu'à présent* (Paris: Veuve de

20 Delaguette, 1757), p. 99, is the author who identifies as a donor of one of the three great roses of the cathedral Jean de Cocquerel, who was mayor in 1241.

20 Georges Durand, *Description abrégée de la cathédrale d'Amiens* (Amiens: Imprimerie Yvert, 1950), p. 26. The windows were destroyed by fire in a Paris *atelier*, where they were being restored by a glazier.

21 Of the twenty-three windows in the seven apse chapels, Durand assembled material describing donors with some degree of probability for ten of them. This included three guilds: the wool-combers, the weavers and the mercers. In addition, there were two windows given by unidentified guilds and three more which probably had guild donors. Finally, there were two windows given by individual burgher donors: one by Etienne Le Clerc (or Cler), grocer, and the other jointly by members of two families, the St-Fuscien and the Conty (G. Durand, *Monographie*, t. I, pp. 555–86). J. Baron, in an earlier manuscript that was not published until 1900 (*Description de l'église cathédrale Notre-Dame d'Amiens*), describes donor 'signatures', that is, work scenes alluding to the donor guilds, in a number of apse chapel windows, which identify candlemakers; mercers; weavers; shoe-makers; 'and others'.

22 A considerable number of chaplaincies were endowed by burghers at the cathedral during the chapel-building period, which often assumed the assistance of the founders in building and decorating the corresponding chapels where they were established or donating art works, missals and sacerdotal gear to them.

23 This was true despite its possession of a number of prestigious relics of St Firmin, St Martin, St Honoré and others, to say nothing of the 'head' of St John-the-Baptist, which was acquired not a dozen years before the building campaign was launched. But the thirteenth century was pre-eminently the era of Mary, whose 'tunic' mag-netized the pilgrims' oboles at Chartres.

24 Edmond Soyez, *Le sanctuaire de la cathédrale d'Amiens* (Amiens: Lambert-Caron, 1873), p. 135.

25 These were all very important rebuilding under-takings, including the collegiate church of St-Firmin-le-Confesseur, the parish church of St-Michel, the city hospital of Hôtel-Dieu and probably also the bishop's palace. The space problems involved are discussed by Jean Massiet du Biest, in 'Y-a-t-il eu à Amiens un bourg épiscopal fortifié complétant à l'est l'enceinte Gallo-Romaine? . . .', *Extrait des Mélanges dédiés à la mémoire de Raymond Monier* (Paris: Montchrestien, 1958), p. 333. Since the Hôtel-Dieu seemed to be very hesitant about abandon-ing its old site near the cathedral, Bishop Arnould de la Pierre promised it a yearly indemnity of 100 l. par. *de bonis fabrice ecclesie nostri* ('of treasure of our church's fabric') to help defray the costs of the new installation. This is quoted by Georges Boudon, in *Cueilloir de l'Hôtel-Dieu d'Amiens* (1277) (Amiens: Yvert & Tellier, 1913), from ms 516 of the Bibliothèque Municipale d'Amiens's documents.

26 One was the fief of Canteraine, an urban hold-ing located among the lowlying branches of the Somme, for which he obtained 100 livres in addition to an annuity of 12 l. The other trans-action, which brought him 180 l., was of excep-tional importance to the burghers since, in addition to some gains of a practical nature, it relieved them of a remnant of the servile state in the form of a head-tax picturesquely called the *Répit St-Firmin*, which all married people had had to pay annually to their bishop since the establishment of the feudal order in the tenth century. Both sources of these transactions are from Aug. Thierry, *Recueil des monuments*, documents no. 52, 1228, pp. 203–5, and no. 49, 1226, pp. 200–1, respectively.

27 Thirty purchases in the 1230s, as listed in the *Cartulaire du chapitre*, attained the important sum of 2,341 l. 6 s. 7 d. par., plus 100 silver marks and one purchase of tithes for which the price was not specified (documents nos 201–3, selected).

28 J. Roux and A. Soyez, *Cartulaire du chapitre*, Document of February 1234. The distribu-tions were also regarded as a method of com-bating widespread absenteeism by canons and dignitaries that plagued many important churches.

29 They were St-Germain, St-Firmin-à-la-Porte and St-Firmin-en-Castillon.

30 These were St-Martin-aux-Waides, St-Rémy and St-Leu. The last was probably built at the end of the eleventh century.

31 Major elements of the church were not actually completed before late in the fifteenth century, no doubt because of the Hundred Years War.

32 Victor Mortet and Paul Deschamps, *Recueil de textes relatifs à l'histoire de l'architecture et à la condition des architectes en France au moyen âge*, t. II: *Douzième et treizième siècles* (Paris: Auguste Picard, 1929).

33 Contrary to the usual practice, the new cathedral had been started at the west rather than at the chevet. This was because St-Firmin-le-Confesseur occupied the site where the chevet had to be built. Rarely during a rebuilding was the old cathedral totally razed at the outset. Operations took place section by section while the rest of the church continued to function.

34 Eugène Viollet-le-Duc, 'La cathédrale d'Amiens', *La Picardie*, t. I (1855), pp. 497–504.

35 F.-I. Darsy, *Bénéfices de l'église d'Amiens ou état des beins, revenus, charges du clergé du diocèse d'Amiens en 1730* ... (Amiens: E. Caillaux, 1869), p. 59.

36 Augustin Thierry, *Recueil des monuments*, document no. 66 (1244), pp. 208–12.

37 This appears from the receipt for payment of the 2,000 livres given the city by Bishop Bernard d'Abbeville, in 1262 (*Inventaire des Archives Communales*, I, Série AA: 28 September 1262, fol. 155 vº). Lack of building funds also is indicated by the fact that the cathedral chapter had to lend money to the fabric in the late 1250s. This is Georges Durand's interpretation (*Monographie*, p. 36) of a document of *c.*1260 listing debtors to the chapter, which includes a reference to 'that which the fabric owes'.

38 It seems indicative of the cool relations between the burghers and the cathedral hierarchy that during this period (1244–53), four handsome gifts from burghers were made not to the cathedral but to another local church, the Abbey of St-Jean (*Inventaire des titres, chartres* [sic], *etc., de l'abbaye de St-Jean d'Amiens, ordre de Premons*..., Archives Départementales, I, 1, fols 12, 59 and 60). The donations included four houses in town and one unspecified gift.

39 These chapels were added on the outside of the already completed nave, set between the pillar-buttresses, after which the original wall was broken through. It was a procedure that was often used (Notre-Dame de Paris is another example, which anteceded the Amiens operation by several decades), to comply with the sudden growth in popularity of chantry chapels and privately sponsored masses, a phenomenon that spread through much of Europe at this time and is largely accounted for by the greatly expanded base of patronage that occurred from the enrichment of the bourgeoisie.

40 Georges Durand, *Monographie*, t. II, pp. 41–2, 46, *passim*. The single possibility of a bourgeois attribution is based on four extant glass panels showing lay donors. But they are not identified as burghers. André Malherbe and his wife are listed as having founded a chaplaincy in this chapel.

41 The original inscription reads as follows: 'LES BONES GENS DES VILLES DENTOUR AMIENS QUI VENDENT WAIDES ONT FAITE CHETE [CETTE] CAPELLE DE LEURS OMONNES.'

42 E. M. Carus-Wilson, 'La guède française en Angleterre: un grand commerce du moyen âge', *Revue du Nord*, t. 35 (1953), p. 97. Miss Carus-Wilson obtained her figure of 3,000 l. for the Picard woad trade in England from the Pipe Roll of 1210/11 ('La guède française', p. 92 and n. 3). The importance of this trade is further corroborated by the fact that in 1237 the Picard woad-merchants were willing to engage themselves to pay 100 livres in the form of a subsidy to the new London water-works, in addition to a yearly tax of 50 l. for the right to sell their woad anywhere in England (*ibid*., p. 94).

43 The pious foundations of André Malherbe, which totalled 2,000 livres or more, were handled mainly by the commune, into whose hands the donor and his wife, Marie, placed properties and money from the earnings of which the annuities were to be paid. Thus, the city's *Registre aux Comptes*, of 1384

(*Inventaire, Arch. Comm.*, IV, Série CC, fol. 17, CC 2: *Aumosnes de la ville*) lists seven foundations by the Malherbes for which it had to pay a yearly total of 70 l. In addition, there were a number of 'esthetic' donations for which Malherbe must have paid in cash. Space does not allow the detailing of all his contributions.

44 Augustin Thierry, *Recueil des monuments*, document no. 100, May 1292.

45 Navigation of the Somme was only possible starting at about 25 kilometres upstream from Amiens and then only by small boat as far as Corbie, still a dozen kilometres from Amiens, where freight would be shifted to barges. Most of the course down the Somme from Amiens had to be done by human draft because of the poor condition of the banks (René Prat, 'Étude historique sur la vallée de la Somme du 12e siècle au milieu du 176 siècle', *Positions de thèses de l'Ecole Nationale des Chartes*, 1934, pp. 137–42).

46 Under feudal terms, to possess the primary seigniory of a property was to withdraw it from any charges or duties except those traditionally owing to the sovereign. As has been often pointed out, the burghers' quest for communal rights was meant to establish them as a group on an equal footing with other classes within the feudal system. Possessing a large part of the basic proprietary seigniory of their city reinforced enormously this posture. The collection of the relatively small annual quitrent from tenants was by no means the only financial benefit accruing to the seignior of a property. For example, any change of tenure, resulting from sale, death or other cause, required payment of a goodly fee. And, above all, seigniorial rights entailed control of justice and other feudal privileges, which could be highly remunerative.

47 Some examples of acquisitions by the commune from leading seigniors were the following: the vidames of the House of Picquigny, who sold it portions of the parish of St-Germain; the bishop, who sold it the important fief of Canteraine in the lower city; the châtelains of the House of Flixiecourt, who sold it areas in the St-Germain and Castillon quarters as well as the suburban sections of Dureaume and Val St-Firmin. And the most extensive purchases were undoubtedly from the count's (later the king's) domain.

48 Jean Massiet du Biest, *La carte et le plan considerés comme instruments de la recherche historique. Études sur les fiefs et censives et sur la condition des tenures urbaines à Amiens, 11e–17e siècle* (Tours: Gibert-Clarey, 1954), pp. 3–4. A document of February 1209 shows the city acquiring by purchase as late as this from the Count of Amiens a vacant square before the church of St-Firmin (which one of the three churches by this title is not designated). This is recorded by Hippolyte Cocheris, in *Notices et extraits des documents manuscrits conservés dans les dépôts publics de Paris et relatifs à l'histoire de Picardie*, t. I (Paris: Durand, 1854–8), document VI. Documents in the city archives also record numerous purchases from individual citizens by the commune, of houses, quitrents and other property, starting in the thirteenth century and especially during the years 1316 and 1317 (*Inventaire des Arch. Comm.*, Série AA 5, fols 26 and ff).

49 Aug. Thierry, *Recueil des monuments*, documents XCIX (1290–2) and C (May 1292). See also Victor de Beauvillé, *Recueil de documents inédits concernant la Picardie*, t. IV (Paris: Imprimerie Nationale, 1881), document 51 (1290–2).

50 Aug. Thierry, documents XCVI (1291) and XCVII (1291). Actually, what was involved was the levy on the weighing of woollens and furs, which had been fiefed to the Sire de Rubempré by the vidame, Jean de Picquigny, to whom the city had to pay 160 l. par. for the release of his rights. The Sire de Rubempré got an annual *rente* of 70 l.

51 *Ibid.*, document XCV (1291) and various others, including *Inventaire des Arch. Comm.*, IV, Série CC: CC 2, *Registre aux Comptes* (1384), fol. 17: *Aumosnes de la ville*. The city bought the tax rights on woad from André Malherbe, who had acquired them from the king in 1291.

52 For example, in 1324, the city bought the 'right' of justice over movable property (Aug. Thierry, document CXLV, 1324). This purchase was from the cathedral chapter, which received an annual *rente* of 20 l. for it.

53 *Ibid.*, documents CXXXIX (1315) and CCXCV

(1387). Regarding the orphans' heritages, see *ibid.*, doc. LXXVIII (1278). Regarding annuities paid by the city on money deposited with it by various burghers, see *Inv. des Arch. Comm.*, IV, Série CC: CC 2, *Registre aux Comptes* (1384), fol. 17: *Aumosnes de la ville*, and fol. 17 v°: *Messes que le ville fait canter, pour certains deniers et pourfis que icelle ville a eu pour ce faire.* . . . The city was still paying the annuities for the two chaplaincies founded by André Malherbe in 1727.

54 At Amiens, the city debt reached 7,800 l. by 1259. By 1382, it was up to 24,000 inflated livres, in addition to 4,300 l. payable for *rentes-à-vie* and about 8,000 l. more due for administrative expenses (see Charles Dufour, 'Situation financière des villes de Picardie sous St. Louis', *MSAP*, 2e série, t. 5, 1858, p. 593). The city's accounts for 1262 and 1263 are given in Arthur Giry's *Documents sur les relations de la royauté avec les villes en France de 1880 à 1314* (Paris: Alphonse Picard, 1885), document XXXVII.

55 For example, the famous lay sisterhood, the Béguines, met up with sharp communal opposition in 1264, after they had received a donation of two houses in the Rue des Cocquerels. Some sensitive nerve of the commune was touched and the Béguines quickly passed the hot poker on to the Dominicans, who then became the centre of a raging conflict with the city. The sisterhood, like the Dominicans shortly thereafter, were forced to leave the city and settle outside the walls (V. de Beauvillé, *Recueil de documents*, doc. CLXX). We find similar situations occurring in other cities; it is a phenomenon that must be understood since it often affected burgher patronage.

56 *Inventaire, Arch. Eccl.* Série G: G. 519 (1263 o.s.).

57 *Inv. des Arch. Comm.*, I, Série AA: AA 2, fol. 15, February 1283.

58 When the bishop finally gave his consent, in 1263, he did so with the condition that the Dominicans would retain their establishment outside the walls, probably as a concession to the commune, since this could relieve the pressure for the mendicants to begin expanding their home inside the city (Anonymous, *Notice*

sur les halles de la ville d'Amiens, Amiens: A. Caron, 1856, p. 18).

59 Edouard Maugis, *Documents inédits concernant la ville et le siège du bailliage d'Amiens. Extraits des registres du Parlement de Paris et du Trésor des Chartes*, t. I, 14e siècle (1296–1412) (Amiens: Yvert & Tellier—Paris: Picard Fils, 1908), *MSAP: Documents inédits concernant la province*, t. 17: document II, 1311. Also in the same work, document XXVI, no. 3, 7 July 1369.

60 The Franciscans established themselves at Amiens in 1244, on a terrain given them by a burgher, Jean Le Monnier, according to L. F. Daire, *Histoire de la ville d'Amiens*, t. II, p. 282.

61 See L. F. Daire, t. II, p. 289, and Pièces Justificatives, pp. 403–7, 4 October 1392: *Fundatio Celestinorum*.

62 *Inv. des Arch. Comm.v* I, Série AA: AA 5, fol. 90, 21 February 1345.

63 Edouard Maugis, 'Essai sur le régime financier de la ville d'Amiens du 14e à la fin du 16e siècle (1356–1588)', *MSAP*, 4e série, t. 3 (1899), p. 622.

64 Lavernier, 'Essai sur l'organisation municipale de la ville d'Amiens . . .', *Mémoires de l'Académie des Sciences, Agriculture, Commerce, Belles-Lettres et Arts du Département de la Somme*, t. 5 (1843), pp. 398–9, gives as his source the 'Registre A, fol. 55', evidently of the city's archives. See also H. Dusevel, *Histoire . . . d'Amiens depuis les Gaulois . . .* (Amiens: R. Machart, 1832), t. I, p. 502, who quotes as his source the 'Registre C des Archives de la Ville', fol. 32 v°.

65 *Inv. des Arch. Comm.*, I, Série AA: AA 1, fol. 209 v° and ff., fol. 219, fol. 219 v° and ff.

66 Albert Demangeon, *La Picardie et les régions voisines: Artois, Cambrésis, Beauvaisis* (Paris: Armand Colin, 1905), pp. 138–40.

67 Jean Massiet du Biest, 'Les ports fluviaux et le *Chemin d'Eau* à Amiens (10e–16e siècles)', *BSAP*, t. 45 (1951–4), pp. 272–5.

68 François Vasselle and Ernest Will, 'L'Enceinte du Bas-Empire et l'histoire d'Amiens', *Revue du Nord*, t. 40 (1958), p. 472.

69 Charles Pinsard, *Recueil de notes relatives à l'histoire des rues d'Amiens*, t. 54: *Le sous-sol*

de la ville d'Amiens, les caves, pp. 20–1
(Manuscript, Bibliothèque Municipale).

70 For example, one cellar in a house beneath the
Rue du Bloc had vaulted ogives with pillars and
capitals (Pinsard, t. 54, p. 67). Another, in the
rue St-Martin, had elegant floral capitals and
keystones (pp. 79ff). Still another, in the rue
André, with charming consoles and keystones,
was of an extraordinary overall beauty, according to Pinsard's sketch (pp. 111ff). The cellar
beneath the Hôtel du Berceau d'Or had several
bays divided off by pillars and had superposed
thirteenth- and fourteenth-century sections.
The beauty of this installation suggested to some
observers that it must have been a chapel but
Pinsard disagreed (pp. 95–6). There are only a
handful of these cellars that have not been filled
and covered over. One of these, in the rue de
Metz-l'Evêque, right behind the cathedral chevet, the owner, Madame Vasse-Robiaud, gra-
ciously allowed my wife and me to visit and
photograph. It has two levels, the lower one of
the twelfth, the upper of the thirteenth century,
the latter having fine vaulting with heavy crossing ogives. These cellars are not as large as some
of those described by Pinsard and others but
parts of them have been filled in, and closed-off
passageways indicate that a whole subterranean
maze existed once in this area.

71 Charles Pinsard (t. 54) has conjectured that
the extent of the cellars was too vast to be
accounted for by storage alone and suggested
that many were used as workshops. This would
not, of course, alter the fact that Amiens's
intense spatial problems were at the source of
such expedients.

72 An additional proof of the great inadequacy
of space within Amiens's medieval walls was
the extraordinary use of storage lofts (called
camerae or *cambres*), which were added at the
tops of houses. These would often be rented
out separately, earnings from which frequently
appear among the pious donations to the Hôtel-
Dieu, for example (*Cueilloir de l'Hôtel-Dieu*,
passim).

73 It is interesting to note here that there were
great cellars right beneath the cathedral *parvis*,
which E. Bienaimé described in an article in the
BSAP, t. 32 (1926–8), pp. 428–55. For the com-

parative size of Amiens cathedral, Viollet-le-
Duc gives the following figures: Amiens, 8,000
sq. metres; Reims, 6,650; Bourges, 6,200; Paris,
5,500 ('La cathédrale d'Amiens', *La Picardie*, t.
I, 1855, p. 502).

74 *Inv. des Arch. Eccl.*, Série G, t. V: G. 653 (1334
o.s. and 1366), in which is described a dispute
between bishop and chapter lasting many years
and which finally ends in a compromise involving limitation of the extent of the cloisters.

75 Antoine Goze, *Histoire des rues d'Amiens*, t. III
(Amiens: Alfred Caron, 1858), p. 177.

76 *Ibid.*, p. 197.

77 H. Dusevel, *Histoire de la ville d'Amiens*, t. I,
p. 163.

78 Antoine Goze, t. III, p. 136.

79 Quoted by Charles Pinsard, t. 33, p. 87.

80 Pierre Dubois, 'Cinq églises amiénoises dispar-
ues', *BSAP*, t. 36, 1935–6, pp. 625ff, which itself
quotes from the Archives Communales, Série
BB: BB 20, fol. 27.

81 Georges Durand, 'Le cimetière St-Denis à
Amiens', *BSAP*, t. 32 (1926–8), p. 206 and n. 2.
The *Epitaphier* was published in 1925 by Roger
Rodière.

82 St-Germain and St-Leu are the only two medieval parish churches still remaining at Amiens.

83 Aug. Janvier, *Les Clabaut, famille municipale
amiénoise, 1349–1539* (Amiens, 1889), pp.
277–81. Pierre's tomb was at the church of St-
Firmin-à-la-Porte. He also arranged for several
handsome bequests to the church in his testament, including one important grant of 20 livres
to its fabric.

84 Louis Douchet (ed.), *Manuscrits de Pagès,
marchand d'Amiens, écrits à la fin du 17e . . .
s.*, t. I (Amiens: Alfred Caron, 1856), p. 89.

85 *Ibid.* We have records of four daily masses
founded at St-Rémy by burghers in the thirteenth and fourteenth centuries and there were
undoubtedly others. Those we know of were
endowed by Elizabeth Chambelane, in 1272;
André Malherbe, 1295; Simon de Bonneville,
1341; and Pierre de Bus, a city barrister, and his
wife, Jeanne Boitel, 1378.

86 *Inventaire, Archives de l'Evêché*, Série G, nos
1–1169: G. 1043 (1341).

87 Ant. Goze, t. III, p. 18. Jacques's wife shared in
this important donation.

88 *Ibid.*, p. 55.

89 *Ibid.*, p. 62.

90 *Manuscrits de Pagès*, t. I, p. 76.

91 *Ibid.*, t. V, p. 371, for the Cocquerel donation; for that of André Malherbe, see *ibid.*, t. I, p. 74, and t. V, p. 75, as well as Pierre Dubois, p. 635, which gives the Archives Municipales, CC 62, fol. 29 as its source for the windows donated by Cocquerel, St-Fuscien and Malherbe. All these affluent citizens were likewise important patrons at the cathedral, a dual outlet of benevolence that was not always matched at other places.

92 Pierre Dubois, p. 637.

93 All the chaplaincies at St-Martin are certainly not recorded, but those that have been include as founders: Liénard Le Secq (*Inventaire de l'Evêché d'Amiens*, 1744–6, Arch. Dépt., G. 650, fol. 120, 1334); Pierre St-Fuscien (*ibid.*, fol. 125, 1365); Colaie le Monnier (*Inv., Arch. Comm.*, Série CC: *Registre aux Comptes*, 1384, CC 2, fol. 17 v°). Pierre de St-Fuscien also paid for the construction of the chapel in which his chaplaincy was established, the foundation document calling for a 'perpetual chaplain ... who will celebrate every day a requiem mass for the above-named souls, in the chapel that I had built . . .'. Toward the end of the fourteenth century, the weekly mass of the famous confraternity, Notre-Dame du Puy, was also held at the Waides. And we should also mention that in all likelihood André Malherbe had a chaplaincy here, since he built a chapel at the Waides and paid for the glazing of three windows in it: see note 43.

94 Edouard Maugis, *Recherches sur les transformations du régime politique et social de la ville d'Amiens des origines de la commune à la fin du 16e siècle. Etudes d'histoire municipale*, t. II (Paris: Alphonse Picard et Fils, 1906), p. 15 and notes 2 and 3.

95 There are many authors that discuss the duties that were performed by the Amiens commune. A number of them have been frequently referred to here, including: Aug. Thierry, *Recueil des monuments*, t. I; L. F. Daire; Albéric de Calonne, *Histoire de la ville d'Amiens*; and others.

96 Ferdinand Lamy, 'Historique de la Hautoye', *BSAP*, t. 30 (1923), pp. 446–7

97 Albéric de Calonne, t. I, p. 267.

98 To give an example: in 1386, the city fathers hired minstrels to celebrate Christmas at the watchtower (*Inv. des Arch. Comm.*, IV, Série CC: CC 3, fol. 39, 1386).

99 Ant. Goze, pp. 218–19.

100 For example, there is an entry in the city's archives, which Antoine Goze first noted (t. III, 1858, p. 220), showing the aldermen paying a sculptor 46 sous for carving two gargoyles ('two beasts') at the watchtower.

101 Gargoyles, 'to cast rainwater away from the terrace', were also added when the old city hall was partially rebuilt in 1398, as described in a document printed by A. Machart from the *Archives de la Ville*, 9e compte, no. 3, of the *Maistre des Ouvrages* ('master of works'), 1398 and 1399, and referred to by Ant. Goze (pp. 202–3). Around the same time, a glazier was paid 4 livres for making ten new windows at the *malemaison*, each of which was inscribed with the arms of the king and the city, as well as for reglazing several others in the meeting room of the aldermen and painting several *ymages* on them (*Inv. des Arch. Comm.*, IV, Série CC, *Impôts et Comptabilités*: CC 6, fol. 138).

102 *Ibid.*, CC 3, 1386. Among the stained-glass paintings described at the Cloquiers was a large one over the entry portal containing the city arms held by an angel and with representations of the symbols of the four Evangelists in the corners.

103 All the city gates were embellished with art, in particular with stained-glass windows with joint arms of king and city as well as images of Christ, the Virgin and St Peter (*Inv. des Arch. Comm.*, IV, Série CC: CC 8, fol. 92 v° fol. 106).

104 *Inventaire-Sommaire des Arch. Communales*, t. IV, Série CC: CC 6, fol. 85.

105 L. F. Daire, pp. 457–8. See also Georges Durand, 'Le cimetière St-Denis à Amiens', *BSAP*, t. 32 (1926–8), pp. 191–2 and notes 1 and 2 on p. 192.

106 G. Durand, *ibid.*, pp. 206, 268, 277ff, 288–97. For a description of the Chapel of St-Jacques at St-Denis, see *ibid.*, pp. 204–6.

107 The great popularity of the Hôtel-Dieu as recipient of donations is best seen in its *Cueilloir* (document F. 497 of the so-called *Cartulaire A 3* in the Arch. Dépt.), which contains 257 entries of gifts made to it during the first forty years of the hospital's existence alone. The *Cueilloir*, which was recorded in 1277, was published in 1913 (Georges Boudon, ed., Amiens: Yvert & Tellier).

108 *Archives des Hospices d'Amiens*, Série A: *Actes de fondations des établissements hospitaliers . . .*, A1, liasse, premier dossier, Arch. Dépt.

109 Arch. Dépt., F. 487: *Hôtel-Dieu, Copies d'actes des années 1184–1301, numerotés I à CXCII et I à XV*, March 1276/7, p. 502. The Bethisy gift brought a net yearly income of 45 livres, which indicates the vast number of quitrents it included, since individually each paid a comparatively small sum, usually a few sous.

110 Among the various sources for burgher donations to the Hôtel-Dieu, the most important is the Arch. Dépt. document C. 3, *Obituaire de l'Hôtel-Dieu (Libellus obitum missarum . . . hospitalariae domus dei . . .), Registre de 1630*. Among the most notable of 100 burgher gifts of the thirteenth and fourteenth centuries were by Henri de Sorchi (alias) Gressin and Marie, his wife (5 November), 'who gave 160 livres and much other property for the construction of the oratory', and by Demicelle Jeanne de May, widow of Jean Du Gard, who gave 1,000 l. tour. for a daily mass and a further 1,000 l. 'for the construction of the cloisters'.

111 The *Maladrerie* was chiefly a recipient of burgher benevolence, as witness the large number of quitrents in its possession within the city (Archives Municipales, AA 10: *Registre et Cartulaire des cens, rentes, louages de maisons, revenus . . . appartenens a le maison de St Ladre . . . encommenchie . . . lan mil ccc et vint six. Sire Pierre Clabaut maieur ou dit an*).

112 Augustin Thierry, *Recueil des monuments*, documents CXVII (1305) and CXXXIV (1312).

113 Victor de Beauvillé, *Recueil de documents inédits concernant la Picardie* (Paris: Imprimerie Nationale, 1860), document no. CLXX: *Description des rues et bâtiments saints et profanes de la ville d'Amiens*.

114 For example, the hospice founded by Liénard Le Secq, which was also called the Hôpital St-Jacques, was provided for by a bequest in his will (Auguste Janvier, *Livre d'or de la municipalité amiénoise*, Amiens: Piteux Frères, p. 18; also L. F. Daire, t. II, p. 345; and others). Another foundation of the same kind was the so-called Hôpital St-Nicolas-en-Cocquerel, which was one of Amiens's most highly endowed hospices and was founded originally by Nicolas Cocquerel. Years later, another member of the family, Colaye Le Monnier, left in her will (1382) a most handsome bequest of 3,000 écus, meant to provide the hospice with twenty beds for forty people. She made over various other funds, including earnings from several mills, which were to be used for heating the home and for providing a daily loaf of bread and a bowl of soup to each inmate. Provision was also made for a permanent chaplain, who was to be selected by the city mayor, who chose the hospice administrator as well. The mayor received the not inconsiderable sum of 100 sous a year for his trouble. If money was left over from all these grants, it was to be used in behalf of two or more indigent bourgeois men or women, who were to receive a weekly stipend of five sous in addition to their food and shelter, to enable them to maintain their dignity for as long as they lived (L. F. Daire, pp. 330–1, 401–2).

115 Jean Massiet du Biest, in 'Les origines de la population et du patriciat urbain à Amiens (1109–14e siècle)', *Revue du Nord*, t. 30 (1948), p. 121, observes that 'from 1138 we find bourgeois lineages joining the cathedral chapter en masse as well as those of other collegiate churches', giving as example the case of Johannes de Cruce, who was a canon of the cathedral in 1138.

116 Augustin Thierry, *Recueil des monuments*, document CCXLVI (1360).

117 J. Massiet du Biest, in 'Les origines de la population . . .', p. 131, gives as examples Jean Le Roux, mentioned in 1261 as husband of Demoiselle Aelis de Halencourt, and Marie de Croy, cited in 1276 as wife of the impecunious

scion of the famous family of châtelains, Bernard d'Amiens.

118 The Du Gard family is on record as possessing noble fiefs from early in the thirteenth century (Ferdinand Pouy, *Longpré-lès-Amiens et les Du Gard, seigneurs dudit lieu, maieurs et échevins d'Amiens . . . à partir du 13e siècle*, Paris: Baur et Détaille, 1870, pp. 10ff). An example among many in the fourteenth century shows the executors of Damoiselle Marie Pesel, wife of the noble Pierre d'Essertaux, selling a piece of their seigniorial property to a burgher, in 1328, for 200 l. tour., with which a chaplaincy was founded at the cathedral (*Inv. des Arch. Eccl.*, t. V, 1902, G. 650, fol. 119).

119 An example was Milon de Ravin, who in 1321 bought the Fief du Hamel de Metz for 900 livres (*Inv. des Arch. Eccl.*, t. VI, Série G, nos 1170–3044, 1910: G. 2434, 1320 o.s.; and G. 2722, January 1332 o.s.). In 1375, Gilles Ravin was named seignior of the fief his ancestor bought in 1321 (*Dictionnaire historique et archéologique de la Picardie*, t. I: *Arrondissement d'Amiens, Cantons d'Amiens, Boves et Conty*, Paris: Picard Fils; also Amiens: Yvert & Tellier, 1909, p. 150).

120 *Inv. des Arch. Eccl.*, t. V, G. 123, 12 May 1377, and t. VI, G. 1500, 1377.

121 *Ibid.*, t. V, G. 448, fol. 21 v°.

122 *Ibid.*, fol. 23 v°.

123 The tendency was greatly increased by the Hundred Years War, as Edouard Maugis shows in *Recherches sur les transformations du régime politique et social de la ville d'Amiens . . .*, pp. 87–8. He furnishes statistics that eloquently illustrate the democratization of the city administration as a result of this disaster.

124 Edouard Maugis, 'Essai sur le régime financier, etc.', p. 157, notes 1 and 2. The 'inventaire après décès' of Clément le Fèvre, tavern-keeper, wealthy burgher, owner of a famous tavern, *Du Bos*, shows that he sold wine both wholesale and retail, had a great stock of wine of a variety of vineyards in several cellars, bought property, loaned money and allowed his better clients to buy wine on credit (H. Duchaussoy, 'Les vignes en Picardie

et le commerce des vins de Somme', *MSAP*, ts 41 and 42, 1926–7, p. 400, quoting as his source the Archives Municipales, FF 1643).

125 Edouard Maugis, 'Essai sur le régime financier, etc.', p. 157, notes 1 and 2.

126 A. Bazot, 'Des ateliers monétaires de la ville d'Amiens', *MSAP*. t. 23 (1873), p. 17.

127 A notorious example of the latter was the provostship (*prévôté*), whose permanent farm the commune had bought in 1292 and which, after royal confiscation, it had to buy back in 1311 and again in 1337, the second time from Philippe-de-Valois (Aug. Thierry, documents CXVII, CXXVIII, CXXIX, CLXVIII and CLXXXI).

128 Aug. Thierry, *Recueil des monuments*, doc. CCXLVI, 1360.

129 Edouard Maugis, 'Essai sur le régime, etc.', pp. 181ff. Fifteen burghers who had never held the post of alderman were elected, including a porter, a dyer and other craftsmen.

130 Edouard Maugis, *Recherches sur les transformations, etc.*, pp. 6–7. The author quotes the complaint of the great *waidiers* to the regent Charles about the matter, suggesting that the royal treasury would incur a great loss as the result of such tactics. Charles complied by ordering his bailiff at Amiens to threaten the interlopers of the woad monopoly with confiscation of their goods.

131 Aug. Janvier, *Livre d'or de la municipalité amiénoise . . .*, pp. 287–9.

132 As for the paintings donated yearly by the famous confraternity of Notre-Dame-du-Puy, which originated in the second half of the fourteenth century as promoters of an annual poetry contest in honour of the Virgin, there is nothing that remains from the early period (A. Breuil, 'La confrérie de Notre-Dame-du-Puy d'Amiens', *MSAP*, t. 13, 1854, pp. 485–662).

3 TOULOUSE

1 Auguste Molinier, 'Etude sur l'administration de Louis IX et d'Alfonse de Poitiers (1226–1271)', note LIX, col. 462–570, in Cl. Devic and J. Vaissete, *Histoire générale de Languedoc*, t. VII, 1879. He sums this situation up as follows: 'The bishop of Toulouse was no more powerful in a temporal sense than any small

baron of the Toulousan or Albigeois region.'
Temporal possessions of a bishopric were normally spread over the entire diocese, bringing
an income that usually ran to thousands of
livres, in addition to the regular contributions
of many hundreds of parishes and other subordinate church units.

2 Devic and Vaissete, t. III (Toulouse: Edouard
Privat, 1872), livre XV, no. XXI, pp. 438–40.
The most important rights claimed at St-Sernin
by Bishop Izarn for the benefit of the Cathedral
St-Etienne included: one-fourth of the oblations; one-third of the grants to the cemetery;
one-third of all acquisitions during Izarn's lifetime, one-half after his death; keys to the tomb
of St-Sernin; abolition of the monopoly of St-
Sernin's burial rights for seigniors and ecclesiastics in favour of St-Etienne in particular;
possession of the 'honors' (holdings) of the three
leading dignitaries of St-Sernin (Elisabeth
Magnou, *L'Introduction de la réforme grégori-
enne à Toulouse, fin XIe-début XIIe siècle*,
Toulouse: Centre Régionale de Documentation
Pédagogique, 1958, pp. 48–9).

3 Elisabeth Magnou, pp. 61ff.

4 *Ibid.*, pp. 10–11.

5 *Ibid.*, p. 69, which quotes from Guillaume de
Catel, *Histoire des comtes de Tolose* (Tolose:
Pierre Bosc, 1623).

6 Pierre Gérard, in 'Aux origines du temporel
de St-Sernin: Ste-Constance de Saverdun, XIe
et XIIe siècles', *Pays de l'Ariège: Fédération
des Sociétés Académiques et Savantes:
Languedoc, Pyrénées, Gascogne* (Actes du
XVIe Congrès d'Etudes, Foix, 28–30 May
1960), p. 101. He points out that some St-
Sernin possessions can be seen to have disappeared from its cartulary, indicating that they
had fallen into lay hands. E. Magnou (p. 5)
names a number of the revenues of St-Sernin
that were lost to it.

7 Guillaume de Catel, p. 166.

8 The St-Raymond Hospital, founded in 1075–8
by Petrus Benedicti judex and which grew to be
the city's biggest unit of this kind, was also
organized at this time (see Célestin Douais,
*Cartulaire de l'abbaye de St-Sernin de Toulouse,
844–1200*, Paris-Toulouse, 1887, nos 546–50,
and John H. Mundy, 'Charity and Social Work

in Toulouse, 1100–1250', *Traditio*, vol. 22, 1966,
p. 211 and notes 23 and 24).

9 Georges Boyer, 'Une hypothèse sur l'origine
de la Daurade', *Annales du Midi*, t. 68 (1956),
p. 48.

10 The exact dating of St-Jacques is not known. It
was certainly established before 1162, since a
document speaks of a bit of property 'where the
said hospital [i.e., the hospice attached to St-
Jacques Chapel] which is now in the St-Etienne
enclosure was formerly located' (*Répertoire de
Claude Cresty*, 1 April 1734–23 June 1737, t. I,
fol. 23).

11 Elie Lambert, *Etudes médiévales*, t. II: *Le sud-
ouest français* (Toulouse-Paris: Privat-Didier,
1956), pp. 157–8.

12 John H. Mundy, in *Liberty and Political Power
in Toulouse, 1050–1230* (New York: Columbia
University Press, 1954), p. 81, points out that
with rent values diminishing rapidly in the
twelfth century, the Toulouse church found its
revenues declining sharply and that no new
donations came to bolster its position.

13 R.-C. Julien, *Histoire de la paroisse Notre-
Dame de la Dalbade* (Toulouse: Edouard Privat,
1891), pp. 2, 123–4. According to Julien, it was
the parishioners themselves who granted the St-
Eloi chapel to the cutlers' guild, giving as his
source the Archives Départementales' *Extrait
de l'enquête de 1776, Couteliers, IXe question*.
The parishioners' active role at Dalbade continued for centuries, its rebuilding in 1381 being
directed by the lay churchwardens.

14 G. de Catel, p. 158.

15 J. Delort, 'Notice sur l'église de St-Pierre-
des-Cuisines', *MSAM*, t. 12 (1880–2), pp.
217–19. The church, which was rebuilt in
the twelfth century, was a favourite meeting
place of the citizens of Toulouse and was the
site of several important transactions between
the consuls and the counts during that century (Jules de Lahondès, *Les monuments de
Toulouse*, Toulouse: Edouard Privat, 1920,
p. 136).

16 Charles Petit-Dutaillis, 'La prétendue commune
de Toulouse', *Académie des Inscriptions et
Belles-Lettres de Paris, Comptes Rendus*, 1941.

17 J. H. Mundy, *Liberty and Political Power, etc.*,
p. 51.

18 R. Limouzin-Lamothe, *La commune de Toulouse et les sources de son histoire, 1120–1249* (Toulouse: Edouard Privat—Paris: Henri Didier, 1932), p. 114.

19 *Ibid.*, pp. 126–7.

20 *Ibid.*, pp. 191–2, 213–15; also J. H. Mundy, pp. 68–72.

21 J. H. Mundy, pp. 58–60.

22 *Ibid.*, pp. 88ff. The author points out also (pp. 149ff) that there was a great increase in participation of the people of Toulouse in the city's affairs during this period. See R. Limouzin-Lamothe, pp. 115–16, 120–1, 126–8, *passim*.

23 *La chanson de la croisade albigeoise*, ed. Eugène Martin-Chabot, II, § XXXV (205) (Nogent-le-Rotrou: Daupeley-Gouverneur, 1931), verses 121–9 and 145–6.

24 J. H. Mundy, pp. 89, 155.

25 *Ibid.*, p. 161.

26 Devic and Vaissete, t. VI (1879), pp. 453, 462, 486ff, 495ff, *passim*. The story is also told in great detail by that excellent epic of the Albigensian 'crusade', *La chanson de la croisade albigeoise*.

27 G. de Catel, pp. 888–92; also Devic and Vaissete, t. VI (1879), p. 244.

28 *Chronique de Guillaume de Puylaurens*, ch. 7. It is quoted by Célestin Douais, in 'Une bulle inédite d'Innocent II en faveur de l'abbaye de St-Sernin de Toulouse, 14 Mai 1216', *BSAM*, t. 14 (1887–94), p. 141, n. 2.

29 Specifically, what Foulques gave the friars were: the church of St-Romain or St-Rome, where Dominick set up his first convent; the Hospital at the Arnaud-Bernard Gate, which was turned over to the Nunnery of Prouille, founded by Dominick for reconverted women heretics; the sixth part of the tithes. This grant was the portion that was supposed to be used for the building and ornamentation of churches in the diocese, an act that beautifully illustrates Foulques's viewpoint of priorities (Devic and Vaissete, t. VI (1879), pp. 468–9).

30 Auguste Molinier, 'Catalogue des actes de Simon et d'Amauri de Montfort', *BEC*, t. 34 (1873), pp. 153–203, 445–501, entry of 4 June 1214. Simon is known to have made other important presents to Foulques, in particular

at Balma, which was built up into an 'episcopal-barony' (Léon Dutil, *La Haute-Garonne et sa région*, Toulouse: Edouard Privat—Paris: Henri Didier, 1928, pp. 374–5; also Al. Du Mège, *Histoire des institutions religieuses, politiques, judiciaires et littéraires de la ville de Toulouse*, t. III, Toulouse: Laurent Chapelle, 1844, p. 95).

31 Philippe Wolff, *Voix et images de Toulouse* (Toulouse: Privat, 1962), p. 58. The author is quoting from St Bernard's disciple and biographer, Geoffroi d'Auxerre. 'Green-Leaf' is English for 'Verte-Feuille', of which Verfeil is a shortened version. The cross-breaking heresy, whose leading exponents were Pierre de Bruys and Henry de Lausanne, attracted many adherents in the south during the first half of the twelfth century.

32 Ernest Roschach (ed.), *Inventaire des Archives Communales de Toulouse antérieures à 1790, Série AA, nos 1–60* (Toulouse: Edouard Privat, 1891), document no. 18, September 1289. The church's reticence in recording gains from confiscations is understandable since future claimants to restitution could always be anticipated into whose hands such papers could fall. Another example is reported by J. H. Mundy in *Liberty and Political Power*, p. 380, telling how the temporal holdings of the important churchman, Archdeacon Pons of Villemur, one of the two judges in Bishop Foulques's usurers' court, was 'considerably enriched by properties' belonging to the Maurand family, which was shot through with heretics. The Order of Trinitarians is also listed as receiving property confiscated from heretics, as are the Franciscans, the Frères Croisiers and the Dominicans (see Yves Dossat, *Les crises de l'inquisition toulousaine au 13e siècle, 1233–1273*, Bordeaux: Imprimerie Bière, 1959, pp. 306–7; also Devic and Vaissete, t. IV, p. 707).

33 Elie Lambert, 'La cathédrale de Toulouse', *MSAM*, t. 21 (1947), p. 147.

34 It is hard to imagine the impoverished Fulcrand being responsible for building the new nave, whereas Raymond de Rabastens served too short a time (1202–5) to undertake such a major project. One does not see Foulques in

this role either, for reasons that we shall soon examine.

35 Raymond Rey, 'La cathédrale St-Etienne de Toulouse', *Congrès Archéologiques de France*, t. 92 (1929), pp. 72–3. The author's source was the Archives de St-Sernin, liasse LXXIX, no. XXI, titre I.

36 For example, St-Denis, Laon, Senlis, the large part of Notre-Dame, Chartres and many others.

37 The extent of France's expropriations at Toulouse is not as well documented as for other regions, such as Poitou or Normandy, where this subject will be more fully studied. None the less, the overall figures of Alphonse's finances for Languedoc for 1258, an 'average' year, show a positive balance of the enormous sum of 31,468 livres (Aug. Molinier, *Etude sur l'administration de St. Louis et d'Alfonse de Poitiers dans le Languedoc, suivie des Actes des Enquêteurs de ces deux princes*, Toulouse: Edouard Privat, n.d., p. 54). Regarding confiscation of property of heretics, Molinier says: 'In the Toulousan region . . . the number of domains sequestrated to the profit of the sovereign was very great' (in Devic and Vaissete, t. VII, p. 516).

38 Pons David was of course a manifest usurer. But there was a certain logic for the tendency of defenders of orthodoxy to link usury with heresy, since the Cathars were evidently indulgent to usurious practices and some authors have even attributed the appeal of this heresy for the bourgeoisie to its realistic attitude to the needs of capitalistic expansion. See, for example, Arno Borst, *Die Katharer* (Stuttgart: Hiersemann Verlag, 1953), p. 189 and note 37. Naming the Hospitallers his principal heir, Pons left one bequest of 2,000 sous with which the Knights were to make restitution for his usuries (J. H. Mundy, *Traditio*, p. 265, n. 200).

39 Devic and Vaissete, t. IV, 1872, pp. 699–701. The authors report that Bishop Raymond donated 4,000 s. toul. to the church fabric, as much more for the capitular hall and as much again for the monks' cells and dormitory. Henri Ramet, in his *Histoire de Toulouse*, p. 150, adds that Raymond left a bequest of 4,000 s. annual income for the Dominicans' clothes,

wine and bread. Toulouse had a strong currency, its livre being worth twice the livre tournois (usually 'tour.'). Recent scholarship has concluded that the Jacobins was built and rebuilt several times, starting with a rather smallish church in 1230, which had a double nave of five bays, flat apse and a wooden vault, hastily constructed to serve as the Dominicans' headquarters-church in their fight against the heresy. This church, finished around 1263, was soon after enlarged and refurbished, with important changes going on into the fourteenth century.

40 The five included: (1) Pierre Cellani and (2) 'Thomas', who gave the Dominicans two houses in 1211, in which they established their first home, one of which later became the headquarters of the Inquisition. They both joined the order and Cellani became prior and was even chief inquisitor for a period (Devic and Vaissete, t. VI, p. 468). (3) *1236 (mid-April)*, Huc Guilhelm in his testament made a bequest of 50 sous (Arch. Dépt., Série E, no. 501). (4) Pons de Capdenier, *1229*, who gave the terrain on which the new Jacobins church was built (see note 43 below). (5) Bernard Bruno, *1275*, who left a bequest of 500 s. toul. for building a funerary chapel as well as other sums for a missal, vestments, etc., and 300 s. toul. for clothing for the monks (Célestin Douais, *Des fortunes commercials à Toulouse et de la topographie des églises et maisons religieuses de Toulouse d'après deux testaments, 13e et 15e siècles*, Paris: Alphonse Picard, 1894). In addition, the chronicle of Bernard Gui includes donations of a garden in 1241 (fol. 112 v°); two houses, 1251 (fol. 113); a house, 1259 (fol. 114); and a gift of 1263 (*Bernardus Guidonis, De Fundatione Conventus Tholosani*, Bibliothèque de Toulouse, ms 490). However, there is no evidence that these donors were burghers.

41 *Ibid.*, fols 112 through 114 v°. The purchases were mainly of houses and were dated from 1241 to 1263.

42 In 1248, Pope Innocent IV protested to the Inquisitors about the luxury of their establishment and the excessive numbers of their servants. Alphonse de Poitiers strongly remonstrated with them on the same subject, in 1269. Since he was

the ultimate recipient of the earnings from confiscations, his interest is understandable (Yves Dossat, *Les crises de l'inquisition toulousaine . . .*, p. 91). The authoritative writer on the Inquisition, Henry C. Lea, in his *A History of the Inquisition of the Middle Ages*, vol. I (New York: Harper, 1888), p. 528, pointed out the possibility of illegal siphoning off of confiscated wealth by inquisitors to be used for other purposes:

> It might, indeed, be a curious question to determine the source when Bernard de Caux, who presided over the tribunal of Toulouse until his death, in 1252, and who, as a Dominican, could have owned no property, obtained the means which enabled him to be a great benefactor of the convent of Agen, founded in 1249.

43 Guilelmus Pelhisso, *De Empcione et adquizicione secundi loci Fratrum Predicatorum Tholose*, 1263.

44 Quoted by Elie Lambert, 'L'Eglise et le couvent des Jacobins de Toulouse et l'architecture dominicaine en France', *Bulletin Monumental*, t. 104 (1946), p. 157.

45 Austin P. Evans, 'Hunting Subversion in the Middle Ages', *Speculum*, vol. 33 (1958), pp. 1–22. Dissident religious movements were widespread. In France, there were a number of foci, which have been overshadowed historically by the Albigensian repression.

46 *Chronique de Guillaume Pelhissonv* translated with commentary by Jean Duvernoy (Toulouse: Ousset, 1958), *passim*.

47 Gatien-Arnoult, 'Jean de Garlande, docteur-régent à l'université de Toulouse, de 1229 à 1232', *Revue de Toulouse et du Midi de la France*. t. 23 (1866), pp. 117–37.

48 H. C. Lea, *A History of the Inquisition in the Middle Ages* (New York, 1888), vol. I, pp. 495–6; vol. II, p. 22.

49 *Chronique de Guillaume Pelhisson*, pp. 28–9.

50 H. C. Lea, vol. II, p. 22.

51 Célestin Douais, *Documents pour servir à l'histoire de l'inquisition dans le Languedoc*, t. II (Paris: Renouard, 1900), documents 1 to 38, selected.

52 C. Douais, t. I, pp. ccxv–ccxvi.

53 H. C. Lea, vol. I, pp. 473–4.

54 Ernest Roschach, *Inventaire des Archives Communales de Toulouse antérieures à 1790*, *Série AA*: AA 5, no. 7, April 1229; also see *Chronique de Guillaume Pelhisson*, p. 51.

55 Guillaume de Catel, *Histoire des comtes de Tolose* (Tolose: Pierre Bosc, 1623), pp. 335ff; also Devic and Vaissete, t. VI, p. 653; t. VII, p. 529.

56 Abbé R.-C. Julien, *Histoire de la paroisse Notre-Dame de la Dalbade* (Toulouse: Edouard Privat, 1891), p. 141. This author's observation is illustrated by an amazing document of the mid-century containing the accumulated grievances of the faithful at that epoch. Aside from exorbitant charges for the sacraments, various other petty tyrannies are listed. If, for example, a man married a woman from another parish, his priest refused to bless the nuptial bed unless the other priest received his fee too. Every curé had the 'right' to partake of the wedding dinner. But if he performed several marriages on the same day, he had to be paid for the meals he could not eat. A person choosing to be buried outside his parish had to pay for funeral services there as well. Discord often resulted but it cannot be construed to mean a complete turning away from the church. Thus, during this very period, a number of the artisans' and tradesmen's guilds and confraternities continued to hold their religious functions at the different churches, and guild statutes from 1279 through 1290 show many of them paying annual rents to sustain a lamp burning day and night at their parishes (see Antoine Du Bourg's two references, *Les corporations ouvrières de la ville de Toulouse . . .*, Toulouse: Sistac et Boubée, 1884, *passim*, and *Coup d'oeil historique sur les diverses corporations de Toulouse*, Toulouse: A. Chauvin & Fils, n.d., *passim*).

57 John H. Mundy, *Traditio*, vol. 22 (1966), p. 236. It should also be made clear that the French did not take possession of the Languedoc *until* the 'mid-century' (1249), whereas almost all the foundations the author offers as evidence for the prosperity he speaks about were established *before* the takeover,

a large part of them dating from what he himself has called Toulouse's 'age of liberty' (*Liberty and Political Power in Toulouse*, p. 159).

58 The enormous cost of the war to the Languedoc cannot be waved away without solid proof either. Aside from the expenses for arms and fortifications, Toulousans were several times forced to pay great sums to the invaders, such as the 30,000 marks Simon de Montfort demanded in 1216 as his price to spare the city from destruction (H. C. Lea, vol. I, p. 185). Later, the cost to Toulouse of the defeat was somewhat tempered by the fact that Raymond VII was allowed to keep control of his county by the Peace of 1229, which nevertheless imposed tremendous payments on Toulouse, such as for the reinforcement of its citadel, the Château-Narbonnais, at a cost of 6,000 marks (P. Wolff, *Voix et images de Toulouse*, pp. 112ff), the maintenance of the garrison there, the launching of the university, for which the count was held responsible for the masters' salaries during the first ten years for a total of 4,000 marks, and indemnities payable to religious groups, which called for 10,000 marks more (*Inv. des Arch. Comm.*, AA 5, no. 4, April 1229). And the greatest loss was undoubtedly due to the war's destruction and devastation of the countryside, to say nothing of the vast expropriations, much of which left the country.

59 According to Professor Mundy's own distribution of twenty-two hospitals, hospices and leper-houses existing at Toulouse in 1250, five dated from the Gregorian Reform period of the late eleventh and early twelfth centuries, eleven from the latter part of the twelfth century and the first decade of the thirteenth and six from after the Albigensian war (*Traditio*, p. 236).

60 *Ibid.*, p. 237. The point should be made also that the foundation of hospitals, hospices and similar units has by no means been carefully studied for the Middle Ages. Though not a specialist on this subject, I have none the less accumulated a considerable amount of heretofore unpublished material regarding it in the cities I have studied. That Toulouse may seem to have been specially favoured by such foundations, as

Professor Mundy believes, may be due to some extent at least to the unusual thoroughness of his investigations.

61 *Ibid.*, pp. 237–8. The author points out that eight of the city's hospitals and leper-houses were equipped with chapels or churches, all built in the pre-1215 period. He himself implies that a substitution of philanthropic objective took place at Toulouse, telling of the complaints of some of the older groups to competition from new churches and chapels.

62 Mireille Castaing-Sicard, 'Donations toulousaines du 10e au 13e siècle', *Annales du Midi*, t. 70 (1958), p. 29 and n. 12. Jean Duvernoy, editor of the *Chronique de Guillaume Pelhisson*, makes the same point, saying that large numbers of people would confess to having dabbled with heresy on their death beds, 'bequeathing their property to an abbey and entering, at least nominally, in the order' (p. 8).

63 J. H. Mundy, *Traditio*, p. 253. He indicates that few of the foundations were actually hospitals in the modern sense. As was general in the Middle Ages, he points out with many illustrations from Toulousan institutions, they 'specialized in one or several of the following categories: the sick, the aged, poor maidens, pregnant women, women, orphans and bastards' (*ibid.*, p. 254 and *passim*).

64 Pierre Gérard, 'Les origines du collège St-Bernard de Toulouse, vers 1150–1335', *Annales du Midi*, t. 69 (1957), pp. 189–205. The immensity of Pons de Capdenier's endowment and the manner of acquisition of his fabulous fortune, by his father and himself, can be followed, property by property, quitrent by quitrent, in the beautiful illuminated cartulary that hired scribes prepared for Pons a few years before his death. It runs from 1161 to 1222 (Arch. Dépt., 7 D 138).

65 J. H. Mundy, *Traditio*, p. 206.

66 *Ibid.*, p. 236, in which the author speaks of 'a new wave of construction and expansion . . . in the twelve-thirties and forties . . .' and of 'the building of many new churches and mendicant convents, aspects of Toulousan enterprise that do not concern us in this essay'.

67 The following list indicates this concentration:
  (1) *St-Sernin*: Partly in the eleventh, partly

in the twelfth and partly built or rebuilt in the thirteenth century (Marcel Aubert, *L'église St-Sernin de Toulouse*, Paris: Henri Laurens, 1933; Jules de Lahondès, *Les monuments de Toulouse*, Toulouse: Edouard Privat, 1920).

(2) *La Daurade*: Sixth century; the nave added in the eleventh (Georges Boyer, 'Une hypothèse sur l'origine de la Daurade', pp. 47–51; also A. Auriol, 'Une page sur chaque église de Toulouse', *BSAM*, 2e série, nos 44–5, 1914–17, pp. 407–16).

(3) *La Dalbade*: Built 1164–1200 (R.-C. Julien, 'Histoire de ... la Dalbade', pp. 123–4); Henri Ramet extends the building period to 1220 (p. 77).

(4) *St-Pierre-des-Cuisines*: Partly eleventh, partly twelfth century (J. de Lahondès, pp. 136–43).

(5) *St-Sernin-du-Taur*: Sixth century for original building, only date known (H. Ramet, p. 85).

(6) *St-Rome (St-Romain)*: Building date unknown, but church was cited in 1176 already. Was given by Bishop Foulques to St Dominick in 1216, who with his monks added a cloister and a dormitory before moving on to the new Jacobins (J. Chalande, 'Hist. des rues de Toulouse', *Mémoires de l'Acad. des Sciences, Inscrip. et B-Lettres de Toulouse*, 12e série, t. 3, 1925, p. 302).

(7) *St-Nicolas*: Romanesque church that was probably completed in the twelfth century, though an extant part is of the eleventh (H. Ramet, p. 81; A. Auriol).

(8) *Templiers*: Arrived at Toulouse in 1136 and came to an agreement with the cathedral chapter a few years later about their establishment (J. de Lahondès, *L'église St-Etienne, cathédrale de Toulouse*, Toulouse: Edouard Privat, 1890, p. 150).

(9) *Hospitaliers*: Arrived at Toulouse in 1115 and made arrangements with St-Etienne for their establishment (*ibid.*).

(10) *Sts-Pierre-et-Géraud*: Pre-1187, date of earliest document (H. Ramet, p. 83).

(11) *St-Quentin*: Already cited 1175 (H. Ramet, p. 85; J. Chalande, MAST, p. 311).

(12) *St-Barthelemy*: Cited at beginning of twelfth century, then not again until 1210 (H.

Ramet, p. 86; J. Chalande, MAST 11e série, t. 4, 1916, pp. 181–2).

(13) *Sts-Pierre-et-Martin*: Twelfth-century priory (H. Ramet, pp. 86–7).

(14) *St-Sauveur*: Church of the cemetery of the same name, the only cemetery in the parish of St-Etienne up to the thirteenth century (J. de Lahondès, *L'église St-Etienne, etc.*, p. 163).

(15) *St-Jacques-de-St-Etienne*: Built in the twelfth century, as we know from note 10 here.

(16) *Capelle Redonde*: Date unknown but probably early twelfth century, according to G. de Catel, p. 158.

(17) *St-Antoine-de-Salins*: Pre-1115 priory, outside the city walls (Devic and Vaissete, t. IV, n. CXLV, pp. 690–2).

(18) *St-Genies*: Pre-1088, date when Bishop Izarn gave it to the chapter (G. de Catel, *Mémoires de l'histoire du Languedoc*, p. 868).

(19) *Ste-Marie-de-Palacio*: Pre-1208, date when Pons David left its fabric 50 sous toul. (Arch. Dépt., H, Malte, Toulouse, liasse 1, no. 17, 17 January 1208).

(20) *St-Rémy*: Pre-1114/19, when several seigniors gave it to the Hospitaliers (Antoine Du Bourg, 'Hôpital et hôtel St-Jean à Toulouse', *MSAM*, t. 11, 1875/80, pp. 249–50).

68 Rebuilding activities at St-Sernin, described by both Aubert and Lahondès, went on throughout most of the thirteenth century but with constant starts and stops. The only other church-building during this century at Toulouse that I have discovered (aside from St-Etienne) included two chapels (Notre-Dame-du-Feretra and the Nazareth) and possibly some work done at St-Julien-du-Bourg. The list of churches rebuilt in part or entirely during the fourteenth and fifteenth centuries includes: the Jacobins, Dalbade, Cuisines, Taur, St-Nicolas, Sts-Pierre-et-Géraud, St-Antoine-de-Salins, Ste-Marie-de-Palacio and others. Emile Mâle's observations are from his *Arts et artistes du moyen-âge*, pp. 87–9.

69 *Répertoire de Claude Cresty*, 1 April 1734–23 June 1737, vols I and II (Archives Départementales); also *Claude Cresty*,

Répertoire... de St-Sernin... les chappelenies sive obits fondés dans leur église... dernier may 1728... 15 du même mois 1730; Inventaire des chartres [sic] et documents des archives du monastère Nostre Dame de la Daurade faict en 1684 (Arch Dépt., 102 H, no. 138).

70 Archives Départementales, *Commanderie de Toulouse du Temple, Inventaire des titres, papiers et documents... qui n'ont pas été repertoriés dans les Inventaires faits par Imbert.* Probably by Claude Cresty, eighteenth century, t. I and especially t. II. No less than eighty-two comparatively important gifts from these sources were counted including such objects as a house, a vineyard, a garden, 10 livres or more in money, etc. Also included were donors of quitrents, whose value to the receiver, as we have pointed out, far exceeded the annual rent that they called for. Dates of the gifts collated ran from 1209 to 1295. Space does not permit their being listed in detail.

71 Thus, J. H. Mundy in his *Traditio* footnotes lists a considerable number of donors to the Hospitallers during the thirteenth century.

72 Aside from the case of Pons David, the wealthy usurer, about which we have already heard, there are various other grave-extraction activities one reads about in the literature of the Inquisition at Toulouse.

73 Ant. Du Bourg, *Ordre de Malte, Histoire du Grand-Prieuré de Toulouse...* (Toulouse, 1882), p. 39.

74 Twenty-five years after Raymond VI's death, papal commissioners heard a hundred and ten witnesses on behalf of his piety (Devic and Vaissete, t. VI, p. 552). But his corpse remained unburied for centuries (H. C. Lea, vol. I, p. 189).

75 R.-C. Julien, pp. 31–2.

76 John H. Mundy mentions several of the Toulousan mendicant groups that disappeared (*Traditio*, p. 206, n. 7).

77 Al. Du Mège, *Histoire des institutions religieuses, politiques, judiciaires et littéraires de la ville de Toulouse*, t. IV (Toulouse: Laurent Chapelle, 1846), p. 614. The author names the two chapel-founders, evidently both of the thirteenth century, as Arnaud Martin, lumber mer-

chant, and Guillaume Pons, also a merchant. Another burgher, Bernard Bruno, bequeathed in his will of 1275, 300 sous toul. to the fabric of the Franciscans' 'great' church (C. Douais, *Des fortunes commerciales, etc.*, pp. 3–4).

78 Gustave Saige, *Les Juifs du Languedoc antérieurement au 14e siècle* (Paris: Alphonse Picard, 1881), p. 86. Treatment of the Jews, even at relatively tolerant Toulouse, was very ambivalent, changing with time and conditions. The same author describes some of the persecutions they suffered even in earlier periods.

79 Célestin Douais, 'Le quartier des Juifs à Toulouse au 13e siècle', *BSAM* (1888), no. 2, p. 118.

80 The act of foundation of the Carmelites is accompanied by a donation by five citizens, one identified as a 'coachmaker', another as 'Pierre called the barber', who turned over some houses to the order (*ibid.*). Douais asserts that the houses were the homes of the donors, but this is clearly incorrect. Guillaume de Catel shows that the men purchased them all at the same time from Jews for the purpose of turning them over to the Carmelites (*Mémoires de l'histoire du Languedoc*, pp. 237–8). Since the quarter was the very valuable Joutz-Aigues, it is much more likely that the Jews had been forced to sell their homes. Such constraint appears clearly in a similar case which is discussed in a letter from Alphonse de Poitiers, dated 3 March 1269, where it is a question of compelling some 'Judeos nostros' to dispose of their homes to the Confraternity of Mont-Carmel (Devic and Vaissete, t. VIII, Preuves, no. 522, cc. 1610ff, XVII, 3 March 1269).

81 Aug. Molinier, *Correspondance administrative d'Alf. de Poitiers*, t. I, 1894, Letter no. 270 (26 June 1267) and Letter no. 405 (21 March 1268). The author says elsewhere that Alphonse actually ordered the suppression of the Confraternity of Carmel, though he does not give the date (see Molinier's article in Devic and Vaissete, t. VII, p. 561, note LIX, cols 462–570). In 1279, it should be further noted, a number of former 'heretics' won royal clemency and were even allowed to return to political life (P. Wolff, *Commerces et marchands de Toulouse*, p. 30).

82 A number of them were to end their lives miser-

ably in North Italy, whence troubadours, sons of burghers, sent bitter 'sirventès' calling the clergy 'ravishing wolves' who won the people's confidence only to betray them to their death (Wolff and Dieuzaide, *Voix et images de Toulouse*, pp. 127–8).

83 Philippe Wolff, in *Les 'estimes' toulousaines des 14e et 15e siècles* (Toulouse: Centre Nationale de la Recherche Scientifique, 1956), pp. 66ff, gives the value of land owned by wealthy Toulousans in 1335, within a radius of fifteen miles from the city, as totalling around 100,000 livres. He estimates that some forty burghers were ennobled between 1322 and 1450 by buying noble fiefs (Philippe Wolff, *Commerces et marchands*, pp. 617ff).

84 The changed attitude toward Toulousan churches in the fourteenth century is reflected in the considerable increase in burgher donations even to older units such as St-Etienne and St-Sernin as shown by the Claude Cresty *Répertoires* previously referred to. The big majority of gifts occur prior to the Hundred Years War, however. The large numbers of gifts to hospitals recorded in the archives had a different impulsion. Coming especially after the first great epidemic of 1348, they reflect a general phenomenon that we can see occurring in many other places: people suddenly became acutely aware of disease and death.

85 Devic and Vaissete, t. IV, pp. 707–8; also A. Du Bourg, *Coup d'oeil historique sur les diverses corporations de Toulouse* (Toulouse: A. Chauvin et Fils, n.d.), p. 94.

86 For example, the military orders, so highly favoured in the thirteenth century, almost disappear in the fourteenth as recipients, according to the same *Inventaire des titres, etc.* that was cited in note 70.

87 Arch. Dépt., 112 H, no. 26, recorded from a *Répertoire* of post-1738.

88 A macabre illustration of this, entirely in the spirit of the time, was the rehearsal arranged, in 1327, for the interment of a capitoul (consul) at the Jacobins. With all the desired pomp, the igniting of countless candles, the wailing of a great chain of mourners, the chanting of the splendid choir and the pealing of bells, he lay in his coffin at the high altar in presence of the entire capitoulate. Then he was carried back home in his bier, where the ghoulish comedy ended with the post-funereal dinner (Charles du Cange, *Glossarium*, t. III, Paris: Didot-Frères, 1844, p. 436, under Funeralia).

89 J. Contrasty, 'Travaux de Jean Maurin aux Jacobins et aux Augustins de Toulouse . . .', *Revue Historique de Toulouse*, t. 9 (1922), pp. 11–15.

90 Arch. Dépt., 112 H, no. 26, 24 November 1369; also Elie Lambert, 'L'église et le couvent des Jacobins de Toulouse, etc.', *Bulletin Monumental*, t. 104 (1946), p. 163.

91 Ch. Higounet, *La chronique de la construction de l'église des Jacobins de Toulouse* (Paris, 1949), p. 97 and notes 1 and 2.

92 Elie Lambert, pp. 166–8, 176.

93 Raymond Rey, *La cathédrale de Toulouse* (Paris: Henri Laurens, 1929), pp. 15–16.

94 Jules de Lahondès, *L'église St-Etienne, etc.*, pp. 68–9; also Raymond Rey, pp. 51–2.

95 Edmond Cabié, 'Testament et autres actes de l'évêque de Toulouse, Bertrand II de Lile, 13e siècle'. Extract from *MSAM*, t. 12 (1881). Devic and Vaissete, t. IV, under 'Bertrand II de l'Ile-Jourdain', claim that the bishop's bequests totalled 120,000 livres tour., which would have sufficed to terminate the cathedral.

96 Devic and Vaissete, t. VI, pp. 803–21. Raymond VII left 10,000 marks sterling in pious alms. Half of this was to go to the Abbey of Fontrevault, where he asked to be buried, and St-Etienne was to come in for 150 l. Alphonse got his experts to trick up arguments to challenge the legitimacy of the will. Some years later, as he was preparing to leave on Crusade, Alphonse turned part of the bequests over to the intended beneficiaries.

97 J. de Lahondès, p. 81; E. Cabié, p. 28; G. de Catel, p. 910.

98 The cathedral canons were even less concerned about continuing the work than were Bertrand's episcopal successors. Whereas in other dioceses, the chapter usually assumed half the building cost, at Toulouse the proportion was less than a fourth (J. de Lahondès, p. 173). The choir vault itself was left incomplete for more than three centuries, closed off with timber. It might never have been finished in

stone but for the fire of 1609 which destroyed the wooden ceiling. Then the stone vaulting was swiftly provided by work lasting only two years (Elie Lambert, p. 161).

99 *Ibid.*, pp. 155–6; Raymond Rey, pp. 15–16.

100 J. de Lahondès, pp. 91ff, 101. The author quotes from the findings of papal investigators of the diocese, on the basis of which the first great amputation was ordered. The second split-off, twenty years later, was featured by another scandal, the sale by Bishop Gaillard de Pressac of 15,000 livres of church property to pay his and his predecessor's personal debts (Claude Cresty, *Répertoire de St-Etienne*, Arch. Dépt., 4 G 3, vol. I, October 1317, Papal Bulls).

101 Claude Cresty, October 1317: 'Chanoines: Prétentions du Saint Siège touchant la nomination des canonicats par grace et que le chapitre ne pouvoit recevoir aucun chanoine sans l'autorité dudit Saint Siège' (fol. 217–217 v°). Even after the second cut, the see of Toulouse's revenues still totalled 40,000 livres (H. C. Lea, vol. I, pp. 514–15).

102 Claude Pécassou, 'Le chapitre cathédrale de Toulouse en 1324. Réforme et réalité', *Annales du Midi*, t. 70 (1958), pp. 339–48.

103 The two exceptions were benefices that were placed at the disposition of the pope, a sop that was accepted, though with bad grace.

104 Some of the family names included were Lautrec, Rabastens, Villeneuve, Orbesson, Graulhet, etc.

105 Claude Pécassou, p. 344. Only three of the new canons were above the age of twenty-two. Seven were less than ten years old.

106 *Ibid.*, pp. 344–5.

107 Elie Lambert, pp. 159–62; also Raymond Rey, 'La cathédrale St-Etienne de Toulouse', *Congrès Archéologiques de France*, t. 92 (1929), p. 83. The four prelates were Gaillard de Pressac (1305–17); Guillaume de Laudun (1327–45); Geoffroy de Vayrolles (1361–76); and Pierre de St-Martial (1392–1401).

4 LYON

1 There are a number of important works that are concerned with these matters, including: Georg Hüffer, *Die Stadt Lyon und die West-hälfte des Erzbisthums in ihren politischen Beziehungen zum deutschen Reiche und zur französischen Krone, 879–1312* (Münster: Aschendorffsche Universitäts-Buchdruckerei, 1878); Horst Bitsch, *Das Erzstift Lyon zwischen Frankreich und dem Reich im Hohen Mittelalter* (Göttingen: Musterschmidt, 1971), particularly pp. 45, 51, 55; Arthur Kleinclausz et al., *Histoire de Lyon*, t. I: *Des origines à 1595* (Lyon: Pierre Masson, 1939), pp. 113–16. The count's title was actually Comte de Lyon et Forez.

2 Ph. Pouzet, in *La vie de Guichard... archevêque de Lyon, 1165–1181* (Lyon: M. Audin, 1929), is the source of the claim that Comte Guigue II's invasion was in reply to the granting of the 'golden bull'. André Steyert, in *Nouvelle histoire de Lyon et des provinces de Lyonnais, Forez, etc.*, t. II: *Moyen-Age, 534–1483* (Lyon: Bernoud et Cumin, 1897), suggests that the archbishop was encouraged to adopt a belligerent posture toward the Comte de Forez by the burghers of Lyon (p. 331).

3 Steyert, *Nouvelle histoire de Lyon et des provinces de Lyonnais, etc.* One of the details of the accommodation provided for was the dropping of the 'Lyon' from the count's title, permitting the archbishop and all the canons to be called 'Comte de Lyon'.

4 The effort, often violent and extending over two centuries and more, to establish the church's sovereignty, had frequently favoured the selection of archbishops who were more gifted as warriors than as churchmen.

5 H. Bitsch, p. 107, notes 314 and 315. Marcel David, in *Le patrimoine foncier de l'église de Lyon de 984 à 1267* (Lyon: Les Impressions E. Vinay, 1942), gives a thorough account of the building up of the church's possessions by Renaud (p. 71 and n. 25; p. 72, n. 26).

6 *Ibid.*, p. 108, n. 317. One of the pensions recorded was for the great sum of 29,000 sous.

7 Jean Beyssac, *Les prévôts de Fourvière* (Lyon: P. Grange, 1908), p. 7.

8 M.-C. Guigue (ed.), *Cartulaire municipal de la ville de Lyon... Recueil formé au 14e siècle par Etienne de Villeneuve, publié d'après le manuscrit original avec des documents inédits du 12e au 14e siècle* (Lyon: Aug. Brun, 1876), appendice I, p. 375. The document was signed

by the archbishop and forty-two canons and had two heavy lead seals appended to it.

9 Lucien Bégule, *Monographie de la cathédrale de Lyon*, with a *Notice historique* by M.-C. Guigue (Lyon: Mougin-Rusand, 1880).

10 Marcel Aubert, 'Cathédrale de Lyon', *Congrès Archéologiques*, t. 98 (1935), pp. 54–90.

11 These have been collated by M.-C. Guigue in his already cited essay in Lucien Bégule's *Monographie*, pp. 6–7.

12 M.-C. Guigue (ed.), *Obituarium lugdunensis ecclesiae. Nécrologe des personnages illustres et des bienfaiteurs de l'église métropolitaine de Lyon du 9e au 15e siècle* (Lyon: N. Scheuring, 1867), pp. 132–40; also the revised edition, begun by Georges Guigue and completed by Jacques Laurent, *Obituaires de la province de Lyon*, t. I: *Diocèse de Lyon*, première partie (Paris: Imprimerie Nationale, 1951), pp. 119–26.

13 A rather extreme example was Dean Arnulphe de Colonges, whose obit, dated 7 September 1250, shows him bequeathing 300 l. for his own anniversary and 120 l. more for one for his parents; another 120 l. for prayers by one or two priests at one of the cathedral altars; and 40 l. more for alms. In addition, he arranged for anniversaries at thirteen other local churches for a total of 300 l. His total bequests were for 880 livres, as against which enormous sum he left exactly 50 sous (2½ livres) to the 'operi majoris ecclesie Lugd.', the cathedral fabric, during a very active construction period (M.-C. Guigue, *Obituarium*, pp. 219–22). The *Obituarium* contains numbers of other similar cases during the first two-thirds of the thirteenth century, when ongoing building operations might have been expected to encourage important donations. Many members of the St-Jean ecclesiastic family are shown in their obits as giving nothing at all to the fabric during this period, while making big bequests for other purposes. For example, Guillelmus Criveus, prévôt de Fourvière, 2 May 1262, who arranged for two anniversaries and left 40 l. (probably a *rente* of that amount) for two chaplains, gave not a cent to the fabric; Guademarus de Jareis, chamberlain and sub-deacon, 31 March 1255, n.st., bequeathed two mills for an anniversary, but gave nothing to the fabric; Petrus Jomari de Baino, priest, 3 April *c*.1251, also set up an anniversary but left nothing to the fabric; Asalitus, canon, cited both in 1217 and 1245/46, left 100 l. for an anniversary, nothing for the fabric; Dalmatius de Sancto Simphoriano, canon, 6 April post-1244, pre-1253, had an anniversary costing 160 l. but left nothing to the fabric; etc.; etc. (collated from G. Guigue et J. Laurent, *Obituaires de la province de Lyon*).

14 Collated from Guigue-Laurent. The gifts of the thirty-three canons totalled 459 livres, 10 sous, plus two miscellaneous donations, for the period 1160–1230.

15 Jean Bellesmains's letter is quoted by M.-C. Guigue in his Introduction to the *Obituarium*, p. xi, n. 3. A. Steyert (*Nouvelle histoire de Lyon . . . * p. 412) asserts that Archbishop Renaud spent half his time in the saddle, making war. M.-C. Guigue discusses the class make-up of the chapter in the *Obituarium* Introduction, p. xxi. For the requirements for the post of canon, see Jean Beyssac, *Les chanoines de l'église de Lyon* (Lyon: P. Grange, 1914, with addition, Lyon: M. Audin, 1931), Introduction, pp. xiii–xiv.

16 The 'Poor Ones of Lyon' were never considered as dangerous as the Cathars and were not expelled from the church for years while efforts were multiplied to reclaim them.

17 A. Kleinclausz, *Histoire de Lyon*, pp. 160ff.

18 Guigue-Laurent, *Obituaires*, 24 March and 19 April, covering the gifts of the Chaponays and Poncie Limanda.

19 My collated list includes seventy-seven lay donors for the entire period of 1160 to 1300. Many of these undoubtedly came from places outside Lyon, and others, though from that city, were hardly burghers, often being merely referred to as *laicus* or *femina*. This record seems the more astonishing in comparison with the important contribution of a group of burghers to an earlier cathedral-building programme, which was symbolized in what was called the 'Furriers' Privilege', a ceremonial reward for the donation by these craftsmen of part of the site of the previous cathedral edifice (L. Bégule, *Monographie*, p. 2).

20 C.-F. Ménestrier, *Histoire civile ou consulaire de la ville de Lyon, justifiée par chartes, titres, chroniques, etc.* (Lyon: Jean-Baptiste & Nicolas de Ville, 1696), p. 371. The number of canons varied from forty-eight to seventy-two, in the twelfth and thirteenth centuries (M.-C. Guigue, *Obituarium*, p. xxiii).

21 H. Bitsch, *Das Erzstift Lyon . . .*, pp. 156–7, 161, 162–3.

22 *Ibid.*, p. 156, n. 494. The pope not only charged Renaud with these atrocities but also accused him of 'violating the public highway and imposing new tolls on merchants', which was the immediate cause of the burghers' rising.

23 *Ibid.*, pp. 156–7.

24 M.-C. Guigue, *Cartulaire municipal*, under September 1208, Appendice, p. 377. For an interpretation of the settlement, see Bitsch, pp. 177–9.

25 My collated list of personal donations of one livre or more to the fabric by clerics for the thirty years, 1241–70, gives a total of 587 livres (383 l. in the decade of the pope's presence at Lyon, 1241–50). This was almost half the total for the entire century, 1,265 l.

26 M. Aubert, 'Cathédrale de Lyon . . .', p. 61.

27 *Ibid.* The author adds that the last bay of the nave was not built until the fourteenth century, while the high windows and vaults were not completed until the end of that century. Nevertheless, the accomplishment of the previous active period of building on the nave is proved by the fact that the cathedral was in a position to contain the 1274 assembly, which was attended by 500 bishops, 70 abbots and 1,000 'prelates', in addition to the various princes and their suites (Georges Guigue, 'La cathédrale de Lyon', p. 83, in Henry Havard, *La France artistique et monumentale*, t. III, Paris: Librairie Illustrée, n.d.).

28 Quoted in C.-F. Ménestrier, p. 334.

29 The basic source of these events is the 'Tractatus de bellis et induciis . . .', which the church published in connection with the inquests that took place afterwards and which C.-F. Ménestrier reproduces in full in his *Preuves*.

30 Jean Beyssac, *Les prévôts de Fourvière* (Lyon: P. Grange, 1908), p. 39.

31 *Ibid.*, p. 30; also C.-F. Ménestrier, p. 380.

32 This is implied in the charge registered against the citizens by the bishop of Autun (the acting archbishop of Lyon), who accused them of sacrileges 'such as the celebration in certain churches of the offices with ringing of bells, despite the interdict . . .' (A. Kleinclausz, *Histoire de Lyon*, t. I, 1939, p. 178).

33 Louis Caillet, 'Le consulat de Lyon et le clocher de St-Nizier', *Bulletin Historique du Diocèse de Lyon*, ts 11–12 (1910/11), pp. 315–28.

34 The major source for these events is the *Cartulaire municipal*, appendice no. 4 (1273), pp. 380–403, which describes the attacks on Ecully and the other villages. The citizens were not only accused of pillaging the buildings of St-Jean cloister (Ménestrier, p. 376) but also of going off with stones from the cloister of St-Just, which they claimed had been taken from the city walls! (Kleinclausz, p. 175). Attacks on residents of the St-Nizier quarter (actually it was the 'Quartier des Changes') were hardly accidental since an author checking names of seventy-four of the burgher insurrectionists found a majority coming from there (B. Vermorel, *Historique des rues de la ville de Lyon . . . en 1350*, Lyon, 1879, p. 2). Some of Lyon's most prestigious names were included.

35 The church claimed its losses were 10,000 livres petits tournois during the 1269 events. But in addition it charged that a series of interventions and seizures by royal agents had cost it 15,000 l. tour. more (Pierre Bonnassieux, *De la réunion de Lyon à la France, étude historique d'après des documents originaux*, Lyon: Auguste Brun, Paris: Honoré Champion, 1875).

36 As compensation for its loss of its temporal justice, the chapter was granted a yearly allowance of 150 l. by the pope, collectable from the archbishop's court's earnings (Kleinclausz, p. 185).

37 P. Bonnassieux, p. 147, n. 1. The chapter's campaign is described by Noël Didier in 'Un procès en annulation d'une sentence pontificale, 1276–1277', *Recueil de mémoires et travaux publiés par la Société d'Histoire du Droit . . .*, Fascicule I, 1948.

38 Kleinclausz, pp. 188–90.

39 P. Bonnassieux (p. 190) reports the purchase of the Comté de Mâcon by St Louis, as does also Bitsch (p. 197). The latter adds that thereafter

the royal bailiff often interfered in the church's autonomy, bringing strong protests from arch-bishops and even popes.

40 Bitsch, pp. 161–8. The cities were Anse, Montbrison and St-Rambert.

41 Georg Hüffer, *Die Stadt Lyon, etc.*, 1878, p. 102.

42 M.-C. Guigue, *Cartulaire municipal*, entries of 28 September 1292; 19 June 1293; various others of 1294, 1295 and 1297; 16 February 1298; 4 February 1300; 9 May 1302 (pp. 411–14, 419–23, *passim*); also A. Péricaud, *Notes et documents pour servir à l'histoire de Lyon depuis l'origine de cette ville jusqu'à l'année 1349* (Lyon: Pélagaud, Lesné et Crozet, 1838), p. 54. It is Pierre Bonnassieux who quotes the king's phrase of 'beloved and loyal Lyonese people' (p. 76).

43 An anomalous feature of this entire episode was that the French king, Philippe-le-Bel, almost lost the support of Lyon's burghers by trying to come to a secret arrangement with the church at their expense. Despite the anger of the citizens at the king's duplicity, in the final phases of France's conflict against the church of Lyon, when the king's troops entered Lyon by boat, there is no question but that a number of burghers joined them for the assault on the archbishop's castle (Pierre Bonnassieux, p. 116; J. Perrier, *Histoire des évêques et archevêques de Lyon*, Lons-le-Saunier: J. Mayet, 1887; and others).

44 Kleinclausz, p. 211.

45 *Cartulaire municipal*, no. LXXII, 21 June 1320, pp. 114–19.

46 Jean Beyssac, 'Philippe et Pierre de Savoie, archevêques de Lyon', *Bulletin Historique du Diocèse de Lyon*, ts 11–12 (1910/11), pp. 171–9. Regarding the indulgences, see Lucien Bégule, *Monographie*, p. 44; and for the quest by the Confraternity of the Fabric, *ibid.*, p. 45.

47 Thus, to regain its most important possessions, those at Anse, that were taken by the English mercenaries in 1362, St-Jean's chapter had to pay a ransom of 32,000 francs, obtained by borrowing from the pope, the city consulate, rich individual burghers, its own canons and a dozen others (Georges Guigue, *Récits de la guerre de cent ans . . .*, Lyon: Vitte et Perrusel, 1886, pp. 114–26). And the war, if anything, was probably more costly to the burghers than to the church. See on this *ibid.*, Pièces Justificatives, no. LXXXII, 1346–78 (pp. 393–419), 'Comptes des fortifications de la ville de Lyon', which lists hundreds of items, totalling as much as 65,000 livres.

48 These wills were inventoried by the nineteenth-century archivist, Vital de Valous, who left an individualized summary of his findings on cards that are available for study at the Archives Départementales in Lyon. A number of the original wills were scrutinized for bur-gher bequests with specific objectives, includ-ing donations to the cathedral fabric, to other church fabrics, to the *Pont du Rhône* con-struction fund, to the archbishop and his 'offi-cial', as well as various aesthetic objects, foundations of chapels and chaplaincies, etc.

49 Rarely would the chapter allow its member-ship prescriptions to be set aside. One recorded exception was an appointee of the pope, Jean de St-Alban, who had no preparation for the priesthood and lived openly with his con-cubine. But it was not these circumstances that the chapter objected to but rather the man's common birth. After papal excommu-nication, the chapter yielded, in 1347 (M.-C. and Georges Guigue, *Bibliothèque historique du Lyonnais. Mémoires, notes et documents, etc.*, Lyon: Vitte et Perrussel, 1886, pp. 313–57).

50 This figure was obtained from my own read-ing of the wills.

51 Arch. Dépt., 4 G 48, fol. 129 v°–134.

52 Arch. Dépt., 4 G 41, fol. 110–13 v°.

53 The fire, which is sometimes blamed on the Waldensians, is reported by J.-B. Martin, *Histoire des églises et chapelles de Lyon*, t. II, under 'St-Nizier'; also by N.-F. Cochard, *Le guide du voyageur et de l'amateur à Lyon, etc.* (Lyon: J.-B. Pezieux, 1826), pp. 164–5.

54 Unfortunately, few of Lyon's medieval churches remain standing, which might have informed us stylistically about what parts were done in the thirteenth century. Those that do remain were in large measure com-pletely rebuilt in later centuries, however, and

bear little or no trace of earlier construction (St-Nizier; St-Bonaventure; Fourvière; St-Just; St-Irénée; St-Georges). Of the churches still erect and maintaining their basically original form (St-Jean; St-Paul; St-Martin-d'Ainay; St-Martin-St-Loup of Île-Barbe; the façade of St-Pierre-les-Nonains), only the cathedral shows important work of the thirteenth century, and we already know at what a dragging pace this went on.

55 M.-C. Guigue, *Cartulaire lyonnais, etc.*, t. I: Documents antérieurs à 1255. St-Just's powerful defences included walls that were four feet thick and almost twelve metres high; there were at even intervals of 15 paces twenty-two square towers (P. Bonnassieux, p. 42, n. 1). Regarding investments of St-Just, the best source is *Cartulaire lyonnais*, ts I and II, *passim*. To illustrate St-Just's great affluence, I counted twenty-eight major possessions for it on the excellent map prepared by René Lacour, *Les possessions des établissements ecclésiastiques séculiers du Lyonnais et du Beaujolais avant la révolution*, Lyon, n.d. The important collegiate church of St-Paul has only twenty-one such possessions, St-Nizier, twelve.

56 See J.-B. Martin, *Hist, des églises et chapelles de Lyon*, under 'St-Nizier', for the grant of the poor fund by the archbishop: Arch. Dépt., *Fabrique*, 15 G 140.

57 The inventory, *Titres de fondations, etc.* (Arch. Dépt., 15 G 1, vol. I), contains entries indicating activity by St-Nizier's canons in connection with various periods of the reparation work. Thus, in 1315, the chapter voted to assign their own prebends for the *second year* to this purpose (pp. 258–9).

58 D. Meynis, *Les anciennes églises paroissiales de Lyon* (Lyon: P. N. Josserand, 1872), p. 157, n. 1.

59 The *Tractatus de bellis et induciis*, published in Ménestrier's *Preuves*, makes the following accusation against the citizens: 'Item, they adopted statutes that no citizen, at death, should have a silk cloth over him, in contempt of the churches. . . .'

60 C.-F. Ménestrier, p. 362.

61 Georges Guigue, 'Le trésor de St-Nizier de Lyon, 1365–1373, etc.', *Revue du Lyonnais*, 1899, pp. 12–24. The Inventory of 1365–73 showed the church's treasury to be possessed of a hundred costly robes and drapes (pp. 7–11). Guigue reports from the *Actes Capitulaires* that numerous meltings down of wax took place at St-Nizier each year (Arch. Dépt., 15 G 10, p. xi, 1338–65).

62 Close to one-fourth of all burgher burials at Lyon took place at St-Nizier. This figure was obtained from the catalogue cards of Vital de Valous at the Arch. Dépt. and my reading of the wills. These show three churches leading all others as burial sites: St-Nizier, St-Paul and St-Bonaventure, with 31, 25 and 20 burials out of 132 counted.

63 From a variety of sources, chiefly from partial readings of the wills at the Arch. Dépt., a considerable number of references to the foundation by Lyon's burghers of chapels, altars and chaplaincies at eighteen of the city's churches have been collated. Chapels totalled 16, with St-Bonaventure (Franciscans) counting 4 and St-Nizier and St-Paul, 2 each. There were likewise 10 altars established by burghers, with 3 at St-Paul and 2 at St-Nizier; and 41 chaplaincies, with 9 at St-Nizier, 8 at St-Paul and 4 each at the Augustins and St-Martin-d'Ainay. Space does not allow full details to be given.

64 Arch. Dépt., Vital de Valous card.

65 Arch. Dépt., 4 G 57, fol. 232 v°–234. Translation: 'This cross was arranged to be made by Clara, widow of Johan Torneon, citizen of Lyon, locksmith'.

66 Vital de Valous card. Testator specified image was to weigh half a pound.

67 Arch. Dépt., 4 G 44, fol. 87 v°–88 v°.

68 I noted two such foundations in the documents: one by Jean de la Mure, who in 1361 bequeathed 40 florins to bring a *rente* of 2½ florins (4 G 48, fol. 129 v°–134), the other by Jean Chanopin, who in 1372 gave 160 florins for a lamp (15 G 1, *Titres de fondations, etc.*, IV, p. 251). The second may be an error, however (see A. Péricaud, *Notes et documents pour servir à l'histoire de Lyon, etc.*, Lyon: Pélagaud, Lesné et Crozet, 1838, p. 10).

69 Arch. Dépt., 15 G 417: St-Nizier, *Prébende de la Rue-Neuve, fondation et érection d'un autel*, 1372.

70 See note 63 on Chaplaincies. As for the yearly obits that were founded at St-Nizier, the church's *Lième des Anniversaires* of 1438 (Laurent-Gras, *Obituaires de la province de Lyon*, t. II, pp. 252–313), which I collated, lists a total of 533. Of these, 151 were founded by identifiable burghers and 145 more by men and women of unknown quality but probably burghers also, for the most part. The total of burgher anniversaries was surely close to 250. About 75 of these have been estimated to be of the fourteenth century.

71 *Obituaires de la province de Lyon*, t. II, pp. 110–58: *Grand Obituaire* (of St-Paul), *c*.1310 with additions up to 1453. About half of the collated 660 anniversaries here were founded by laymen, according to my calculations, and slightly over 50 per cent of those were established in the thirteenth century.

72 The St-Paul *Obituarium* lists twelve investments between 1202 and 1250 for a total of 857 livres 10 sous. The St-Paul *Polyptique* lists sixteen more (two without mention of price) for a total of 646 livres. The overall total thus is 1,503 l. 10 s. (M.-C. Guigue, *Polyptique de l'église collégiale St-Paul de Lyon. Dénombrement de ses tenanciers, possessions, etc., au 13e siècle*, Lyon: Aug. Brun, 1875, *passim*). Before the development of the city's most active commercial centre between the two rivers, Lyon's concentration of trade activities was on the west bank of the Saône, which had grown up around its great cluster of churches. The commercial development here gave a strong impulsion to the Abbey of St-Paul in later centuries, which remained the sole church unit with important burgher participation on this side of the Saône after the growth of the new commercial quarter across the river.

73 J.-B. Martin, *Histoire des églises et chapelles de Lyon*, t. II, pp. 414–15. Other chapels at St-Bonaventure were paid for by a variety of guilds, including the tavern-keepers, painters, curriers, clothshearers and others (L. Morel de Voleine, pp. 151–4; also L. A. Pavy, *Les Grands Cordeliers de Lyon, ou l'église et le couvent de St-Bonaventure, depuis leur fondation jusqu'à nos jours*, Lyon: Librairie

Ecclésiastique de Sauvignet, 1835, pp. 22–7). Another chapel was founded by the merchants of Troyes who traded at Lyon (L. Morel de Voleine, 'Monuments de Lyon. Notes corrigées et rectifiées, etc.', *Lyon-Revue*, 1885, pp. 152–3).

74 *Inventaire des titres du chapitre d'Ainay*, Arch. Dépt., 11 G 20, entry for 17 September 1343. The *Inventaire* is not signed, but René Lacour, formerly Director of the Archives Départementales du Rhône, told me that it was probably done by Christophe Gouvillier in 1781.

75 Other members of Etienne's family continued to add to his foundation. Thus, Aynard de Villeneuve made a grant in 1400 of 40 florins of annual pension for a 'great mass to be sung every day' (*Inventaire*, 25 November).

76 *Obituaires de la province de Lyon*, t. II: 'Livre des Sépultures', pp. 191–247, Introduction. There was, seemingly, no limit to the number of participating priests that the richer testators might ask for. As one example among many, Martin Genas, in his will, called for twenty chaplains to officiate at his funeral (Arch. Dépt., 4 G 42, fol. 136–137 v°). And Thomas Pignioli, in 1370, wanted no fewer than sixty priests to function at his (4 G 50, fol. 28).

77 Vital de Valous card. Among other large bequests to the poor were: Jean de Viste, *1383*, who asked that it be announced to all the poor of Lyon that they would get an 'obole' if they came to his funeral (4 G 55, fol. 149–54); *1308*, Aymon Ravastelly, who left up to 160 l. for the poor (Vital de Valous card); *1348*, Guichard de la Mure, who left 200 florins for them (Vital de Valous card); *1355*, Léonard de Varey, who left 200 florins 'to the poor of Jesus Christ' (Charles Le Laboureur, *Les masures de l'Île-Barbe*, Lyon: Vitte et Perrussel, 1887, p. 658).

78 Vital de Valous card. Even the cathedral supplied a procession but the 10 florins it cost meant that it was only for the rich. The friars charged only 10 sous for their processions, a sixteenth of the St-Jean fee, according to the will of Pierre Saburin, tavern-keeper (Vital de Valous card).

79 Arch. Dépt. 4 G 57, fols 179–82.

80 A. Kleinclausz, p. 196; also C.-F. Ménestrier, p. 371.

81 For the wealth of the St-Pierre establishment and the luxury of the nuns' life, see J. Tricou, 'Notes et souvenirs d'Antoine Sabatier sur les églises et chapelles de Lyon, 1768–1770', *Bulletin Hist, du Diocèse de Lyon*, 1922, pp. 141–62; also Alfred Coville, 'Une visite de l'abbaye de St-Pierre de Lyon en 1503', *Revue d'Histoire de Lyon*, t. 11 (1912), pp. 240–72. Its proprietary wealth was early established by princely gifts, to which the abbesses were able to add great urban holdings in later centuries. A recent publication by Joseph Picot (*L'Abbaye de St-Pierre de Lyon*, Paris, 1970), gives in detail this double source of St-Pierre's riches (pp. 138, 155–6, 166ff). Similarly, the author of a manuscript history of the abbey, at the Bibliothèque Municipale de Lyon (Gaspard de Berges de Moydieu, *Tableau historique de l'abbaye royale de St-Pierre à Lyon*, 1783, p. 142) reports that there were at that time eight hundred 'articles' of property in the abbey's 'patrimony' located in the city's commercial area. These possessions made St-Pierre one of the most prosperous church units of Lyon. The fact that the Abbey of St-Pierre did not benefit much from burgher benevolence was substantiated to me by Joseph Picot.

82 J. Tricou, *Notes et souvenirs d'Antoine Sabatier . . .*, pp. 156, 157 and note 1.

83 *Ibid.*, pp. 195–7; also D. Meynis, *Les anciennes églises paroissiales de Lyon* (Lyon; P. N. Josserand, 1872), p. 88; and Gaspard de Berges de Moydieu, *Tableau historique de l'abbaye royale de St-Pierre à Lyon, 1783*, a copy of the original manuscript at the Bibliothèque Municipale, published in 1880, pp. 159–62.

84 M.-C. and Georges Guigue, *Bibliothèque historique du Lyonnais, etc.*, 'La fête des merveilles', pp. 166–9. The reference to 'John as baptizer' was a reminder of Professor Meyer Schapiro to the author.

85 *Ibid.*, pp. 171ff; also A. Kleinclausz, *Histoire de Lyon*, p. 165, who adds that the 'fête' was not finally abandoned until the fifteenth century. When Archbishop Pierre de Savoie signed the treaty recognizing France's sovereignty, one of the rights reserved for the church was that of 'coercion and punishment against those who are recalcitrant or delinquent in carrying out their duty with regard to the Festival [of Miracles]': M.-C. and G. Guigue, p. 173.

86 The burghers asked for suppression of the manifestation in 1363, 1364, 1382, 1383 and 1395 at least (*ibid.*, pp. 174–5). It should be noted that a bridge over the Saône had been up for over a century before work on the Pont du Rhône was first begun. It was built by Archbishop Humbert (1052–77) (A. Kleinclausz, p. 166). A weaker current and a shorter span permitted retention of its wooden form for much longer than was possible with the great bridge, though repairs were constantly required on it, as we can judge from the continuing bequests left to it in burghers' wills.

87 I lived at Avignon for several months one winter and spring and observed many times the flow of the river when swollen with rainwater upstream. There is a sharp bend in the Rhône just before the old Pont d'Avignon is reached (only part of which remains today), which the downflowing stream sometimes strikes with great force. But this breaks the strength of the current sharply before it reaches the emplacement of the bridge.

88 Horst Bitsch quotes the original document describing the accident (*Das Erzstift Lyon zwischen Frankreich und dem Reich im hohen Mittelalter*, Göttingen: Musterschmidt, 1971, p. 171, n. 554).

89 A. Croze, 'La question des origines de l'Hôtel-Dieu', *Revue d'Histoire de Lyon*, t. 10 (1911), p. 464.

90 *Ibid.*, Pièces Justificatives, no. 13, p. 467. Urban IV confirmed the Frères Pontifes in possession of these houses, in 1261 and 1264 (J.-B. Martin, *Conciles et Bullaire*, no. 1504, p. 370).

91 See note 54.

92 A. Croze, Pièces Justificatives, no. 12, p. 471.

93 M.-C. Guigue, *Recherches sur Notre-Dame de Lyon . . . Origines du Pont de la Guillotière et du Grand Hôtel-Dieu* (Lyon: N. Scheuring, 1876), p. 48, note 1.

94 *Cartulaire municipal*, 2 July 1328, p. 22, shows Pope John XXII corroborating these accusations made by the burghers. Another source claims that when the city took over the work

again, the two first arches were hardly completed (A. Bleton, *Le Pont de la Guillotière*, n.d.).

95 The author's own check of the wills showed over one-third of the testators making donations to the Pont du Rhône. Half of these donations cluster around the decade of 1341–50, which was just following the takeover of the work by the capitoulate. Many of these donations were very big, running to 20 florins or even more.

96 In the wills of Etienne Brunel, 1343 n.st. (Arch. Dépt., 4 G 41, fol. 44–45 v°), Etienne Daveine, 1342 (Vital de Valous card) and Péronin de Durches, 1348 (4 G 44, fol. 61 v°–62 v°), for example.

97 *Cartulaire municipal*, p. 188; also Arch. Dépt., *Inventaire . . . contenant les anciens actes du couvent des FF Precheurs de Lyon*, 1781, t. IV, fol. 121, which shows a woman, Françoise, wife of Ennemond de Sivrieu, grocer, being granted a full indulgence, in July 1384, for having become a member of the confraternity.

98 *Inventaire des titres recueillis par Samuel Guichenon, précédé de la Table du Lugdunum Sacrophanum de P. Bullioud* (Lyon: Louis Perrin, 1851), no. 135.

99 M.-C. and G. Guigue, *Bibliothèque historique . . .*, 'La fête des miracles', p. 175.

100 *Inventaire . . . par Samuel Guichenon*, no. 103. This was in 1385.

101 Jean Beyssac, *Les prieurs de Notre-Dame-de-Confort* (Lyon: Emmanuel Vitte, 1909), p. 18. The burgher was Aynard de Villeneuve, whose chaplaincy was to be alternated between the Dominican church and the Chapelle du St-Esprit du Pont du Rhône.

102 M.-C. Guigue, *Recherches, etc.*, p. 60.

103 *Ibid.*

104 The seals also show other buildings on both sides of the river, which could represent the auxiliary structures that went up in association with the bridge.

105 Arch. Dépt., 4 G 49, fol. 123–126 v°.

5 STRASBOURG

1 Paul Wentzcke (ed.), *Regesten der Bischöfe von Strassburg bis zum Jahre 1202*, I

(Innsbruck: Verlag der Wagner'schen Universitäts-Buchhandlung, 1908), pp. 282–7.

2 *Ibid.*, pp. 343–6.

3 Alfred Hessel, 'Die Beziehungen der Strassburger Bischöfe zum Kaisertum und zur Stadtgemeinde in der ersten Hälften des 13. Jahrhunderts', *Archiv für Urkundenforschung*, VI, Erstes Heft (1916), pp. 266–75.

4 Aloys Meister, *Die Hohenstaufen im Elsass, mit besonderer Berücksichtigung des Reichenbesitz und des Familiengutes derselben im Elsass, 1079–1255*. Doctoral dissertation (Mainz: Druck von Joh. Falk III, 1890). The author gives full details on the Hohenstaufens' vast acquisitions in Alsace, mainly through dynastic inheritance and purchase and tells how they were able to establish their claims over certain of them only 'after a long conflict with the Strasbourg bishop' (pp. 1–2). These struggles are described in even greater detail by Lily Greiner, in 'La seigneurie de Strasbourg jusqu'en 1274 et les origines de la supériorité territoriale', *Positions de Thèses*, 1949, pp. 83–9.

5 This was very exceptional and a highly significant coincidence that played its part in our story. Aloys Schulte, in *Frankreich und das linke Rheinufer* (Stuttgart-Berlin: Deutsche Verlags-Anstalt, 1918), p. 73, reports that of forty-three bishops of Strasbourg from 925 to 1704, only nine came from Alsace. Those were concentrated mainly around our period.

6 Paul Wentzcke, *Regesten der Bischöfe*, vol. I; and Alfred Hessel and Manfred Krebs, vol. II (1924), *passim*. For example, during the critical cathedral-building period of 1212–50, the following military exploits by Strasbourg's prelates are recorded: in 1212(2); 1214; 1216; 1227; 1228; 1229; 1233; 1246(2); 1247(2); 1248(2); and 1250.

7 A. Hessel (p. 273) points out that Strasbourg was the only Rhenish city at the time that opposed Frederick II, which made its help to the bishop that much more precious.

8 Georg Winter, *Geschichte des Rathes in Strassburg von seinen ersten Spuren bis zum Statut von 1263* (Breslau, 1878), pp. 30ff.

9 One author has reported that the gap in work at the transepts, for example, allowed rain and

wind to penetrate the uncovered masonry, causing erosion, traces of which are still visible today (Robert Will, 'La cathédrale romane', pp. 35–50, in Hans Haug *et al.*, *La cathédrale de Strasbourg*, Strasbourg: Éditions des Dernières Nouvelles, 1957).

10 The Hohenstaufen king, Philipp, whose choice was opposed by Bishop Konrad von Hunenburg, conducted two destructive campaigns against Alsace, in 1198 and 1199. During the latter, he placed Strasbourg under siege, wrecking a large part of the suburbs and especially the abbey of St Arbogast, which had to be rebuilt (Karl Hegel, *Die Chroniken der oberrheinischen Städte: Strassburg*, Leipzig: S. Hirzel, 1870/71, vol. I, pp. 22–3; also Rodolphe Reuss, *Les collectanées de Daniel Specklin, chronique strasbourgeoise du seizième siècle*, Strasbourg: J. Noiriel, 1890, p. 70). Emil von Borries, in *Geschichte der Stadt Strassburg* (Strasbourg, 1909), p. 43, declares that Bishop Konrad's opposition to King Philipp was occasioned by 'family interests', which were endangered by the 'rich possessions in Alsace' of the Hohenstaufens.

11 Fridtjof Zschokke, *Die romanischen Glasgemälde des strassburger Münsters* (Basel: Benno Schwabe, 1942), footnote, p. 23.

12 See note 6.

13 Georg Dehio, 'Historisches in den Glasgemälden des Strassburger Münsters. Die Königbilder', *ZGOR*, Band 22 der neuen Folge (1907), p. 471.

14 I read this argument as given in the *Papiers Boisseré*, a manuscript of the nineteenth century from Cologne, a photostat of which was shown me by Joseph Fuchs, archivist of the Archives Municipales at Strasbourg. The date when the cathedral canons were reportedly supplying money for the St Peter construction was around 1200. The manuscript's source of this information was evidently Daniel Specklin, whose original papers were destroyed in the 1870 bombing of Strasbourg by the Germans.

15 Georg Dehio was among the first to point out that the Gothic cathedral was hardly any larger than Werner's church, on whose foundations, strengthened, much of the new structure was built.

16 Hans Haug, 'La cathédrale dans la cité', in H. Haug *et al.*, pp. 11–32; also Robert Will, pp. 49–50.

17 Adalbert Erler, *Das Strassburger Münster im Rechtsleben des Mittelalters*, 1954.

18 All important events involving burghers took place here (Peter Wiek, 'Die Strassburger Münster. Untersuchungen über die Mitwirkung des Stadtbürgertums am Bau bischöflicher Katedralen im Spätmittelalter', *ZGOR*, Bd 68, 1959, p. 87). As for the carvings there, though most of them have also vanished, their iconography can be identified from old works, too. It was entirely in keeping with the use which the portal area served, that is, the idea of justice. Beginning with the Judgment of Solomon on the central pillar, the sculpture mounted to the climax of the great 'trial' of Church versus Synagogue. The famous contending figures still exist, though not so the twelve Apostles who constituted the jury. And presiding over all was Jesus Christ, the eternal judge.

19 Various sources and especially the city's printed archives (Wilhelm Wiegand, *Urkundenbuch der Stadt Strassburg*, Erster Band: *Urkunden und Stradtrechte bis zum Jahr 1266*, Strasbourg: Karl J. Trübner, 1879) show the prominent burgher role in these nunneries.

20 *Daniel Specklin*, pp. 98–9. The nunnery of St Stephan, an independent foundation, was a noblewomen's convent *par excellence*, which was frequently condemned for its *voluptuosam vitam*. Various bishops tried to reform the nunnery, 'without success' (*Archives de l'église d'Alsace*, vol. 13, nouvelle série, 1962/3).

21 Lucien Pfleger, *Kirchengeschichte der Stadt Strassburg im Mittelalter* (Kolmar: Alsatia Verlag, 1941), p. 90. The author states that about six *béguines* were set up in the thirteenth century and many times that in the fourteenth. Many upper-class young women undoubtedly remained unmarried because inheritance rules left younger sons impoverished. But can this explain the sudden appearance of so many nunneries?

22 L. Pfleger, p. 86.

23 *Regesten der Bischöfe von Strassburg*, nos 1494, 1495, 1502; also L. Pfleger, p. 60.

24 Ernest Lehr, *L'Alsace noble*, t. III (Paris: Veuve

Berger-Levrault & Fils, 1870), Appendice, pp. 296–7.

25 Karl Hegel, *Die Entstehung des deutschen Städtewesens* (Leipzig: S. Hirzel, 1898), pp. 103–4.

26 J. Brucker, in *Inventaire-Sommaire des Archives Communales de la ville de Strasbourg antérieures à 1790* (Strasbourg: R. Schultz, 1878), reproduces a document of 1129 in which King Lothar II confirms this privilege.

27 Rodolphe Reuss, *Histoire de Strasbourg depuis ses origines jusqu'à nos jours* (Paris: Librairie Fischbacher, 1922), pp. 33–4.

28 The new bishop had already incurred the city's anger when as cathedral provost he had fought the repeal of emergency police measures which Bishop Heinrich had adopted during a period of violence, which the citizens claimed had long since ended (*Regesten der Bischöfe*, under 24 May 1256 and document 1492).

29 *Ibid.*, p. 179.

30 R. Reuss, pp. 35–6.

31 *Regesten der Bischöfe*, document 1630.

32 *Ibid.*, document 1633; also *UB* I, no. 471; and Lucien Pfleger, 'Die Stadt und Ratsgottesdienste im Strassburger Münster', *Archiv für elsässische Kirchengeschichte*, XII (1937), p. 5. Regarding the *Frühaltar*, see Jos. Walther, 'La topographie de la cathédrale au moyen-âge', *BSACS*, II, deuxième série (1935), pp. 61–3. The common was a big area, where the city's markets were located and parts of which were rented out (Ernst Kruse, 'Verfassungsgeschichte der Stadt Strassburg, besonders im 12. und 13. Jahrhundert', aus *Westdeutsche Zeitschrift für Geschichte und Kunst*, Ergänzungs-Heft I, 1884, p. 12).

33 *Regesten der Bischöfe*, document 1635.

34 *Ibid.*, document 1639. The prelate's interdict covered even the sick and the children. The city was able to bring in three priests from outside Strasbourg, however, who conducted mass at the 'Morning Altar'.

35 *Ibid.*, document 1639.

36 *Ibid.*, documents 1652 and 1656. Graf Rudolf took over from the bishop's supporters Colmar, Mulhouse and other important points. He became the first Habsburg king in 1273 and his cherished position in the hearts of Strasbourg's citizens was consecrated around 1291 when the burgher fabric administrators of the Münster mounted his statue on the façade pinnacle along with those of the legendary Frankish kings, Clovis and Dagobert. This was only shortly after King Rudolf of Habsburg's death, a circumstance which rendered the erection of his great commemorative monument in such venerated company all the more extraordinary.

37 *Ellenhardi Argentinensis, Annales et Chronica. Monumenta Germaniae Scriptorum*, XVII (Hanover: Hahn, 1861): *Bellum Waltherianum*, pp.105–14.

38 *Regesten der Bischöfe*, documents 1653 and 1657.

39 *Ibid.*, document 1668.

40 Georg Winter, in *Geschichte des Rathes in Strassburg von seinen ersten Spuren bis zum Statut von 1263* (Breslau: Wilhelm Koebner, 1878), p. 90, footnote, says that this sally was led by the archbishop of Trier. Its exact timing is unclear.

41 *Bellum Waltherianum.*

42 Philipp Jaffe, editor of the *Monumenta*, likewise gives a short account of Ellenhard's life and collates the documents concerning him. The *Bellum Waltherianum* is also available in an old German version, translated in 1362, by the chronicler Closener.

43 *Bellum Waltherianum*, para. 20.

44 *Ibid.*, para. 23.

45 Wilhelm Wiegand, *Bellum Waltherianum* (Strassburg: Karl J. Trübner, 1878, p. 72). The author reports that the possession of battle-axes by the Strasbourg burghers appears in another chronicle of the battle, written in 1265 by the monk Richerius.

46 Paul Wentzcke, 'Urkunden und Regesten zur Baugeschichte des Strassburger Münsters', *Strassburger Münsterblatt*, IV, no. 8 (1907), under 1262.

47 *Inventaire-Sommaire des Archives Communales . . ., Série AA*, 1ère partie: AA 1394. The *Urkundenbuch* I contains a series of documents dated after Hausbergen showing the payment of ransoms ranging from 40 to 600 marks. A number of those paying were *ministeriales*, members of the bishop's 'fam-

ily', who from their service in various local capacities had come into close working relations with the burghers, even serving prominently on the Rat. Unfortunately for them, they chose the bishop's side when the break with Walther came, a number of them being killed at Hausbergen. The great majority of the rest left the city after the bishop's defeat, passing out of history (Karl Achtnich, *Der Bürgerstand in Strassburg bis zur Mitte des 13. Jahrhunderts*, Leipzig: Quelle & Meyer, 1910, p. 50).

48 Philippe Dollinger, *Strasbourg du passé au présent* (Strasbourg: Editions des Dernières Nouvelles, 1962), pp. 17–18. Strasbourg, given the prestigious name of 'free city', owed the emperor neither taxes nor military service, giving the latter occasionally at its own choice. 'Strasbourg was truly, despite its tiny territory, an independent republic within the empire', the author sums up. Though Strasbourg's position was more advanced than any other German city of the period (Dollinger, p. 18), it should be added that in many other places where prelates held the seigniory, similar developments occurred (Peter Wiek, pp. 40–1).

49 Rodolphe Reuss, pp. 40–1.

50 *Regesten der Bischöfe*, document 1288.

51 *UB* I, document 519, contains the basic agreement between the bishop and the city (see also *Inventaire-Sommaire des Arch. Comm.*, AA 1395). Further, the Stadtgericht, the city's court, had its jurisdiction recognized for the entire diocese (Karl Hegel, *Die Chroniken der Oberrheinischen Städte*: Strassburg, 1870–1, vol. I, p. 31); every craft was allowed to have its own chief; and it was specified that the toll officer must be a burgher (*UB* I, document 519).

52 Jos. Walther, 'La typographic de la cathédrale . . .', p. 61.

53 The reservation must be made, however, that two bays and part of a third were evidently already done when building operations were resumed in 1263 (Hans Kunze, 'Der Stand unseres Wissens um die Baugeschichte des Strassburger Münsters', *Elsass-Lothringisches Jahrbuch*, XVIII, 1939, p. 94). Peter Wiek (p. 90) tends to credit to burgher initiative the entire nave of Strasbourg cathedral, holding that the fabric was during its construction

period 'completely dependent on burgher donors'. He gives no sources for this blanket assertion, however.

54 Jos. Walther, p. 61.

55 Peter Wiek, pp. 62–5.

56 *Ibid.*, p. 94. The Viennese cathedral, the Stefansdom, was in great part built in the fifteenth century.

57 C. A. Hanauer, *L'oeuvre Notre-Dame de Strasbourg* (Rixheim: F. Sutter, 1901), p. 9. This transference was decided between bishop and chapter at the time of the broad agreement settling the church-city controversy and can be assumed to have been done with the city's knowledge and consent.

58 Peter Wiek, pp. 63–4.

59 My collation of burgher donations contained in the several volumes of the *Urkundenbuch* reveals only four gifts from 1246 to the 1280s, occurring in 1246, 1263, and two in 1266. Suddenly, in the 1280s, after the city took over the fabric, burgher donations surged and never receded thereafter though at times they assumed an accentuated rate due to individual circumstances that will be studied. The lack of burgher donor entries in the *Urkundenbuch* prior to 1280 need not be considered definitive, however, since it was only after the city's assumption of the fabric that it would have tended to keep a close check on such donors in its archives.

60 Jos. Walther, pp. 61–3.

61 Lucien Pfleger, *Kirchengeschichte der Stadt Strassburg im Mittelalter . . .*, p. 9 and note 1. The manuscript *Liber Donationum* was prepared some time between 1318 and 1328 (Peter Wiek, p. 68). Hence, it is likely that many names of earlier donors may have been overlooked or lost. Several scholars have published analyses of the *Liber*, notably Louis Pfleger, 'Das Schenkungsbuch des Strassburger Münsters', *Elsassland Lothringer Heimat*, 1935, pp. 101–6, and especially Antoinette Joulia, *Etude sur le Livre des Donations de la cathédrale de Strasbourg. Mémoire pour l'obtention du diplôma d'études supérieures*, 20 June 1960.

62 Bishop Konrad seemed to be quite expert in doing things for the fabric that did not cost him anything. Though his own record of gifts is

pristine, he had the total number of years of indulgence accruing to other donors published twice during his episcopate (*UB* II, 1886: 14 November 1279 and 26 October 1289).

63 Peter Wiek, p. 45.

64 *UB* II: 28 January 1275 (no. 42).

65 Paul Wentzcke, 'Urkunden und Regesten zur Baugeschichte des Strassburger Münsters', *Strassburger Münsterblatt*, t. 4, no. 8 (1912), pt. 3, pp. 1–6.

66 *Regesten der Bischöfe*, document 1990.

67 Paul Wentzcke, 'Urkunden und Regesten . . .'.

68 *Ibid.*

69 *Regesten der Bischöfe*, under Konrad III von Lichtenberg, *curriculum vitae*, pp. 282–5.

70 *Ibid.*, introductory section and documents, *passim*.

71 *Ibid.*, document 2438, which reports such burgher support in April 1298, for example. It should be said, however, that a chief reason for the citizens' support of their bishop's military exploits on this occasion was evidently because Konrad had opted for Albrecht, son of Rudolf von Habsburg, as his successor to the throne.

72 *Ibid.*, document 2499: 29 July 1299.

73 J. Knauth, 'Erwin von Steinbach', *Strassburger Münsterblatt* (1912), pp. 7–52; see also John Harvey, 'The Development of Architecture', in Joan Evans (ed.), *The Flowering of the Middle Ages* (London: Thames & Hudson, 1966), p. 123.

74 Hans Haug, 'La cathédrale dans la cité', p. 19.

75 In 1248, Pope Innocent IV himself had specified that no new church was to be permitted in any parish of Strasbourg without consent of the bishop and cathedral chapter (*UB* IV–1). The 'third' city charter, of 1249, contained a provision that Rat members must swear to uphold this ban (Adam W. Strobel, *Vaterländische Geschichte des Elsasses . . .*, I, Strassburg: Verlag von Schmidt & Grucker, 1841).

76 Charles Schmidt, *Les Dominicains de Strasbourg au treizième siècle . . .*, 1854, p. 5.

77 The friars' earlier implantation in Strasbourg was not, of course, solely or even mainly the result of the burghers' support. Most impor-

tant was, no doubt, the papal protection they got.

78 *UB* I, document of 5 November 1265.

79 *UB* II, document of 1 September 1285.

80 My collation from the *Urkundenbuch* shows a total of seventeen donations by Strasbourg citizens to the fabric during the last two decades of the century. Most of them were very important gifts, two of them entailing all the donors' worldly goods, ten others being of one or more houses and two more of other property.

81 By my reckoning, the Dominicans and their nunneries received a total of twenty-seven donations from citizens during the same 1280–99 period, fourteen of which went to the main convent, all but two consisting of a house or other property. The burghers, in their accusations against the Dominicans, used the picturesque word, *Erbschleicherei*, 'inheritance-trickery' (Lucien Pfleger, *Kirchengeschichte der Stadt Strassburg im Mittelalter . . .*).

82 One example was the case of Burkard Bone, burgher, who had left all his worldly goods to the nunnery of St Katherine. His widow was evidently displeased, especially after she remarried and had two children, in whose name she contested the bequest. The bishop made an evidently satisfactory adjustment (*UB* I, document 425).

83 Jean Adam (ed.), *Inventaire des archives du chapitre de St-Thomas . . .* (Strasbourg, 1937), document 131. The sequence of events starting in 1283 is described in Charles Schmidt, 'Notice sur le couvent et l'église des Dominicains de Strasbourg jusqu'au seizième siècle', *Bulletin de la Société pour la Conservation des Monuments Historiques d'Alsace*, t. IX, 2ème série (1874/75), p. 180.

84 *UB* II, document 120, dated 26 May 1287. The Rat's letter was written in German, the phrase in question reading: 'daz unsir stat kurzlich alle ir eigen were worden', the use of the conditional indicating that the city felt its action had definitively halted the process.

85 Charles Schmidt, *Notice sur le couvent et l'église des Dominicains*, 1876, p. 3.

86 Jean Adam, document 135a; Charles Schmidt, *Les Dominicains de Strasbourg au 13e siècle*, extrait de la *Revue d'Alsace* (1854), p. 11. This

was only the first act of 'friendship' by the Franciscans toward the burghers. In the crisis that followed, when Strasbourg was excommunicated for several years, these friars allowed the citizens to evade the interdict by participating in offices held by members of their so-called *tercia regula*.

87 C. Schmidt, *Notice, etc.*, p. 179.

88 *UB* II, document 120.

89 *Ibid.*

90 C. Schmidt, *Les Dominicains . . . au 13e siècle . . .*, p. 18.

91 Jean Adam, *passim*; also C. Schmidt, *Notice, etc.*, pp.181–9.

92 Canon Mattias proved especially effective in countering actions by other churchmen of the diocese in support of the Dominicans' cause.

93 Jean Adam, document 147.

94 *Ibid.*, document 161.

95 *UB* II, 28 December 1288.

96 C. Schmidt, *Notice, etc.*, p. 193.

97 *Les collectanées de Daniel Specklin*, p. 161.

98 For the effects of the fire on the building campaign, see J. Knauth, 'Erwin von Steinbach', *Strassburger Münsterblatt* (1912), pp. 12, 22–3.

99 For example, in the period of 1330 to 1365, the city spent 3,000 marks in purchasing properties from the bishop and chapter located in several towns (*Inv.-Somm. des Arch. Comm.*: AA 1399 and 1400). In addition, in 1343, the city bought off the church's toll rights in the city for 2,100 marks (*UB* V, document 120). The city archives from early in the fourteenth century are crowded with details of its manifold political and military activities, most of which were very costly: attending assemblies of Alsatian seigniors and towns, signing treaties, engaging in campaigns, ransoming prisoners, etc. (*UB* II and III, *passim*).

100 Johann Schilter, *Chronike von Jacob (Twinger) von Königshoven, Priestern in Strassburg, von Anfang der Welt biss ins Jahr nach Christi Geburth 1386* (Strassburg: Verlegt und gedruckt durch Josias Städel, 1698), Anhang, pp. 1101–4. Also Hans Haug, *L'Hôtel de ville de Strasbourg à travers les siècles* (Strasbourg, n.d.).

101 *Urkundenbuch* IV-2, 1888. King Ludwig's acknowledgment is mentioned in Hans Haug *et al.*, *La cathédrale de Strasbourg . . .*, p. 19.

102 This occurred very infrequently at Strasbourg, however, especially after the city took over the fabric. A rare exception was an act of 1294, by the diocesan synod, on Bishop Konrad von Lichtenberg's request, when all church incomes were taxed by a quarter over a period of four years (*Regesten der Bischöfe*, II, 1924, document 2358).

103 The fabric possessed its own landed property and other sources of permanent revenue (Peter Wiek, p. 74). Its income for 1338, as reported by Heilmann von Nördlingen, one of the three fabric administrators, was 550 l. 10 d. (*UB* V, 1896, document 83).

104 Supporting this assumption, it would seem, would be the number of such annuities founded by burghers which have been collated by the present author from the *Urkundenbuch* (vols III and VII). They total forty, earning altogether about 50 livres a year, enough to pay the annual salary of five masons.

105 Peter Wiek (p. 46) finds but a single cathedral canon listed as a donor to the fabric in the *Urkundenbuch* up to 1332, with nine other clerical donors from other Strasbourg churches. In contrast, he counts sixty-eight burgher donors during the same period. It should be said, however, that the city's *Urkundenbuch* may not be as trustworthy a source for clerical donors as would the *Liber Donationum,* in which 98 donors between 1257 and 1324 have been identified as churchmen by Antoinette Joulia.

106 *Regesten der Bischöfe*, II, document 2615.

107 The archives and registers are replete with listings of bishops either borrowing or selling property to help pay their military debts. One example among many was in 1251, when Bishop Heinrich III von Stahleck sent a dunning letter to Rome, declaring that he had had to sell much church property in order to buy the support of important individuals in the fight against Frederick II. Pope Innocent IV gave the prelate permission to disregard the claims of his creditors, even if they had been backed up by his oath! (*Regesten der Bischöfe*, II, documents 1350 and 1351).

108 In 1294, for example, when the three chapters of Strasbourg permitted the bishop to collect incomes from vacant prebends for four years 'to help pay his debts' (*UB* II, document 191).

109 Philippe Dollinger, 'Patriciat noble et patriciat bourgeois à Strasbourg au quatorzième siècle', *Revue d'Alsace*, vol. 90 (1950/51), pp. 75ff; also Wilhelm Dettmering. *Beiträge zur älteren Zunftgeschichte der Stadt Strassburg* (Berlin: E. Ebering, 1903), pp. 112ff.

110 *Regesten der Bischöfe*, II, document 2390.

111 Ph. Dollinger, pp. 62–3. For example, Heinrich von Müllenheim was treasurer to King Albrecht, Rudolf von Habsburg's son, by the end of the thirteenth century and loaned Albrecht's son, Friedrich, 3,900 marks in 1314. This was the scope of operations of another great moneylender, Johann Merswin, who specialized in loans to Strasbourg's bishops (*ibid.*, pp. 68–9).

112 *Ibid.*, p. 71 and note 5. Strasbourg was also known for its grey cloth, which found its way onto the stalls of the famous Fairs of Champagne (Etienne Martin St-Léon, *Histoire des corporations des métiers*, Paris: PUF, 1941, p. 310).

113 Philippe Dollinger, *Strasbourg du passé au présent* . . . (1962), p. 19; also his *Patriciat noble, etc.*, pp. 60–1 and notes 3 and 4.

114 R. Reuss, *Histoire de Strasbourg depuis ses origines* . . . (Paris, 1922), p. 50. The author gives as indicative statistics the multiplication of the price of wheat by the factor six between 1278 and 1294 while a measure of wine went up twelvefold in a similar space of time. Debasing of the currency was also an important factor here.

115 Philippe Dollinger, *Les villes allemandes au moyen-àge. Les groupements sociaux* (Bruxelles: Librairie Encyclopédique, SPR 2, 1956), pp. 387–9; and by the same author, *Strasbourg du passé au présent* . . ., p. 19. Also see on this subject Ernest Lehr, *L'Alsace noble*, t. III (Paris: Veuve Berger-Levrault & Fils, 1870), Appendice, p. 298; *Les collectanées de Daniel Specklin*, p. 182; and Wilhelm Dettmering, p. 121.

116 A common practice was non-payment for work done or other similar extortions. Some of the poor artisans, many of whom belonged to no guild, were driven to the point of putting themselves under the protection of armed knights, which was tantamount to voluntary serfdom, from which the commoners had striven for two centuries to free themselves (Rodolphe Reuss, p. 50).

117 The *Chronike von Jacob Twinger von Königshoven*, Anhang, p. 1104, contains a reproduction of the painting. Another evidence of the importance of the military function in the lives of Strasbourg's burghers is the large number of them who can be seen bequeathing their arms in their wills. I recorded ten such bequests from the *Urkundenbuch*. They would list them affectionately, piece by piece, as did Henselin Judenhenselin, baker, when making over his fighting gear to the cathedral fabric in 1390 (*UB* VII, 1900, document 2522).

118 Aloys Schulte, 'Das Geschölle der Zorn und Mülnheim, 1332', ZGOR, NF, VIII (1893), pp. 494–516.

119 *Inv.-Somm. des Arch. Comm.*: AA 43, under 1319.

120 Jung St Peter is still erect, as are the chapels founded by these two great Strasbourg families, as well as by a third, the Kagenecks. Many of their tombstones can still be seen in the chapels or are immured in the cloister walk. The Zorn family, especially, favoured this important church and a number of its members held high dignities in it (Wilhelm Horning, *Die Jung-Sankt-Peter-Kirche und ihre Kapellen*, Strassburg: Vomhoff, 1890, p. 33).

121 F. C. Heitz, *Das Zunftwesen in Strassburg* (Strassburg: F. C. Heitz, 1856), pp. 19–21; also Aloys Schulte, p. 510.

122 *UB* VII, document 1068.

123 *Chronike von . . . Königshoven*, Anmerckung 15, pp. 782–801, which gives a full report of the testimony of witnesses that were called to the hearings that were subsequently held. One gets from this amazing account a sense of the heavy pall of fear that hung over Strasbourg, causing witnesses, when asked to identify one who had struck a lethal blow, suddenly to turn cautious: 'I didn't recognize him.'

124 Aloys Schulte, p. 515.

125 Philippe Dollinger, *Patriciat noble et patriciat bourgeois* . . ., p. 75. Since a large number of the guild representatives came from the patri-

ciate (while a number of the less 'noble' trades did not have recognized guilds as yet), it was inevitable that the oligarchy would re-establish itself to a considerable degree.

126 The idea for the kings' cycle was once attributed to Ellenhard, the famous bourgeois chronicler, who had, it was argued, meant it as an apotheosis of Rudolf von Habsburg, Strasbourg's great friend. However, it was later shown that this cycle was begun around 1250, long before 1284, when Ellenhard took charge of the fabric. This suggests a less specific iconographic intention, probably a glorification of the Holy Roman Empire as defender of the church, hence a purely hieratic concept, doubled by a retrogressive style.

127 Fridtjof Zschokke (*Die romanischen Glasgemälde, etc.*) is the source that there were originally twelve apostles and sixteen prophets in the south windows. They were replaced by the new glass starting around 1331. The two cycles on either side of the nave had been glazed starting in 1250, when burghers were already functioning on the fabric. Either they gave tacit consent to the iconography or did not concern themselves with it. A few decades later, when Strasbourg's citizens had become masters both of the city and the cathedral, a more down-to-earth scenario was evidently required. Though stained-glass style in general had become more 'humanized' in the latter part of the thirteenth century, what is noteworthy in this case is the extraordinary aplomb shown by the fabric's bourgeois administrators in changing the *subject matter*.

128 *UB* V, document dated 12 January 1349. The Cologne Rat had written to Strasbourg on 10 August 1348, asking if it was true that six Jews had been condemned to death there for having allegedly poisoned wells. It also sent similar inquiries to other cities and the replies were such, it declared later, that it had reached a decision not to allow 'the Jews of our city to be in any way molested by such fleeting rumours'. At Strasbourg, it was the bishop who finally made the decision that the city's Jews 'must be done away with' (*Code historique et diplomatique de la ville de Strasbourg*, I, Strasbourg: G. Silbermann, 1843, pp. 131–5). One of the charges against the Jews was that they had prepared a special horn with which to betray Strasbourg to its 'enemies' from the top of the city wall. This was nothing but the ceremonial 'shofar' but the Rat later had a special horn made and twice-nightly had it sounded from the walls as a reminder of the peril that was narrowly averted and of the 'Jews' disgrace and shame' (*Chronike von . . . Königshoven*, p. 1113). This custom was continued until the French Revolution (Jacqueline Rochette, *Histoire des Juifs d'Alsace des origines à la révolution*, Paris: Lipschutz, 1938). A sculptured figure of a watchman blowing a horn was also put at the top of the cathedral (Otto Schmidt, *Gotische Skulpturen des Strassburger Münsters*, Frankfurt/Main: Frankfurter Verlags-Anstalt, 1924).

129 *Chronike von . . . Königshoven*, pp. 294ff. Two brothers, Peter and Johannes Swarber, mayor and guild-chief (Ammeister) respectively, had gained a stranglehold on the city after 1332. Both had been given lifetime tenures by the Rat, thus effectually removing them from democratic control. Criticism of the Ammeister was particularly bitter, his broad powers over trade and industry having led to renewed oppressive abuses.

130 Philippe Dollinger, *Patriciat noble et patriciat bourgeois . . .*, pp. 77–9.

131 *Code historique et diplomatique de la ville de Strasbourg*, t. I, which reprints essential parts of the Königshoven chronicle; the section regarding the 1349 events is on pp. 131–5.

132 *UB* V, documents 300 and 302.

133 Although the greater amount of burgher patronage that is recorded is listed for the fourteenth century, this to a considerable degree is due to the fact that the archives are more informative for that period. But a great deal of church building in addition to the cathedral took place at Strasbourg in the thirteenth century. Among the available sources, the authority F. X. Kraus lists much detail on the subject, including information about the churches of Jung St Peter, St Stephan, St Thomas, St Wilhelm, St Andreas, etc. (*Kunst und Alterthum im Unter-Elsass . . .*, Band I, 1876, *passim*). For an example of a great patron, the case of the wealthy financier,

Heinrich von Müllenheim, may be considered. He appears in the archives as an almsgiver of extraordinary largess, especially in connection with two monuments, the church of St Wilhelm and the magnificent Oratoire de la Toussaint, which he himself built and endowed munificently. Data regarding the latter can be found in various works, notably in the *Inventaire-Sommaire des Archives Départementales*, Série G (Strasbourg, 1872): G 6197 and ff. He also had a grandiose mausoleum built at the Toussaint which was destroyed during the Revolution. However, an old drawing of it was recently published (Victor Beyer, *La Sculpture strasbourgeoise au 14e siècle*, Strasbourg et Paris: Compagnie des Arts Photomécaniques, 1955).

I have collated a great number of chapels, altars and chaplaincies that were founded by Strasbourg burghers in local churches and other religious units. This information was derived from a variety of sources and most particularly from the *Urkundenbuch*, vols I, II, III, V and VII. The most favoured churches (exclusive of the Münster) were Jung St Peter (24 important foundations); Dominicans or its nunneries (16); All Saints Oratory, that is, Toussaint (15); Grünen Wörth (13); St Nicholas (12); St Stephan (11); and St Thomas (9). In summary, the burgher foundations consisted of 14 chapels, 9 altars, 2 oratories, 2 hospitals, 2 convents, 1 leprosary and over 159 chaplaincies. As for the cathedral itself, 38 chaplaincies, 15 altars and 1 chapel were collated for it.

134 Luzian Pfleger, *Kirchengeschichte der Stadt Strassburg im Mittelalter* (Kolmar, 1941), pp. 73–4.

135 While members of the Great Choir were not supposed to call themselves canons (to distinguish them from the nobles holding this office on the Great Chapter), they had all the other honours that could be claimed by a canon of a collegiate church (*ibid.*, pp. 71–2).

136 Victor Beyer, *La sculpture strasbourgeoise au quatorzième siècle*, p. 41.

137 Hans Reinhardt, 'Les textes relatifs à l'histoire de la cathédrale de Strasbourg . . .', *BSACS* (1960): the entry for 1372 shows that the 'master-of-works', Cuntz, was named member of the Rat in 1372, 1374, 1376, 1380 and 1382.

138 In 1338, the Rat had formally undertaken full responsibility for the fabric, including all its debts (Peter Wiek, p. 74).

139 *Ibid.*, p. 73.

140 Johannes Fritz (ed.), *Urkunden der Stadt Strassburg*, Bd VI: *Politische Urkunden, 1381–1400* (Strasbourg: Karl J. Trübner, 1899), doc. 721.

141 *Ibid.*, doc. 722.

142 *UB*, VI, doc. 700. The document shows a total of 1,466 guildsmen being summoned up. In addition there were many others mobilized by city districts covering those who did not fight under the guild banners. This included most of the horsemen, those guarding the gates and walls, etc.

143 *UB* VI, doc. 783.

144 Hans Reinhardt, 'Les textes relatifs à l'histoire de la cathédrale de Strasbourg, etc.', pp. 11–29.

145 *UB* VI, doc. 149. The way the decree read was that in case of bequests being made to a convent, the nearest heirs had the right to reclaim any property involved at half the calculated value. Excluded from the ban were only donations made on behalf of divine offices.

146 *UB* VI, doc. 342.

147 Three of the Dominicans' leading nunneries were in open revolt. Their monastic guardians were accused of having seduced a number of the nuns by aid of their 'worldly habits, short tunics, elegant shoes and hair put up in curls', and also of having 'executed dance steps, provoking the nuns to lightness'. In short, several of the sisters became pregnant (Charles Schmidt, 'Notice sur le couvent et l'église des Dominicains de Strasbourg jusqu'au 16e siècle . . .', p. 209).

148 Rudolf Schwarz, 'Zur Baugeschichte der Leutkirche St Niklaus in Strassburg', *Elsass-Lothringer-Jahrbuch*, VI (1927), pp. 177–93. My collated listings of donations to all churches, hospitals, etc. by Strasbourg's burghers show that these took a great leap during the last three decades of the century. Gifts totalled 138, 144 and 116 respectively for the ten-year periods, as compared to 59 for the

best prior period. All churches shared in this upturn except the Dominicans and their seven nunneries, which went down to 22 received gifts for the thirty years, or about one-third of any comparable period.

149 One was established in 1386 at the Dominican convent (*UB* VII, doc. 2262), the other, in 1387, at St Margaret Nunnery (*ibid.*, doc. 2318).

150 These donations were collated by me from the *Urkundenbuch*. The fabric's revenues listed for the single year of 1386 attained the extraordinary total of 1,797 livres (*UB* VI, doc. 543). A summary of all burgher gifts to the fabric follows. It covers the period of 1246 to 1398. Though all burgher donations are by no means contained in the *Urkundenbuch* volumes, nevertheless, the large number that are included in them furnish a striking idea of the scope and quantity of these benefactions.

Summary of 246 Burgher Donations to Cathedral Fabric 1246–1398

Types of donations

(1) *Omnia bona, omnia mobilia*, or large parts of	99
(2) One or more houses, often with lot, etc.	31
(3) Important miscellaneous property	18
(4) Money gifts of 10 livres or more	14
(5) Annuities (*rentes*)	40
(6) Horses and/or arms	13

Note: Excluded were gifts of clothes, which were often very valuable but impossible to estimate. Money gifts totalled about 1,000 livres; annuities about 50 l., hence were based on investments totalling 1,000 l. Assuming an average value of 25 l. for a house or other property and 100 l. for seven particularly important units of this kind, the total for (2) and (3) is about 2,000 l.

Total Donors by Decade

1240–49	1	1320–29	20
1250–59	0	1330–39	9
1260–69	2	1340–49	8
1270–79	0	1350–59	12
1280–89	7	1360–69	15
1290–99	11	1370–79	53
1300–09	13	1380–89	66
1310–19	10	1390–99	19

Donors of Omnia Bona by Decade

1280–89	2	1340–49	1
1290–99	0	1350–59	3
1300–09	3	1360–69	5
1310–19	1	1370–79	27
1320–29	4	1380–89	41
1330–39	3	1390–99	9

151 An example is the donor who gave 220 l. to repair the damages to the cathedral from the fire of 1384. This was Anna von Bütenheim, widow of Jacob Mansze. As a reward, the fabric gave her a daily mass which was to be celebrated at its own Altar of the Virgin, beneath the roodscreen.

152 See note 150. Included in the listing were also large fractions of the *omnia bona* (or *universa bona*, as it was sometimes written), especially the one-third of a couple's communal property that frequently appears in women's grants. This at times was explained to be the acquisitions made during a couple's married life, independent of a woman's dowry, for instance, over which she was shown at times to have had free disposition and which on occasion she may even have added to her third of the communal property in making her bequest to the fabric.

153 Peter Wiek, for one (p. 92), refers to the burghers' traditional interest in the church tower. Again, it is significant that the city seal revealed its attachment to the tower since apart from the Virgin and Child, which evidently alluded to the subject of its altar at the roodscreen, the seal also contained a reproduction of the great tower (Ph. Dollinger, *Strasbourg, du passé au présent*, p. 17).

6 YORK

1 Hugh the Chantor, *The History of the Church of York, 1066–1127*, translated from the Latin and with Introduction by Charles Johnson (London: Nelson, 1961).

2 *Ibid.*, p. 14.

3 W. H. Dixon and James Raine, *Fasti Eboracenses, Lives of the Archbishops of York* (London: Longman, Green, Longman & Roberts, 1863), p. 234. (Cited hereafter as Dixon and Raine.)

4 *Ibid.*, pp. 237ff. Also see Charles Brunton

Knight, *A History of the City of York*, 2nd edn (York and London, 1944), p. 157.

5 Dixon and Raine, p. 249.

6 *Ibid.*, p. 243. Archbishop Richard's curse is quoted by A. F. Leach, 'A Clerical Strike at Beverley Minster in the 14th cent.', *Archaeologia*, LV(1896), p. 14.

7 James Raine (ed.), *Historical Papers and Letters from the Northern Registers* (London: Longman, 1873), nos XXXVII, XLVII, etc.

8 *The Register of Archbishop Henry of Newark* (Durham: Publications of the Surtees Society, vol. 128, 1917), p. xl and note 4. The English mark was worth two-thirds of a pound.

9 The first ten years of Gray's collected documents are missing but the size of the bribe comes from another source. See J. Solloway, in A. Hamilton Thompson (ed.), *York Minster Historical Tracts, 627–1927* (London: Society for Promoting Christian Knowledge, 1927).

10 Dixon and Raine, p. 293. Thomas Stubbs, a fourteenth-century Dominican friar, is the source of the Romeyn attribution (see C. B. Knight, *A History of the City of York*, p. 177).

11 John Browne, *The History of the Metropolitan Church of St Peter, York . . .* (London: Longman, 1847), pp. 58ff; also Gordon Home, *York Minster and Neighbouring Abbeys and Churches* (London: Dent, 1947), pp. 42–4

12 Quoted in Dixon and Raine, p. 299.

13 J. Raine (ed.), *Historical Papers, etc.*, no. VI.

14 James Raine (ed.), *The Historians of the Church of York and its Archbishops*, vol. III (London: Eyre & Spottiswoode, 1894), no. CXXX.

15 Dixon and Raine, p. 308. Giffard made four disbursements totalling 2,150 marks in 1267 alone.

16 *The Register of Walter Giffard, Lord Archbishop of York, 1266–1279* (Durham: Publications of the Surtees Society, vol. 109, 1904), no. 388. This Ancher Panteleone or Panthéléon was a native of the French town of Troyes like his uncle, Pope Urban IV, to whom he owed his rise (see note 36).

17 *The Register of William Wickwane, Lord Archbishop of York, 1279–1285* (Durham: Publications of the Surtees Society, vol. 114, 1907), *Libera de Anno Secundo*, p. 329. One

remittance on a loan of £1,000, made by Wickwane, is dated 4 June 1284.

18 James Raine quotes several examples of the York archbishopric going from father to son (*The Register, or Rolls, of Walter Gray . . . with Appendices of Illustrative Documents*, Durham: Publications of the Surtees Society, no. 56, 1872, Preface, p. xxviii).

19 *The Registers of John le Romeyn, 1286–1296*, Part II (Durham: Publications of the Surtees Society, vol. 128, 1917), Introduction, p. xiv.

20 *Ibid.*, no. 1432. In addition to his many borrowings, Romeyn also gave the order to his proctor to sell his houses in Paris to help realize money: no.1457.

21 *Ibid.*, Introduction, p. xxxii. Romeyn got into deep trouble by trying to establish the 'right of visitation' over the powerful Bishop Anthony Bek of Durham, nominally a suffragan of York. An Earl Palatine of the kingdom, Bek was sustained by Edward I, whereas Romeyn was imprisoned in the Tower of London, tried and condemned to pay a huge fine (Dixon and Raine, pp. 347–9).

22 *The Registers of John le Romeyn passim*. There may be some duplication in the calculation of Romeyn's borrowings since at times the entry is for a loan asked, at others for a payment on a loan. Also, several of the payments were in the form of yearly pensions, for which I took the liberty of calculating the principals on a 5 per cent basis. The highest expenditures recorded in the fabric rolls for the fourteenth century (there are none extant for the thirteenth) were those of 1371, under Archbishop Thoresby, when the total was £622 9s. 4d. A somewhat larger sum was spent under Archbishop Bowet, another great builder (£629 6s. 5d.), but that was in the fifteenth century, 1415 (James Raine, *The Fabric Rolls of York Minster*, Durham: Publications of the Surtees Society, vol. 35, 1858, nos II and VII). Actually, there is no *proof* of how much building on the nave and chapter-house Romeyn was responsible for.

23 *The Register of William Greenfield, Lord Archbishop of York, 1306–15*: Surtees Society, vols. 145 (1931), 149 (1934), 151 (1936), 152 (1938) and 153 (1938), shows that he did make

four gifts to the fabric: 21 August 1312: 100 marks; 26 May 1314: 50 marks; 28 May 1315: 50 marks; and 22 November 1315: £14. This total of £147 is very respectable, considering his Roman debts and losses in the war with the Scots. The entries in the Greenfield register regarding his payments to Rome are endless and total many thousands of pounds.

24 *Ibid.*, vol. 145, no. 399.

25 Dixon and Raine, pp. 364–5. The authors observe: 'The cost of Greenfield's stay at Rome and the sums which he was obliged to disburse to hasten his consecration were enormous. He came back to England literally a beggar. . . .'

26 It should be noted that every English see had to pay a 'fee' to Rome for its acceptance of a new prelate (Herbert B. Workman, *John Wyclif, a Study of the English Medieval Church*, Oxford: Clarendon Press, 1926, vol. II, p. 88, n. 5). York was particularly vulnerable in this regard, however, because of its controversy with Canterbury. One author lists the revenues of the Masham prebend as 250 marks, according to the 'old taxation' (James Torre, *The Antiquities of York Minster, considered in its (1) Fabrick . . . (2) Ecclesiasticall Government . . . Collected out of the Records of the Said Church and some other authorities*. Manuscript volume of the seventeenth century at York Minster Library, p. 1124).

27 H. B. Workman, p. 87.

28 An example of such payments on borrowings from Rome can be seen in Greenfield's register (Durham: Surtees Society, vol. 152, 1938), no. 2160, in which the prelate sends a mandate on 26 June 1307, to one 'Francesco', 'payable in the Curia on St. John the Baptist's day'. The payment included a patent for £90 7s. 9d. 'in which [Francesco] was bound to the archbishop for wool sent by the archbishop's bailiff of Beverley'. For the role of religious houses in wool production, see Eileen Power, *The Wool Trade in English Medieval History* (Oxford University Press, 1941). Miss Power refers specifically to the part played by Italian merchants in this trade (pp. 53–4) as well as to the famous Pegolotti handbook of the early fourteenth century, where this representative of the Bardi house recorded English abbeys and priories where wool was obtainable and in what quantities (p. 23). See also on this Herbert E. Wroot, 'Yorkshire Abbeys and the Wool Trade', *Publications of the Thoresby Society*, vol. 33 (1935): *Miscellanea* of 1930, 1931, 1932, pp. 1–21.

29 Charles T. Clay, *York Minster Fasti*, vol. II, Yorkshire Archaeological Society Record Series, vol. 124 (1958), pp. vii–x. The author shows that from 1216 to 1317, of about 190 canon-prebends, 27 per cent were filled by papal action, all but 2 per cent going to foreigners.

30 *Register of Walter Giffard*, no. 753.

31 A. H. Thompson, 'Cathedral Church of St. Peter, York', *The Victoria History: Yorkshire*, vol. III (London: Constable, 1913), p. 378. The author collated Corbridge's register, fol. 189d *et seq.*, as well as that of Melton, fol. 68d–122.

32 *Register of William Greenfield*, vol. 145 (1931), Appendix, pp. 289ff.

33 Charles T. Clay, pp. 19–20.

34 *Register of William Greenfield*, no. 200.

35 Charles T. Clay, p. xi.

36 Cardinal Ancher Panthéléon, not satisfied with his York prebend at Warthill, demanded a second and had to be given a pension of 100 marks a year before surrendering his claim. But in 1272, a papal provision (his uncle's) granted him the more profitable prebend of North Newbold, which he held until his death in 1286, a critical fourteen years in the building history of the church of St-Urbain of Troyes, with which he was occupied for over twenty years (*ibid.*, p. x). Urban himself died in 1273. See also A. H. Thompson, 'Ecclesiastical History', *Victoria History: Yorkshire*, vol. III, p. 29 and n. 51.

37 A. H. Thompson (ed.), *York Minster Historical Tracts, 627–1927*, article by the same, 'The Fourteenth Century'. From 1343 to 1385, three successive Roman cardinals held the York deanery. James Torre, in *The Antiquities of York Minster*, sets the dean's 'ancient revenues' at £373 6s. 8d. (p. 548) and the treasurer's at £243 6s. 8d. (p. 619).

38 L. Peter Wenham, *Gray's Court (St John's College), York*, n.d. but post-1963.

39 Dixon and Raine, *Fasti Eboracenses*, p. 298.

40 Archbishop Bovill put up a fight against this outrageous procedure and in Matthew Paris's quoted words was ordered 'to be ignominiously excommunicated throughout all England, with tapers lighted and bells ringing'. He was deprived of his office but did not long outlive his disgrace (*ibid.*, p. 299).

41 When Edward III came on the Continent in 1338, at the beginning of the Hundred Years War, a factor of the London subsidiary of the Perruzzi house of Florence accompanied him (Armand Grunzweig, 'Compte-rendu de Armando Sapori, *I libri de commercio dei Perruzzi*, Milan, 1934', in the *Revue Belge de Philologie et d'Histoire*, t. 16 (1937), pp. 750–60).

42 James Raine (ed.), *The Historians of the Church of York and its Archbishops*, no. CXLVI. This document gives 'An accounting of the sums paid in by the receivers of the temporalities of the see of York to the exchequer of the king during several vacancies'. The highest sum paid was during the year of 1255 (May to May), following Archbishop Gray's death: £3,255 13s. 7d. The average collected by the king during the following six vacancies, which included the period after Archbishop Corbridge's death in 1303, was about £2,145, for a total of almost £13,000 in 48 years.

43 *Register of William Greenfield*, vol. 149 (1934), Introduction by A. H. Thompson, pp. xvi–xviii.

44 A. H. Thompson, 'Cathedral Church of St. Peter, York', *Victoria History*, vol. III, pp. 375–82; and A. H. Thompson, 'Ecclesiastical History', in *ibid.*, p. 33. Seven prebends in York diocese alone brought Bogo de Clare £933 a year, besides his big income from the treasurer's post (Charles T. Clay, *York Minster Fasti*, Yorkshire Archaeological Association, vol. 123, 1957, pp. 26–7).

45 Thus, when the important chapter statutes of 1291 were adopted, only eight canons were present. In 1310, three canons met in chapter to arrange for the election of a new dean. When the choice was actually made, only nine canons were present in person for the vote. When the man designated, William

Pickering, died eighteen months later, there were only six canons at the session called to choose his successor. The election was postponed but at the next meeting only seven canons appeared, when William's brother, Robert, was named (A. H. Thompson, *Cathedral Church of St Peter*, p. 378; also see *Register of William Greenfield*, vol. 145 (1931), Introduction, pp. xvi–xvii). Archbishop Walter Gray seems to have accepted absenteeism as incorrigible when he instituted the required hiring by every canon of a vicar, the entire group, which came to be known as the Vicars-Choral, conducting the Minster's sacerdotal functions thereafter.

46 *Register of Walter Giffard*, Introduction, p. xv.

47 Dixon and Raine, p. 288. The authors' source is Matthew Paris.

48 James Raine, *Historical Papers . . . from the Northern Registers*, nos 160, 173 and 175; also Dixon and Raine, p. 406.

49 J. Raine, *Historical Papers . . .*, no. 184.

50 E. Miller's 'Medieval York', pp. 86–7, in P. M. Tillott (ed.), *A History of Yorkshire: The City of York* (London: Institute of Historical Research, 1961), goes into detail to show how numerous artisans were kept busy preparing arms and other material for the fighting force. He concludes: 'War and the presence of the government, in other words, were good for business. . . .' York's population in the late fourteenth century has been estimated by one authority at 13,000, but in the earlier part of the century, before the series of epidemics began, it ran to more than twice that number (Maud Sellers, *York Memorandum Book*, Part II, Durham: Publications of the Surtees Society, vol. 125, 1915, p. iii; also by the same, 'Social and Economic History', in *Victoria History*, p. 441).

51 F. Harrison, *The Painted Glass of York* (London: Society for Promoting Christian Knowledge, 1927), pp. 31–5; 54–60.

52 Nevertheless, this source of assistance to the Minster fabric must be seen in proper perspective. The fact remains that overall, work on the nave progressed only fitfully all through this period, proving that more solid and steady

support was required for so mammoth a project as the building of a cathedral (John Browne, *The History of the Metropolitan Church of St Peter*, pp. 113ff).

53 J. Raine, *Historical Papers . . .*, no. 179.

54 Dixon and Raine, p. 425.

55 *Ibid.*, p. 433.

56 *Ibid.*; also J. Raine, *Historical Papers . . .*, no. 179.

57 John Browne, *Fabric Rolls and Documents of York Minster, or a Defence of 'The History of the Metropolitan Church of St Peter, York'* (York: Author, 1863), p. 34, the source being from the Melton *Register*, fol. 62b. The two gifts were dated 7 June 1338, and 4 February 1339. The fact that the great west window was glazed in Melton's time might give the impression that the nave was completed under him. This was not true since we know that the nave was not lead-vaulted until under Thoresby, in 1354, sixteen years after the window was glazed (Gordon Home, *York Minster and Neighbouring Abbeys and Churches*, p. 45).

58 Dixon and Raine, pp. 429–30.

59 *Ibid.*, p. 436. To illustrate the tremendous earnings of the York archbishopric, Melton got from prebends and other 'preferments' an annual income of £311 6s. 8d. (*Miscellanea*, I, *A List of Benefices in the Diocese of York Vacant between 1316 and 1319*: Yorkshire Archaeological Society Record Series, vol. 61, 1920, p. 137).

60 Quoted in L. F. Salzman, *Building in England down to 1540* (Oxford: Clarendon Press, 1952), pp. 54–5

61 John Browne, *Fabric Rolls of York Minster*, p. 169.

62 James Torre, *The Antiquities of York Minster*, p. 4.

63 John Browne, *Fabric Rolls . . .*, pp. 52–4.

64 Dixon and Raine, p. 484 and notes. John Browne is also highly informative on this account. Over and over he emphasizes that accomplishment was dependent on the amount of funds available (*Fabric Rolls . . .*, pp. 85, 87, 88–9, 102, *passim*). Browne reports one case from Thoresby's *Register* in which he is shown paying out 20 livres for 24 oaks he had bought

for the fabric (*History of the Metropolitan Church of St. Peter*, p. 150).

65 John Browne, *History of the Metropolitan Church*, p. 160.

66 *Ibid.*, pp. 152–4 and p. 154, note 1. Thoresby is said to have proposed the dramatic idea, in 1370, that every man and woman of York place one penny on the high altar every year to help the building-fund (reported in a manuscript at the Minster Library, incorrectly attributed to James Torre, *Catalogue of the Archbishops, Deans, etc. of York. Also extracts from the Registers of Torre*).

67 John Browne, *Fabric Rolls*, p. 103. On Thoresby's settlement of the Canterbury and Bootham controversies, see Dixon and Raine, p. 457; Gordon Home, p. 50; and E. Miller, pp. 68–9.

68 Thomas Frederick Simmons and Henry E. Nolloth (eds), *The Lay Folks' Catechism, or the English and Latin Versions of Archbishop Thoresby's Instruction for the People* (London: Kegan Paul, Trench, Trübner, 1901).

69 Dixon and Raine, p. 493. There was one item, however, in a codicil in which he added 100 livres to the 40 marks bequeathed to his two relations, Margaret and Agnes de Thoresby— but it was money owing to him!

70 After Thoresby's death, fabric revenues dropped enormously (J. Browne, *Fabric Rolls . . .*, pp. 86–7).

71 The fabric rolls of 1418 contain this significant note: 'Received by oblations at the tomb of Master Richard le Scrope, late archbishop of York, for wages for masons, 150 l.' (quoted by J. Browne, *The History of the Metropolitan Church . . .*, p. 217). The fabric rolls of 1409 contain the following passage: 'It is agreed . . . that the offerings coming to the tomb of Richard [Scrope], late Archbishop, be applied to the work of the fourth column . . .' (quoted by L. F. Salzman, *Building in England, etc.*, p. 404). James Raine (ed.), *The Fabric Rolls of York Minster*, p. 196, is the source for the king's angry order.

72 The canonization of William Fitzherbert (York's archbishop in 1143–7 and 1154), a notorious simoniac who was once deposed by the pope, was an astute bit of public relations worked

up three-quarters of a century after his death by Walter Gray, with the evident purpose of helping him to gather funds for the erection of his transept. But it never 'took' with the people. St William's tomb at the Minster brought in the least of all shrines, as little as 2s. 10d. in one recorded year (John Browne, *History of the Metropolitan Church*, p. 63; also J. Raine, *The Fabric Rolls* ..., no. VII, 22 December 1415).

73 F. Harrison, *The Painted Glass of York*, p. 100.

74 *Ibid.*, pp. 72, 73–4, 76, 88, 89, *passim*; also J. Torre, *The Antiquities of York Minster*, pp. 52ff.

75 F. Harrison, p. 2. Several authors have suggested that donors may have made their payments for glass lancets directly to artisans or contractors. This would account for the absence of any mention of them in the documents. However, such donors could have been ecclesiastics or members of the nobility as well as burghers.

76 There was another window that was paid for by a rich artisan, Sir John Petty, glazier and Lord Mayor of York, who was depicted in it wearing a rich, scarlet robe. But its inscribed date was 1508 (J. Torre, p. 46). Another window that was paid for by a merchant, Richard Russell, was once located over the door of a 'vestibule' but has disappeared. This was almost certainly fifteenth-century glass since Russell died in 1435 (R. Beilby Cooke, 'Early Civic Wills', *AASRP*, vol. 34, pt I, 1917, p. 204).

77 J. Browne, *The History of the Metropolitan Church*, p. 159.

78 The dates of these benefactions run from 1227 to 1399. There are about a dozen other bequests to the fabric in the wills of burghers, of a pound value (20 shillings each) but they are all strictly on a *quid pro quo* basis.

79 The five burger chantries founded at the Minster include:

1292: Founded by Henry de Milforde in behalf of a churchman, Dean William de Langton, his patron or friend (William Brown (ed.), 'Yorkshire Inquisitions', *YAS, Record Series*, vol. 23, 1897, no. 90). There is some question, however, whether Henry de Milforde was a burgher. When Edward I granted the licence for this chantry he called Milforde 'Our beloved' (John Browne, p. 113).

The four other chaplaincies are included in the master list prepared by George Benson in his 'Later Medieval York, 1100 to 1603', *Yorkshire Philosophical Society*, 1917/24:

1318: Ralph Fenton, whose chantry is listed at the St William Chapel of the Minster. However, I was not able to determine whether he was a burgher.

1328: Richard Tunnoc, about whom we have already heard.

1368: John Stonegate.

1376: Maud Alnwick.

80 James Raine, *The Fabric Rolls of York Minster* (Durham: Publications of the Surtees Society, vol. 35, 1859), Preface, p. xxiii. Even if Canon Raine's remark were applied only to the Minster's clerical family, it would be far from true, as I have verified. The full quotation from Canon Raine reads as follows: 'Indeed, so widely diffused was the spirit of sacrifice and the wish to decorate one of the noblest of God's temples, that there were few wills in which there was no bequest to the fabric....' For a detailed analysis of Raine's sloppy archival work in his preparation of the fabric rolls for publication, see John Browne, *Fabric Rolls and Documents of York Minster, etc.*, Introduction.

81 York's wills are found in two places, chiefly. Those from the dean-and-chapter's court are at the Minster Library; those from the archbishop's court, at Borthwick Institute. The church had jurisdiction over the preparation and registration of wills in the Middle Ages and those at York were divided between the two main church authorities under which the parishes were instituted. The dean-and-chapter wills, though less numerous because of the fewer parishes under its jurisdiction, are more important nevertheless since they date from 1321, whereas those from the archbishop's court begin only in 1388. Space requirements do not permit printing all the donors' names. Only a short summary can be given, as follows:

Summary of Burgher Donors to Minster Fabric

	Wills read	Donors	% of donors
Dean-and-chapter's court	140	37	26.4
Archbishop's court	216	53	24.5
Total of both courts	356	90	25.3

Totals corrected when those asking burial at Minster are deducted, unless they are donors of over twenty shillings in money or value (chantries included)

	Wills read	Donors	% of donors
Dean-and-chapter's court	140	20	14.3
Archbishop's court	216	52	24.1
Total of both courts	356	72	22.8

82 Will of John de Snaweshyll, archbishop's court, fol. 110. And a number of similar expressions can be found in the wills. The 'qualification' referred to concerns almost exclusively wills from the dean-and-chapter's court, where the Minster fabric may be mentioned in some other context than an outright gift to the building-fund. The fundamental reason for this is that only people in the chapter's parishes could have had a direct sacerdotal relationship to the Minster. This was in practice confined usually, however, to burial, while even funeral services and of course the other sacraments were handled at the parishes. Confusion in interpretation could also stem from the fact that the Minster fabric carried out a number of duties in addition to its authority over building operations, receiving payment for several of them. However, if a donation was intended for the building-fund the will either said so categorically or the sum offered was so much in excess of the usual burial fee (which ran from 3s. 4d. to 20s., depending on the person's financial circumstances) that this purpose could safely be assumed. James Torre (*The Antiquities of York Minster*, pp. 141, 145, 277, 278, 289, *passim*) lists twenty-six burghers as having funerary monuments at the Minster, dating from the period of our study. However, many of these were clearly only *requests for burial* and we cannot be sure that they were always granted.

83 See the Summary under note 81.

84 Matilda de Alnewyk, widow of Alan de Alnewyk, goldsmith; will of 20 February 1376 (n.s.), dean-and-chapter's court, fol. 62. Henry de Blythe, painter, in his will of 1365, makes the same kind of offer, 20s., for burial at the Minster and 13s. 4d. to the church of the Augustin friars, 'if it is not possible for me to be buried [at the Minster] for the said sum' (*Testamenta Eboracensia*, Durham: Publications of the Surtees Society, vol. 4, 1836, no. 57).

85 James Torre, *The Antiquities of York Minster*, p. 84.

86 Robert de Holme, merchant, will of 15 September 1396, archbishop's court, vol. I, fol. 100.

87 James Neville Bartlett. 'Some Aspects of the Economy of York in the Latter Middle Ages, 1300–1500', thesis submitted for the degree of Ph.D. in the University of London, May 1958, p. 253.

88 It probably did not help the touchy canons to reach a positive decision when they read Holme's testamentary requirement that they sign a contract—in three copies—'faithfully' to carry out the provisions of his chaplaincy!

89 Charles Gross, *The Gild Merchant* (London: Oxford University Press, 1897), p. 109. The grip that was put on Yorkshire from the beginning by the Conqueror was a harsh one. The northern province had reacted vehemently to the defeat, which William countered finally by sending up a 'pacifying' army which spread such devastation in both province and city that its effects were felt for decades after (Thomas Widdrington, *Analecta Eboracensia . . .*, London: C. J. Clarke, 1897, p. 51, n. 2).

90 As quoted from John A. Knowles, *Essays in the History of the York School of Glass-Painting*, p. 44.

91 *Ibid.*

92 J. S. Purvis, *The Condition of Yorkshire Church Fabrics, 1300–1800* (London and York: St Anthony's Press, 1958). As occurred in Lyon with regard to the *Festival of Miracles*, the York burghers turned against their obligatory role in the Corpus Christi plays. The evidence of the *York Memorandum Book* of civic documents leaves no doubt that they were less than popular with the performers because of the heavy outlay they required for costumes and sets,

especially. 'One point emerges clearly', Maud Sellers concludes, 'the men themselves found the upkeep of the plays an intolerable burden' (*York Memorandum Book*, part II, Durham: Publications of the Surtees Society, vol. 125, 1915, Introduction, p. xliv).

93   The fourteenth-century glass that still remains at some of York's parishes gives us an idea of what riches they must have once contained. Thus, F. Harrison reports that half a century ago there were still seventy windows with some old glass in fifteen of the city's parishes. Among those he lists (*The Painted Glass of York*, 1927), some were destroyed in the last war.

94   Unfortunately, space does not permit listing the 106 chaplaincies founded at parish churches by burghers before 1400 that I have collated. These came from a great variety of places, including wills and other documents, registers, histories, repertories and many miscellaneous sources, often unexpected. Most surprising, no doubt, as an occasional source were the listings, published by the Yorkshire Archaeological Society, of the so-called *Pedes Finium*, or Feet of Fines, as for example in its Record Series, Vol. 42 (1910), p. 47. The term Feet of Fines was derived from the final summary sentence taken from decisions in certain early suits over property. Actually, the suits were fictitious but were the only method available for conveying freehold property other than by feoffment. Since the latter entailed much inconvenience, this collusive suit was used, the decision involving a fine which when paid made the contract binding after the lapse of a short period of time. I noticed that in reading these cases with some care, a certain number turned out to be pious gifts of property, at times in support of a permanent chantry.

The best printed source for York's burgher chantries is George Benson, who has named about fifty of them founded in parish churches, in his 'Later Medieval York, 1100 to 1603', *Yorkshire Philosophical Society* (1917/24). The most recent work on the subject that I have found is R. B. Dobson's 'The Foundation of Perpetual Chantries by the Citizens of medieval York', which appeared in G. J. Cumming, *Studies in Church History*, Vol. IV: *The Province of York* (Leiden: E. J. Brill, 1967), pp. 22–38. Professor Dobson cites 'approximately 140' chantries within York city's walls but adds that at least 56 of them were established at the Minster, leaving only 84 at the parish churches themselves. His collection also includes a number that were founded after 1400, which is beyond the period of my listings. It is clear, in any case, that he is premature when he remarks that 'it now seems unlikely that future research will be able to add more than a very few new names' to those already gathered (p. 24) since my group contains 106 names of citizen founders, and I am certain that this list is incomplete. In detail, too, we differ in our findings. He cites but one parish with as many as 8 chantries, St Saviour's. I found one, St Mary, Castlegate, with 9, and two others with 8, Holy Trinity, King's Court, and St Martin, Micklegate, while four parishes have 7 each: St Martin, Coney Street, All Saints, Pavement, Holy Cross and St William's Chapel, Ousebridge. Curiously, my own total for St Saviour's is only 5, which again calls for care in assuming definitive figures, though my smaller number may be due to the restrictions as to time and type of founder (burghers) that I have set. On the other hand, Professor Dobson cites only three chantries in parishes by the thirteenth century; I have found ten of these.

95   *York Memo Book*, fol. 9, p. 24, and Introduction, p. lvii. Twenty examples in which the city or parishioners had the presentation of chantries can be found in James Torre, *The Antiquities of York Citie; York Memo Book*, I-II; or were found elsewhere by me.

96   *The History and Antiquities of the City of York*, vol. II, p. 308. The parishioners were given the presentation of this chantry, whose yearly income was just short of £2.

97   Angelo Raine, *Medieval York* (London: John Murray, 1955), p. 47

98   L. F. Salzman, *Building in England down to 1540*, p. 430; and Robert H. Skaife, 'Civil Officials of York & Parliamentary

Representatives', nineteenth-century ms. at York Library, vol. I. In the case of St Martin's, Coney Street, the parishioners are shown contracting with a carpenter to build six houses, for which they pledge to pay him £62 plus a robe if the job is done according to specifications and in the allotted time, three months. If not, they direly warn, the carpenter would be excommunicated by the chapter of York, to whom the church belonged.

99 Skaife, vols II and III. He gives two examples, both members of bourgeois families, Sir Gilbert de Louth (1282) and Sir John Sampson (1309).

100 J. Solloway, in 'York Churches, with Special Reference to an Anonymous Visit Made to Them in the Year 1843', *AASRP*, vol. 28, pt I (1905), pp. 413–34, lists nineteen Maisons-Dieu at York. *Victoria History . . . Yorkshire*, vol. III, gives some useful detail involving burghers for several of these as well as regarding hospitals of York.

101 Details of the construction work on the Merchant Adventurers Hall, starting in 1357, can be gleaned from the treasurer's book of 1357–64 of the Gild of Jesus Christ and the BVM, which notes the large expenditures undertaken as well as a number of donors (Surtees Society, vol. 129, 1917, *passim*; and Angelo Raine, pp. 73–5).

102 St Leonard's Hospital had its origin in pre-Conquest days, receiving its most munificent grant in 936 from the Saxon king Athelstane, a thrave of 'corn' from every carucate of land in the diocese (*History and Antiquities of the City of York*, II, p. 363). Donations from people of all walks of life continued to St Leonard's in the succeeding centuries, its evaluated income in 1280 being £1,062 7s. 2 1/2d. (George Benson, 'St Leonard's Hospital, York', in *AASRP*, vol. 40, pt I, 1930, p. 113).

103 E. Miller, in P. M. Tillott, *A History of Yorkshire*, p. 49. Donors to Fountains and Whitby are listed in John Burton, *Monasticon Eboracense and the Ecclesiastical History of Yorkshire* (York: Author, 1758), pp. 78ff, 208. Burton also records a large number of York donors to other priories and abbeys of Yorkshire.

104 The remark about the comparative rarity of

burgher gifts is a mere conjecture, since dated gifts to St Mary's by burghers, with a few exceptions, are altogether lacking for this period.

105 Sir William Dugdale, *Monasticon Anglicanum*, section on the 'Abbey of St Mary, York', pp. 529–73. The church was richly ornamented with sculpture, remnants of which still exist, as well as stained glass, all vanished, but which is recorded in an early manuscript of the late thirteenth or early fourteenth century (John Solloway, 'St Mary's Abbey, York', *AASRP*, vols 26–30, 1901/08, pp. 231–42).

106 In the collection of 356 fourteenth-century wills of burghers that I read, I found 102, or almost 29 per cent, containing bequests to one or more of the four major mendicant orders (Dominicans, Franciscans, Carmelites, Augustins).

107 Of the 102 testators making bequests to the four groups, 21, or about 20 per cent, definitely mentioned some *quid pro quo* specification. However, I had a strong impression that prayers, whether cited or not, were an almost unfailing reward for any bequest, varying in number and duration according to the importance of the gift.

108 My collated list of burial churches mentioned in the wills includes: Minster, 35 times; St Michael-le-Belfrey, 26; All Saints, North Street, 12; St John Evangelist, Micklegate, 12; Holy Trinity, King's Court, 11; St Martin, Coney Street, 9. The total for thirty churches was 192 burials.

109 John de Quenby, abp court, fol. 65.

110 Robert H. Skaife, I, under Robert de Ampleford, whose second wife, Joan, was buried near him and thus located.

111 Emma de Stayngate, d.c. court, fol. 52.

112 The first quotation is from the will of Constantine del Dame, abp court, III, fol. 4, the burial church being St Martin, Coney Street. The second is from the will of William dictus Markeman, d.c., fol. 9, the church designated being the Minster.

113 Walter Bempton's will, abp court, I, fol. 86; buried at Minster.

114 Henry de Blythe (J. Raine, *Testamenta Eboracensia*, Durham: Publications of the Surtees Society, vol. 4, 1836, no. 57, 1365, p. 74).

115 Thomas Verdenell, d.c. court, fol. 16; and others.

116 Thomas Fenton, merchant, abp court, I, fol. 89. His will is dated at Danczyck, 16 September 1395, where he asks burial at the Preachers' church, indicating that his death may have come suddenly.

117 I counted twelve wills in which burial in an out-of-town church is requested; sixteen more where a donation was made to such a church without such a request being specifically made.

118 Robert de Holme, abp court, I, fol. 100: a bequest of 100s. to the fabric of the church of St Peter at 'Howm', '*ubi fui orund*'.

119 Since the subject is of special interest to this investigation, I collated examples from the wills where mention of an aesthetic gift or donation to a parish fabric was made. Such gratuities totalled fifty-five.

120 F. Harrison, *The Painted Glass of York*, p. 65.

121 C. F. R. Palmer, 'The Friar Preachers, or Black Friars of York', *The Yorkshire Archaeological and Topographical Journal*, vol. 6 (1881), p. 410 (1391).

122 Alice de Ripon, 17 July 1393, abp court, I, fol. 58.

123 Agnes Russell, 13 August 1396, d.c., fol. 114; and Katherine de Craven (R. B. Cooke, 'Some Early Civic Wills of York', *AASRP*, vol. 32, 1913, p. 317).

124 Agnes Elevelay, 9 February 1394, o.s., abp, I, fol. 79; also Katherine de Craven, note 151: 'Also I bequeath to adorn the image of Our Lady in the Minster of St Peter, York, my best girdle and one set of best beads with gold necklace. . . . Also I bequeath to adorn the image of Our Lady in the chapel of St Mary's Abbey, near York, one set of amber beads with gold clasp.'

125 Margaret de Knaresburgh, 31 January 1397, o.s., abp, II, fol. 14.

126 Peter de Barleburgh, taillor, 21 December 1390, abp, I, fol. 17.

127 Constantine del Dame, apothecary, 21 July 1398, abp, III, fol. 4.

128 Alan de Alnewyk, 13 September 1374, d.c., fol. 59.

129 An editor of John Wyclif's works reports that French was a sealed language to most English people by the end of the fourteenth century. Early in that century, it was still being taught to children of gentlemen and merchants, but no longer in the second half, when use of French in court was prohibited because it was so little known (Herbert B. Workman, *John Wyclif, a Study of the English Medieval Church*, Oxford: Clarendon Press, 1926, pp. 156, 180–1). The *York Memo Book*, I, reproduces a number of late-fourteenth-century guild charters written in French but they were doubtless holdovers from the earlier period.

130 William Mowbray, Junior, 4 July 1391, abp, I, fol. 27.

131 John de Croxton, 7 March 1393, d.c., fol. III. This specific request for burial in the Minster cemetery reminds us that when a Minster-burial was asked for it by no means meant that a privileged spot inside the cathedral was expected.

132 John de Carlele, 21 September 1390, abp, I, fol. 40.

133 Rich. de Dalton, 29 October 1392, abp, I, fol. 64.

134 Alice Waterton, 1337, d.c., fol. 22.

135 Isabell de Wele, 5 February 1397, o.s., abp, II, fol. 13.

136 Robert de Holme, 15 September 1396, abp, I, fol. 100.

137 E. Miller, 'Medieval York', in P. M. Tillott (ed.), *A History of Yorkshire, The City of York* (1961), p. 104.

7 POITIERS

1 Abbé Auber, in 'Répertoire archéologique du département de la Vienne', *BSAO*, t. 9 (1860), pp. 219–337, analyses the style of almost two hundred churches of the *département*. Of these, 118, or 60 per cent, were of the eleventh or twelfth centuries and an additional 35, or 18 per cent, in transitional style. Only 29, or 15 per cent, were of a prevailing Gothic mode of the thirteenth or fourteenth centuries while 15, or 7 per cent, were flamboyant, being built in the fifteenth century or later.

2 André Mussat, *Le style gothique de l'ouest de la France, 12e–13e siècle* (Paris: A. & J. Picard, 1963), pp. 261, 267, *passim*.

I recognize the complexity of this question of evolution of a style. Many countries certainly were much slower in developing the Gothic than were France and England and the speed of adoption of this style varied from region to region in these countries themselves.

4 Elisa Maillard, *Les sculptures de la cathédrale St-Pierre de Poitiers* (Poitiers, 1921), p. 161.

5 Camilie Enlart, in *Manuel d'archéologie française depuis les temps mérovingiens jusqu'à la Renaissance*, Première partie . . . I, *Architecture religieuse* (Paris: Alphonse Picard & Fils, 1902), pp. 436, 499. Henri Focillon, in *Art d'Occident*, t. 2: *Le moyen âge gothique* (Paris: Armand Colin, original edition, 1938; in Livre de Poche, n.d.), p. 115, is more shaded on the subject:

> The ogive, in its own form and constructive capacity, was applied early [in Normandy] in the vaulting of edifices, spreading from there into the royal domain. But it is in the Île-de-France that it developed all its possibilities and gave birth to a style.

We shall not quarrel with the way earlier authors interpreted this style. Some recent writers have gone so far as to deny its application to certain early examples of architecture formerly characterized as 'Gothic'.

6 As for example by Auguste Molinier, in *Correspondance administrative d'Alfonse de Poitiers*, t. I (Paris: Imprimerie Nationale, 1894–1900), Introduction, p. lxxxi.

7 Jacques Boussard, *Le gouvernement d'Henri II Plantagenet* (Paris: Librairie d'Argences, 1956), pp. 472ff; also Alfred Richard, *Histoire des comtes de Poitou, 778–1204* (Paris: Alphonse Picard & Fils, 1903), pp. 176ff.

8 Léopold Delisle and Elie Berger, *Recueil des actes de Henri II, roi d'Angleterre et duc de Normandie, concernant les provinces françaises et les affaires de France*, 2 vols (Paris: Imprimerie Nationale, 1916/20), *passim*. In his will, besides, Henry left 41,000 silver marks and 500 gold marks for churches (L. Delisle, 'Des revenus publics en Normandie au 12e siècle', *BEC*, t. 10, 1848/9, p. 288).

9 Jacques Boussard, in 'Les mercenaires au 12e siècle, Henri II Plantagenet et les origines de l'armée de métier', *BEC*, t. 105 (1944), pp. 189–224, estimates that 6,000 was probably the maximum number of mercenaries used by Henry II or his sons at any particular time (p. 220). The same author, in 'Les institutions financières de l'Angleterre au 12e siècle, *Cahiers de Civilisation Médiévale*, t. I (1958), pp. 475–94, reports that the mercenary was paid one denier a day (or 1 livre per year), plus his arms. Henry's army was largely financed by the payment of a tax in lieu of service, called 'scutage', by holders of feudal fiefs. In 1159, he raised 8,000 l. by this tax in Normandy and England for his campaign in Languedoc (J. Boussard, 'Les mercenaires, etc.', p. 199).

10 J. Boussard, in 'Les mercenaires, etc.', tells about the system of châteaux built by Henry II. They played a key role in the movement of supplies, besides, giving his army an unprecedented mobility (pp. 204–7).

11 René Crozet, in 'Le vitrail de la Crucifixion à la cathédrale de Poitiers', *Gazette des Beaux-Arts* (1934), pp. 218–34, reminds us that the donor panel that we see today was the work of a nineteenth-century restorer. There is a drawing done in 1824, prior to the restoration, which shows the original painting of the crowned couple with 'several children'.

12 André Rhein, in 'Cathédrale St-Pierre', *Congrès Archéologiques*, t. 79 (1912), pp. 252–69, tells us that an early sixteenth-century author, Jean Bouchet, using documents now lost, asserts that the cathedral-building programme, which had been going slowly for many years, 'took on new life under Alphonse de Poitiers'. One wonders about these lost documents. In any case, at Alphonse's death, in 1271, only two of the four nave bays were as yet completed. Since the entire choir and transept were already completed by the early years of the century and some work on the first two nave bays was carried out in the four decades before Alphonse's accession, the accomplishment during the nearly three decades of his appanage was thin indeed.

13 Dom Fonteneau, in t. 2 of his great collection of transcriptions at the Bibliothèque Municipale of Poitiers, has copied out the lengthy 'procès-verbal' of the Huguenot pillage and destruction at the cathedral (pp. 455–517).

14 For the initiation of the new cathedral, see Bélisaire Ledain, *Histoire sommaire de la ville de Poitiers* (Fontenay: Auguste Baud, 1889), p. 71; and by the same author, 'Note sur l'architecte et la date de la cathédrale de Poitiers', *BSAO*, t. 7, 2e série (1895), pp. 80–6; also A. Mussat, *Le style gothique de l'ouest . . .*, p. 246.

15 M. de Longuemar, *Essai historique sur l'église royale et collégiale de St-Hilaire-le-Grand de Poitiers* (Poitiers, 1857), p. 9.

16 *Documents pour l'histoire de l'église de St-Hilaire de Poitiers* (*MSAO*, 1852), t. II, reports the number of 'full and equal' prebends as 28, in addition to 8 *portiones* and 36 chaplaincies. There was, besides, the considerable sum of 400 l. available for daily distributions to the canons (Fonteneau, t. 60, p. 213). The cathedral chapter, on the other hand, had only 18 prebends, divided among its 24 canons, some of whom therefore had to be content with a half-prebend (H. Beauchet-Filleau, *Pouillé du diocèse de Poitiers*, Niort: L. Clouzot, Poitiers: M. Oudin, 1868, pp. 148–52).

17 *Documents pour l'histoire, etc.*, t. I (or *MSAO*, t. 14, 1847, no. 298), lists the big foundation grants of the dukes of Aquitaine to St-Hilaire in the tenth century. There were many other donations as well during the same period and running into the eleventh and twelfth centuries, but mainly from seigniors and churchmen. An occasional burgher gift can be seen but this is usually in the thirteenth century (*Inventaire-Sommaire des archives départementales antérieures à 1790*, edited by Louis Rédet and Alfred Richard, Poitiers: Imprimerie Tolmer, 1883, t. I, *Archives Ecclésiastiques*, série G: G. 490, 494, 615, 630, 732, 855, 1029, 1037). Regarding the roles of the two countesses, Emma and Agnès, as well as of Gautier Coorland, see A. de la Bourlière, *Notice historique et archéologique sur l'église de St-Hilaire-le-Grand de Poitiers*, 2nd edn (Fontenay-le-Comte: Auguste Baud, 1891), pp. 35ff; also Elisa Maillard, 'Le problème de la reconstruction de St-Hilaire-le-Grand au 11e siècle', *BSAO*, t. 10, 3e série, pp. 323–8; and René Crozet, 'Textes et documents relatifs à l'histoire des arts en Poitou', *Société des*

Archives Historiques du Poitou, t. 53 (1942), no. 86.

18 There are a number of authors who have concerned themselves with the reconstruction of St-Hilaire, including Eugène Lefèvre-Pontalis, in his two articles in the *Congrès Archéologiques*, t. 70 (1903) and t. 79 (1912); also René Crozet, in *L'art roman en Poitou* (Paris: Henri Laurens, 1948), pp. 85–9; and Marcel Aubert, 'Saint-Hilaire de Poitiers', *Congrès Archéologiques*, t. 109 (1951), p.51.

19 Fonteneau, t. 2, p. 41; also Jos. Berthelé, *Recherches pour servir à l'histoire des arts en Poitou* (Melle: Ed. Lacuve, 1889), pp. 205ff.

20 At Poitiers itself, the temporal holdings of bishop and chapter were limited, a large part of the city being in the count's hands. The churchmen had neither political authority nor justice in the city though they were stronger in both regards beyond the walls (Prosper Boissonnade, Introduction in E. Audouin, *Recueil de documents concernant la commune de la ville de Poitiers*, Poitiers: Nicolas Renault, 1923, t. I, pp. xix–xx).

21 A. Mussat, pp. 249–59; Elisa Maillard, *Les sculptures de la cathédrale . . .*, pp. 12–13, 38, 50, 71, 85; and R. Grinnell, 'Iconography and Philosophy in the Crucifixion Window at Poitiers', *Art Bulletin*, vol. 28 (1946), p. 173.

22 The churches of Poitou found Alphonse intractable in his demands for payment of 'amortization', the customary royal fee on their acquisitions, which pious princes might overlook. In 1261, he ordered the seizure of church property belonging to units that had not yet settled up. Flat-sum settlements were ordered equal to two years' revenues. The bishopric of Poitiers likewise suffered great losses due to the illegal imposition by Alphonse of the 'right' of regalia (Louis Rédet, 'Cartulaire de l'évêché de Poitiers ou Grand-Gauthier', *AHP*, t. 10, 1881, no. 32, etc.; and Bélisaire Ledain, 'Les maires de Poitiers', *MSAO*, t. 20, 2e série, 1897, pp. 232–3). As for any documented donations to the cathedral fabric by Alphonse, they are non-existent.

23 Lecointre-Dupont, 'Jean Sans-Terre, ou essai historique sur les dernières années de la domination des Plantagenets dans l'Ouest de la

France', *MSAO* (1845), pp. 194–6; also Alfred Richard, *Histoire des comtes de Poitou, 778–1204*, t. II (Paris: Alphonse Picard & Fils, 1903), pp. 449–54. B. Ledain, in *Histoire sommaire de la ville de Poitiers*, reports that when Philippe-Auguste invaded Poitou, the burghers of Poitiers sent their militia to help him take over the province. This was handsomely rewarded three months later with the grant of a charter based on the famous *Etablissements de Rouen*.

24 Léopold Delisle, *Catalogue des actes de Philippe-Auguste . . .* (Paris: Auguste Durand, 1856), nos 887, 952, 997, *passim*.

25 *Ibid.*, no. 966. Alphonse visited this 'distant' province of Poitou exactly eight times from 1241 to 1270; after 1251 he never went there again until 1270, just before leaving for the Crusade (Pierre-Fr. Fournier and Pascal Guébin, *Enquêtes administratives d'Alfonse de Poitiers . . . et textes annexes, 1249–1271*, Paris: Imprimerie Nationale, 1959).

26 Robert Grinnell, 'Iconography and Philosophy', p. 174. Among the various signs of cutting corners, this author includes 'the re-use of many of the embellishments and perhaps entire wall-surfaces from the previous structure'.

27 A. Mussat, *Le style gothique, etc.*, p. 249; also A. Rhein, *Cathédrale St-Pierre*, p. 256.

28 René Crozet, 'Survivances romanes à la cathédrale St-Pierre de Poitiers', *BSAO*, t. 3, 4e série (1955), pp. 245–8.

29 See A. Mussat, p. 257, for example.

30 Louis Grodecki, 'A Stained-Glass Atelier of the Thirteenth Century', *Journal of the Warburg and Courtauld Institutes*, vol. II (1948), pp. 87–111. It is interesting that the author makes that claim regarding the first Gothic lancets of Poitiers. He states that the returning glazier also brought with him influences that he had picked up at Bourges, and that while the Poitiers workshop continued to follow some of the local traditions, after 1225 it 'was subjected ever more strongly to the influence of the Île-de-France'. This was, to be sure, years before Alphonse de Poitiers came to Poitiers and could allegedly charm the people there out of their antagonism to the conquerors.

31 All authors are in agreement about this gap in

work at the cathedral, basing their conclusions on stylistic analysis.

32 Jacques Bidaut, 'Eglise Ste-Radegonde de Poitiers', *Congrès Archéologiques*, t. 109 (1951), pp. 96–117. The author suggests that stylistic examination indicates that the first two-and-a-half nave bays of the four were completed in the first half of the thirteenth century but that the rest were not begun until thirty or forty years later, in a different building campaign, being completed in the early fourteenth century (pp. 104–6).

33 To be sure, the Radegonde artistans could have merely been excellent imitators.

34 The record is fully documented in this extraordinary affair, with papers on hand regarding the purchase of annuities by the city with Gabet's money or by the churchman himself on behalf of the city (*Inventaire ou répertoire des privilèges, dons, octrois . . . autrefois appartenant aux maire, eschevins et bourgeois de la ville de Poitiers . . .*, Bibliothèque Municipale, ms no. 36 (1506), pp. 171, 172, 179–80, 202, 314, 315, 346, 390).

35 There were on occasion such conflicts at Poitiers, particularly at St-Hilaire, between the powerful treasurer and his own chapter (*Documents pour l'histoire de l'église de St-Hilaire*, t. II, nos 306 and 313).

36 *Copia testam. dm. G. Gabeti scolatrici p. bacal. ec. pict.* ('Copy of the testament of Master Guillaume Gabet, superintendent of diocesan schools of the church of Poitiers'), 1290, Archives Départementales, G. 346.

37 As it happened, also, the burghers were at the time concerned with the establishment of an important civic alms-dispenser, the so-called *Aumônerie de l'Echevinage*, which could have appealed to the benevolent churchman (E. Audouin, pp. lxxxvii–lxxxviii).

38 After 1204, the west was in constant turmoil, with revolts by barons and seigniors calling for intervention of French rulers in 1214, 1224, 1227, 1230 and 1242 (Walter W. Shirley (ed.), *Royal and Other Historical Letters Illustrative of the Reign of Henry III*, London, 1862 and 1866, nos XXIV, 30, 36, 42, 79, 106, *passim*). The records are replete with accounts of the passage of great sums of money used as bribes

to assure either side of the loyalty of powerful seigniors. (See also A. Bardonnet, 'Le terrier du grand fief d'Aulnis, texte français de 1246', *MSAO*, t. 38, 1874, pp. 56–7; and Bélisaire Ledain, 'Savary de Mauléon ou la réunion de Poitou à l'unité française', *MSAO*, t. 13, 2e série (1890), pp. xli–xlii). It was the house of Lusignan and La Marche that benefited most richly by exploiting the English-French duel, to the extent of several hundred thousand livres, becoming in the process, for a few years at least, one of the greatest sovereignties of France. Prudent Boissonnade gives details of the huge bribes to these princes by the French, from 1212 on ('L'Ascension, le déclin et la chute d'un grand état féodal du centre-ouest. Les Taillefer et les Lusignan, comtes de la Marche et d'Angoulême, et leurs relations avec les Capétiens et les Plantagenets, 1137–1314', *Bulletins et Mémoires de la Société Archéologique et Historique de la Charente* (1935), pp. 5–258).

39 Edgard Boutaric, *St Louis et Alfonse de Poitiers* (Paris: Henri Plon, 1870), pp. 43–54; also Prudent Boissonnade, pp. 233–53, and various others. The hatred felt by large sections of the population, particularly in the cities of the west, for the warring barons is typified in a series of letters written during this period by the burgher leaders of such cities as Niort, St-Jean-d'Angely and especially La Rochelle, to Henry III, complaining of devastation of property, extortions and violence to which they were subjected (A. Bardonnet, Letter nos 1030, 1031, 1032, 1035, 1045, 1047). These reports are substantiated by letters of the English king's seneschal of Poitou and Gascogne (Walter W. Shirley, Letter nos XXIV, 30).

40 The major printed sources are: Auguste Molinier, *Correspondance administrative d'Alfonse de Poitiers*, t. I (Paris: Imprimerie Nationale, 1894); Abel Bardonnet, 'Comptes d'Alfonse de Poitiers, 1243–1247', *AHP*, t. 4 (1875); 'Comptes et Enquêtes d'Alphonse, Comte de Poitou, 1253–1269', *AHP*, t. 8 (1879); and Fournier and Guébin, *Enquêtes administratives d'Alfonse de Poitiers*.

41 Bélisaire Ledain, *Histoire d'Alphonse ... et du Comté du Poitou sous son administration, 1241–1271* (Poitiers: Henri Oudin, 1869). The author tells how before debarking at Aigues-Mortes for his last Crusade, in May 1270, Alphonse wrote his will, freeing all his serfs and their children and giving endless numbers of bequests to churches (pp. 98–9).

42 Abel Bardonnet, 'Comptes et enquêtes d'Alphonse, Comte de Poitou, 1253–1269', *AHP*, t. 8 (1879), pp. 38–72.

43 Fournier and Guébin list investigators as being in the Poitou in 1251, 1259, 1261, 1262, 1263, 1264, 1266, 1267, 1268 and 1269. We also know that they were there in 1247 and Auguste Molinier cites an inquest for 1258–9 (p. xxxvi).

44 Fournier and Guébin, Pièce 2, nos 23 and 36, for example.

45 B. Ledain, p. 281, for example.

46 Fournier and Guébin, Pièce 24, for example. Aug. Molinier, in *Correspondance administrative d'Alfonse de Poitiers*, t. I, reproduces several documents with a total of fifty names of people whose claims were turned down (nos 1919 and 1923).

47 Aug. Molinier, pp. xxxvff.

48 The Enquête of 1247 ordered for Poitou by St Louis covered about 500 cases alone (B. Ledain).

49 See A. Bardonnet, in the two already cited works on Alphonse's accounts, for 1243–7 and 1253–69, *passim*.

50 *Ibid.*

51 Prudent Boissonnade, pt II, pp. 40–2.

52 B. Ledain, *Enquête ordonnée par le roi St Louis en 1247, AHP*, pp. 252ff.

53 *Ibid.*, p. 254: *Contra Eustachium Galardon.*

54 *Ibid.*, p. 280.

55 *Ibid.*, p. 281.

56 *Ibid.*, p. 285.

57 *Ibid.*, p. 277.

58 Fournier and Guébin, Pièce 2 (April 1251), no. 204.

59 *Ibid.*, Pièce 2, no. 30.

60 B. Ledain, pp. 273–88. There are about fifty cases listed for Poitiers of the 500 total.

61 *Ibid.*, p. 246.

62 *Ibid.*, p. 282.

63 *Ibid.*, p. 288.

64 Auguste Molinier, *Correspondance administrative*, no. 1946.

65 Louis Rédet, 'Cartulaire de l'évêché de Poitiers ou Grand-Gauthier', *AHP*, t. 10 (1881), no. 41.

66 Aug. Molinier, no. 1946.

67 B. Ledain, *Histoire d'Alphonse . . . et du Comté de Poitou sous son administration, 1241–1271 . . .*, pp. 38–9. The author reports that Alphonse had 100,000 livres in his coffers when he left on his first Crusade in 1249, which was only a part of the money he gathered for this expensive venture. For the Crusade of 1270, Alphonse, with much more time to gather funds, was able to put together four or more times as much (see Edgard Boutaric, *St Louis et Alphonse de Poitiers*, pp. 347–9).

68 *Ibid.*, pp. 115, 117.

69 Aug. Molinier, p. xlii.

70 Dr Vincent, 'Les juifs du Poitou, au bas moyen âge', *Revue d'Histoire Économique et Sociale*, t. 18, no. 1 (1930), pp. 265–313. It was especially in preparation for the Crusade of 1270 that Alphonse, as part of the national policy established by St Louis, took steps leading to the complete expropriation of the Jews. These measures, which Molinier qualifies as 'odious' (p. xlvi), are described at length by this writer.

71 Edgard Boutaric, pp. 347–9.

72 This categorical statement is based essentially on negative indication. Whatever documentation or direct evidence has survived (since so many of the structures themselves have disappeared without a trace) indicates that the thirteenth century saw only partial elements done on churches, if any work at all took place. The list would include the following:
(1) *St-Hilaire-la-Celle*, a tiny church of only two bays, whose nave was erected in the first two decades of the thirteenth century (François Eygun, 'Saint-Hilaire-de-la-Celle de Poitiers', *Congrès Archéologiques*, t. 109, 1951, pp. 71–95).
(2) *Notre-Dame-la-Grande*, whose cloister was probably built in the thirteenth century (Gaston Dez, 'Notre-Dame-la-Grande de Poitiers', *Congrès Archéologiques*, t. 109, 1951, pp. 118–37).
(3) *St-Germain*, whose *absidiole* was built early in the thirteenth century whereas its south lateral tower was added later in that century (René Crozet, 'Deux anciennes églises de Poitiers, St-Nicolas et St-Germain', *BSAO*, t. 10, 3e série, 1934, pp. 585–97).
(4) *Baptistry of St-Jean*, whose apse was 'probably' vaulted in the thirteenth century while the wall paintings which once covered the entire church were originally added in the twelfth and thirteenth centuries (André Rhein, 'Baptistère Saint-Jean', *Congrès Archéologiques*, t. 79, 1912, pp. 243–8).
(5) *St-Hilaire-le-Grand*, mural painting of Judgment Day, at the end of the north transept, was done late in the thirteenth century, judging from its style (René Crozet, 'Peintures murales du 13e siècle a St-Hilaire-le-Grand de Poitiers', *BSAO*, t. 3, 4e série, 1955, pp. 137–40).

73 Arch. Départementales, 1 H 18, liasse 76, articles 1–37; also 1 H 18, no. 263, Inventaire de 1788: 'Table alphabétique et raisonnée des titres des Dominicains de Poitiers', documents cited under 'Donations', ch. I.

74 The property taken over by the Franciscans had evidently belonged to the shortlived Friars-of-the-Sack, whose quarters were turned over to the former by the bishop (T.-M. Dufour, *De l'ancien Poitou et de sa capitale*, Poitiers: Mmes Loriot, 1826, p. 394). The two other major mendicant groups, the Carmelites and the Augustins, had to wait until the fourteenth century for their establishment in Poitiers.

75 Excluding the cathedral and the mendicant churches from our listing of church construction dates, the most important source is the famous *Pouillé* of Bishop Gauthier de Bruges, which was prepared in the thirteenth century and was amended from the 1326 accounts of the Apostolic Chamber of Avignon (H. Beauchet-Filleau, *Pouillé du diocèse de Poitiers*, Niort: L. Clouzot–Poitiers: M. Oudin, 1868, pp. 347–59). Sources for information about the less-known churches include the following: René Crozet, 'Deux anciennes églises de Poitiers, St-Nicholas et St-Germain', *BSAO*, t. 10, 3e série (1934), pp. 585–97; *Cartulaire du Prieuré de St-Nicolas de Poitiers*, in *AHP*, t. I (1872), pp. 1–51; T.-M. Dufour, *De l'ancien Poitou et de sa capitale* (1826); *Congrès Archéologiques*, t. 79 (1912) and t. 109 (1951),

with articles on various churches of Poitiers; François Eygun, 'St-Porchaire de Poitiers', *BSAO*, 4e série (1955), pp. 89–114; B. Ledain, 'L'église de St-Nicolas de Poitiers', *BSAO*, t. 5, 2e série (1889–91), pp. 502–7; René Crozet, 'Textes et documents relatifs à l'histoire des arts en Poitou', *Société des Archives Historiques du Poitou*, t. 53 (1942); Abbé Auber, *L'Eglise St-Paul de Poitiers* (Poitiers: A. Dupré, 1863); Notes to Léon Babinet's 'Le siège (épiscopal) de Poitiers en 1562', *MSAO*, t. 11, 2e série (1888), pp. 577–9. Summarizing the available data:

Dating of Twenty-Seven Poitiers Churches

(1) St-Germain: Pre-1083, date when it was given to Montierneuf (Dufour, p. 427).

(2) St-Paul: Pre-1083, date when given to Montierneuf (Dufour, p. 269). It was 'reconstructed' at the end of the eleventh and beginning of the twelfth centuries (Auber, p. 16).

(3) St-Saturnin: Pre-1077, date when given to Montierneuf (Dufour, p. 454).

(4) Notre-Dame-la-Petite: Pre-1083, date when given to Montierneuf (Auber, p. 12).

(5) St-Pierre-es-Liens: Pre-1083, date when given to Montierneuf (*ibid.*).

(6) St-Nicolas: Founded 1049 or 1050 by Countess Agnès de Bourgogne; somewhat later was turned over to Montierneuf (B. Ledain).

(7) Baptistère de St-Jean: Partly fourth to seventh centuries; partly early eleventh; vault of apse, thirteenth; murals, twelfth and thirteenth (André Rhein, in *Congrès Archéologiques*, 1912, pp. 243–8).

(8) St-Pélage: Was already 'owned' by the Abbey of La Trinité by 1119; hence was most probably built in eleventh century (Notes to Léon Babinet's 'Le siège (épiscopal) de Poitiers en 1569', *BSAO*, t. 11, 2e série, 1888).

(9) St-Cybard: Very early since it was built from a 'Roman edifice' (*ibid.*, p. 546).

(10) St-Triaise: Cited already in 965; modillions of portal indicate church of eleventh century though rest is modern (Dufour, p. 417).

(11) Notre-Dame-de-la-Chandelière: Already cited in 997 (*ibid.*, p. 419).

(12) St-Grégoire: Already cited 1119; hence probably eleventh century (*ibid.*, p. 424).

(13) Ste-Luce: Was given to Abbey of Noaillé in 1119; hence probably eleventh century (*ibid.*, p. 264).

(14) St-Hilaire-de-la-Celle: It was already called 'old' at the end of the tenth century (*ibid.*, p. 340).

(15) St-Hilaire-entre-Églises: Destroyed by the Normans, was rebuilt around eleventh century, according to a document of 1096 (*ibid.*, pp. 365–6).

(16) St-Pierre-le-Puellier: Founded by Countess Adèle in 958 (*ibid.*, pp. 367–70; also Arch. Dépt., 2 H 2, under Abb. de la Trinité, no. LV).

(17) St-Porchaire: Built pre-950, its porch pre-1068 (Eygun, pp. 89–91).

Sources for following collegiate, abbey and priory churches are more fully listed in note 77.

(18) Montierneuf: Built 1075–96; changes in fourteenth century.

(19) St-Hilaire-le-Grand: Built by 1080 with twelfth-century additions.

(20) Notre-Dame-la-Grande: Built 1083–99; additions in thirteenth and fourteenth, etc. centuries.

(21) Ste-Radegonde: Built *c.*1083–99; changes in thirteenth century discussed in text.

(22) Abbaye-de-la-Fontaine-le-Comte: Founded 1127–37.

(23) Abbaye-de-St-Cyprien: Church consecrated 936.

(24) Abbaye-de-la-Trinité: Built by Adèle, daughter of Edward the Confessor, King of England; foundation confirmed in 963 (Dufour, pp. 373–4).

(25) Prieuré-de-la-Résurrection: Its small church was built at cost of a cathedral canon; consecrated in 937 (Pouillé).

(26) Prieuré-de-St-Denis: Was given by bishop to the monastery of Noyers in 1120; hence probably eleventh century (Dufour, p. 375).

(27) Prieuré-de-St-Léger: A papal bull of 1119 confirms its possession by La Trinité; hence probably eleventh century (*ibid.*, p. 376 and note).

76 Elisa Maillard, in *Les sculptures de la cathédrale St-Pierre de Poitiers*, Poitiers, 1921, p. 159, makes the undocumented statement: 'By reason of the recent [meaning late] construction of the majority of churches of Poitou, the necessity to build new ones was not felt for many years.'

77 Additional documentation on collegiate and abbey churches:

St-Hilaire-le-Grand: Dedicated in 1049; completed in 1080; additions and reconstruction in first half of twelfth century (René Crozet, *Textes et documents relatifs à l'histoire des arts en Poitou . . .*, no. 86; René Crozet, *L'Art roman en Poitou*, pp. 51, 85–8; A. de la Bouralière, *Notice historique et archéologique sur l'église de St-Hilaire-le-Grand de Poitiers*, Fontenay-le-Comte: Auguste Baud, 1891; Marcel Aubert, 'St-Hilaire de Poitiers', *Congrès Archéologiques*, t. 109, 1951, pp. 44–5; Eugène Lefèvre-Pontalis, *Congrès Archéologiques*, t. 79, 1912, pp. 302–15, and t. 70, 1903, pp. 1–44; Elisa Maillard, 'Le problème de la reconstruction de St-Hilaire . . . au 11e siècle', *BSAO*, t. 10, 3e série, 1934, pp. 323–8).

Notre-Dame-la-Grande: 1083–99 (Gaston Dez, 'Notre-Dame-la-Grande de Poitiers', *Congrès Archéologiques*, t. 109, 1951, pp. 9–19; André Rhein, *Congrès Archéologiques*, t. 79, 1912, pp. 279–90).

Montierneuf: 1075–96 (Jacques Bidaut, 'Eglise St-Jean-de-Montierneuf de Poitiers', *Congrès Archéologiques*, t. 109, 1951, pp. 118–37; R. Crozet, *L'Art roman en Poitou . . .*, p. 69; M. de Chergé, 'Mémoire historique sur l'abbaye de Montierneuf de Poitiers', *MSAO*, 1844, pp. 169, 186, 255).

St-Cyprien: Church consecrated in 936 (Louis Rédet, 'Cartulaire de l'abbaye de St-Cyprien de Poitiers', *AHP*, t. 3, 1874, Avant-Propos, pp. xi–xxxii; documents, pp. 1–350: document no. 4).

Ste-Radegonde: First building *c*.1083–99 (R. Crozet, *L'Art roman en Poitou*, pp. 72–3). Basic reconstruction in thirteenth century with additional changes in fourteenth century, as discussed in text and annotated.

78 The Abbey of Fontaine-le-Comte was founded in 1127–37 by Duke Guillaume VIII (Louis Rédet, 'Notice historique sur l'abbaye de Fontaine-le-Comte, près Poitiers', *MSAO*, t. 3, 1ère série, 1837, pp. 229–30, 254–5).

79 From Dom Fonteneau's printed volumes, I was able to collate a total of almost 350 donations by laymen alone to churches of Poitiers and the surrounding area. Donations in the earlier centuries were overwhelmingly land-based elements: fields, prairies, vineyards, manses, woods, salines, mills, winepresses, quitrents, fiefs, tithes, even serfs and often churches. All of which characterizes the donors as chiefly of rural, even seigniorial derivation.

80 Founders of the two hospices were Durand de la Charité, who in 1218 endowed an almonry for twelve poor people (E. Audouin, *Recueil de documents . . .*, p. lxxxvii and p. 87, footnote) and had a chapel built to go with it (B. Ledain, *Histoire sommaire de la ville de Poitiers*, pp. 80–1); and Guillaume Le Bourguignon, who left all his possessions to the city in 1291 on behalf of his foundation (*Recueil de documents*, p. lxxxviii and document no. 148).

81 Arch. Dépt., 1 H 18, liasse 1 and Registre no. 245, 'Inventaire des titres du dépôt du couvent de Poitiers', 1756.

82 Notes to Léon Babinet, 'Le Siège de Poitiers en 1569', *MSAO*, t. 11, 2e série (1888), p. 545.

83 I have collated some donations to churches by Poitiers burghers in the thirteenth and fourteenth centuries but they are hardly worth recording. It is clear that a number of other sources must have disappeared. René Crozet, in 'Aspects sociaux de l'art du moyen âge en Poitou', *BSAO*, t. 3, 4e série (1955), p. 19, lists one single donor to the cathedral, Jeanne Marchande, a woman from the rural town of Vivonne, who made her gift in 1264. He conjectures that there must have been 'many others' whose names have been lost because of the 'innumerable destructions'. Other authors are similarly vague on bourgeois patronage. As for surviving direct evidence of donors of stained-glass lancets at St-Pierre, this is unfortunately impossible to check since in the pillage of 1562 the Huguenots destroyed most of the lower panels, in which donor 'portraits' or 'signatures', if any, would have been displayed. There is, therefore, in summary, hardly anything that can be said about the burghers'

role as patrons of the cathedral during its building period.

84 Even in the twelfth century there were some known wealthy citizens at Poitiers and in 1243, the mayor, Guillaume Grossin, is shown to be owner of a 'domain' as far off as La Rochelle (B. Ledain, 'Les maires de Poitiers', *MSAO* (1897), p. 80). Two other mayors, Philippe Larchier and Hilaire Foucher, are seen as purchasers of 'cuts of wood' from Alphonse de Poitiers's forest at Moulière, in 1242 and 1243 (*ibid.*, pp. 229 and 231).

85 Besides the fact that the city charter was very late in coming, its content was never as extensive as that of many other cities, such as the important manufacturing and trading centres of north-eastern France, Flanders and the Rhine region. This weakness was attributable in great degree to the intermittent military occupancy to which the city was subjected. Philippe-Auguste, who had often found the burghers a strong aid in the prosecution of his political ambitions in the crown domains, issued the first actual charter to Poitiers, based on the famous *Etablissements de Rouen*, in 1204, as a reward for military help received from its burghers in bringing other cities of Poitou into the French fold. The same king extended the city's privileges in 1214 and especially in 1222 (E. Audouin, 'Les chartes communales de Poitiers et les Etablissements de Rouen', *Bulletin Historique et Philologique du Comité des Travaux Historiques et Scientifiques*, 1912, pp. 125–58; also *Inventaire des archives de la ville de Poitiers*, nos 3–6).

86 Thus, we find on various occasions the city's troops being ordered out by the royal seneschals to quell some refractory seignior or town (B. Ledain, *Histoire sommaire*, p. 82; also B. Ledain, 'Les maires de Poitiers', p. 220).

87 *Recueil de documents*, t. I, p. lxiii. As a matter of fact, in this respect the Poitiers charter was weaker than were those of other cities in the region, such as Niort, La Rochelle, etc.

88 P. Boissonnade, *Recueil de documents*, t. II, p. xlii.

89 *Inventaire des archives de la ville de Poitiers*, no. 479 (1339).

90 For the original grant, see Louis Rédet, *Mémoire sur les halles et les foires de Poitiers* (Poitiers: A. Dupré, 1846), pp. 5–6.

91 'Les maires de Poitiers', p. 246, which incorrectly sets the amount paid as 150 livres, however. This is corrected by E. Audouin, in the *Recueil de documents*, no. 151, who adds the significant remark: 'This sum was apparently taken by the commune from the bequest of Guillaume Gabet', as proven by an insertion in the bill of sale by the nobleman owner, Renaud de Pressigny.

92 Pertinent dates can be found in *Inventaires . . . de la ville de Poitiers*, for the years 1198, 1288, 1302, 1307. Another tax privilege owned by a church was that on the sale of salt at the Old Market, which Ste-Radegonde enjoyed from 1063; it also had one-third of the tithe collected on bread and wine stored in the city's cellars (*Recueil de documents*, t. I, p. xxii).

93 For the original grant by King Richard, see Gaston Dez, 'Notre-Dame-la-Grande de Poitiers', *Congrès Archéologiques*, t. 109, 1951, pp. 9–19.

94 In 1507, Notre-Dame was still seen getting the keys, the mayor putting them into the hands of its dignitaries at the Porte de Pont at Joubert (Fonteneau, t. 20, p. 685).

95 Paul Deschamps, 'Peintures de la voûte du choeur de Notre-Dame-la-Grande de Poitiers', *Congrès Archéologiques*, t. 109 (1951), p. 24.

96 Eugène Lefèvre-Pontalis, 'Saint-Hilaire de Poitiers. Etude archéologique', *Congrès Archéologiques*, t. 70 (1903), p. 390.

97 See note 32. The gap in work at Ste-Radegonde during the mid-century is also discussed by A. Mussat, in *Le style gothique*, p. 266.

98 André Mussat (p. 265) corroborates this intention of continuing the nave toward the east. This could have been done only by suppression of the old chevet.

99 An example of the way churches lost revenues as a result of the war can be obtained from two references regarding Notre-Dame-la-Grande: in 1350, the chapter reduced the rent due on a house in the city, which 'had been burnt by the English'; and in 1357, the *chapelains* and *bacheliers* cut in half the rents due on property they owned at nearby Cissé, 'in

consideration of the wars and the mortality . . .'
(Archives Départementales, *Inventaire* in manuscript of 1846, no. 11).

100 R. Crozet, 'Deux anciennes églises de Poitiers,
St-Nicolas et St-Germain', *BSAO*, t. 10, 3e série
(1934), p. 595.

101 J. Salvini, *Le diocèse de Poitiers à la fin du
moyen âge, 1346–1560* (Poitiers: Université de
Poitiers, n.d.), p. 31.

102 Abbé Auber, *L'Eglise St-Paul de Poitiers*
(Poitiers: A. Dupré, 1863), p. 16.

103 André Rhein, 'Saint-Porchaire', *Congrès
Archéologiques*, t. 79 (1912), pp. 298–302.

104 Mme L. Labande-Mailfert, 'Le Palais de Justice
de Poitiers', *Congrès Archéologiques*, t. 109
(1951), pp. 27–43.

105 Jacques Bidaut, 'Eglise St-Jean-de-Montierneuf',
Congrès Archéologiques, t. 109 (1951), pp.
118–37. Two other rare exceptions of work
done in the fourteenth century should be mentioned here: (1) Frescoes in the choir of Ste-
Radegonde (Abbé Auber, 'Mémoire sur les
anciennes peintures à fresque de l'église de
Ste-Radegondede Poitiers', *BSAO,* 1837, pp.
83–7); and (2) Lateral chapels at St-Hilaire (E.
Lefèvre-Pontalis, 'St-Hilaire-le-Grand', *Congrès
Archéologiques*, t. 79, 1912, p. 302). The
Judgment Day mural at this church was probably done in the very late thirteenth century
(René Crozet, 'Peintures murales du treizième
siècle à St-Hilaire-le-Grand de Poitiers', *BSAO*,
t. 3, 4e série, 1955, pp. 137–40).

106 André Rhein, in 'St-Jean-de-Montierneuf,
Congrès Archéologiques, t. 79 (1912), p. 292,
reminds us that the great abbey church lost
the first three bays of its elongated nave in the
nineteenth century.

8 ROUEN

1 Georges Lanfry, *La cathédrale dans la cité
romaine et la Normandie ducale* (Rouen: Les
Cahiers de Notre-Dame de Rouen, 1957), pp.
51–2.

2 *Ibid.*, p. 70. The author singles out alterations
in the style of the tribune, for example.

3 Louise Pillion, *Les portails latéraux de la
cathédrale de Rouen* (Paris: Alphonse Picard et
Fils, 1907), p. 221. Philippe-Auguste's citadel
was torn down in 1490, declared 'unnecessary'.

4 Jean Lafond, in his monograph on the stained-
glass lancets, in Armand Loisel's *La cathédrale
de Rouen* (Paris: Henri Laurens, n.d.), pp.
110ff, dates all the lower windows as originally
pre-1250. The upper lancets were entirely
replaced by later work, he adds, and some of
those in the nave chapels were also in part
replaced while retaining portions of the original glass. Some of the work of the ambulatory
chapels was also redone, notably that of the
Chapel of the Virgin, early in the fourteenth
century.

5 Armand Loisel and Maurice Allinne, *La
cathédrale de Rouen avant l'incendie de 1200:
La tour de St-Romain* (Rouen: Lecerf Fils,
1904), p. 72. The authors add in a footnote that
Philippe-Auguste is only mentioned in the
cathedral obituary for the foundation of an
anniversary, for which he paid 300 livres.

6 Léopold Delisle (and Élie Berger), *Recueil des
actes de Henri II, roi d'Angleterre et duc de
Normandie, concernant les provinces françaises
et les affaires de France*, t. I (Paris: Imprimerie
Nationale, 1916), nos 8, 52, 53, 395.

7 François Farin, *Histoire de la ville de Rouen*
(Rouen: Louis de Souillet, 1731, originally published in 1668), t. II, 6e partie, p. 27. The same
author also notes various gifts by Henry II to
the Priory of Mont-aux-Malades, to which the
church of St-Thomas belonged. On the Vicomté
de l'Eau, the duke's major source of revenue from
the river commerce, see Ch. de Beaurepaire, *De
la Vicomté de l'Eau de Rouen* (Evreux: Auguste
Hérissey, 1866), pp. 46, 47, 49.

8 *Inventaire-Sommaire des archives départementales antérieuresà 1790 . . .*, Série G (Paris:
Paul Dupont, 1866), G. 1104. Léopold Delisle
dates the gift as of 1195 (*Catalogue des actes
de Philippe-Auguste*, Paris: Auguste Durand,
1856, no. 31). Richard also founded, in 1190,
four chaplaincies at the cathedral, called the
Quinze-Livres, since each had an annuity of
that amount (Julien Loth, *La cathédrale de
Rouen*, Rouen: Fleury, 1879, p. 66).

9 He was a freethinker, according to current
rumour (Sidney R. Packard, 'King John and
the Norman Church', a reprint from *Harvard
Theological Review*, XV, January 1922, pp.
15–40).

10 Achille Deville, *Revue des architectes de la cathédrale de Rouen* (Rouen: Alfred Péron, 1848), p. 8. The gift was in livres angevines, however, which had a lower value than much other currency. For the desperate condition of John's treasury in Normandy at the time, see Lechaudé d'Anisy, 'Grands rôles des échiquiers de Normandie', *MSAN*, 2e série, t. V (1846), *passim*. John had also founded four prebends in 1189 at the cathedral, called the *Quinze-Marcs* because of their annual revenues (Julien Loth, p. 65).

11 *Cartulaire de l'église cathédrale de Rouen. Copié d'après le manuscrit original de la bibliothèque publique de cette ville: Bibliothèque Nationale, Nouv. acq. latin 1363, no. 129 (fol. 87 vº).*

12 François Farin, *Histoire de la ville de Rouen*, p. 95.

13 Same source as in note 11. Farin, p. 60, has an interesting observation to the effect that in the building of the previous cathedral, in the eleventh century, part of the money raised for the task was 'by impositions on the people'.

14 Georges Ritter, *Les vitraux de la cathédrale de Rouen* (Cognac: Impressions d'Art des Etablissements Fac, 1926), *passim*; also Jean Lafond, pp. 112–14.

15 The dating is by the specialist on Rouen's glass, Jean Lafond, 'Le vitrail en Normandie de 1250 à 1300', *Bulletin Monumental*, CXI (1953), pp. 317–58.

16 Charles Ouin-Lacroix, *Histoire des anciennes corporations d'arts et métiers et des confréries religieuses de la capitale de Normandie* (Rouen: Lecointe Frères, 1850), ch. 32. See also on Rouen's confraternities Christine Lereboullet, 'Recherches sur les confréries de métiers à Rouen du XIIIe au XVe siècle', *Positions de thèses* (1960), pp. 67–74.

17 The cathedral's *Necrologio* (Arch. Dépt., G. 2094) lists over 500 obits, few of which have been dated, unfortunately. Since the founders are not identified either, it is difficult to decide which of them are burghers or even laymen.

18 G. Ritter, *Les vitraux de la cathédrale de Rouen.*

19 Dom Pommeraye, *Histoire de l'église cathédrale de Rouen* (Rouen: Imprimeurs Ordinaires de l'Archeveschté, 1686), p. 685.

20 F. Farin (p. 35) asserts that the 'privilege' may date back to the twelfth century. But other dates, some very early, have been suggested.

21 J. Loth, *La cathédrale de Rouen* (Rouen: Fleury, 1879), p. 49.

22 A large number of gifts by burghers to the cathedral in the thirteenth century are recorded in the *Inventaire-Sommaire*, série G, ts II and III.

23 *Inventaire-Sommaire*, série G: G. 3545 (1266).

24 *Polyptychum Rotomagensis dioecesis*, partially printed in *Recueil des historiens des Gaules et de la France*, t. 23, p. 230, which shows Ace le Tort as the founder of another chaplaincy, at the church of St-Vigor.

25 Of thirty-one lay chaplaincies collated by me at Notre-Dame, five are definitely dated in the thirteenth century, all in its second half.

26 Adolphe Chéruel, *Hist. de Rouen pendant l'époque communale, 1150–1382* (Rouen: Nicétas Periaux, 1843), pp. 41–4; also Achille Deville, *Tombeaux de la cathédrale de Rouen* (Paris: A. Lévy, 1881), p. 200. The latter quotes a papal bull telling of the mutilations: '*Quosdam membris genitalibus turpiter et nefarie detruncaverunt.*' Also see Arch. Dépt., G. 2080, liasse 2. The burghers' hatred of these enclaves bears a strong resemblance to the modern trade unionists' opposition to the 'open shop'. The consequences in the medieval period could be disastrous for a city's economic control whereas the unions today are usually powerful enough to render the closed shop unnecessary.

27 *Cartulaire de l'église cathédrale*, nos 129, 136, 138, 140; also Arch. Dépt., G. 2080, liasse 2: for 11 October 1194, 15 May 1195, and 3 and 4 June 1198.

28 A. Chéruel, p. 54.

29 *Ibid.*, Introduction, p. lxix.

30 *Ibid.*, pp. 15–17.

31 Arthur Giry, *Les Etablissements de Rouen* (Paris: F. Vieweg, 1885), p. 26. Actually, Rouen never won satisfactory rights of justice, a large number of seigniors in the city, particularly ecclesiastic ones, retaining their independent jurisdictions to which Rouen's citizens were at

times arbitrarily subjected (A. Chéruel, pp. 72–3).

32 Lucien Valin, *Recherches sur les origines de la commune de Rouen* (Rouen: Imprimerie Cagniard, 1911), p. 24; also Jacques Boussard, *Le gouvernement d'Henri II Plantagenet* (Paris: Librairie d'Argences, 1956), pp. 188–9.

33 A. Giry, p. 33. J. Boussard, however, justly remarks (p. 191) that the overall organization of cities in the west was 'clearly inferior to that of the rest of the kingdom'.

34 F. M. Powicke, *The Loss of Normandy, 1189–1204* (Manchester University Press, revised edn, 1961), pp. 263–4. J. R. Strayer notes that the more rebellious nobles passed over to England, while those that remained adapted to the new regime surprisingly rapidly (*The Administration of Normandy under St Louis*, Cambridge, Mass.: The Mediaeval Academy of America, 1932, p. 19).

35 See the previous chapter, note 38.

36 See the previous chapter, note 39, especially A. Bardonnet, Letters 1030, 1031, 1032, 1035, 1045, 1047.

37 A number of authors give eloquent testimonial to these facts, including F. M. Powicke, pp. 112, 115–16, 186–9, 221–4, 234–5, 240, and 299, note 92; Léopold Delisle, 'Des revenus publics en Normandie au 12e siècle', *BEC*, t. X (1848–9), p. 289; and William Stubbs, *Historical Introduction to the Rolls Series* (London, New York, Bombay: Longmans, Green, 1902), pp. 295ff.

38 Lechaudé d'Anisy, 'Grands rôles des échiquiers de Normandie', *MSAN*, t. VI (1852), p. 75.

39 F. M. Powicke, p. 235; also F. Lot and R. Fawtier, *Le premier budget de la monarchie française: le compte général de 1202–1203* (Paris: Honoré Champion, 1932), p. 138.

40 Charles Petit-Dutaillis, *Querimoniae Normannorum*, in A. G. Little and F. M. Powicke (eds), *Essays in Medieval History Presented to Thomas Frederick Tout* (Manchester: Subscribers, 1925), p. 100; also Borrelli de Serres, *Recherches sur divers services publics du 13e au 17e siècle*, t. I (Paris: Alphonse Picard & Fils, 1895), pp. 419–20; L. Delisle, *Cartulaire Normand*, nos 87, 88, 89, 91, 96, 98, 101, 104, *passim*; and L. Delisle, *Catalogue des actes de Philippe-Auguste* (Paris: Aug. Durand, 1856), nos 838, 846, 1877, 1911, *passim; Inventaire-Sommaire*, série G: G. 4009.

41 J. R. Strayer, *The Administration of Normandy*, pp. 91–3, 95–6

42 *Ibid.*, pp. 84, 102.

43 *Ibid.*, pp. 41–2.

44 *Ibid.*, p. 52, which adds in note 7 that the subsidy brought in about 35,000 l. from Normandy by the end of the thirteenth century. Eudes Rigaud, a Franciscan, who had been for years Master of the Exchequer for St Louis, was far more geared to finance than he was to theology. This is endlessly revealed in the remarkable record he left of his 'visits' to the churches of his archdiocese during his lengthy office, 1247–75 (Th. Bonin, *Journal des visites pastorales d'Eudes Rigaud, archevêque de Rouen, 1248–1269*, Rouen: Auguste Le Brument, 1852). While querying his respondents dutifully about moral offences, he was clearly more interested in revenues and expenditures, placements and debts and stocks on hand. By his cogent advice he was able to put many a desperately burdened monastery back into financial stability.

45 J. R. Strayer, p. 106. Borrelli de Serres (Appendice A) records in a table the 'Revenu brut des prévôtés', which shows the Norman bailliages bringing in about 60,000 livres in 1230 and two-and-a-half times as much by 1286. Strayer is fairly dithyrambic about the French administration of Normandy, declaring that it 'was one of the best governed and most prosperous regions in France in the thirteenth century; in fact it is hard to think of a region in France, or even in Europe, in which it would have been better to live at that time . . .' (pp. 107–8). Yet when he breaks this prosperity down into detail, he loses some of his assurance:

> How widespread this prosperity was is another question. Individual nobles and monasteries became badly involved in debt during the reign of St Louis; a little later the lower classes of Rouen were driven to revolt by their misery; and throughout the century the poorer peasants were losing their holdings because they could not pay the rent . . . (pp. 108–9).

The loss of holdings was also due to over-borrowing, as is pointed out by Robert Genestal, *Rôle des monastères comme établissements de crédit, étudié en Normandie du 11e à la fin du 13e siècle* (Paris: Arthur Rousseau), pp. 204–6.

46 Léopold Delisle, *Querimoniae Normannorum, Anno 1247*, in *Recueil des historiens des Gaules et de la France*, t. 24, 1ère partie (Paris: Imprimerie Nationale, 1904), pp. 1–73; also see Charles Petit-Dutaillis, *Querimoniae Normannorum*, pp. 99–118; and Ch.-V. Langlois, 'Doléances recueillies par les enquêteurs de St Louis et des derniers Capétiens directs', *Revue Historique*, XCII (September–October 1906), pp. 1–41.

47 Petit-Dutaillis (pp. 104, 107–8) points out that confiscations are mentioned in more than a hundred of 551 articles appearing in the *Querimoniae*, which covered only one-fourth of Normandy. The big majority of complainants were rural seigniors, whose deprivations must have totalled 2,000 livres a year over a period of twenty-five years, with a number going beyond that.

48 *Inventaire-Sommaire*, série G: G. 4021 (1249). A *vidimus* of 1322 lists all the donations made to Royaumont by St Louis as well as by his father and mother, together with later acquisitions by the abbey (*Répertoire Numérique des Archives Départementales*, série H, t. II, 1927, 11 H 1).

49 *Inventaire-Sommaire*: G. 4021.

50 Robert Genestal argues that peace in Normandy in the thirteenth century made possible development of the system of *rente*-loans as an aid to cultivators in improving their exploitations (p. 197). Urban leaders are known to have made great profits through this financial innovation. Léopold Delisle, in *Etudes sur la condition de la classe agricole et l'état de l'agriculture en Normandie, au moyen âge* (Evreux: A. Hérissey, 1851), p. 635, develops the same idea.

51 In 1210, for example, Rouen merchants were shut out of English ports (A. Chéruel, *Histoire de Rouen pendant l'époque communale*, p. 113).

52 Charles de Beaurepaire, *De la Vicomté de*

l'Eau de Rouen (Evreux: Auguste Hérissey, 1866), pp. 31–2.

53 Ernest de Fréville, *Mémoire sur le commerce maritime de Rouen depuis les temps les plus reculés jusqu' à la fin du 16e siècle* (Rouen: Le Brument–Paris: Auguste Durand, 1857), p. 199.

54 *Ibid.*

55 A. Chéruel, p. 153. In a decision of 1258, the parlement of Paris, the royal appellate court, refused to allow Rouen's merchants to bring their goods from the bridge of Mantes to Paris unless they joined the Paris guild of merchants (Edgard Boutaric, *Actes du Parlement de Paris*, 1ère série, de l'an 1254 à l'an 1328: t. I, 1254–99, Paris: Henri Plon, 1863, no. 220). What this meant actually was that Rouen's merchants had to share their profits with the Parisians.

56 A. Chéruel, p. 203. Even foreign boats could get out of paying Rouen a toll by exhibiting a free-passage from the king, for which they had to pay, of course. Finally, the policy, 'If you can't beat them, join them', began to spread among wealthy Rouen merchants, some of whom, like the des Essarts family, shifted their headquarters to Paris.

57 E. de Fréville, p. 125.

58 The apparent continuity of the Rouen cathedral's building record does not mean that it was built as expeditiously as possible. Even if a building crew was always kept on the premises, its numbers could be reduced to a fraction of what was required to keep construction going at full speed.

59 *Inventaire-Sommaire*, série G. Introduction.

60 Aside from the building of the two churches of the Dominicans and the Franciscans, the literature records only a few minor structures that went up at Rouen in the thirteenth century. Following is a partial list of the construction dates of Rouen's churches:

Tenth century: St-Sever.

Eleventh century: Abbey of St-Amand; Priory of Bonne-Nouvelle; Abbey of St-Ouen; Abbey of Ste-Trinité-du-Mont; St-Gervais; St-André-hors-Ville; St-Etienne-des-Tonneliers; St-Laurent; St-Sépulchre; St-Antoine; St-Pierre-le-Portier; St-Jean-sur-Renelle; St-

Sauveur; and in addition a few others of uncertain dating but which were built 'very early': St-André-dans-la-Ville; St-Paul; St-Godard; and St-Martin-sur-Renelle.

Twelfth century, first half: Priory of St-Lô; Priory of La Madeleine; Priory of the Mont-aux-Malades; Notre-Dame-la-Ronde; St-Cande-le-Vieux; St-Vincent; St-Jean-des-Prés; St-Jacques; St-Gilles; St-Nicolas-le-Peinteur. *Second half*: St-Maclou; St-Thomas-Martyr; Priory of Grammont; Ste-Croix-St-Ouen; St-Vivien; Templiers's 'first' church; St-Denis; St-Nicolas-de-Beauvoir; Priory of St-Julien; Chapel of St-Marc; and in addition three other churches that were probably built in the twelfth century: St-Patrice; St-Herbland; St-Pierre-du-Châtel.

Fourteenth century: St-Nicaise; St-Ouen (rebuilt); Ste-Croix-St-Ouen (rebuilt); Filles-Dieu and Hospital of Billettes. There was also some repair work done on several churches in the fourteenth century.

61 An exception to this negative pattern appears to be available at one fairly intact church, St-Laurent, where a study of the galleries is instructive. Here the vaults can be seen to move fitfully from one style to another more advanced, as though to illustrate a constantly resumed evolution of form which was just as repeatedly interrupted. Farin (p. 124) says that the church was badly damaged by the 1248 fire and 'was reestablished only with much difficulty'.

62 Charles de Beaurepaire, *Inventaire du fonds de St-Mathieu dit les Emmurées*, a nineteenth-century manuscript of the Archives Départementales, 68 H, which records the whole series of gifts by St Louis to this nunnery, starting in 1261 and reaching a high point in 1269, with the donation of the site of the convent with buildings, fields, garden, etc., plus the 400 l. *rente* and the chapel of 'Glapion'.

63 L. Delisle's *Cartulaire Normand*, no. 450.

64 *Inventaire-Sommaire*, série G: G. 3658.

65 Jean Oursel, in *Les beautez de la Normandie, ou l'origine de la ville de Rouen*... (Rouen: Jean Oursel, 1700), p. 87, lists the following fires in the thirteenth century at Rouen: 1200, 1203, 1210, 1211, 1225, 1228, 1248, 1284.

66 Auguste Longnon reports tithes paid to the Abbey of St-Amand as 940 l.; to St-Maclou, 180 l.; to the great Abbey of St-Ouen, 6,639 l. His figures were based on registers of church revenues of the thirteenth century with important additions of 1337, as published in his *Pouillés de la province de Rouen* (Paris: Imprimerie Nationale, 1903).

67 The 1248 date for the big fire is cited by all historians of St-Ouen, as for example by A.-P.-M. Gilbert, *Description historique de l'église de St-Ouen de Rouen* (Rouen: Imprimerie de Crapelet, 1822), p. 16.

68 *Ibid.*, p. 16.

69 According to the abbey's *Inventaire* of 1642 (Arch. Dépt., ms 14 H 4), the first abbot to be buried in the choir after the fire was Jean I (1273–87), who had lived away from the abbey, however, all during his office.

70 It was about this time, too, that St-Ouen was given the greater part of the revenues of the parish church of St-Vivien (*Répertoire Numérique des Archives Départementales*, Série H: 14 H 466).

71 This phenomenon was matched by the numbers of Rouen merchants who became associated with Paris houses, some of them, like Simon de Paris and Martin and Pierre des Essarts, even migrating to the capital, where they became patrons of the cathedral and other churches.

72 Jules Quicherat, 'Documents inédits sur la construction de St-Ouen de Rouen', *BEC*, 3e série, t. III (1852), pp. 464–76; also *Inventaire* of 1642.

73 André Masson, *L'Eglise abbatiale St-Ouen de Rouen* (Paris: Henri Laurens, 1927), which includes a special memorandum by Jean Lafond, 'Vitraux', pp. 74–91.

74 A.-P.-M. Gilbert, p. 27; also *Etat et inventaire des chartes, titres... de l'abbaïe... St-Ouen de Rouen*, t. I (1729), pp. 46–7 (Archives Départementales, 14 H 8).

75 J. Quicherat; also A. Deville, *Observations sur l'achèvement de l'église de St-Ouen de Rouen* (Rouen: Alfred Péron, 1844), p. 3.

76 Francisque Michel, *Chronique des abbés de St-Ouen de Rouen* (Rouen: Edouard Frère, 1840, printed from the fourteenth-century original), pp. 44–6.

77 *Ibid*. There is possibly an error in the *Chronique's* arithmetic, my total being 15,692 l. 6s. 4d.

78 *Ibid*. The quaint old French is very sad: 'toute l'iglise et especialment son dit moustier furent mout grandement greveys en son temps'.

79 *Ibid*., pp. 91–2.

80 *Ibid*. In 1380, King Charles VI, on request of his uncle, the Duke of Burgundy, seemed to be trying to make good the damage done to the abbey's building programme by the fine of 1355 through a grandiose donation of 3,000 livres to its fabric. But it evidently was too late to get the arrested building impulse going permanently again.

81 Already by the end of the fourteenth century, Rouen had become an important ship-repair centre for the crown (Charles Bréard (ed.), *Le compte du Clos des Galées de Rouen au 14e siècle, 1382–1384, recueilli par René de Bourdellès*, Rouen: E. Cagniard, 1893). The parish church of St-Etienne-des-Tonneliers also attests to the developing importance of Rouen as a shipbuilding centre. Originally a very modest parish, it was rebuilt magnificently in the fifteenth and sixteenth centuries, with the aid of wealthy shipbuilders who had become its parishioners (Ch. de Beaurepaire, *Notes historiques et archéologiques*, pp. 167–9).

82 J. Quicherat, *Documents inédits sur la construction de St-Ouen de Rouen* . . .

83 Churches undergoing important construction in the fifteenth and sixteenth centuries include: St-Maclou; St-Lô; Priory of La Madeleine; St-Thomas-Martyre; Priory of Grammont; St-Gervais; Abbey of St-Ouen; St-André-dans-la-Ville; St-André-hors-Ville; St-Cande-le-Jeune; St-Etienne-des-Tonneliers; St-Laurent; St-Godard; St-Pierre-le-Portier; St-Jean-sur-Renelle; St-Sever; St-Vincent; St-Vivien; St-Martin-sur-Renelle; St-Herbland; St-Denis; St-Nicolas-le-Peinteur; St-Pierre-du-Châtel; St-Pierre-l'Honoré; St-Patrice; Notre-Dame-la-Ronde; St-Vigor; St-Michel; Ste-Marie-la-Petite; churches of Carmelites and Augustins.

84 Charles Ouin-Lacroix, *Histoire de l'église et de la paroisse de St-Maclou de Rouen* (Rouen: Mégard, 1846); also *Inventaire-Sommaire*, série G: G. 6872 (*Cartulaire de la fabrique de St-Maclou*); and G. 6873 (*Registre Chartrier*, of St-Maclou).

85 Armand Loisel and Maurice Allinne, *La cathédrale de Rouen, etc.*, pp. 19–20.

86 *Ibid*., p. 64. In 1370 already, the cathedral chapter decided that the section over the main portal must be strengthened by the addition of an 'O' ('ogive'?) (*Inventaire-Sommaire*, série G: G. 2115, *Registre: Acta in capitulo Rotho*).

87 *Cartulaire de la fabrique de la cathédrale de Rouen*, Arch, Dépt., G. 2008, fols 250ff. It contains a 'Declaration de la sonnerie ordinaire de legle nte dame de Rouen, ordonnée en chappitre général 1476'.

88 E. H. Langlois, *Stalles de la cathédrale de Rouen* (1838).

89 *Comptes de la fabrique*: Archives Départementales, G. 2492–G. 2503.

INDEX

Note: Information presented in illustrations is indicated by page numbers in *italics*. Information presented in endnotes is indicated by an "n" and the note number following the page number.